The Other Side of the Frontier

American and European Economic History
Joel Mokyr and Robert Margo, Series Editors

*The Other Side of the Frontier: Economic Explorations into
Native American History,* edited by Linda Barrington

*The British Industrial Revolution: An Economic Assessment,
Second Edition,* Joel Mokyr

The Other Side of the Frontier

Economic Explorations into Native American History

EDITED BY

Linda Barrington
Barnard College

Westview Press
A Member of the Perseus Books Group

American and European Economic History

Copyright © 1999 by Westview Press, A Member of the Perseus Books Group

Published in 1999 in the United States of America by Westview Press, 5500 Central Avenue, Boulder, Colorado 80301-2877, and in the United Kingdom by Westview Press, 12 Hid's Copse Road, Cumnor Hill, Oxford OX2 9JJ

A CIP catalog record for this book is available from the Library of Congress.
ISBN 0-8133-3395-4 (hc)—ISBN 0-8133-3396-2 (pb)

The paper used in this publication meets the requirements of the American National Standard for Permanence of Paper for Printed Library Materials Z39.48-1984.

10   9   8   7   6   5   4   3   2   1

Contents

PART 3
WESTWARD EXPANSION

PART 4
TWENTIETH-CENTURY FEDERALISM

Preface

Over the last decade or so, there has been increasing interest in producing a "diversity-friendly" economics curriculum. In 1992 a panel at the annual meetings of the American Economics Association (AEA) titled Alternative Pedagogies and Economic Education produced three papers discussing the need for greater inclusiveness in the general economics curriculum (Bartlett and Feiner 1992; Conrad 1992; Shakelford 1992). Three years later, a guidebook titled *Economics 190 R&G: Introductory Economics from a Race and Gender Perspective* (Bartlett 1995) was distributed at a pre-AEA conference workshop detailing a more inclusive introductory economics course. Both the workshop and guidebook generated much interest. Bartlett provides an excellent summary of methods to add diversity into the introductory economics course in her 1996 article, and recently published book on the subject (1997). And beginning in 1996, three additional faculty development conferences, coordinated by Susan Feiner and sponsored in part by the National Science Foundation, will focus on techniques for teaching female economics students.

The field of economic history has included itself in this movement to diversify the economics curriculum. Textbooks now routinely include research on the economic history of slavery, the reconstruction experience for African Americans, and women's labor force participation. Further, research on Asian American economic history is increasingly making its way onto course syllabi. Examples of such work are Patricia Cloud and David W. Galenson's "Chinese Immigration and Contract Labor in the Late Nineteenth Century" (1987) and Maseo Susuki's "Success Story? Japanese Immigrant Economic Achievement and Return Migration, 1920–1930" (1995). Akira Motomura and Pamela Nickless (1994) find greater treatment of gender, race, and ethnicity issues in the most popular economic history texts than in economics textbooks in general. Yet despite these trends, Native American economic history is still quite underrepresented in the standard economic history curriculum. And, as Ronald Trosper (1975) argues for African Americans and Native Americans, lessons drawn from the discrimination history of one group are not necessarily applicable to another.

More than lip service to indigenous peoples is needed. Including the Native American experience in the economic history curriculum must involve more than an apologetic note on land confiscation and the loss of indigenous life and heritage. Although these losses were tremendous and tragic, such statements are not sufficient. A detailed and accurate account of the economic history of the United States and the indigenous peoples within its borders requires substantive economic historic research into Native American experiences. Such research does exist, but opportunities for further study are unlimited. This volume provides ready examples of what is available and, by default, what is still lacking; I hope it will stimulate research to fill the void.

Describing the scope of research on the industrial revolution, Joel Mokyr wrote: "It is an ongoing project to disentangle how economic, technological, and social elements affected one another" (1993, 5). This imagery applies equally well to the study of Native American economic history. The economic history of Native Americans evolves with that of the United States in a web of economic, technological, and social interactions. Compared to the study of the Industrial Revolution, or its extension to North America, research on the interwoven economic histories of the United States and Native Americans is sparse. The opportunities are great for research that starts to disentangle the different strands of development in order to see how they have impacted each other. This volume includes many of the principal authors of research on Native American economic history and contains some of the seminal work in the field.

Linda Barrington

References

Bartlett, Robin L. 1995. *Economics 190 R&G: Introductory Economics from a Race and Gender Perspective.*

_____. 1996. "Discovering Diversity in Introductory Economics." *Journal of Economic Perspectives* 10, no. 2 (Spring):141–153.

———. 1997. *Introducing Race and Gender ito Economics.* New York: Routledge.

Bartlett, Robin L., and Susan F. Feiner. 1992. "Alternative Pedagogies and Economic Education: Balancing the Economics Curriculum. Content, Method and Pedagogy." *American Economic Review Papers and Proceedings* (May):559–564.

Cloud, Patricia, and David W. Galenson. 1987. "Chinese Immigration and Contract Labor in the Late Nineteenth Century." *Explorations in Economic History* 24:22–42.

Conrad, Cecilia A. 1992. "Evaluating Undergraduate Courses on Women in the Economy." *American Economic Review Papers and Proceedings* (May):565–569.

Mokyr, Joel. 1993. *The British Industrial Revolution: An Economic Perspective.* Boulder, Colo.: Westview Press.

Motomura, Akira, and Pamela Nickless. 1994. "Reflections on the Coverage of Gender, Race, and Ethnicity in the U.S. Economic History Texts." Unpublished manuscript.

Shakelford, Jean. 1992. "Feminist Pedagogy: A Means for Bringing Critical Thinking and Creativity to the Economics Classroom." *American Economics Review Papers and Proceedings* (May):570–576.

Susuki, Masao. 1995. "Success Story? Japanese Immigrant Economic Achievement and Return Migration, 1920–1930." *Journal of Economic History* 55, no. 4 (December):889–901.

Trosper, Ronald L. 1975. "Minority Groups—Discussion." *The American Economic Review* 65, no.2 (May): 59–62.

Acknowledgments

I am indebted to Carol Wipf-Miller for her hours of assistance in compiling the manuscript for this collection and to Ann Carlos for her interest and words of encouragement. The Columbia University Seminars, under the direction of Aaron Warner, provided financial assistance for the preparation of the manuscript for publication. The underlying body of work for this volume was presented to the University Seminar on Economic History at the conference Furthering Research into the Past: Current Research on the Economic History of Native Americans, held on May 6–7, 1994, at Columbia University and cosponsored by the University Seminars and the Barnard College Gildersleeve Fund. My appreciation goes to Jeremy Atack, Michael Edelstein, Bernard Elbaum, Larry Neal, Robert Puth, Hugh Rockoff, Richard Sylla, and Ronald Trosper, who contributed to this volume through their participation in the initial conference as discussants and chairs. I am grateful to Robert Margo and Alan Dye, who provided valuable suggestions and advice, and to Westview Press for remaining interested in this project through various personnel changes. Finally, I wish to acknowledge my daughter Alana Katherine who provided great, daily distraction at the end of this project, and my colleague, husband, and friend, Alan, who knew when to shield me from the distractions and when to share them with me.

L.B.

Editor's Introduction: Native Americans and U.S. Economic History

LINDA BARRINGTON

Pre-Colonial Endowments

Population Estimates at Contact

The 500th anniversary of the arrival of Christopher Columbus in the New World revived interest in precontact indigenous civilizations and population estimates thereof. Accordingly, William M. Denevan produced a second edition of his 1976 (edited) volume *The Native Population of the Americas in 1492*. In the 1992 edition, Denevan lowered his previously published estimate of the indigenous population of North America (excluding Mexico and Hawaii) in 1500 by 610,000 to 3,790,000.[1] Higher estimates put the preconquest indigenous population north of the Rio Grande at 7 to 12 million (Shaffer 1992, 4). A summary of the estimates that Denevan reported for particular tribes or regions at or near contact appear in Table I.1. Map I.1 shows the settlement areas of the indigenous population at first contact. Letters preceding the tribes listed in Table I.1 identify their precontact location on Map I.1.

Another good source for the demographic story of indigenous North Americans is A. J. Jaffe's *The First Immigrants from Asia: A Population History of the North American Indians*, also published in 1992. Here Jaffe presented the demographic history of American Indians from their assumed initial arrival from Asia through the 1980 Census of the Population of the United States. In Jaffe's text the first contact with Europeans is treated as just one episode in a population history that covers many millennia.[2] Jaffe estimated the indigenous population within the present-day borders of the United States (excluding Alaska and Hawaii) to be just 1 million near the

TABLE I.1   Existing Population Estimates for Various Regions or Tribes at or Near Contact

Region or Tribe (not mutually exclusive)	Population Estimate	Source(s)
North America (Excluding present day Mexico)	3,790,000	Denevan, Table 1
A. New England	72,000–144,000	Cook 1976b Snow 1980 Salisbury 1982
B. Mohawk	13,700–17,000	Snow 1980
C. Virginia Algonquian	14,300–22,300	Feest 1973
D. Arikara	30,000	Holder 1970
E. Pawnee	100,000	Holder 1970
F. Iroquois[a]	20,000–110,000	Trigger 1976 Engelbrecht 1987 Clermont 1980
G. Huron	23,000–30,000	Trigger 1985 Dickinson 1980
H. Micmac	12,000–50,000	Snow 1980 Miller 1976, 1982
I. Pueblo	100,000	Reff 1991
J. Timucuan	722,000	Dobyns 1983

[a]Writings from Cartier in 1535 record that the Iroquois village of Hochelaga contained fifty longhouses and some 1,000 people. This was the largest indigenous town noted by the French in the period of early contact; James P. Ronda, "Black Robes and Boston Men: Indian-White Relations in New France and New England, 1524–1701," in *The American Indian Experience, A Profile: 1524 to the Present,* ed. Philip Weeks (Arlington Heights, Ill.: Forum Press, 1988), 7.

Source: Summarized from William Denevan, ed., *The Native Population of the Americas in 1492,* 2nd ed. (Madison: University of Wisconsin Press, 1992), xix–xx and xxviii, Table 1.

time of first contact (1992, 246). Even adding in his estimates for Canada (210,000), Jaffe's numbers are still much lower than those of Denevan. With regard to the population beginnings of the New World, Jaffe concluded that the research suggests "the probability of a northeast Asia origin is very high" (1992, chap. 2). Yet there are those who doubt that all American Indians descended from immigrants who crossed the Bering Strait at the end of the Ice Age. More radical theories suggest multiple sources of "first" immigrants, possibly including ocean-faring Polynesians. Mainstream archaeologists, in particular, have questioned the theory that South America was populated solely by the continuous migration of hunters from the north. Most recently, an archaeological find in the Brazilian Amazon adds credence to the theory that not all indigenous South Americans are the descendants of North American high

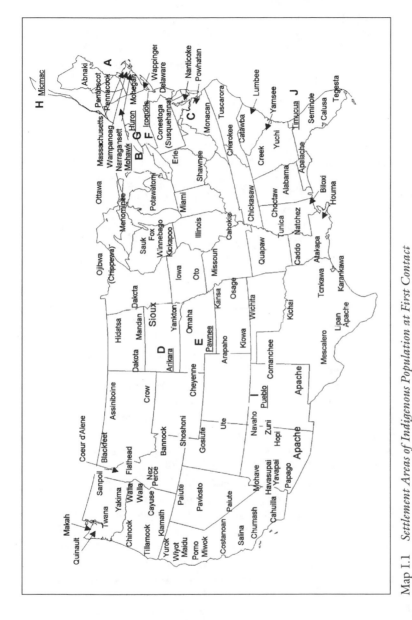

Map I.1 *Settlement Areas of Indigenous Population at First Contact*

Source: Compiled using Kenneth Jackson, ed. Atlas of American History, (1978), 8–9; Mark Carnes and John Gar-
raty, ed. Mapping America's Past: A Historical Atlas, (1996), 24; Hilde Heun Kagan, American Heritage Pictorial
Atlas of United States History, (1966), 23.

Note: Corresponding population estimates appear in Table I.1 for regions and underlined tribes marked A through J.

plains residents who moved southward in a single migration. Excavations have revealed an Amazonian population "contemporary with the Clovis tradition [11,200 to 10,900 years before the present—B.P.] but more than 5000 miles to the south" (Roosevelt et al. 1996), suggesting that a more complex migration pattern resulted in the population of the Americas.

The population estimates presented in Table I.1 focus on Native American societies located within the present-day boundaries of the forty-eight contiguous states at the time of first contact by Europeans. In the study of indigenous North Americans, the distinction is typically made between American Indians and the indigenous peoples of Alaska and Hawaii. Although peoples of all three categories are Native Americans, for our purposes the term "American Indian" will refer only to those indigenous peoples of the continental United States. Tribal affiliation is preferred to the overly general term "American Indian" and will be used when the discussion is tribe specific. As the policies and legislation of the colonial and federal governments often lumped together indigenous peoples of all tribes, the term "American Indian" will be used, by necessity, to denote collective members of multiple mainland tribes. The term "Native American" will refer to members of mainland tribes or to the peoples of Alaska and Hawaii.

Although there are historical differences in the contact and conquest histories of Native Americans, one experience common to Native Americans of all regions is devastation from disease (see Cook 1943, 1955; Milner 1980; McNeill 1976; Thornton 1987). For Hawaii, contact with white empires and diseases came two-and-a-half centuries after Columbus landed in the Caribbean. The first white "discovery" of Hawaii is generally attributed to Captain James Cook in 1778. Significant U.S. immigration to the islands began only after 1820. The conquest of Hawaii is often described as a condensed, but equally deadly, version of the conquest of the mainland. Only 120 years passed between Cook's first visit and the Annexation Treaty with the United States in 1898. This is less than half the time span between the first permanent Europeans settlements on North America's eastern seaboard and the Battle of Wounded Knee. Although there were fewer outright violent encounters between conquering and indigenous peoples in Hawaii, epidemics followed foreign presence on the islands, resulting in a massive depopulation of Hawaii similar to that experienced by other Native American communities. Estimates are that the indigenous population of Hawaii fell from 800,000 to just 48,000 within 100 years of Cook's arrival (Crosby 1992).

Precontact Economies

As long as people have populated North America, economic incentives have been at work. Economic history textbooks, however, start the time line of economic analysis several hundred, if not thousands, of years too late (see

Vernon L. Smith, Chapter 1 in this volume). The first immigrants to what would become the United States of America were not the pilgrims, the Spanish, or even the Vikings. The ancestors of indigenous populations in North America arrived more than 20,000 years before the Niña, the Pinta, and the Santa María. If population growth reveals the existence of at least minimal success in adapting to one's surroundings, then surely the population increase alone from zero to perhaps more than 3 million by 1492 would reveal the versatility and inventiveness of the first Americans within the present-day borders of the United States and Canada.

Archaeological records are the sole historical source for most of the pre-European history of indigenous civilizations in the present-day United States. Nonetheless, a long, rich history has been revealed throughout North America above the Rio Grande. Even a simple overview of the "highlights" of production practiced by a variety of precontact peoples provides a good sense of the sophistication of their ability to organize production. For example, highly advanced textiles were produced early on. Some 10,000 years ago, the weavings of indigenous peoples in the Southwest were "as advanced as anywhere in the world . . . [probably] using looms" (Goldberg 1996). In some cases, indigenous hunting techniques called for a remarkable degree of cooperation and organization. As early as 8200 B.C. on the Great Plains, bison hunts involved the organization of 100 persons or more to slaughter herds of bison by stampeding them over a cliff. Settled agriculture was also practiced quite early in prehistory. By 3000 B.C. domesticated corn was being grown north of present-day Mexico. Prior to the arrival of the Spanish, impressive architectural works had also been built north of the Rio Grande. Preserved in Mesa Verde National Park in Colorado are the multiroom cliff dwellings that the Anasazi (A.D. 1000–1300) built atop and into the sides of rock mesas. The Anasazi also built a system of dams and irrigation canals to support their agriculture. In the Mississippi River Valley, as early as 1400 B.C. large conical and bird-shaped earthen mounds were constructed at Poverty Point. Several thousand years before the European "discovery" of the New World, the Mississippian mound-building civilization used the Mississippi River system to conduct trade in flint and copper between Poverty Point and settlements along the Arkansas, Missouri, and Ohio rivers (see Linda Barrington, Chapter 2 in this volume). Without steel or iron tools, wheeled vehicles, gunpowder, large sailing ships, or keystone arches or domes, Native peoples within the present-day borders of the United States maintained extensive trade routes, practiced irrigated agriculture using dams and canals, and built cities that supported populations estimated in the tens of thousands[3] (see Mintz 1995, 1–11, for above and further discussion of prehistoric civilizations in North America).

By the time the Spanish arrived in 1492, the Anasazi had abandoned their 100-roomed Cliff Palace, their dams and irrigation canals; and Cahokia, the most successful Mississippian mound-building center, once populated with upwards of 30,000 people, was past its apex. The reason for the decline of these highly organized societies is still a matter of debate. Theoretical causes for their collapse include drought, environmental degradation, indigenous wars, and pre-European epidemics (Bryson and Murray 1977, chap. 3; Shaffer 1992, 81–83). Whatever the cause, the decline of these great communities did not mean the end of organized, indigenous economies. Spanish records indicate that indigenous trade routes were in operation, and significant inter- and intratribal socioeconomic distinctions were clearly present during the last decade of the fifteenth century. In northern North America, despite the lower population density, trading routes covering long distances also existed at the time of first contact with Europeans. The Huron, for example, maintained precontact trade routes reaching from one end of the Great Lakes region to the other (Ronda 1988, 8).[4] One should not be surprised, then, that indigenous traders expanded their trading networks to incorporate the new arrivals from Europe and the merchandise they offered.

Colonial Political and Trade Alliances

Economic aspirations of Europeans and European Americans have been the driving force in the history of the United States. Although many immigrants came to North America seeking greater social and religious freedoms and others were brought by force, economic opportunities were by far the major draw. Fulfillment of European American aspirations also drove Native American history. Inherent in the "frontier economy" characterization of the economic history of the United States is the westward expansion of the nonindigenous population. As the expanding white population swept westward, it undeniably obliterated or irreversibly altered indigenous nations.

Beginning as a fragile minority on the North American continent, Europeans and their descendants quickly became the majority population. It is likely that the nonindigenous population outnumbered that of indigenous societies as early as the middle of the eighteenth century.[5] Looking at two relatively early settlement regions, the Southeast and New Mexico, we find indigenous peoples losing their majority standing certainly before 1800. Peter Wood (1989) estimated that in the Southeast the nonindigenous population became the majority before 1715; in New Mexico, this did not occur until 1780 (Gutierrez 1991). The population time series of both these regions are presented in Figures I.1 and I.2. Although New England probably became majority white no later than the Southeast, the western regions of the continent were settled by nonindigenous populations much later. Indigenous societies in these western regions, however, also had lower population densities than those of the South and East. Population estimates for all of the United States and Canada for the years 1570, 1650, 1825, and 1935 are available from Angel Rosenblat (1954). According to his estimates, Native Americans composed almost 86 percent of the population of Canada

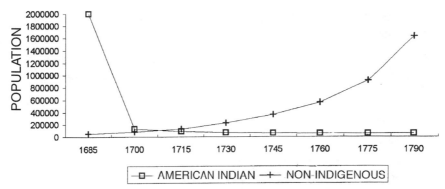

Figure I.1 *Indigenous and Nonindigenous Population, Southeastern United States*
Source: Populaion estimates from Peter Wood, "The Changing Population of the
Colonial South: An Overview by Race and Region, 1685–1790," in *Powhatan's Man-*
tle: Indians in the Colonial Southeast, eds. Peter H. Wood, Gregory A. Waselkov, and
Tomas M. Hartley (Lincoln: University of Nebraska Press, 1989), 38–39, table 1.

Note: Regions covered by population estimates include Virginia (east of the mountains), North Carolina (east of the mountains), South Carolina (east of the mountains), Florida, Georgia, Alabama, Creek, Cherokee, Choctaw, Chickasaw, Natchez,
Louisiana, east Texas, and Shawnee Interior.

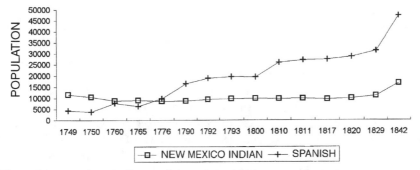

Figure I.2 *American Indian and Spanish Population, New Mexico*
Source: Population data from Ramon Gutierrez, *When Jesus Came, the Corn Mothers*
Went Away: Marriage, Sexuality, and Power in New Mexico, 1500–1846, (Stanford:
Stanford University Press, 1991), 167, table 4.2.

and the United States in 1650 and under 4 percent in 1825 (see Figure I.3).
Although Rosenblat's data do not contradict the suggestion that the mid-
eighteenth century was the "crossover" point, neither does it provide any real
supporting evidence for that theory.

Mercantilist competition among the European empires is typically the frame
in which the beginnings of North American economic history is set. Whereas
competition and alliances between European powers are emphasized, the alliances actively sought between European colonizers and indigenous nations
are largely overlooked. How important the alliances between colonial and in-

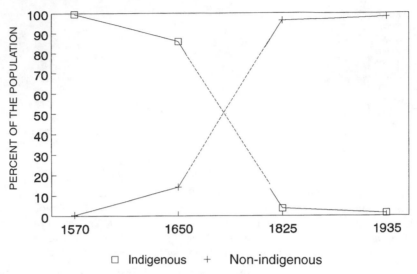

Figure I.3   *Indigenous and Nonindigenous Composition of Population, United States and Canada*
Source: Population data from Angel Rosenblot, *La Poblacion Indigena yel Mestizaje en America* (Buenos Aires: Editorial Nova, 1954), 1:21, 37, 59, 88.

digenous nations were to the delineation and maintenance of these mercantilist colonies is rarely discussed. Political and trade relations with Native American societies were fundamental to the early colonization and settlement.

In northern North America, the French formed alliances with the Algonquian and Huron, and the British with the Iroquois Confederacy—inheriting in 1644 relations first established by New Netherlands Dutch traders (Wolf 1982, 163–170). The Iroquois Confederacy, which included the Cayuga, Mohawk, Oneida, Onondaga, and Seneca, is also referred to today as the Six Nations.[6] Precolonial animosities between the Mohawk of the Iroquois Confederacy and the Huron provided an indigenous template upon which the British-French mercantilist competition was laid in the New World (Roback 1992, 14–16).[7] In the southeastern regions of North America, the French and British formalized political and trade alliances with the Choctaw and Chickasaw, respectively. Like the peoples of northern North America, the indigenous population of the Southeast could provide valuable furs for export. During the eighteenth century the most consistent export from French Louisiana was deerskin.[8] Between 1720 and 1780 an average of 50,000 deerskins were exported from Louisiana annually, with an approximate value of 100,000 livres. About one-third of the value of Louisiana's exports at midcentury was in deerskins. Similarly, peltry was an important export from South Carolina. As late as 1748, 22 percent of the export value of South Carolina was from deerskins (rice provided the majority of the export value). Roughly 100,000 deerskins were exported annually from South Carolina during this decade (Usner

1992, 246–247; see Edward Murphy, Chapter 5 in this volume, for further discussion of the southeastern fur trade).

Although gold is typically identified as the treasure sought by mercantilist conquest, trade with the indigenous nations did prove complementary to mercantilist goals as well. Historian Dale Miquelon wrote:

A large portion of the hardware and dry goods was destined for the Indian trade and, so far as the white population was concerned, filled an economic role similar to that of most of the barrelled beef exported to Martinique, which sustained the sugar export economy by feeding the slaves. The Indian fitted into the mercantile economy better than did the slave because he not only provided an export staple, but was a good consumer of manufactures, perhaps a better customer than a French peasant. Indian or white, the Canadian population showed the same dependence upon French manufactures that characterized the Creole populations. (Quoted in Usner 1992, 259)

And according to Daniel Usner, the French were exchanging 5,000 ells of limbourgh cloth and 4,000 pounds of gunpowder annually in trade with the Choctaw by 1750 (1992, 259).[9]

Although the history of Native American–white interaction is often the story of a victimized and exploited indigenous people, evidence can be found in early trade relations to the contrary. By the mid-eighteenth century those tribes indigenous to locations of the first colonial settlements had been decimated by dislocation, violence, and disease. However, for a time, some large tribes of the hinterland of North America held a significant degree of bargaining power in interactions with the French, British, and Spanish. Prior to British colonial domination of North America, American Indians could and did play European traders against one another rather effectively. Tribes with strategic locations were able to break monopoly price fixing and obtain goods declared contraband by one or another of the European powers (Curtin 1984; Worcester 1988, 37). In the 1730s the governor of Louisiana agreed to raise the price paid for Choctaw furs because of fears that more furs would otherwise flow northeast to the English. And two decades later, concern was still present over Choctaw "malcontents who have gone to trade their skins to the English." During the 1770s Spain tried repeatedly to prevent the trade of guns and ammunition to the Texas Indians, but their efforts were futile. The indigenous populations of east Texas could obtain these goods easily through trade in Louisiana and Illinois (Usner 1992, 252, 134).

Trade was not the only realm in which European competitive aspirations surfaced in the New World. North America also became an auxiliary military battlefield for the four European wars fought between 1689 and 1763. The European military and trade conflicts heightened indigenous tensions, often intentionally. In 1721 Louisiana officials, for example, offered "'one gun, one pound of powder, and two bullets' for each Chickasaw scalp and eighty livres of merchandise for each Chickasaw slave" (Usner 1992, 65). By this time the

Chickasaw had established a strong alliance with British South Carolina. Furthermore, the introduction of the horse and firearms—prized European goods—altered the traditional balance of weapons power, creating an arms race among indigenous tribes. This, in turn, increased the value of European trade to their Native allies. (For a discussion of institutional change resulting from the introduction of the horse, see Terry L. Anderson and Steven La-Combe, Chapter 3 in this volume.)

The importance of Native political and trade alliances to the eventual pattern of development in the New World is hard to measure, but the intensity of European solicitation of such relations suggests it was considered paramount at the time. Historian Clarence Vandiveer ([1929] 1971) went so far as to suggest that had the British not benefited from the buffer zone provided by the Iroquois, the majority of North America would be French. David Wolf agreed that the British armed the Iroquois to slow French expansion westward, but added that the French also had an interest in keeping the Iroquois strong. The dominance of the Iroquois prevented the British from opening direct trade with the Ottawa and thus, paradoxically, protected French traders who did business west of the Iroquois (Wolf 1982, 169). The French in Louisiana had similar perverse desires to weaken yet not destroy the Chickasaw: Although the Chickasaw were British allies, their presence prevented the French-allied Choctaw from becoming too powerful (Usner 1992, 81–82). Work by Ann M. Carlos and Frank D. Lewis (Chapter 4 in this volume) makes clear that the British and French each responded to the competitive threat posed by the other by increasing fur trade activities with the surrounding tribes. Wherever the exclusive dominance of trade relations was challenged, the purchase of furs by Europeans increased beyond the monopolist optimum. As economic and political relations were strongly linked, such evidence can suggest the importance of indigenous relations in both realms. That the European powers monopolized, by the use of government agents, all interactions with both individual American Indians and their tribal governments also shows the value placed on such relations (see Roback 1992, 11–13, for a discussion of British monopolization of purchases of American Indian lands).

The fur trade established an interdependency between American Indians and Europeans, but what balance of power existed initially was eventually lost. Westward expansion of white settlers and reductions in animal populations resulted in increased competition between indigenous tribes. Increased resource scarcity heightened rivalries between some tribes and caused the displacement others. Further conflict arose when displaced tribes relocated in already-occupied territory. Such widespread upheaval made impossible the formation of lasting and widespread Indian alliances that might otherwise check white settlement. And as the British empire came to dominate larger regions of the continent, even the most powerful tribes were subsumed within its area of influence. The bargaining power of indigenous nations diminished once they no longer had bordering empires to play against one another (Smith 1988, 52; Usner 1992, 284).

Colonial Policy and the Revolution

Much attention has been paid to the role that the Navigation Acts played in the American Revolution, and the consensus is that the net economic cost to the colonies was relatively small. With mercantilist goals in mind, the British Crown tightly regulated colonial issuance of money and the manufacture and trade of goods through the Navigation Acts. But imperial policies also subsidized goods approved for colonial production and provided military protection of the colonies and colonial shipping. The net burden of being under Britain mercantilist rule has been estimated to be between 3 percent and less than 1 percent of estimated colonial income (McClelland 1969; Thomas 1965).

Although also listed among the grievances stated in the Declaration of Independence, the closure of land west of the Appalachian Mountains to British colonial settlement was another economic stimulant of the American Revolution, one that has been far less often discussed.[10] In the two decades prior to the Declaration of Independence the British Crown made two declarations in an attempt to protect American Indian lands from future settlement and thereby lower military costs on the colonial frontier. In 1763 the king drew a demarcation line along the Appalachian Mountains, creating a protected area for American Indians west of this line. Only traders with permits were to be allowed beyond the Appalachian Mountain border (Roback 1992, 16–17). Indigenous power was strong enough in this region that the Crown assumed, perhaps incorrectly, that the cost of further aggravating the Native inhabitants in the Old West would be greater than the benefit of placating colonists bent on expanding settlement westward.[11] In 1774, intensifying the frustrations of colonists, the Crown then declared the area between the Appalachian Mountains and the Ohio River to be an Indian reservation and ceded the land between the Ohio and Mississippi rivers to Quebec (the Quebec Act).[12] Overlapping claims had been made on this land by the colonies of Connecticut, Massachusetts, and Virginia, and the forced loss of future settlement land was not taken lightly. The colonists' responded to the "loss" of the Old West with an import boycott. This is the same tactic used to protest the Sugar Act (1764) and the Townshend Act (1767) (Atack and Passell 1994, 68–69, 252). George Washington, an owner of western lands in the contested area, threatened to fight the British in Boston at his own expense after the Quebec Act was enacted (Hughes 1990, 45). The strong reaction provoked by the Quebec Act suggests that restricting the "right" of westward expansion was considered by the colonists to be at least as damaging as the mercantilist regulations more commonly discussed by economic historians.

With hindsight we can see that removing these lands from white settlement would probably have altered the pattern of economic growth to a much greater degree than did the Navigation Acts and similar legislation. But what was the expected opportunity cost of the settlement ban at the time? Would the expected losses have been greater than the 0.5 percent of annual income that Thomas estimated as the net cost of mercantilist restrictions? Given the size of the land mass under question, we might conjecture that colonists had high expectations for future economic gain from the lands declared off-limits to settlement. To date, however, no quantitative study of the contribution of Indian land policy to the causes of the American Revolution has been published.

Indian Territory Policy of the United States: Removal, Concentration, and Allotment

The creation and management of Indian Territory by the U.S. government passed through three phases between the establishment of U.S. nationhood and the Indian Reorganization Act of 1934. The three phases were removal, concentration, and allotment. The misguided premise underlying removal was that there existed some distant land to which American Indians, whose homelands were in the path of westward expansion, could be once and for all relocated. It was thought that removal would both clear the way for white settlement and protect the indigenous people from destruction. The policy of removal gave way to that of concentration as white desire for land increased. The belief that American Indian tribes would fare better if located away from white settlement was also the underpinning of the policy of concentration. But as priority was given to the expansion of white settlement, rather than maintaining the integrity of American Indian territory, indigenous tribes had to be concentrated within smaller areas in order to keep whites and American Indians separate.

Since first contact with the indigenous peoples of North America, the Europeans had as a goal the "civilizing" of the New World inhabitants. Becoming civilized was generally synonymous with becoming assimilated. It was thought that the isolation of the American Indians from white settlements would allow them to assimilate at their own pace. But the relocation and concentration of the American Indian tribes did not, in fact, lead to complete assimilation into the dominant culture, especially with regard to land tenure. Allotment, a more active intervention into American Indian land tenure, followed the removal and concentration policies. Allotment required that all American Indian territory be divided into individual allotments, with each recognized tribal member receiving a parcel of land to be held individually. This restructuring was seen to have two beneficial results. First, allotment would advance assimilation by imposing individual rather than communal landholding, allowing American Indians to capitalize their land assets if desired. Second, "surplus" lands remaining after allotment could be opened to white settlement. The policies of removal, concentration, and allotment are each discussed in turn below.

Westward Expansion, the Land Acts, and Removal from the Old Northwest

Westward expansion is not only inseparable from the economic history of the United States but has been put forward as, perhaps, the primary factor contributing to the long-run economic growth of the nation. The frontier both created economic opportunity for a large segment of the population and supported the entreprencurial spirit necessary to take advantage of this unique access to economic resources (see North 1990, 98–99; North and Rutten, 1987). There is no agreement on the extent to which the historical paths of growth of the current industrialized countries can serve as models for less-developed countries (Sen, 1983; Hirschman, 1981). In identifying factors contributing to U.S. economic growth that may or may not be transferable to today's developing countries, the history of westward expansion should not be considered in isolation from the expropriation of the lands of indigenous peoples. Many less-industrialized countries are currently struggling with issues of indigenous rights to land and cultural preservation.[13]

Westward expansion, and the economic history of United States in general, was indelibly shaped by land and settlement policy. Although policy governing the use and disbursement of federal land continually changed with the dynamics of the nation, there are three pieces of legislation that stand out as monumental in the history of white settlement. The Land Ordinance of 1785 detailed the process for surveying and the rules for purchasing government lands in the Old Northwest. The uniform patchwork quilt pattern one sees today when flying over the Midwest is a testament to the once radical notion of systematic establishment of townships and privately purchased lots. The Northwest Ordinance of 1787 outlined both the political structure of this new territory and the procedures for obtaining statehood. Finally, the Homestead Act of 1862 made ownership of land possible for just a ten-dollar registration fee and five years of continuous residence (see Hyman 1986 for an overview of the Homestead Act).

Each wave of frontier-opening legislation and settlement was preceded necessarily by governmental action on the "Indian question." White settlers regularly encroached on Native lands ahead of the official opening of a territory. Violence between the indigenous residents and encroaching settlers as

TABLE I.2   Nonindigenous Population of the Old Northwest, 1790–1860
(in thousands)

	Ohio	Indiana	Illinois	Michigan	Wisconsin
1790	–	–	–	–	–
1800	45.4	5.6	–	–	–
1810	230.8	24.5	12.3	4.8	–
1820	581.3	147.2	55.2	8.8	–
1830	937.9	343.0	157.4	31.6	–
1840	1519.5	685.9	476.2	212.3	30.9
1850	1980.3	988.4	851.5	397.7	305.4
1860	2339.5	1350.4	1712.0	749.1	775.9

Source: Gary M. Walton, "River Transportation and the Old Northwest Territory," in *Essays on the Economy of the Old Northwest,* eds. David C. Klingaman and Richard K. Vedder (Athens: University of Ohio Press, 1987). Reprinted with the permission of Ohio University Press, Swallow Press, Athens.

well as clashes among the settlers themselves (who had no court-enforceable title) probably sped the official opening of frontier lands. Prior to the opening of new lands to white settlement, the federal government always undertook some "legal" action to deal with Native American land claims. The broad official policy that was applied first to indigenous residents of the Old Northwest and later to residents of all lands east of the Mississippi was removal. At best, removal of indigenous peoples beyond the frontier of white settlement was considered the only way to prevent their wholesale destruction. At worst, removal was a compromise accepted by land-hungry settlers who otherwise preferred genocide.[14]

Ohio was the first region of the Old Northwest coveted for white settlement by the new nation. In less than seventy-five years, 2,000,000 European Americans had settled in Ohio, replacing the upwards of 20,000 American Indians of various tribes who had resided there at the time of the Revolutionary War (Knepper 1988, 87, 94).[15] Table I.2 presents the nonindigenous population in the Old Northwest between 1790 and 1860.

Congress acknowledged that prior to implementation of the Land Ordinances, Indian title to this land had to be removed. The Northwest Ordinance of 1787 stated explicitly that

> The utmost good faith shall always be observed toward the Indians; their land and property shall never be taken from them without their consent; and in their property, rights and liberty, they shall never be invaded or disturbed, unless in just and lawful wars authorized by Congress, but laws founded in justice and humanity shall from time to time be made, for preventing wrongs being done to them, and for preserving peace and friendship with them. (Northwest Ordinance, 1787, Third Article, as found in Prucha 1990)

The first treaty removing Indian title to land was signed in 1785 at Fort McIntosh, Pennsylvania, following the passage of the Land Ordinance of that year. Contested by unrepresented tribes and individual American Indians, the Fort McIntosh treaty did not definitively or universally remove title from the Native residents of Ohio. Military action and four more treaties (the last being the Treaty of Greenville in 1795) were employed by the United States over the next decade to secure the southeastern two-thirds of the future state of Ohio (Knepper 1988, 91–94). The year after the Treaty of Greenville was signed, the first land offices were opened in Pittsburgh and Cincinnati under the Land Act of 1796 (Atack and Passell 1994, 258, table 9.1). Removal of the Ohio tribes from the remaining third of the future state would wait till after the War of 1812. The last of the organized tribes was removed from Ohio in 1842 (Knepper 1988, 82).

Land cessions and white settlement of Indiana began after 1800. These further encroachments brought to prominence two Shawnee Indians: Tenskwatawa and Tecumseh. The Shawnee brothers, whose pan-Indian alliance united members of the Kickapoo, Menomini, Ottowa, Potowatomi, Shawnee, Winnebago, and Wyandot tribes, led the last resistance in the Old Northwest (Mintz 1995, 27). Tenskwatawa was killed by future President Benjamin Harrison at the battle of Tippecanoe.[16] Tecumseh fought on the side of the British and died in the War of 1812. By 1819 the American Indian nations from the Mississippi River to the Atlantic Ocean had finally lost the last of their potential for playing empire against empire. The United States had gained 828,000 square miles in the Louisiana Purchase (1803), beaten the British in the War of 1812, and acquired the Spanish holdings in the Southeast (1810 and 1819).

Cotton, Slaves, and Removal from the South

Although the phrase "westward expansion" typically elicits images of log cabins and dugout prairie houses spreading across the Midwest and Plains, the cotton South experienced its own antebellum westward expansion. Eli Whitney's invention of the cotton gin expanded greatly the viable cotton lands, and "in the 1820s and 1830s there was an almost explosive rush into Alabama, Tennessee, and Mississippi" (Atack and Passell 1994, 300). This westward spread of cotton has been explained by the attraction of higher yields that these new lands could provide (Atack and Passell 1994, 300). Map I.2 illustrates this boom in cotton production between 1821 and 1859.

This spread of the cotton economy, like the expansion of white settlement into the Midwest, is intertwined with the removal of indigenous peoples. The southeastern Native Americans, some of whom occupied coveted potential cotton lands, were members of the Cherokee, Creek, Choctaw, Chickasaw, and Seminole tribes. These peoples were also known as the Five

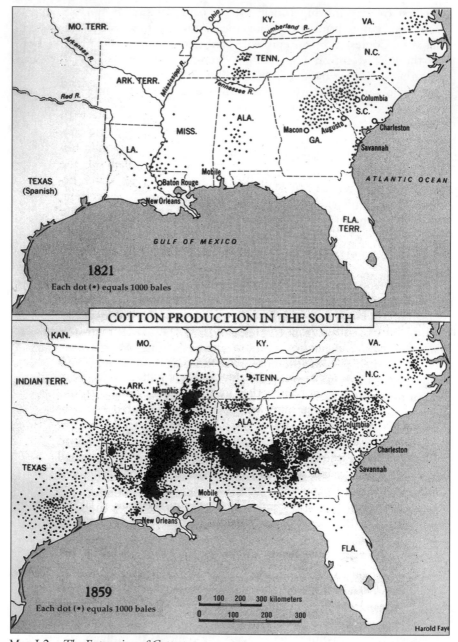

Map I.2   *The Expansion of Cotton*
Source: Gavin Wright, The Political Economy of the Cotton South *(New York: Norton, 1978), 16. Reprinted by permission of W. W. Norton. Adapted from USDA, Atlas of Agriculture, Part 5, Advance Sheets, December 15, 1915.*

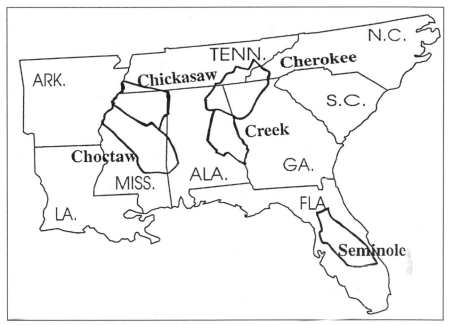

Map I.3   *Southeastern Tribal Lands of the Chickasaw, Cherokee, Choctaw, Creek, and Seminole Prior to Removal*
Source: Philip Weeks, Farewell My Nation: The American Indian and the United States, 1820–1890 *(Wheeling, Ill.: Harlan Davidson, 1990), 20. Adapted with permission of Harlan Davidson, Inc.*

Civilized Tribes. Together, these tribes had some 60,000 members in the present-day states of Georgia, Alabama, Mississippi, North Carolina, Tennessee, and Florida (Foreman 1934, vii). Map I.3 illustrates the general location and lands occupied by Cherokee, Creek, Choctaw, Chickasaw, and Seminole Indians. On the southern frontier, white residents' intolerance of American Indian homelands in the region increased with the growth of the cotton industry. In addition, the 1828 discovery of gold on Cherokee lands in Georgia further magnified state determination to take control of indigenous lands. Just one month after the discovery of gold on Cherokee lands, the Georgia legislature passed sweeping restrictions on the Cherokee Nation that prohibited the meeting of the Cherokee governmental body, Cherokee mining on their own lands, all contracts between whites and Cherokee, and Cherokee testimony against any white in court (Anders 1981, 228).[17] The Indian Removal Act was passed by Congress in 1830 requiring the removal of American Indians residing east of the Mississippi.

The southeastern tribes responded in varying ways to increased pressure from their white neighbors. The Choctaw, Chickasaw, and Creek ceded land quickly; within two years of the passage of the Indian Removal Act, the Choctaw, Chickasaw, and Creek signed treaties ceding their southeastern territories in exchange for lands west of the Mississippi River (Weeks 1990, 28). The Cherokee and Seminole, on the other hand, continued to resist removal, albeit in dramatically different ways. The Cherokee resisted removal through assimilation and through battles in the U.S. courts; the Seminole undertook armed resistance to wage a defensive war against U.S. Army troops. In the end, however, none fared better than the others. All of the Five Civilized Tribes were removed to Indian Territory west of the Mississippi. It was assumed that this removal would protect the tribes from further white encroachment. But encroachment continued and, within decades, all tribes removed under the Indian Removal Act would suffer additional territorial losses.

Map I.4 provides a summary of the removal of tribes from the South and the Old Northwest. Approximate locations of lands ceded and location within the Indian Territory are shown by tribe. Although the vast majority of American Indians suffered removal, a minority of tribal members did escape the ordeal and remained within preremoval regions. Among the Cherokee, there were two notable North Carolina communities that survived removal, despite being within the borders of the Cherokee Nation. Members of the Snowbird community bought back over 1,200 acres of their land from the state of North Carolina. Since North Carolina did not allow Indians to own land until after the Civil War, this purchase was made under the names of three sympathetic whites within weeks of removal. Some fifty Cherokee families within the area of today's Qualla Reservation became citizens of North Carolina, forsaking their Cherokee citizenship at that time (Neely 1991, chap. 1).

For quite some time the Cherokee had demonstrated their desire to avoid removal and remain in their southeastern homelands through selective adoption of and allegiance with white society. Cherokee, along with Chickasaw and Choctaw and some Creek tribal members, had fought on the American side in the War of 1812. In 1819, in an attempt to stay white settlement, the Cherokee government passed a law making unapproved land sales a capital offense. The Cherokee replaced their tribal governance structure with a republican government in 1827. Their constitution was modeled after the Constitution of the United States. The Cherokee Council established a national newspaper under the editorship of Elias Boudinot. *The Cherokee Phoenix*, a bilingual (Cherokee and English) publication, began its publication in 1828 (Foreman 1934, 292).

In contrast to popular images of indigenous societies, many Cherokee had adopted southern, "white" agricultural practices. Many Cherokee were slave holders and, perhaps most significantly (given contemporary rhetoric that equated civilized society with settled agriculture), the majority of antebellum

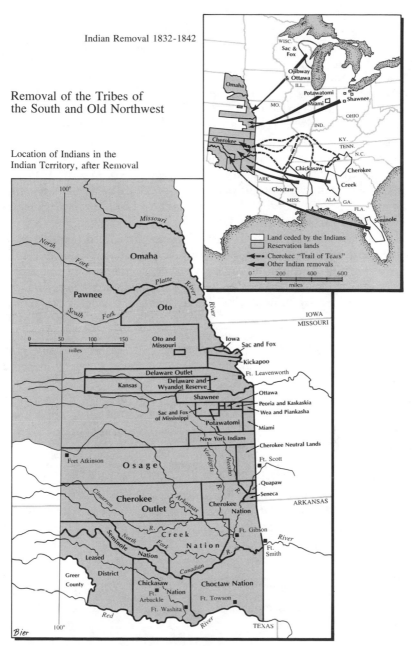

Indian Removal 1832-1842

Removal of the Tribes of
the South and Old Northwest

Location of Indians in the
Indian Territory, after Removal

Map I.4   *Tribal Lands Before and After Removal*
Source: Philip Weeks, Farewell My Nation: The American Indian and the United
States, 1820–1890 *(Wheeling, Ill.: Harlan Davidson, 1990), 20. Reprinted by permission of Harlan Davidson, Inc.*

Cherokee farms were producing marketable surpluses (Wishart 1995).[18] (David Wishart's discussion of the agricultural productivity and capital accumulation of the Cherokee prior to removal can be found in Chapter 6 in this volume.)

The Cherokee also used the U.S. court system to fight actively against removal and state-imposed restrictions. It appeared they had won a significant legal battle against removal in 1832 when the U.S. Supreme Court ruled in *Worcester v. Georgia* that state law did not extend to the Indian Nations. This legally freed the tribes from state harassment efforts. However, showing his great contempt for as well as the inherent weakness of the separation of powers, President Andrew Jackson simply refused to enforce the Court's ruling—making this an important case in constitutional as well as American Indian history. Removal of the Cherokee was carried out forcibly by the federal army in 1838, despite the assimilation of many Cherokee.

By contrast with the Cherokee, the Seminole of Florida resisted both removal and assimilation. The U.S. government's refusal to accept the Seminole presence in the Florida territory resulted in a costly seven-year war. Over 10,000 U.S. Army and Navy troops were committed to the war effort; they were joined by some 30,000 citizen soldiers. Roughly 14 percent of army and navy troops died in action or from disease. Some estimates of the dollar expenditures on the Seminole Wars are as high as 40 million dollars. At the end of the Seminole Wars, 3,000 Seminole were eventually removed to the Indian Territory west of the Mississippi. Perhaps several hundred escaped capture and remained in Florida (Mahon 1967, 325–326). Among the Creek, Choctaw, and Chickasaw some 28,000 to 30,000 survived removal from their southeastern homelands. It is estimated that 4,000 of the 18,000 Cherokee who began the removal march from the Southeast died en route (Perdue 1988, 110–113; Weeks 1990, 32). Because so many died in the removal, the trek westward is known as the Trail of Tears. The path of the Cherokee Trail of Tears is identified on Map I.4.

Although generalizations can be made on the tribal level, the degree of acculturation of individual tribal members varied greatly within as well as among tribes. Disputes between "progressives" and "traditionalists" plagued the tribes both before and after removal. Cultural differences between and within the Five Civilized Tribes further worsened the already appalling experience of removal. A low-intensity civil war lasted for seven years (1839–1846) among the Cherokee after removal, and the issue of slavery eventually split allegiances between the North and the South during the U.S. Civil War.[19]

Concentration of the Indian Territory

The growing western movement of the white population during the 1840s turned the policy of "protective" removal of American Indians into a failed

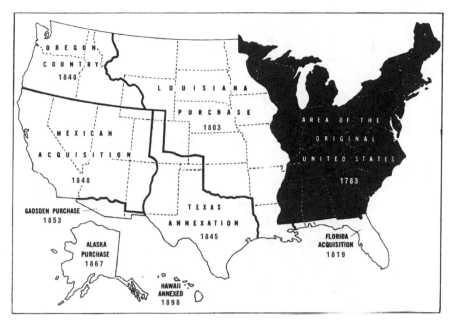

Map I.5   *The Territorial Expansion of the United States*
Source: Gary M. Walton and Hugh Rockoff, History of the American Economy, 8th
cd. *(New York: Harcourt, Brace, 1998), 161, map 8.1. Reprinted with permission of
Harcourt, Brace, and Co.*

policy. Despite the remoteness of Indian Territory west of the Mississippi
just decades earlier, American Indians were now in the direct path of westward expansion. Within just three years, the United States annexed the Republic of Texas (1845), obtained the Oregon Territory south of the forty-
ninth parallel (1846), and took control of an additional 1.2 million square
miles of western lands at the end of the Mexican War (1848) (Weeks 1990,
51) (see Map I.5). Accompanying the acquisition of these new territories
was an unprecedented reduction in the time it took to travel westward. Over
the first half of the nineteenth century, canals were extended into the Old
Northwest, steamboats were introduced for river travel, and railroads expanded into previously isolated areas. Between 1830 and 1857 travel time
for this trip fell from just over two weeks to under three days. In 1857 one
could travel the entire width of the continent, from the East to the West
Coast, in as little as three weeks (see Maps I.6, I.7, I.8). Between 1800 and
1830 the nonindigenous population in the North Central Region of the
country increased from 51,000 to 1,610,000.[20] By 1860 the population in
this region was over nine million (U.S. Bureau of the Census 1975, series
A172). Additionally, on the Pacific Coast, the Gold Rush prompted a population explosion in California, pulling further traffic across the Plains. Be-

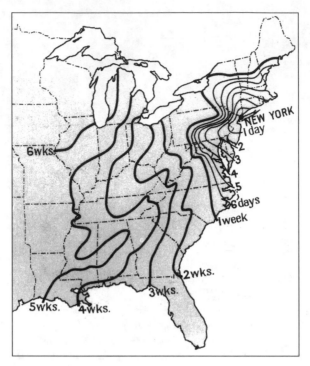

Map I.6   *Rates of Travel, 1800*
Source: Charles O. Paullin, Atlas of the Historical Geography of the United States *(Washington, D.C.: Carnegie
Institution, 1932), plate 138A. Reprinted with permission of Carnegie Institution.*

tween 1849 and 1851 the non-Indian population in California increased
from 14,000 to nearly 500,000 (Weeks 1990, 49).

Along the western trails, the Plains tribes (who were still dependent upon
hunting) bore the burden of westward expansion most directly through the
reduction in available game. This ecological crisis was the result of both
hunting and habitat encroachment by travelers (see Map I.9 for the location
of the Bozeman and Oregon Trails in relation to the eventual location of the
Sioux reservation). The response of the Plains tribes may appear remarkably
similar to that of Western institutions dealing with international traffic and
commerce: They imposed duties or tolls for passage on the "foreign" white
travelers. Along the Oregon Trail, for example, the Sioux responded to the
externalities created by westward-bound travelers by forcibly collecting a
compensating toll from those passing across their lands. However, charges
that the Sioux were harassing whites traveling the trail bombarded Washing-

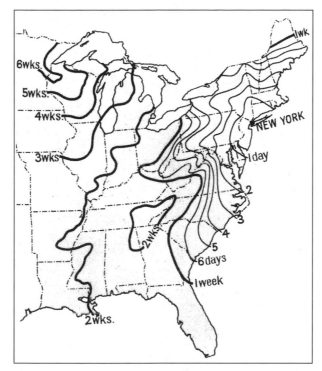

Map I.7   *Rates of Travel, 1830*
Source: Charles O. Paullin, Atlas of the Historical
Geography of the United States *(Washington, D.C.:
Carnegie Institution, 1932), plate 138B. Reprinted with
permission of Carnegie Institution.*

ton, and the federal government responded in 1847 by establishing forts
along the trail to protect citizens. In doing so, the government effectively
prohibited the collection of compensating tolls by the Sioux (Weeks 1990,
57–58). This was an implicit refusal, on the part of the U.S. government, to
acknowledge Sioux sovereignty to tax within its own borders.

At the time of the Indian Removal Act, the land designated as Indian Territory was thought to be so far removed from the lands desired for white settlement that this removal would be final. However, as land from coast to
coast came under U.S. domain and as the cost of moving westward fell, the
size of the Indian "sanctuary" west of the Mississippi—which lay between
the Red River to the south and the Missouri River to the north (see Map
I.4)—seemed increasingly excessive. Territorial organization in the large
"unorganized" region of the continent seemed a necessity (see Map I.10).

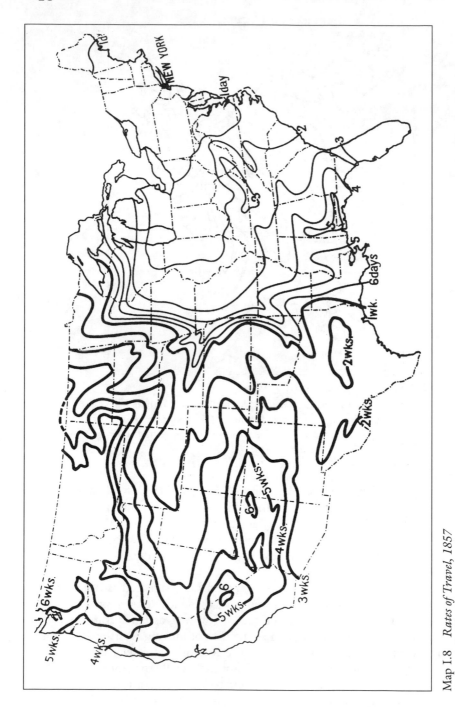

Map I.8   *Rates of Travel, 1857*
Source: Charles O. Paullin, Atlas of the Historical Geography of the United States (Washington, D.C.: Carnegie Institution, 1932), plate 138C. Reprinted with permission of Carnegie Institution.

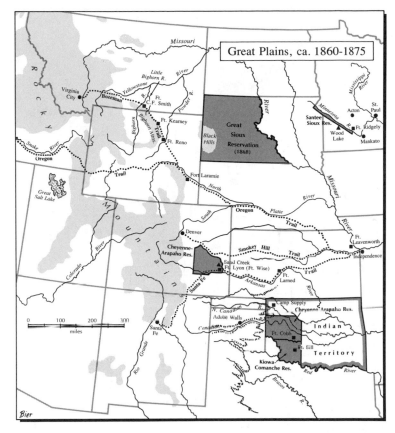

Map I.9   *Location of the Bozeman Trail, the Oregon Trail, and the Santa Fe Trail*
Source: *Philip Weeks,* Farewell My Nation: The American Indian and the United States, 1820–1890 *(Wheeling, Ill.: Harlan Davidson, 1990), 74. Reprinted by permission of Harlan Davidson, Inc.*

Although in 1850 the middle plains remained "unorganized," the population density of white settlers was increasing in the new states west of the Mississippi River. In particular, the populations of Missouri and Arkansas were denser in 1850 than those of Georgia and North Carolina just sixty years prior (see Map I.11). So as the second half of the nineteenth century began, the solution to the "Indian question" turned from removal westward to concentration within a smaller territory (Weeks 1990, 60–71). The Indian Appropriations Act was passed in 1851. This act authorized $100,000 to be used in negotiating the reduction of Indian Territory and relocating

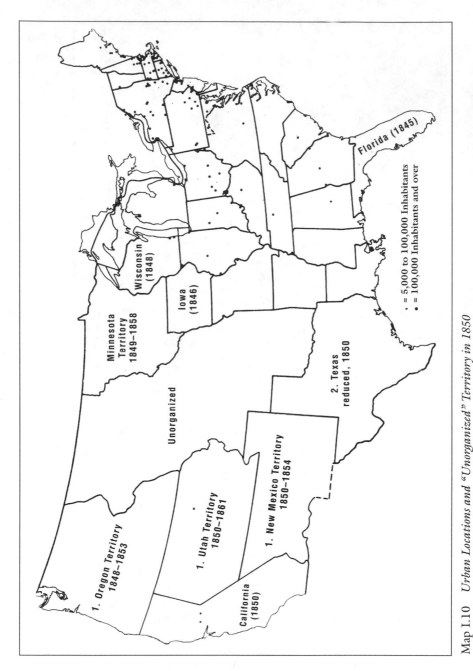

Map I.10   *Urban Locations and "Unorganized" Territory in 1850*
Source: *Charles O. Paullin, Atlas of the Historical Geography of the United States (Washington, D.C.: Carnegie Institution, 1932), plate 63. Reprinted with permission of Carnegie Institution.*

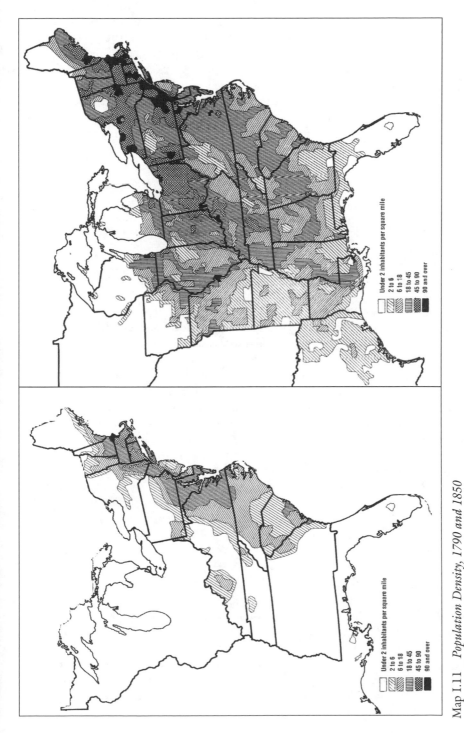

Map I.11 *Population Density, 1790 and 1850*
Source: Charles O. Paullin, Atlas of the Historical Geography of the United States (Washington, D.C.: Carnegie Institution, 1932), plates 76, 77. Reprinted with permission of Carnegie Institution.

the Native Americans from these ceded lands. The Kansas-Nebraska Act, passed in 1854, opened up the Indian Territory north of the present-day state of Oklahoma for white settlement (Weeks 1990, 62, 65). By 1856 Indian lands had been shrunk by some 174 million acres through the negotiation of some fifty treaties.

The policy of concentration meant that Oklahoma was to become a new home to many tribes other than the Five Civilized Tribes of the Southeast. Map I.12 illustrates the eventual relocation of many American Indian tribes from their original locations in the East and the West to Oklahoma. In all, American Indians from some sixty different tribal identities were relocated to Oklahoma during the nineteenth century (*American Indian Digest* 1994, 34).

The War Between the States and Reconstruction

The Five Civilized Tribes and the Confederacy

Indian Territory that lay beyond the western border of the Union was both above and below the Mason-Dixon Line, geographically and institutionally: Although the bulk of American Indians were being relocated to Oklahoma, south of the thirty-sixth parallel many still resided in Kansas and other "free" territories. Although the Indian Territories were officially not part of the United States of America and therefore neither within the Union nor the Confederacy, they were nonetheless drawn into the Civil War. In the antebellum period there were both slaveholding American Indians and American Indian abolitionists. Consequently, when war broke out residents of Indian Territory were not unanimous in their allegiances. Divisions were drawn between and within tribes and, as with the white population during the Civil War, brother would fight against brother among the American Indian population. Among the tribes in Indian Territory, the Five Civilized Tribes felt the impact of the Civil War most directly. These tribes, or more accurately, factions therein, joined the Confederacy through official action of the tribal government.[21] These were the only American Indian tribes to join the Confederacy explicitly as allied nations and thereby gain representation in the Confederate Congress.

Given the southern states' active role in the removal of the Five Civilized Tribes just four decades earlier, it might seem surprising that any alliance was formed with the Confederacy. Annie Heloise Abel, however, provides a lengthy and carefully documented discussion of the reasons for an American Indian–Confederate alliance in *The American Indian as Slaveholder and Secessionist* (1992a), the first volume of her trilogy *The Slave Holding Indians*. Between the Trail of Tears and the outbreak of the Civil War, the Cherokee, Creek, Choctaw, Seminole, and Chickasaw tribes had not fared well under federal authority. The Kansas-Nebraska Act was followed by further en-

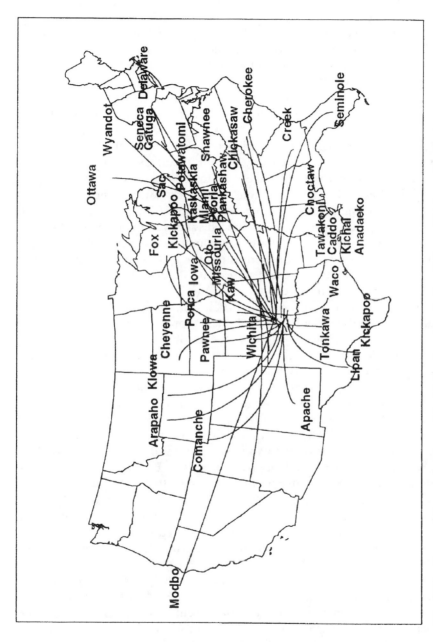

Map I.12 *Eventual Removal of Some of the Major American Indian Tribes to Oklahoma Territory*
Source: American Indian Digest (*Phoenix, Ariz.: Thunderbird Enterprises, 1995*), 35. Reprinted with permission of publisher.

croachment by white settlers and demands that all Indians be removed from Kansas. Further, it was apparent that tribes removed from Kansas and north would very likely be relocated on the lands held exclusively for the Five Civilized Tribes (Abel 1992b, 33–36). In consequence, these tribes were drawn to the Confederacy. Secessionists argued that the federal government planned to open the remaining Indian lands south of the thirty-seventh parallel to white settlement as W. H. Seward (a Republican party insider, later appointed secretary of state) had explicitly suggested during the 1860 presidential campaign. Pro-secessionist forces quoted Seward as saying "the Indian Territory, also, south of Kansas, must be vacated by the Indians" (Abel 1992b, 58). Additionally, unlike officials from Washington, D.C., representatives of the Confederacy actively sought alliance with the Five Tribes. Agents from southern states were sent to negotiate with leaders of the Cherokee, Creek, Choctaw, Seminole, and Chickasaw, and the deal they offered was better on several accounts. At the time of southern secession the Cherokee had been trying to sell to the federal government an 800,000-acre tract of land that had been infiltrated by squatters. The Confederate Indian commissioner was given permission to pay the Cherokee their asking price, after the federal government had refused it (Perdue 1979, 126). Furthermore, American Indian representation in the U.S. Congress had been discussed for years, but such representation had never been forthcoming. The Confederacy, on the other hand, established representation for the Five Civilized Tribes in the House of Representatives of the Confederate Congress. The treaties of alliance with the Confederacy also provided the Five Civilized Tribes with the right to tax trading post operators, to legal protection in court (for example, the right to be a witness and obtain counsel), and to travel and drive stock through Confederate states.[22] These were all benefits the tribes had not been able to procure from the U.S. government. And, of course, there was also the issue of slave ownership; slavery had been practiced by tribal members prior to and after removal from the South. Wishart reports that prior to removal, approximately 8 percent of Cherokee households held slaves (see Chapter 6 in this volume). In 1859 a recorded 4,000 African Americans lived among the 21,000 Cherokees in Indian Territory (Anders 1981, 229). The Confederate treaties declared slavery within the Five Civilized Nations to be "legal [having] existed from time immemorial" and provided for the mutual "return of fugitive slaves" (quoted in Abel 1992b, 157–180).

Secessionists also argued that tribes, not just individual slaveholders, had financial interests in a southern alliance. Of the $3,449,241 held in trust for the American Indian tribes, roughly 70 percent was held in southern state bonds (see Table I.3). Southerners lobbying for an alliance with the Five Civilized Tribes in 1861 informed tribal leaders that these securities would be forfeited by the war if tribes allied themselves with the Union (Abel

TABLE I.3   Indian Trust Fund (List of Stocks Held by the Secretary of the Interior in Trust for Indian Tribes)

	Amount
Arkansas	$ 3,000.00
Florida	132,000.00
Georgia	3,500.00
Indiana	70,000.00
Kentucky	183,000.00
Louiusiana	37,000.00
Maryland[a]	131,611.82
Missouri	63,000.00
Missouri	484,000.00
North Carolina	562,000.00
Ohio	150,000.00
Pennsylvania[a]	96,000.00
South Carolina	125,000.00
Tennessee	218,000.00
Tennessee	143,000.00
United States	251,330.00
Virginia	796,800.00
Total	3,449,241.82

[a]Taxed by the state.
Source: Commissioner of Indian Affairs, *Report* (Washington, D.C.: GPO, 1859), 452.

1992b, 61). Confidence in the federal government had fallen to such a degree that tribal leaders did not trust that the Union would secure them completely against such a loss. Together these factors supplied reasonable incentive for the Cherokee, Creek, Choctaw, Seminole, and Chickasaw to form an alliance with the Confederacy, despite the mistreatment and hostility suffered at the hands of southern citizens and state governments prior to the tribes' removal. Treaties of alliance were ratified by the Confederate Congress in December 1861. Regarding the rights of the Five Civilized Tribes under Confederate rule, Abel summarizes: "In general, their rights, civil, political, and judicial, as men and as semi-independent communities were now specified under conditions as made for what in times past would have been regarded as full recognition, and even for enlargement. Indian rights were at a premium because Indian alliances were in demand" by the South (1992b, 167, 205–206).

The gains made by the tribes through the Confederate alliance treaties lasted only as long as the Confederacy. The tribes of the Oklahoma territory underwent postwar occupation and Reconstruction along with their southern white allies; but one could argue that the negative impact was greater on the inhabitants of the Indian Territories than it was on the citizenry of the Old South. Casualties were high among the Five Civilized Tribes. Among the Cherokee, the death toll due to the Civil War is estimated to have been as high as one-third of adult males (Anders 1981, 230). But in addition, the alliance with the South provided the victorious North with the rationale for voiding all treaties with the Five Nations, both those made with the Confederacy and those in effect prior to the War Between the States. Within the Indian Territories, the Reconstruction treaties of 1866 not only abolished slavery but also required that ex-slaves be given access to tribal land and granted tribal membership. The stipulations of these Reconstruction treaties, however, were not limited to abolition and equality for the freedmen. The federal government also took the opportunity to assist the continuing westward expansion of the white population by opening Indian lands to settlement and transportation. The Five Civilized Tribes had their antebellum landholdings reduced by half to allow for the resettlement of newly displaced members of the Plains tribes. And to further the flow of white migration westward, the tribes were required to grant right-of-way to railroads (Gibson 1988, 194).

Repercussions of the War Between the States on the Plains

While the Civil War raged in the South and on the southern frontier, westward expansion slowed some, but it did not halt. Even as federal military resources shifted away from the western frontier to the war with the South, six new territories were organized in the West. Gold had been discovered in Colorado (1858), and a steady stream of white settlers pushed westward. The governmental enforcement of Indian-white boundaries, such as it had been on the frontier, was reduced even further. Racial violence escalated, and some of the worst atrocities of Indian-white conflict followed. Both Colorado and Minnesota experienced infamous incidents of brutality. The underlying stimuli of each was the same: conflict between tribal "progressives" and "traditionalists," white insistence on strict enforcement of Indian territorial borders, and desperate food shortages among the American Indian population. The Sand Creek Massacre of the Colorado Cheyenne (1864) and the Santee Sioux uprising in Minnesota occurred within two years of each other. The Santee Sioux uprising occurred in 1862, interestingly the same year the Homestead Act was passed. Lasting over three decades, the Sioux Wars would eventually end with the tragic 1890 Battle of Wounded Knee (Weeks 1990, 89–105).

Events on the Plains from the 1860s to the 1890s were in fact a small part of the long history of Indian-white relations. However, these events have formed the strongest and most lasting memories and myths of Indian-white interactions and are the backdrop for the majority of the Hollywood westerns (Brown 1970, xvii). Consequently, our stereotypes of American Indian life and culture, which are molded to a large degree by commercial westerns, center upon American Indian societies at a period when they were in a relatively degenerate political state. The decades from which these powerful images arose followed the displacement of American Indians by white expansion westward. This uprooting of American Indians from their former lands not only caused tribes to compete with each other for the reduced land mass, but it also destroyed the indigenous institutions that had provided property rights and political rights that had ensured economic and political stability.

Allotment and the Market

Philip Weeks nicely summarizes the history of federal governmental frontier policy as seeking "to realize three goals: promoting westward expansion and settlement, protecting American settlers, and guaranteeing Indians' land and rights. These goals, however, were inherently conflicting" (1988, 174). By the 1870s it was recognized that the policies of removal and concentration had achieved only the first goal. Allotment was the next hope. Under allotment, each registered American Indian (including former slaves) would receive an allotment of land to be held as private property. Indian territorial lands left in excess after allotment was complete would be opened to white settlement. Developers of this policy felt that a "civilized" lifestyle and economic prosperity would follow from assigning well-defined property rights to the individual American Indian. Peace would come to the frontier because federal laws would now protect Indian lands in the same manner that they protected the property rights of all citizens. If only individual Native Americans held land privately, market forces could be called upon to help realize all three long-held federal goals.

The General Allotment Act, or Dawes Act, legislated the new allotment policy. This act, passed by Congress in 1887, provided that each registered American Indian (including ex-slaves) would receive an allotment of land, generally 160 acres, to be held in trust for twenty-five years.[23] In response to the Dawes Act, thousands of blacks and whites from nearby states flooded into the territory of the Five Civilized Tribes, claiming to be freed slaves or of sufficient American Indian blood to be eligible for an allotment. A commission eventually awarded allotments to only 25 percent of all claimants (Gibson 1988, 200).

The Five Civilized Tribes, along with many other tribes, resisted allotment. Because of intense congressional lobbying, the Osage, Miami and Perola, Sac and Fox, Nebraska Sioux, New York Seneca, and the Five Civilized Tribes kept their lands exempt from the original allotment of the Dawes Act.

However, by 1907, under various additional congressional amendments and the threat of jail for resisting allotment, most tribal lands were partitioned into individually held parcels.[24] Between 1887 and 1920 American Indian landholdings fell from 138 million acres to roughly 50 million acres (Parker 1989, 47–53). The allotment program was brought to an end in 1934 with the Indian Reorganization Act.

Leonard Carlson provides an overview of allotment in the introduction to Part 4 of this book. Carlson's past work on this subject concludes that prior to allotment, well-defined individual property rights in land already existed. Allotment, ironically, discouraged, rather than stimulated, American Indian farming (Carlson 1981a, 1981b). In fact, on "some reservations Indian land holdings were so reduced or divided that future development plans were hindered by fragmented land holdings or too little remaining land" (Carlson 1983, 34). McChesney, on the other hand, tends to blame the incomplete assignment of property rights for the failure of the allotment policy. He points to the fact that under allotment American Indians were not even able to alienate land to fellow tribal members. This inhibited the consolidation of fragmented holdings and did nothing to protect the "Indian way of life," as this restriction prevented sales to other tribesmen. Both Carlson and Mc-Chesney agree with the general consensus that American Indians were not the primary beneficiaries under the allotment program. McChesney emphasizes that the Indian Office bureaucracy acted in its own self-interest in implementing restrictions and then terminating privatization of tribal lands. Carlson argues that Indian Office actions were correlated more to "white economic interests than to the goal of aiding Indian farmers" (1983, 44).

Although the rhetoric surrounding the Dawes Act was that allotment would provide American Indians with property rights that would increase their access to markets, an undeniable result was the transfer of lands from American Indians to whites and the hindrance of Indian economic development. Allotment, it had been argued, would provide private property and thus the incentive, capital, and legal institutions to allow Native Americans to integrate themselves into the market economy, improving their economic conditions and "becoming civilized" in the process. However, much preallotment evidence exists that suggests that federal Indian policy did not consistently encourage market activity. The more reasonable historical generalization is that while the federal government was discussing the need to define property rights better in one realm, it was almost simultaneously changing rules and weakening the security of such rights in another. In the brief time span between removal and allotment, there is much evidence of market activity in the Indian Territory as well as evidence of government action that repeatedly limited or eliminated the success of such "entrepreneurial spirit." With regard to the Five Civilized Tribes, the two most widely discussed examples are the Cherokee Tobacco Case and the Cherokee Outlet leasing. In both cases, economic success resulting from Native

American use of "the market" was met with legislative prohibition of the successful activity.

After the Civil War, the Cherokee attempted to take advantage of a "sleeper clause" included in the otherwise restrictive Reconstruction treaties. This clause stipulated that tribal citizens could "produce, manufacture, ship, and market any product throughout the United States without restraint, exempt from federal tax." Two Cherokee entrepreneurs bought and imported a tobacco plant from Missouri to produce snuff and chewing and pipe tobacco within Indian Territory. These tobacco products were sold successfully on and off the reservation at a lower (untaxed) price. Complaints from tobacco producers in neighboring states prompted Congress to pass a law revoking this clause of the treaty. A lawsuit ensued (the Cherokee Tobacco Case) in which the Cherokee claimed that congressional legislation could not supersede federal treaties. The U.S. Supreme Court ruled that treaties with Native American nations were not the same as treaties with foreign nations; congressional law was superior to the former but not the latter. Within months of the 1870 Supreme Court ruling, a congressional resolution was issued stating that treaties would no longer be negotiated with American Indian tribes. Congressional law and administrative rulings would henceforth govern U.S.-Indian affairs (Gibson 1988, 195–196).

An even more successful use of the market banned through act of Congress was the leasing of the Cherokee Outlet prior to 1889. The Cherokee sought to make use of the whites' demand for their lands while not relinquishing tribal ownership by first taxing and then leasing the land to white cattlemen. The section of land called the Cherokee Outlet was established as a hunting ground and buffer zone, separate from other Cherokee holdings in the Indian Territory. Lee Alston and Pablo Spiller (1992) have provided an excellent political economic analysis of the Cherokee Outlet case. As early as 1867 the Cherokee began charging a tax per cattle head passing through the Outlet. A leasing arrangement with white cattlemen for $100,000 per year was then approved by the Cherokee legislature and the secretary of the interior in 1883. Both the cattle taxes and leasing arrangements were backed by the power of the cavalry. This enforcement included the expulsion of tax-evading cattlemen and squatting farmers. In 1888, however, the secretary of the interior said leasing of the Outlet could no longer continue. Cattlemen who had agreed to increase their annual rental payment to $200,000 were told by the federal government that they had eight months to remove all cattle from the Outlet. Several cattlemen offered to purchase the Outlet for as much as $30 million. The federal government refused to approve this sale, yet in 1891 the Cherokee were "obliged" to let the federal government buy the Outlet for $8.6 million. In less than two years the Outlet was opened for white settlement. Alston and Spiller (1992) concluded that members of Congress acting in the interests of their constituents (the squatters and future settlers) served on relevant committees and exercised great influence over the legislative process. Consequently, they managed to defeat the lobbying activities of the better-organized Cherokee and cattlemen. Encouraging Cherokee participation in "the market" was neither the legislative motivation nor the outcome.

Present-Day State of Affairs

Currently there are 319 federally recognized American Indian tribes in the continental United States, with 1.2 million enrolled members and 1.9 self-identified Indians. The federal government recognizes 300 reservations composing some 55 million acres. Only 22 percent of the American Indian population lives on reservations. Of the total reservation acreage, 44 million acres are range and grazing, 5.3 million acres are in commercial forest, and 2.5 million acres are in crop land. Additionally, reservation land contains "4% of U.S. oil and gas reserves . . . 40% of U.S. uranium deposits . . . [and] 30% of western coal reserves" (*American Indian Digest* 1994, 22–34). Although many reservations do contain valuable natural resources, gaming (that is, gambling) has become an increasingly important and publicized economic endeavor. Table I.4 lists federally recognized reservations and notes the presence of gaming facilities.

Gaming facilities have received much attention through press coverage and self-promotion. A recent joke articulates the opportunity for economic development that some foresee in casino investment: Two pilgrims and two American Indians stand talking on the shores of America. One pilgrim says to the other, "Give 'em some beads and we'll take the land." The American Indian replies to his tribesman, "Give 'em gambling and we'll take it all back." The scenario suggested by this joke is more real than one may think. In Michigan, both the Sault Ste. Marie Chippewa tribe and the Upper Peninsula's Mills Indian Community have indicated interest in building off-reservation casinos in Detroit (Barkholz 1994). Supporters argue that the jobs created would help alleviate Detroit's depressed economy; opponents counter that gambling developments would crowd out other, healthier forms of economic development in Detroit.

The verdict is still out on the degree of long-term economic success that the gambling industry can bring to American Indian reservations. Although the 1993 annual gaming revenue from all American Indian establishments was some $2.6 billion, one-third of that went to just two tribes: the Mashantucket Pequot and the Shakopee Sioux.[25] Some 200 tribes currently have gaming establishments. The three most financially successful gaming reservations, however, support a combined population of less than 500 ("Indian Gaming Having Little Effect on Poverty" 1995). In fact, in May 1995 the Hopi Nation recently voted down a referendum to establish a gambling facility on their reservation for fear it would diminish support for traditional culture ("Hopis Turn Down Gambling" 1995). Many supporters of gam-

TABLE I.4 Reservation and Gaming Facilities by Bureau of Indian Affairs Administrative Regions

Reservation	State	Gaming	Reservation	State	Gaming
Aberdeen Area					
Devils Lake Sioux	ND	✓	Crow Creek	SD	✓
Fort Berthold	ND	✓	Flandreau Santee Sioux	SD	✓
Turtle Mountain	ND	✓	Lower Brule	SD	✓
Ponca	NE	✓	Rosebud	SD	✓
Santee Sioux	NE	✓	Yankton	SD	✓
Omaha Reservation	NE-IA	✓	Sisseton-Wahpeton	SD-ND	✓
Winnebago	NE-IA	✓	Standing Rock	SD-ND	✓
Cheyenne River	SD	✓	Pine Ridge	SD-NE	✓
Albuquerque Area					
Southern Ute	CO	✓	Ramah (Navajo)	NM	
Ute Mountain	*	✓	San Felipe Pueblo	NM	✓
Acoma Pueblo	NM	✓	San Ildefonso Pueblo	NM	
Alamo (Navajo)	NM		San Juan Pueblo	NM	✓
Canoncito (Navajo)	NM		Sandia Pueblo	NM	✓
Cochiti Pueblo	NM		Santa Ana Pueblo	NM	✓
Isleta Pueblo	NM	✓	Santa Clara Pueblo	NM	
Jemez Pueblo	NM		Santo Domingo Pueblo	NM	
Jicarilla Apache	NM	✓	Taos Pueblo	NM	✓
Laguna Pueblo	NM		Tesuque Pueblo	NM	✓
Mescalero Apache	NM	✓	Zia Pueblo	NM	
Nambe Pueblo	NM		Zuni Pueblo	NM-AZ	
Picuris Pueblo	NM		Ysleta Del Sur Pueblo	AZ	✓
Pojoaque Pueblo	NM	✓			
Anadarko Area					
Iowa	MT	✓	Sac & Fox	MT	✓
Kickapoo	MT	✓	Alabama-Coushatta	MT	✓
Pottawatomi	MT	✓	Kickapoo	WY	✓
Billings Area					
Blackfeet	MT	✓	Rocky Boy's	MT	✓
Crow	MT	✓	Northern Cheyenne	MT	✓
Fort Belknap	MT	✓	Wind River	WY	✓
Fort Peck	MT	✓			
Eastern Area					
Poarch Creek	AL	✓	Penobscot	ME	
Mashantucket Pequot	CT	✓	Pleasant Point	ME	
Mohegan Nation	CT	✓	Mississippi Choctaw	MS	✓
Big Cyprus (Seminole)	FL		Eastern Cherokee	NC	✓
Brighton (Seminole)	FL		Allegany (Seneca)	NY	✓
Hollywood (Seminole)	FL	✓	Cattaraugus (Seneca)	NY	✓
Miccosukee	FL	✓	Cayuga Nation	NY	
Chitimacha	LA	✓	Oil Springs (Seneca)	NY	
Coushata	LA	✓	Oneida	NY	✓

*CO-NM-UT

(*continues*)

TABLE I.4 (*continued*)

Reservation	State	Gaming	Reservation	State	Gaming
Jena Band-Choctaw	LA		Onondaga	NY	
Tunica-Biloxi	LA	✓	St. Regis Mohawk	NY	✓
Gay Head Wampanoag	MA	✓	Tonawanda	NY	
Aroostook Band	ME		Tuscarora	NT	✓
Houlton Maliseet	ME		Narragansett	RI	
Indian Township	ME		Catawba Nation	SC	
Minneapolis Area					
Sac & Fox	IA	✓	Prairie Island Community	MN	✓
Bay Mills	MI	✓	Red Lake	MN	✓
Grand Traverse	MI	✓	Shakopee Mdewakanton	MN	✓
Hannahville Community	MI	✓	Upper Sioux Community	MN	✓
Isabella	MI	✓	White Earth	MN	✓
L'Anse Reservation	MI	✓	Bad River	WI	✓
Lac Vieux Desert	MI	✓	Ho-Chunk Nation	WI	✓
Little River–Ottawa	MI	✓	Lac Courte Oreilles	WI	✓
Little Traverse–Odawa	MI	✓	Lac du Flambeau	WI	✓
Pokagon Potawatami	MI	✓	Menominee	WI	✓
Sault Ste. Marie	MI	✓	Oneida	WI	✓
Bois Forte	MN	✓	Potawatomi	WI	✓
Fond du Lac	MN	✓	Red Cliff	WI	✓
Grand Portage	MN	✓	Sokaogon Chippewa	WI	✓
Leech Lake	MN	✓	St. Croix	WI	✓
Lower Sioux Community	MN	✓	Stockbridge-Munsee	WI	✓
Mille Lacs	MN	✓	Pine Creek Reservation	MI	
Muskogee Area					
Osage	OK	✓			
Navajo Area					
Navajo	*				
Phoenix Area					
Ak-Chin	AZ	✓	Dresslerville Colony	NV	
Camp Verde	AZ	✓	Duck Valley	NV	
Cocopah	AZ	✓	Duckwater	NV	
Fort Apache	AZ	✓	Ely Colony	NV	
Fort McDowell	AZ	✓	Fallon Colony	NV	✓
Gila Bend	AZ		Fort McDermitt	NV	✓
Gila River	AZ	✓	Las Vegas Colony	NV	✓
Havasupai	AZ		Lovelock Colony	NV	
Hopi	AZ		Moapa River	NV	✓
Hualapai	AZ		Pyramid Lake	NV	
Kaibab	AZ	✓	Reno-Sparks Colony	NV	✓
Pascua Yaqui	AZ	✓	Summit Lake	NV	
Payson Community	AZ	✓	Te-Moak (4 Bands)	NV	✓
Salt River	AZ		Walker River	NV	
San Carlos	AZ	✓	Washoe	NV	

*AZ-NM-UT

(*continues*)

TABLE I.4 (*continued*)

Reservation	State	Gaming	Reservation	State	Gaming
San Juan Southern Paiute	AZ		Winnemucca Colony	NV	
San Xavier	AZ	✓	Yerington	NV	
Tohono O'Odham	AZ	✓	Yomba	NV	
Yavapai-Prescott	AZ	✓	Goshute	NV-UT	
Colorado River	AZ-CA	✓	Northwestern Shoshoni	UT	
Fort Yuma (Quechan)	AZ-CA	✓	Paiute	UT	
Fort Mojave	*	✓	Skull Valley	UT	
Chemehuevi	CA	✓	Uintah & Ouray	UT	
Carson Colony	NV				
Portland Area					
Coeur d'Alene	ID	✓	Makah	WA	✓
Fort Hall	ID	✓	Muckleshoot	WA	✓
Kootenai	ID	✓	Nisqually	WA	✓
Nez Perce	ID	✓	Nooksack	WA	✓
Flathead	MT	✓	Ozette	WA	
Burns Paiute	OR	✓	Port Gamble (S'Klallam)	WA	✓
Coos, Lower Umpqua	OR	✓	Port Madison (Suquamish)	WA	
Coquille	OR	✓	Puyallup	WA	✓
Cow Creek	OR	✓	Quileute	WA	✓
Grand Ronde	OR	✓	Quinault	WA	
Siletz	OR	✓	Sauk-Suiettle	WA	
Umatilla	OR	✓	Shoalwater	WA	✓
Warm Springs	OR	✓	Skokomish	WA	
Chehalis	WA	✓	Spokane	WA	✓
Colville	WA	✓	Squaxin Island	WA	✓
Hoh	WA		Stillaquamish	WA	
Jamestown Klallam	WA	✓	Swinomish	WA	✓
Kalispel	WA		Tulalip	WA	✓
Lower Elwah	WA	✓	Upper Skagit	WA	✓
Lummi	WA	✓	Yakama	WA	✓
Sacramento Area					
Aqua Caliente	CA	✓	Mesa Grande	CA	
Alturas Rancheria	CA		Middletown Rancheria	CA	✓
Augustine	CA		Montgomery Creek	CA	
Barona Rancheria	CA	✓	Mooretown	CA	
Benton Paiute	CA		Morongo	CA	✓
Berry Creek Rancheria	CA	✓	North Fork Rancheria	CA	
Big Bend Rancheria	CA		Pala	CA	✓
Big Lagoon Rancheria	CA	✓	Pauma & Yuima	CA	
Big Pine	CA		Pechanga	CA	✓
Big Sandy Rancheria	CA		Picayune Rancheria	CA	
Big Valley	CA	✓	Pinoleville Rancheria	CA	
Bishop Reservation	CA		Potter Valley Rancheria	CA	
Blue Lake Rancheria	CA		Quartz Valley Rancheria	CA	
Bridgeport Indian Colony	CA		Ramona	CA	

*AZ-CA-NV

(*continues*)

TABLE I.4   (*continued*)

Reservation	State	Gaming	Reservation	State	Gaming
Buena Vista	CA		Redding Rancheria	CA	✓
Cabazon	CA	✓	Redwood Valley	CA	
Cahuilla	CA		Resighini Rancheria	CA	✓
Campo Reservation	CA	✓	Rincon	CA	
Capitain Grande	CA		Roaring Creek	CA	
Cedarville Rancheria	CA		Robinson Rancheria	CA	✓
Chicken Ranch Rancheria	CA	✓	Rohnerville Rancheria	CA	
Chico Rancheria	CA		Round Valley	CA	
Cloverdale Rancheria	CA	✓	Rumsey Rancheria	CA	✓
Cold Springs Rancheria	CA		San Manuel	CA	✓
Colusa Rancheria	CA	✓	San Pasqual	CA	✓
Cortina Rancheria	CA		Santa Rosa Rancheria	CA	✓
Coyote Valley Rancheria	CA	✓	Santa Rosa	CA	✓
Dry Creek Rancheria	CA		Santa Ynez	CA	✓
Elk Valley Rancheria	CA		Santa Ysabel	CA	
Enterprise Rancheria	CA		Scotts Valley Rancheria	CA	
Fort Bidwell	CA		Sheep Ranch Rancheria	CA	
Fort Independence	CA		Sherwood Valley	CA	
Greenville Rancheria	CA		Shingle Springs	CA	
Grindstone Rancheria	CA		Smith River Rancheria	CA	
Guidiville Rancheria	CA		Soboba	CA	✓
Hoopa Valley	CA	✓	Stewart's Point	CA	
Hopland Rancheria	CA		Sulphur Bank Rancheria	CA	✓
Inaja-Cosmit	CA		Susanville Rancheria	CA	
Jackson Rancheria	CA	✓	Sycuan	CA	✓
Jamul Indian Village	CA	✓	Table Bluff Rancheria	CA	
Karuk Tribe	CA		Table Mountain	CA	✓
La Jolla	CA		Timbi-Sha W. Shoshone	CA	
La Posta	CA		Torres-Martinez	CA	
Laytonville Rancheria	CA		Trinidad Rancheria	CA	✓
Likely Rancheria	CA		Tule River	CA	✓
Lone Pine	CA		Tuolumne Rancheria	CA	
Lookout Rancheria	CA		Twenty-Nine Palms	CA	✓
Los Coyotes Rancheria	CA		Upper Lake Rancheria	CA	
Lytton Rancheria	CA		Viejas	CA	✓
Manchester Point	CA		XL Ranch	CA	
Manzanita	CA		Yurok Tribe	CA	

Source: American Indian Digest (Phoenix, Ariz.: Thunderbird Enterprises, 1995), 38–45. Reprinted with permission of publisher.

ing, however, claim that a backlash against Indian casinos is being propagated to a large extent by non-Indians and is just another attempt to block successful use of the market by Native Americans.

Outline of the Book

As one might expect, the body of research on Native American economic history is still in its infancy. Nonetheless, in the past few years important contributions have been made, and these indicate the need for developing an integral picture of North American history that recognizes the continuity and incorporates the interactions of indigenous nations as nonindigenous settlement progressed westward. This book presents some of the recent economic explorations into key episodes of Native American economic history.

In addition to offering a good introduction to the breadth of Native American economic history topics currently under study, the following chapters highlight the diversity of tools and data available for New Economic History studies of Native American experiences. Throughout this book, the focus of the analyses changes in order to address the immediate questions or more salient issues of the different time periods. For the precolonial history and the earliest period of contact, the establishment and alteration of institutions is a natural focus. As the demographics shifted from majority Native American to majority European American, the balance of power in trade relations also shifted. Issues of bargaining power and dependency came more to the forefront. As the frontier expanded westward, the center of Native-white economic interactions moved westward as well. And, finally, the rise of federal activism in the twentieth century shifted the focus to bureaucratic strategies.

Part 1 of the book focuses on fundamental issues in the economic organization of precolonial civilizations as well as the roles of and changes in economic institutions. Vernon L. Smith's Chapter 1, "Economy, Ecology, and Institutions in the Emergence of Humankind," discusses the importance of opportunity costs and human capital accumulation in the evolution of human culture and its habitation in North America. In the next chapter, "The Mississippians and Economic Development Before European Colonization," Linda Barrington surveys the economy of the Mississippian civilization prior to colonization and argues that the institutions of trade and labor organization in the precolonial Mississippian economy may have had important implications for colonial economic development in the South later on. Terry L. Anderson and Steven LaCombe, in Chapter 3, "Institutional Change in the Indian Horse Culture," describe the impact that the introduction of the horse had on American Indian institutions even before much Indian-white interaction took place. They argue that once the domestic horse was adopted in tribal society, it brought about radical and discontinuous change in institutions and in the way tribes produced and consumed.

Part 2 focuses on the interactions of early colonial and indigenous societies through trade. Chapter 4, by Ann M. Carlos and Frank D. Lewis, and Chapter 5, by Edward Murphy, both emphasize the early importance of the fur trade for tribes in both northern and southeastern North American colonies. Murphy, in "The Eighteenth-Century Southeastern American Indian Economy: Subsistence Versus Trade and Growth," estimates the volume of the deerskin trade in South Carolina to show the importance of that commodity for both colonial and indigenous participants in the southeastern economy. Carlos and Lewis also illustrate the importance of the trade in beaver pelts for the northern indigenous economy. Viewing Native Americans "as central players rather than passive agents in the [fur] trade," Carlos and Lewis analyze the interactions of the French, British, and Native Americans in the eighteenth-century northern fur trade. They conclude that competition between the French and British for furs supplied by Native Americans resulted in relatively higher prices paid to the Indians, which encouraged greater depletion of the beaver population. Contact with the European trading system resulted in the dislocation of tribes in the St. Lawrence, Great Lakes, and Hudson Bay regions. Carlos and Lewis conclude that this dislocation inhibited the formation of property rights among the American Indians and that such rights might have impeded the depletion.

The chapters in Part 3 focus on the economics of westward expansion. Chapters 6 and 7 present quantitative exercises intended to reconstruct a statistical record for Native American societies in the nineteenth century. Using a detailed 1835 census of Cherokee holdings, David M. Wishart fills the quantitative void in Cherokee historiography by providing estimates of productivity in Cherokee agriculture. In Chapter 6, "Could the Cherokee Have Survived in the Southeast?" Wishart demonstrates that the agricultural achievements of Cherokee farms prior to removal were greater than removal advocates claimed. In Chapter 7, "Land, Population, Prices, and the Regulation of Natural Resources: The Lake Superior Ojibwa, 1790–1920," James W. Oberly examines an economy much different from that of the Cherokee. Unlike the Cherokee economy based on market-oriented agriculture, the mid-nineteenth century economy of the Ojibwa in Wisconsin was based on subsistence fishing, hunting, and gathering, supplemented by treaty payments. Oberly has gathered information about the relative heights of indigenous peoples of Wisconsin to infer the quality of life of the Ojibwa subsistence economy. He finds, contrary to common assumptions about subsistence, that the Ojibwa did not regularly underproduce relative to the needs of their population. Only after the Civil War, with the onslaught of logging and the implementation of allotment, did population decreases and tuberculosis outbreaks signal a severe deterioration in the quality of life. Finally, in their Chapter 8, entitled "The Political Economy of Indian Wars," Terry L. Anderson and Fred S. McChesney examine the Machiavellian "choice" of war over the Coasian "choice" of negotiating a mutually beneficial exchange. They find that with regard to the history of American Indian–white relations, one can generalize that war was more likely than negotiation when (1) the goods produced and technology used by the two races were more unequal, (2) the casualties of war were suffered by a standing army instead of by the parties inciting the conflict, (3) there existed differential expectations of military capabilities, and (4) negotiation costs were high.

The fourth and final part of this book looks at two cases of bureaucratic federal programs in the twentieth century allegedly set up to serve the interests of Native Americans. Leonard A. Carlson, in Chapter 9, "The Economics and Politics of Irrigation Projects on Indian Reservations, 1900–1940,"

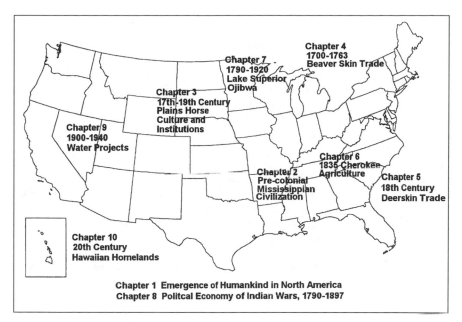

Map I.13 *Chapters and Topics of The Other Side of the Frontier: Economic Explorations into Native American History*

concludes from his analysis of irrigation developments in the West that actions of the Bureau of Indian Affairs were not undertaken solely for the benefit and protection of American Indians; rather, they were the result of interest group competition, where bureaucrats themselves were among the self-interested, competing actors. American Indians probably benefited from federal irrigation projects in areas where white land interest was limited or as a by-product when others were the intended beneficiaries. Carlson also suggests that the change in tribal administration following the 1930s Indian Reorganization Act had little impact on the development of irrigation resources in Indian reservations. Sumner J. La Croix and Louis A. Rose put similar emphasis on the self-interest of bureaucrats in Native American matters. In Chapter 10, "The Political Economy of the Hawaiian Home Lands Program," they review the history and discuss the inefficiency of a program that was established in 1921 to assure that land remained in Native Hawaiian hands. They conclude that this program has not effectively accomplished its goal and is in need of reform. However, as with most established bureaucratic programs, institutional barriers to implementing reforms are great.

A visual orientation to the chapters included in this book is presented in Map I.13. From this map it is apparent that although a variety of time periods and Native American peoples have been considered in the current research, much is still waiting to be written.

Notes

I wish to thank Hugh Rockoff and Ann Carlos for their comments on an earlier version of this chapter.

1. As no actual population count exists, statistical estimates are necessary and commonly constructed using models of mortality rates from epidemics. Denevan relies heavily upon the claim of Daniel F. Reff (1991) that 90 percent of the indigenous population died prior to 1678. For the sake of comparison, Denevan's estimate of 3.8 million for the United States and Canada is greater than his estimate of 2 million for Central America, but quite small compared to his 13.8 million estimate for Mexico (Denevan 1992, xxviii, table 1). Denevan also noted that the estimated loss of life between 1492 and 1650, for all of the New World, is 48.3 million—"a human toll of a magnitude comparable to that suffered during World War II" (xxix).

2. Other population histories of Native Americans include Dobyns 1983; Stannard 1992; and Thornton 1987.

3. For discussion of the indigenous economies south of the Rio Grande, in particular, the empires of the Aztec, Maya, and Inca, see Lockhart and Schwartz 1983; Berdan 1982; Collier, Rosaldo, and Wirth 1982; and Wauchope 1970.

4. In precontact northern North America, there is no evidence of tribute-reliant hierarchies comparable to the evidence that exists for the southeastern and southern regions of the continent. This is consistent with the lower population density and greater reliance on seasonal travel for hunting that characterized the northern indigenous nations. For more on the relationship between population density, settled agriculture, and tribute, see Boserup 1981.

5. As no complete population data exist prior to 1850, we must rely on estimates. Many estimates of population at contact exist (see Table I.1), but few time series over the eighteenth century have been estimated.

6. The sixth tribe, the Tuscarora, joined the confederacy later than the others. They moved to the north from the Carolina-Virginia frontier to join the linguistically related Iroquois Confederacy after losing a two-year struggle with southern white settlers. The violent conflict was prompted by settler encroachment and slave raids (Smith 1988, 57).

7. Using indigenous peoples to fight against one another had also been a successful tactic for the Spanish conquest of Mexico 100 years earlier (Lockhart and Schwartz 1983, 82–83).

8. The discussion of the southern colonial deerskin trade presented here draws heavily from Usner 1992, chapter, 8, an excellent source for the history of this trade.

9. For a detailed list of items supplied by the French through trade with indigenous residents of Louisiana, see Usner 1992, tables 6 and 7, 260–265.

10. "[The King] has endeavored to prevent the population of these States; . . . refusing to . . . encourage their migration hither, and raising the conditions of new appropriations of lands" (Declaration of Independence). Also included in the Declaration of Independence was an explicit complaint regarding the king's alliances with Native nations: "[He] has endeavored to bring on the inhabitants of our frontiers, the merciless Indian savages." Complaints regarding frontier policy did not stop, however, with independence from Britain. Just as they had before 1776, settlers from within the U.S. borders continually took up residence on Indian lands, beyond legal

boundaries demarcated by federal authorities, and then expected U.S. military protection.

11. Just months earlier the British had suffered great losses in the Old Northwest during the so-called Pontiac's Rebellion of 1763.

12. It should be noted that the Crown and its representatives did not consistently protect and respect the indigenous nations during the mid-eighteenth century. Although the British sought to respect Indian territorial borders at the time of the American Revolution, just two decades earlier, during the French and Indian War, official resolutions sanctioned the murder of American Indian men, women, and children. In 1755 the governor of the Massachusetts Bay province declared the tribes inhabiting "the Eastern and Northern Parts of His Majesty's Territories of New-England, the Penobscot Tribe only excepted," to be traitors and offered a bounty for each American Indian killed: "For every Male Indian Scalp, brought in as Evidence of their being killed, Forty Pounds. . . . For every Scalp of such Female Indian or Male Indian under Twelve Years of Age, brought as Evidence of their being killed, as aforesaid, Twenty Pounds" (Shirley [1755] 1994, 13).

13. The United Nations designated 1993 as the year of the World's Indigenous People and 1994–2003 as the International Decade of the World's Indigenous Peoples to draw attention to the continued destruction of the land and cultures of indigenous peoples. Also drawing global attention to the current situation of indigenous people has been Nobel Prize winner Rigoberta Menchu, an activist for her people, the Quiché of Guatemala. (For more on world indigenous peoples and economic development see *Seeds of a New Partnership* 1994; Young 1995; and Beauclark, Narby, and Townsend 1988.)

14. "Nits make lice" was Colonel John Chivington's dictum. Chivington was the commander responsible for the Sand Creek Massacre, where many children were among those slaughtered (Weeks 1990, 102–104). Such violent rhetoric directed at indigenous peoples, unfortunately, has not been left only to our past. Within the last decade or two conflict over Native American rights to traditional use of natural resources has increased. Signs bearing such odious slogans as "Too bad Custer ran out of bullets" have appeared at recent protest rallies (see Trahant 1995, 17, photo by Andrew Lichtenstein, Impact Images). Arguments characterizing the historical policies of the U.S. government toward indigenous peoples as genocidal can be found in Churchill 1994 and Jaimes 1992.

15. Among the tribes represented in Ohio at the time of the passage of the Northwest Ordinances were the Miami, Wyandot, Ottawa, Mingoe, Seneca, Delaware, Shawnee, Ojibwa, and Iroquois (Knepper 1988).

16. The battle was later championed in Harrison's campaign chant "Tippecanoe and Tyler too," John Tyler being Harrison's vice presidential candidate (Goebel and Goebel 1945, 112).

17. Georgia's early nineteenth century push for removal was stronger than that of her neighboring states due in part to the Georgia Compact of 1802. This compact involved the federal government's payment of $1,250,000 to Georgia and a promise to eliminate all Indian land holdings in Georgia in exchange for Georgia's relinquishing claim to all western lands (Gage 1969, 283).

18. Anecdotal evidence of the standard of living among the Cherokee prior to removal can also substantiate the success of some Cherokee. Arrell Morgan Gibson

quotes an 1820s visitor from the North who commented that the Cherokee "seemed to have more money than the whites in our settlements; they were better clothed . . . raising beef and pork in abundance; butter and milk everywhere. We were at an election for delegates among the Cherokees to form a constitution" (1988, 190).

19. The Senate had stipulated that Cherokee lands in the West should be limited to the north by the thirty-sixth parallel. This was to preserve the Missouri Compromise upon the arrival of Cherokee slaves with their masters (Gage 1969, 292).

20. The North Central Region, as defined here, includes the present-day states of Ohio, Indiana, Illinois, Michigan, Wisconsin, Minnesota, Iowa, Missouri, North Dakota, South Dakota, Nebraska, and Kansas (U.S. Bureau of the Census 1975, text for series A 172–194).

21. The alliance with the southern states was not a unanimous decision on the part of tribal members. Many pro-Union tribal members fled into Kansas, often under threat of attack from their secessionist tribal kin.

22. Confederate treaties were also made with the Osage, Seneca, Shawnee, Quawpaw, Wichita, and Comanche. These treaties, however, did not include the same provisions for protection and allegiance as did those with the Creek, Choctaw, Cherokee, Seminole, and Chickasaw (Abel 1992b, 157–158).

23. Allotment size to both American Indians and their ex-slaves and descendants did vary between the Five Civilized Tribes. Ex-slaves of Cherokee, Creek, and Seminole masters received the same sized plots as their former masters, 110 to 160 acres. The plots assigned to ex-slaves of Choctaws and Chickasaws were smaller—40 acres, whereas the non-freedmen members of these tribes received 320 acres (Gibson 1988, 200).

24. Some tribes did escape allotment altogether. For example, the Pueblo communities of the Southwest were never allotted, and the Sioux did retain some common tribal property (Carlson 1983, 35; Parker 1989, 48).

25. The Mashantucket Pequot have recently expanded their economic base to include the production of a new generation of high-speed ferryboats. The new Pequot River Shipworks produces boats intended both to carry gamblers from New York City to the Pequot casino and for the commercial market in North and South America (Johnson 1997, B1).

Bibliography

Abel, Annie Heloise. 1992a. *The American Indian in the Civil War, 1862–1865.* Lincoln: University of Nebraska Press.

_____. 1992b. *The American Indian as Slaveholder and Secessionist.* Lincoln: University of Nebraska Press.

Alston, Lee, and Pablo Spiller. 1992. "A Congressional Theory of Indian Property Rights: The Cherokee Outlet." In *Property Rights and Indian Economies: The Political Economy Forum,* ed. Terry L. Anderson, 85–107. Lanham, Md.: Rowman and Littlefield.

American Indian Digest: Facts About Today's American Indians. 1994. "Contemporary Demographics of the American Indian." Phoenix, Ariz.: Thunderbird Enterprises.

Anders, Gary C. 1981. "The Reduction of Self-Sufficient People to Poverty and Welfare Dependence: An Analysis of the Causes of Cherokee Indian Underdevelopment." *The American Journal of Economics and Sociology* 40, no. 3 (July):226–237.

Atack, Jeremy, and Peter Passell. 1994. *A New Economic View of American History: From Colonial Times to 1940.* New York: Norton.

Barkholz, David. 1994. "Cities Likely to Add Casinos to Entertainment Mix." *Crain's Detroit Business,* 19 December, 20.

Beauclark, John, Jeremy Narby, and Janet Townsend. 1988. *Indigenous Peoples: A Fieldguide for Development.* Development Guidelines, no. 2. Oxford, Eng.: Oxfam.

Berdan, Frances. 1982. *The Aztecs of Central Mexico: An Imperial Society.* New York: Holt, Rinchart, and Winston.

Boserup, Ester. 1981. *Population and Technological Change: A Study of Long-Term Trends.* Chicago: University of Chicago Press.

Brown, Dee. 1970. *Bury My Heart at Wounded Knee: An Indian Story of the American West.* New York: Henry Holt.

Bryson, Reid A., and Thomas J. Murray. 1977. *Climates of Hunger: Mankind and the World's Changing Weather.* Madison: University of Wisconsin Press.

Carlson, Leonard A. 1981a. "Land Allotment and the Decline of American Indian Farming." *Explorations in Economic History* vol. 18:128–154.

––––––. 1981b. *Indians, Bureaucrats, and Land: The Dawes Act and the Decline of Indian Farming.* Westport, Conn.: Greenwood Press.

––––––. 1983. "Federal Policy and Indian Land: Economic Interests and the Sale of Indian Allotments, 1900–1934." *Agricultural History* 57, no. 1. (January):33–45.

Churchill, Ward. 1994. *Indians Are Us? Culture and Genocide in Native North America.* Monroe, Maine: Common Courage Press.

Collier, George A., Renato I. Rosaldo, and John D. Wirth, eds. 1982. *The Inca and Aztec States, 1400–1800: Anthropology and History.* New York: Academic Press.

Cook, Sherburne. 1943. "The Indian versus the Spanish Mission." *Ibero-Americana* 22:1–294.

––––––. 1955. "The Epidemic of 1830–1833 in California and Oregon." *University of California Publications in American Archaeology and Ethnology* 43:303–325.

Crosby, A. W. 1992. "Hawaiian Depopulation as a Model for the Amerindian Experience." In *Epidemics and Ideas: Essays on the Historical Perception of Pestilence,* eds. Terence Ranger and Paul Slack, 75–202. Cambridge: Cambridge University Press.

Curtin, Philip D. 1984. *Cross-Cultural Trade in World History.* Cambridge: Cambridge University Press.

Denevan, William M., ed. 1992. *The Native Population of the Americas in 1492.* Madison: University of Wisconsin Press.

Dobyns, Henry F. 1983. *Their Number Become Thinned: Native American Population Dynamics in Eastern North America.* Knoxville: University of Tennessee Press.

Foreman, Grant. 1934. *The Five Civilized Tribes.* Oklahoma: University of Oklahoma Press.

Gage, Duane. 1969. "Oklahoma: A Resettlement Area for Indians." *The Chronicles of Oklahoma* 47, no. 3 (Autumn):282–297.

Gibson, Arrell Morgan. 1988. "To Kill a Nation: Liquidation of the Five Indian Republics." In *The American Indian Experience, A Profile: 1524 to the Present*, ed. Philip Weeks, 189–206. Arlington Heights, Ill.: Forum Press.

Goebel, Dorothy Burne, and Julius Goebel. 1945. *Generals in the White House*. New York: Country Life Press.

Goldberg, Carey. 1996. "Oldest Mummy 'Found' on Museum Shelf." *New York Times*, 27 April.

Gutierrez, Ramon. 1991. *When Jesus Came, the Corn Mothers Went Away: Marriage, Sexuality, and Power in New Mexico, 1500–1846*. Stanford: Stanford University Press.

Hirschman, Albert O. 1981. "The Rise and Decline of Development Economics." In *Essays in Trespassing: Economics to Politics and Beyond*, ed. Albert Hirschman. Cambridge: Cambridge University Press.

"Hopis Turn Down Gambling." 1995. *Native Americas: Akwe:kon's Journal of Indigenous Issues* 7 (3) (Fall):3.

Hughes, Jonathan. 1990. *American Economic History*. New York: HarperCollins.

Hyman, Harold M. 1986. *American Singularity: The 1781 Northwest Ordinance, the 1862 Homestead and Morrill Acts, and the 1944 GI Bill*. Athens: University of Georgia.

"Indian Gaming Having Little Effect on Poverty." 1995. *Native Americas: Akwe:kon's Journal of Indigenous Issues* 7 (3) (Fall):3.

Jaffe, A. J. 1992. *The First Immigrants from Asia: A Population History of the North American Indians*. New York: Plenum Press.

Jaimes, M. Annette, ed. 1992. *The State of Native America: Genocide, Colonization, and Resistance*. Boston: South End Press.

Johnson, Kirk. 1997. "After Foxwoods, Pequots Turn to Building Ferries." *New York Times*, June 12.

Knepper, George W. 1988. "Breaching the Ohio Boundary: The Western Tribes in Retreat." In *The American Indian Experience, A Profile: 1524 to the Present*, ed. Philip Weeks, 81–95. Arlington Heights, Ill.: Forum Press.

Lockhart, James, and Stuart B. Schwartz. 1983. *Early Latin America: A History of Colonial Spanish America and Brazil*. Cambridge Latin American Studies. Cambridge: Cambridge University Press.

Mahon, John K. 1967. *History of the Seminole War, 1835–1842*. Gainesville: University of Florida Press.

McClelland, Peter. 1969. "The Cost to America of British Imperial Policy." *American Economics Review* 59:370–381.

McNeill, W. H. 1976. *Plagues and Peoples*. New York: Anchor Books.

Milner, George. 1980. "Epidemic Disease in the Postcontact Southeast: A Reappraisal." *Midcontinental Journal of Archaeology* 5:39–56.

Mintz, Steven. 1995. *Native American Voices: A History and Anthology*. New York: Brandywine Press.

Neely, Sharlotte. 1991. *Snowbird Cherokees: People of Persistence*. Athens: University of Georgia Press.

North, Douglass. 1990. *Institutions, Institutional Change, and Economic Performance*. New York: Cambridge University Press.

North, Douglass, and Andrew Rutten. 1987. "The Northwest Ordinance in Historical Perspective." In *Essays in the Economy of the Old Northwest*, eds. David C. Klingaman and Richard K. Vedder, 19–36. Athens: Ohio University Press.

Parker, Linda S. 1989. *Native American Estate: The Struggle over Indian and Hawaiian Lands.* Honolulu: University of Hawaii Press.

Perdue, Theda. 1979. *Slavery and the Evolution of Cherokee Society.* Knoxville: University of Tennessee.

_____. 1988. "The Trail of Tears: Removal of the Southern Indians." In *The American Indian Experience, a Profile: 1524 to the Present*, ed. Philip Weeks, 96–117. Arlington Heights, Ill.: Forum Press.

Prucha, Francis Paul, ed. 1990. *Documents of United States Indian Policy.* Lincoln: University of Nebraska Press.

Reff, Daniel F. 1991. *Disease, Depopulation, and Culture Change in Northwestern New Spain, 1518–1764.* Salt Lake City: University of Utah Press.

Roback, Jennifer. 1992. "Exchange, Sovereignty, and Indian-Anglo Relations." In *Property Rights and Indian Economies: The Political Economy Forum*, ed. Terry Anderson, 5–26. Lanham, Md.: Rowman and Littlefield.

Ronda, James P. 1988. "Black Robes and Boston Men: Indian-White Relations in New France and New England, 1524–1701." In *The American Indian Experience, A Profile: 1524 to the Present*, ed. Philip Weeks, 3–34. Arlington Heights, Ill.: Forum Press.

Roosevelt, A. C., M. Lima Da Costa, C. Lopez Machado, M. Michab, N. Mercier, H. Vaslladas, J. Feathers, W. Barnett, M. Imazio da Silveira, A. Henderson, J. Sliver, B. Chernoff, D. S. Reese, J. A. Holman, N. Toth, and K. Schick. 1996. "Paleoindian Cave Dwellers in the Amazon: The Peopling of the Americas." *Science* 272 (19 April):373–384.

Rosenblat, Angel. 1954. *La Poblacion Indigena Yel Mestizaje en America.* Vol. 1. Buenos Aires: Editorial Nova.

Seeds of a New Partnership: Indigenous Peoples and the United Nations. 1994. New York: United Nations.

Sen, Amartya. 1983. "Development: Which Way Now?" *Economic Journal* 93 (December):745–762.

Shaffer, Lynda Norene. 1992. *Native Americans Before 1492: The Moundbuilding Centers of the Eastern Woodlands.* Sources and Studies in World History. Armonk, N.Y.: M. E. Sharpe.

Shirley, William. [1755] 1994. Proclamation. In *American Indian Digest: Facts About Today's American Indians,* 13. Phoenix, Ariz.: Thunderbird Enterprises.

Smith, Dwight L. 1988. "Mutual Dependency and Mutual Distrust: Indian-White Relations in British America, 1701–1763." In *The American Indian Experience, A Profile: 1524 to the Present*, ed. Philip Weeks, 49–65. Arlington Heights, Ill.: Forum Press.

Stannard, David E. 1992. *American Holocaust: Columbus and the Conquest of the New World.* Oxford: Oxford University Press.

Thomas, Robert Paul. 1965. "A Quantitative Approach to the Study of the Effects of British Imperial Policy upon Colonial Welfare: Some Preliminary Findings." *Journal of Economic History* 2:615–638.

Thornton, Russell. 1987. *American Indian Holocaust and Survival: A Population History Since 1492.* Norman: University of Oklahoma Press.

Trahant, Mark N. 1995. "Surfing the Republican Wave: Native Politics in Threatening Times." *Native Americas: Akwe:kon's Journal of Indigenous Issues* 7 (3) (Fall):15–21.

U.S. Bureau of the Census. 1975. *Historical Statistics of the United States, from Colonial Times to 1970.* Washington, D.C.: GPO.

Usner, Daniel H., Jr. 1992. *Indians, Settlers, and Slaves in a Frontier Exchange Economy: The Lower Mississippi Valley Before 1783.* Chapel Hill: University of North Carolina Press.

Vandiveer, Clarence A. [1929] 1971. *The Fur Trade and Early Western Exploration.* New York: Cooper Square Publishers.

Wauchope, Robert, ed. 1970. *The Indian Background of Latin American History: The Maya, Aztec, Inca, and Their Predecessors.* New York: Knopf.

Weeks, Philip. 1988. "Humanity and Reform: Indian Policy and the Hayes Presidency." In *The American Indian Experience, A Profile: 1524 to the Present,* ed. Philip Weeks, 174–188. Arlington Heights, Ill.: Forum Press.

_____. 1990. *Farewell My Nation: The American Indian and the United States, 1820–1890.* Wheeling, Ill.: Harlan Davidson.

Wishart, David M. 1995. "Evidence of the Surplus Production in the Cherokee Nation Prior to Removal." *The Journal of Economic History* 55 (March):120–138.

Wolf, Eric R. 1982. *Europe and the People Without History.* Los Angeles: University of California Press.

Wood, Peter H. 1989. "The Changing Population in the Colonial South: An Overview by Race and Region, 1685–1790." In *Powhatan's Mantle: Indians in the Colonial Southeast,* eds. Peter H. Wood, Gregory A. Waselkov, and Thomas M. Hartley, 35–103. Lincoln: University of Nebraska Press.

Worcester, Donald E. 1988. "Spaniards, Frenchmen, and Indians: European-Indian Relations in the Greater Southwest." In *The American Indian Experience, A Profile: 1524 to the Present,* ed. Philip Weeks, 35–48. Arlington Heights, Ill.: Forum Press.

Wright, Gavin. 1978. *Political Economy of the Cotton South: Households, Markets, and Wealth in the Nineteenth Century.* New York: Norton.

Young, Elspeth A. 1995. *Third World in the First: Development and Indigenous Peoples.* London: Routledge.

Part One

Pre-Colonial Civilizations

Introduction

Relative Prices, Civilizations, and Evolving Institutions

LINDA BARRINGTON

Economic historians have increasingly come to acknowledge the interactive dance that takes place between institutions, macroeconomic growth trends, and microeconomic decisionmaking. Economic growth allows for the development of institutions, and the path along which these institutions evolve influences further economic growth. In addition, although any optimization decision is constrained by formal and informal rules, the optimization of economic self-interest simultaneously influences the creation of these rules. Institutions affect incentives, and incentives mold institutions.

Part 1 provides glimpses into varying preconquest civilizations and their institutions. These three chapters reveal how, before the arrival of Europeans, indigenous peoples reacted to economic forces—establishing and adapting their civilizations in response to comparative advantage.

Vernon L. Smith, in Chapter 1, presents the big picture of prehistoric human evolution and settlement. He describes how economic concepts such as comparative advantage and the tragedy of the commons can explain global prehistory. Prehistoric settlement of the American continent and the evolution of its indigenous civilizations are part of this long economic history of humankind. In his chapter, Smith presents several generalized principles or hypotheses. Among them: (1) Hunters and gatherers invented technologies and created institutions that allowed them to obtain affluence manifested in terms of nutrition, health, and leisure. Skeletal records of late-Pleistocene humans and studies of nineteenth- and twentieth-century hunting and fishing peoples in Africa, Australia, the Pacific Northwest, Alaska, Malaya, and Canada reveal little disease or malnutrition and notable quantities of time spent in leisure activities. (2) Opportunity cost has directed the development of humankind. For example, the horse increased the opportunity cost of settled agriculture for the Cheyenne by making hunting more productive—a shift in relative costs that resulted in a dramatic change of lifestyle and culture. (3) Both the tragedy of the commons and the origin of property rights are probably quite ancient. Prior to the evolution of states, the enforcement of property rights was accomplished through mutual dependence, kinship ties, and tribute; however, the lack of property rights in large animals may provide an economic explanation for the global correlation between human settlement and the regional extinction of large mammal species. (4) Biological and economic development, like baseball, is characterized by long stretches of limited activity followed by great flurries or leaps of activity. Each new plateau has been the cause or result of changing relative costs prompting humankind to adapt behavior and institutions, invent relatively cheaper "technologies," and add to the stock of knowledge.

In Chapter 2, Linda Barrington describes the level of economic development of the Mississippian civilization of southeastern North America prior to European contact. Contrary to common perception, the Mississippian civilization was not limited to a hunting and gathering economy. The Mississippian economy was characterized by the existence of long-distance trade routes and the specialization of production. The power structure was one of hierarchical rule in which the elite benefited from the institutions of tribute and slavery. The remains of the great Mississippian earthen mounds, still visible at sites like Cahokia Mounds in Illinois, provide physical evidence of prehistoric economic and social institutions capable of the mass coordination of labor and production. Barrington concludes by suggesting that these indigenous institutions may have influenced European colonial settlement and development of the region.

Terry L. Anderson and Steven LaCombe, in Chapter 3, examine how changing costs and benefits led to institutional change among the Native American cultures of the Great Plains. The horse spread northward from Mexico between 1600 and 1740. With it, the authors argue, came the transformation of the peoples of the Plains from semiagriculturalists and pedestrian hunters to a horse-dependent culture almost completely reliant on buffalo meat. Prior to the advent of the horse, large, communally organized social groups were optimal for pedestrian hunting, with smaller bands joining together seasonally to hunt buffalo. Anderson and LaCombe find that the introduction of the horse increased the mobility of the Plains Indians, ended the use of mass slaughters of buffalo as a hunting technique, and reduced the scale economies of hunting and the optimal size of social organizations. The changes in relative costs of transportation and hunting made it possible for bands to live independently of one another. Lessened need for cooperation in hunting meant greater conflict between tribes as encroachment into others' hunting grounds increased. In response, political structures became more centralized, tribes delineated private hunting grounds, and personal property rights in horses allowed individuals to accumulate great wealth and prestige. The horse altered the relative costs of production for the Plains Indians and their institutions changed accordingly.

Part 1, while discussing a limited selection of preconquest North American peoples, reveals the universality of humankind's response to economic forces. The ever changing relative prices of the resources available for production has meant and will continue to mean the evolution of human civilizations and their institutions.

1

Economy, Ecology, and Institutions in the Emergence of Humankind

VERNON L. SMITH

This chapter is about who we were in prehistory and how we were shaped by economic principles.[1] Of the many models that one encounters in the antiquities literature of humankind, unabashedly economic models are rare, almost nonexistent. Such models are easily dismissed as reductionist economic determinism because they appear not to account for the richness of culture. The tale of humankind that I will relate is a relatively simple model of the influence of opportunity cost and human capital accumulation on our development from bipedalism through tool manufacturing to anatomically modern *Homo sapiens*, with big-game hunting, art, language, and the beginning of agriculture. I think it is an exciting story—perhaps humanity's most important story.

Life Emerged Early, Bipedalism and *Homo* Very Late

The earth and other planets, formed by the condensation of gas that produced our solar system, are about 4.5 billion years old. Elementary life forms, whose remains have been found in Australia and South Africa, appeared 3.8–3.5 billion years before present (B.P.), which is about as early as life as we know it could have emerged. But multicellular animals are not found in the fossil record until much later, some 650 million years B.P., and those of modern form that are believed to be antecedents of humankind appear about 550 million years B.P.

In Africa, sometime between 10 and 5 million years ago, bipedal protohumans almost certainly split off from the forerunners of today's chimpanzees and gorillas. This is indicated directly by the fossil record and by genetic comparisons between living humans and other primates. Thus compelling evidence for the oldest hominid yet found, the new species *Australopithecus ramidus*, has been recovered in the form of dental, cranial, and postcranial specimens dated about 4.4 million years B.P. (White, Suwa, and Asfaw 1994). During this period a globally cooler and drier climate shrunk forests in favor of grasslands and savannas (Klein 1989, 29–35, 180–181; Laporte and Zihlman 1983). This was a conditioning factor. Grassland ungulates (hoofed mammals) increased in number and diversity as the cost of harvesting their food declined, and the resulting economic stress on forest dwellers brought the extinction of many ape species in Eurasia. But at least one ape species in Africa adapted by becoming more of a ground dweller (Klein 1989, 181). These environmental changes may have made bipedalism an economizing response in several ways: It was easier to carry food and young; heat stress would have been reduced by exposing less body surface to direct sunlight; the hands were freed for using, carrying, and later fabricating tools; the energy requirements of locomotion were decreased; and, finally, it led to an improved ability to see over obstructions, grass, and shrubs. Although bipedalism predates the earliest recorded stone tools, early prehumans may have used wood, bamboo, and other perishable material for simple fabricated tools, much as chimpanzees (genetically the nearest relative of humans) will make, transport, and use sticks to reach for food.[2] In fact it can be argued that an elementary reliance on implements may have predated bipedalism and helped to account for our protohuman ancestors' ability to flourish in savanna environments (Laporte and Zihlman 1983, 105–107). Although bipedalism was an important opportunistic response (for us), it was not nature's only experimental adaptation to the demands of a savanna environment. Apparently the other response was the evolution of a more effective quadrupedal knuckle-walker, to evolve into the modern chimpanzee and continue to exploit woodland as well as Savanna environments (Zihlman 1991). If our ancestral protohumans were adaptively attempting bipedalism as grasslands expanded, then mutations favoring bipedalism would have economic value.

At some point, perhaps 4–3 million years B.P. (proposed in Zihlman and Cohn 1988), early bipedal hominids lost much of their body hair and developed thermoregulatory (body-cooling) sweat glands. Hair reduction would have necessitated skin pigmentation to protect against ultraviolet radiation. These developments, especially in combination with bipedalism, would have greatly enhanced survival and foraging productivity in open grassland and savanna mosaic environments.

The cooler dryer trend in climate that is associated with the emergence of bipedalism accelerated from 2.5 to 2 million years B.P. This coincided with rapid evolutionary change in hominids and other African mammals, leading to a more carnivorous, larger-brained, and more tool-dependent lineage of *Homo* whose expanding niche may explain the decline of other African carnivores (Vrba 1985; Walker 1984). The earliest firmly documented stone tools (attributed to *H. habilis*) are found at the Hadar site in northeast Ethiopia adjacent to the Red Sea; they are conservatively dated at 2.5–2.4 million years B.P., but could be as old as 3.1 million years B.P. (Harris 1983). These and other sites in Zaire, Olduvai, and elsewhere show that stone tools were widely used in southern and eastern Africa by 2 million years B.P. These early tools, though crude by later standards, were diverse, but their diversity (based upon experimental replication) appears to have been controlled by the random shape of the original blank rather than by deliberate design (Toth 1985). The tool kit and the tools' suggested uses included flakes (for cutting and splitting), scrapers (for butchery), and cobble missiles (for hunting or defense). The combination of such stone tools with fragmentary animal bones clearly demonstrates an increased interest in meat by *H. habilis* over earlier hominids, but it cannot be definitely said that they were great hunters. Most of the assemblages are found near ancient stream or lake beds where animals would have congregated. Although the bones often show evidence of scarring from stone tools, this does not prove that meat was obtained by hunting rather than by scavenging the kills of other carnivores. Whether it was more cost efficient for these early humans to take meat from such formidable carnivores than to dispatch the prey themselves is an open research issue. A recent study of Hazda scavenging found that "scavenging returns were highly variable, depending on carcass encounter rates, carcass size and completeness on encounter, and success at displacing the original predators" (O'Connell, Hawkes, and Jones 1988, 356). The authors conclude that even if early hominids had no difficulty displacing competing carnivores, scavenging could only have been intermittently successful in savanna environments comparable to those in the Hazda study.

At the beginning of the Pleistocene, approximately 1.8–1.7 million years ago, *H. habilis* was replaced by *H. erectus*, generally thought to be the direct ancestor of *H. sapiens* and of you and me. We are still in the Pleistocene epoch (or Quaternary), conventionally called the Holocene, enjoying a warming interglacial period that began about 14,000 years B.P.[3] The significance of the Pleistocene is that the evolutionary, cultural, and economic development of humankind accelerated during the ebb and flow of the earth's cycles in glaciation. There have been seventeen major glaciations in the last 1.7 million years and eight during the last 730,000 years. At the peak glaciation nearly a third of the earth's surface was covered by ice sheets, and the sea level dropped 400–500 feet. This caused the joining of land masses that were isolated in the warm stages: Siberia with Alaska, Australia with New Guinea, and Southeast Asia with Java. Gulfs such as the Persian were river valleys above sea level. Within the past million years interglaciations as warm as the one we are now experiencing have lasted only about 10,000 years, whereas the periods of glaciation have lasted closer to 100,000 years. (Perhaps this will comfort those concerned with global warming.) Consequently our ancestral development occurred under mostly glacial conditions, to which we adapted well. These cycles of glaciation made possible a worldwide redistribution of plants, animals, and humankind (Klein 1989, 34–35).

Out of Africa: Exodus I

A prominent contemporary view of the emergence of modern humans is the "out-of-Africa model," in which humankind first evolved in Africa then spread throughout Eurasia (Gould 1988; Stringer 1990) in an initial wave beginning about 1 million years B.P. In Africa the displacement of *H. habilis* by *H. erectus* may be explained by the increased emphasis on tool use and by carnivorousness. *H. erectus* was much better endowed with a locomotor skeleton, had a larger brain, and the typically human external nose.[4] These endowments suggest improved exertion capacity and hunting, gathering, or scavenging skill. The greater adaptability of *H. erectus* is demonstrated by this people's colonization of previously unoccupied dry regions of Africa about 1.5 million years B.P. and by their dispersal to northern Africa and thence into colder regions such as Eurasia and China and, after 1 million years B.P., to Java. Generally, in the African and eastward expansion paths of *H. erectus* one finds evidence of tool use that required more investment in human capital—planning, foresight, and preparation effort—than is associated with *H. habilis.* Thus the finding that most of our current growth is due to investment in human capital probably applies with even greater force to the last 2 million years of hominid development. The tool kit now included hand axes, cleavers, and other large bifacial tools used for butchery, bone breaking, and perhaps woodworking (wood spears appear toward the end of this period). Also it is likely that *H. erectus* could control the use of fire; the oldest evidence dates from 1.5–1.4 million years B.P., although more convincing evidence (of a tended hearth rather than a natural fire) does not appear until 500,000 years ago (see Klein 1989, 171, 218 for references; for recent new evidence dating back to 465,000 years, see the report by Balter 1995).

A long-standing puzzle is the geographical distribution of these tools in Southeast Asia; here the tools are less standardized, and there is a paucity of hand axes but no shortage of chopper tools. At one time this led to the conclusion that *H. erectus* was culturally retarded, that they had minimal capacity for standardizing the manufacture of stone tools. Yet it is hard to believe that the same race of people who made hand axes in Africa and northwest Asia and who had trekked to Southeast Asia had unintentionally lost this sophisticated craft. A hypothesized solution has now been offered by the observation that the line across Southeast Asia below which one finds alleged "cultural retardation" corresponds to the distribution of naturally occurring bamboo. This is an area that today contains over 1,000 species of bamboo, a raw material that can be fabricated into knives, spears, projectile points, and traps (Pope 1989). It would appear that *H. erectus*, far from having suffered cultural degeneration in bambooland, simply responded to the locally high opportunity cost of making standardized tools, such as hand axes, from stone.

Out of Africa: Exodus II

With the exception of some early *Homo sapiens*, most known human fossils dated 500,000–400,000 years B.P. or earlier are those of *H. erectus* (found in Java, China, and Africa). Whereas the European fossils of this period exhibit some similarity with the later Neanderthals, the African fossils suggest that *H. erectus* evolved in the direction of modern *H. sapiens*. Fossils in Southeast Asia, on the other hand, maintain their similarity to *H. erectus*, as is evidenced in the artifacts of the region, which are dominated by flake and chopping tools with an absence of hand axes. The hand axes of early *H. sapiens* and other stone artifacts are better made because *H. sapiens* had apparently invented a technique for predetermining flake size, allowing tools to be more deliberately designed. Such artifacts are generally uniform in function and style over wide areas and a long period of time (Klein 1989).

Neanderthals—at one time traditionally believed to be our immediate ancestors—are thought to be a Eurasian descendant of *H. erectus*. They appeared 130,000 years ago or earlier, had a brain case at least as large as living people, and, judging from the skeleton and muscle/ligament markings on the bones, had exceptional physical strength (Trinkaus 1986). They were adapted to cold climates and made tools of wood (for example, spears) and in rare instances of bone. Judging from the animal bones at numerous sites, Neanderthals successfully hunted deer, bison, aurochs (wild cattle), sheep, goats, and horses. They cared for family members who were handicapped or incapacitated and were the first people who practiced intentional burial, perhaps with ceremony; they may have adorned their bodies with ocher. But their unusual adaptations were not viable, and they disappeared about 30,000 years ago (Klein 1989; Gould 1988).

Although traditionally anthropologists thought modern *H. sapiens* or Cro-Magnons originated 50,000–40,000 years B.P., overlapping with Neanderthals, recent research claims to have found anatomically modern humans as early as 90,000 years B.P. (Valladas et al. 1988). Thus Neanderthals may have overlapped Cro-Magnons for more than 50,000 years and according to one view are not central stock but a side branch. The contemporary view, supported by fossil and genetic evidence, is that modern humans evolved initially within the period 200,000–50,000 years B.P. in Africa. A controversial study placed our common mitochondrial DNA ancestor at 200,000 B.P. (see Vigilant et al. 1991; and two rebuttal notes, Templeton 1992; Hedges et al. 1992). A recent corroborating study of the paternally inherited DNA polymorphism in the Y chromosome found no sequence variation in a worldwide sample of thirty-eight human males. "The invariance likely results from either a recent selective sweep, a recent origin for modern *Homo sapiens,* recurrent male population bottlenecks, or historically small effective male population sizes" (Dorit, Akashi, and Gilbert 1995, 1183). This leads to an expected time since a common ancestral male lineage of 270,000 years, but with a 95 percent confidence interval of 0 to 800,000 years.

Prior to this time body form and behavior (based on tool assemblages) evolved together (Klein 1989, 1992). Subsequently behavioral evolution accelerated within a constant bodily form. Thus the "people of Cro-Magnon carved intricate figures of horses and deer and painted their caves with an esthetic power never exceeded in the history of human art" (Gould 1988, 16). After 40,000–35,000 years B.P. artifact assemblages varied tremendously across neighboring regions, and the pace of change accelerated dramatically (Klein 1989, 360–398). Cro-Magnons fashioned bone, ivory, and antler into projectile points, awls, punches, needles, and art objects (for the evolution of Cro-Magnon weapons see Knecht 1994). Compared to those of the Neanderthals, their stone crafts included more blades with longer cutting edges and numerous shouldered projectile points of the kind suitable for spears, arrows, and darts. Their graves, houses, and fireplaces were also more elaborate. Ceramics and fired clay appeared about 28,000 years B.P. Eurasian Cro-Magnons hunted in savannas and grasslands principally for mammoth, bison, reindeer, antelope, and horse—all large gregarious herbivores—which provided meat, hide, and sinew as well as bone, antler, and ivory. It is likely that, like the American Indians and the plains settlers, they burned the dried droppings ("buffalo chips") of large animals where wood was unavailable (Klein 1989, 366).[5] After 20,000 years B.P. the artifacts included the atlatl (spear thrower), arrows, stone inserts in antlers, harpoons, leisters (three-pronged fish spears), eyed needles, and all manner of clothing—jackets, shirts, trousers, and so on. Conclusive evidence for the bow and arrow appears 12,000–10,000 years B.P. (Tyldesley and Bahn 1983), but a much earlier origin is probable given the frequent occurrence of stone points similar to those used for arrow tips in historical times.

From Europe 34,000–11,000 years B.P. there is widespread evidence that humankind had the means of making large numbers of kills of a single species. They ate ungulates, fish, mollusks, birds, and seals. The staples were reindeer, red deer, horse, ibex, and bison. Evidence of the mass slaughter of horse and reindeer suggest they were driven into cliff-enclosed canyons or off "jumps." The Cro-Magnons were adept at the battue (beating underbrush to drive game), the drive line, the stampede, and the pit trap.

Humankind:
Super Predation and World Expansion

Modern *H. sapiens* spread from Africa through Europe and Asia in the last 50,000 years, jumped to Australia by about 40,000 years B.P., entered Alaska about 12,000–11,000 B.P., the lower forty-eight states of North America by 11,000 B.P., and within the next 1,000 years reached the southern tip of South America. The last destinations of this worldwide expansion were Madagascar, New Zealand, and Antarctica, which were occupied by humankind only in the last 1,000 years.

A plausible theoretical hypothesis is that North America was discovered by advanced Paleolithic people who crossed the exposed Bering land bridge, connecting Asia with Alaska, some 12,000–11,000 years ago:

> The settlement of Beringia (extending from the Verkhoyansk Range on the west to the Mackenzie River on the east) began (approximately) 12,000 yr B.P. . . . The continued presence of the land bridge permitted rapid colonization of western and eastern Beringia. The lack of occupations in other regions of the New World that are firmly dated to before 11,200 yr B.P., despite apparent access to these regions from Alaska and the Yukon by at least 14,000 yr B.P., suggests the absence of a Beringian population before 12,000 yr B.P. (Hoffman, Powers, and Goebel 1993, 51)

The Bering terrain was unsuitable for gathering plants, but the subarctic grasses supported the cold-adapted mammoth, bison, and caribou. Communal hunting parties, armed with stone weapons and able to control fire, were big-game hunters par excellence. Their descendants found an exposed land corridor between the western and midcontinental ice sheets in Canada (Klein 1989, 390), ultimately made their way into Montana, and then spread south and east throughout the United States. As suggested by Paul S. Martin (1990), they entered a continent that was an unprecedented "home-on-the-range" for now-extinct mammoth, mastodon, ground sloth, two now-extinct species of bear, cheetah, the giant beaver (*Castoroides*, the largest North American rodent—roughly the size of a black bear), horse, tapir, two species of peccary, camel, llama, two now-extinct species of deer, the stag moose, pronghorn, shrub ox, two species of musk ox, yak, two subspecies of bison (*B. occidentalis* and *B. antiquus*—both larger than the surviving *B. bison* known to the plains settlers), the dire wolf, a saber-toothed and a scimitar-toothed "tiger," and many other less-familiar megafauna.

Many of these animals, such as the ground sloth, were slow and could be easily hunted. Others, like the mammoth, mastodon, and horse, were large gregarious herd animals whose herding behavior implied low search cost for hunting parties armed with stone projectile points and strategic knowledge of animal behavior. Additionally, their great size meant high value per kill. Some prey, such as the extinct plains bison, may have been easier to hunt than their living relatives. Since there were no property rights in live animals, only in harvested animals, there was no incentive to stay the spear in anticipation of tomorrow's reproductive value as with modern domesticated cattle—descendants of the Old World auroch. The resulting mass harvesting pressure on animals may have caused or contributed to the extensive megafauna loss on the North American continent by 11,000 years B.P.

Hunting parties left behind Clovis fluted points—a work of craftsmanship in stone—found from Florida to Nova Scotia, in the high plains, the southwest, across the midwest, and in the south. These points are 7–15 centimeters long and 3–4 centimeters wide with concave bases, and they have a fluting extending from the base to one-half the length of the point. They were flaked by percussion, and the base edges were ground down to prevent cutting of the thongs securing them to a throwing or thrusting spear—a design that would allow the weapon to sustain lateral stress if it remained in the hand of the hunter after penetrating the prey.

That Clovis hunters killed mammoth is well documented. Numerous mammoth kill sites in the western United States show that the mammoth were harvested by hunters. Evidence also suggests that these animals had become extinct by 11,000 years B.P. (Haynes 1964, 1988), although they "had been in North America for over one million years" (Martin 1990, 111).[6] Some sites also contain the bones of camel and horse,[7] but no incontrovertible evidence exists that these animals were hunted in North America, even though the horse was one of the most widely hunted animals in the Paleolithic Old World. The horse became extinct in North America (where it originated) only about 10,000 years B.P. (Mead and Meltzer 1984, 446). It was reintroduced by the Spanish in the sixteenth century and has thrived in the wild down to the present under the arid conditions of Arizona, Nevada, and Utah.

The Clovis point was replaced by the Folsom point between 11,000 and 10,000 years B.P.; it is less widely dispersed than the Clovis and is associated with the extinct *Bison antiquus*. The Scottsbluff and similar projectile points date from about 9,000 years B.P. and are associated with the slightly smaller, extinct *Bison occidentalis*. It appears probable that Paleoindian procurement of Bison occurred in mass kills, sometimes of several hundred animals at a time. This is illustrated at the Olsen-Chubbuck site in Colorado (Wheat 1967), where, 8,500 years B.P., two hundred *B. occidentalis* were stampeded into an arroyo five to seven feet deep and dispatched with Scottsbluff projectile points. At least fifty of the animals apparently represented a wastage kill, since they showed no evidence of butchery for consumption. Dozens of such kill-butchery sites are found in Colorado, Wyoming, Montana, and Nebraska (Frison 1986; Todd 1986). Many sites are stampede jumps or traps that had several thousand years of use. Near the Montana border in Alberta there is a cliff site, Head-Smashed-In, that forms a natural amphitheater used for over fifty-five centuries as a jump for stampeding bison to their deaths. It has been estimated that "the remains of nearly 123,000 bison lie on the prairie east of the kill site" (Fagan 1989, 38). Boiling pits were used for rendering the fat to make pemmican, a storable mixture of fat and pounded meat.

Bison may have survived in the form of the plains bison by dwarfing (Edwards 1967); indeed, this could have been an adaptive response to the greater vulnerability of the larger subspecies to predation.[8] Despite the enormous carrying capacity of the land from Alberta to Texas (which historically supported perhaps 60 million bison), we were left with far fewer large species than the fossil record of the Pleistocene would lead one to expect.

Martin (1967, 1984, 1990) has summarized the evidence for the worldwide extinction of late Pleistocene megafauna. In Africa and Asia, 15–20 percent of the genera disappeared 80,000–60,000 years B.P.; in Australia, 94 percent were lost from 40,000–15,000 years B.P.; North and South America experienced a 70–80 percent loss in the last 15,000 years, with an abrupt North American loss of mammoth, mastodon, ground sloth, and such dependent predators and scavengers as the saber-toothed cat and (in much of its range) the condor 11,000 years ago. The horse and two subspecies of bison were gone by 9,000–8,000 years B.P.. This worldwide pattern correlates suspiciously with the chronology of human colonization, leading to Paul Martin's hypothesis that extinction was directly or indirectly due to "overkill" by exceptionally competent hunter cultures. This model explains the light extinctions in Africa and Asia where modern humankind "grew up"; local fauna may have gradually adapted to humankind's accumulating proficiency as a superpredator. It explains the abrupt massive losses in Australia and the Americas—the only habitable continents that were colonized suddenly by advanced Stone-Aged humans. But the control cases for Martin's "experiment" are the large oceanic islands such as Madagascar and New Zealand; both were colonized within the last 1,000 years, and both suffered a wave of extinctions at this time (Dewar 1984; Trotter and McCulloch 1984; Anderson 1989).[9]

One wonders why—if extinction was due to climatic change—Madagascar extinctions were not coincident with those of Africa 220 miles off its coast, and why Australian extinctions were not coincident with those of New Zealand. Similarly, we might ask why European and Ukrainian mammoths became extinct 13,000 years B.P., whereas in North America they survived another 2,000 years. Previous great extinction waves had affected plants and small animals as well as large animals, but the late-Pleistocene extinctions are concentrated on the large gregarious herding, or slow moving, animals—the ideal prey of human hunters. Such large genera are also the animals that are slower growing, have longer gestation periods, require longer periods of maternal care, and live longer. Consequently they were more vulnerable to hunting pressure because reductions in biomass require more time to recover. The theory is bold—some say fanciful.

A counterargument is that there is little direct evidence of hunting, that Paleolithic peoples "probably" relied on plants. But if the fossil record of hunting is "small," the fossil evidence of gathering is virtually nonexistent (Klein 1989, 219, 364–365). A second counterargument is that there would not have been an incentive to overproduce in excess of immediate needs, that this occurs only in modern exchange economies (Frison 1986, 213). But this argument fails to recognize that in the absence of private property rights, there is no intertemporal incentive to avoid the kind of waste associated with large kills. What controls the slaughter of domestic cattle is the comparative value of dressed versus live beef (Smith 1975, 745). Since no one owned the mammoth, their harvest value (net of hunting cost) contrasted sharply with their zero live procreation value to the individual hunter. A third argument finds it incomprehensible that mere bands of men could have wiped out the great mammoth and two subspecies of bison.[10] It takes a particularly skilled modern rifleman to stop a charging African elephant in time to prevent injury, and extant bison react quickly and violently when they sense danger (Frison 1986, 188–192).

Such observations may simply tell us that these particular subspecies have survived because they were selected for their successful defensive characteristics. We know nothing of the behavioral properties of extinct species, which may have been far more approachable than their surviving relatives. Although African and Indian elephants are both members of the same genus, their fossil similarities fail to inform us that the Indian elephant is docile and easily trained for circus display, whereas the African elephant is not. No one has successfully domesticated the African zebra; in contrast the Tarpan horse has been domesticated since ancient times (5000–2500 B.P.). *Equus* includes horses, asses, and zebras—all behaviorally distinct animals.

Interpretations and Hypotheses from the Prehistoric Record

Several principles and hypotheses stem from our brief survey of the prehistorical record.

1. *Hunting and gathering provided the technology and institutions for the first affluent society.* One of the great myths of modern humankind is the belief that life in the Paleolithic was intolerably harsh, or as presumed (without evidence) by Thomas Hobbes, "solitary, poor, nasty, brutish and short." It may have been none of these. What is just as likely is that hunting and gathering provided the first affluent society (Sahlins 1972); it sustained and promoted humankind for almost all of their 2.5 million years of existence. The

Hobbesian belief obscures the striking continuity in the ability of prehistoric humans to adapt to changes in their environment by substituting new inputs of capital, labor, and knowledge for old and to fabricate new products when effort prices were altered by the environment or new learning. The skeletons of late Pleistocene humans show a mortality pattern like that of historic hunter-gatherers and "rarely show evidence of serious accidents or disease" (Klein 1989, 385). Their teeth were healthy, probably because their diets contained little sugar. Historically, among the hunting and fishing peoples of Africa, Australia, the Pacific Northwest, Alaska, Malaya, and Canada, malnutrition, starvation, and chronic diseases were rare or infrequent. Studies of the African Kung Bushman (Lee 1968) show that these people work only twelve to nineteen hours per week, their hunting and gathering activities scored well on several measures of nutritional adequacy, and their labor bought much leisure in the form of resting, visiting, entertaining, and trance dancing.[11] Similarly, the African Hazda hunters work no more than two hours per day, with plenty of time left for gambling, other social activities, or investment. Much of the great diversity in our ancestral development must have been due to the extent to which different peoples employed time released from subsistence for different forms of investment in human capital.

Although studies of the prehistoric record place great emphasis on the intellectual development of humans—brain size, tool use, the control of fire—their prowess as hunter-gatherers was probably also due to their physical superiority over other animals. After all, tool development was slow and limited until the explosive development of the late prehistoric period. But human physical superiority is striking. As J. B. S. Haldane once noted, only humans can swim a mile, walk twenty, and then climb a tree.

2. *Opportunity cost has conditioned the cultural and economic development of humankind.* This principle was articulated succinctly by the Kung Bushman who was asked by an anthropologist why he had not turned to agriculture (as his neighbors had done). His reply: "Why should we plant when there are so many mongongo nuts in the world?" (Lee 1968, 33). Why indeed, unless tastes and opportunity cost combine to demand it? Bipedalism itself occurred at a time when the cost of an arboreal existence was stressing primate populations. An economical adaptation was to subsist in the spreading savannas and grasslands that were replacing the forest. The great migrations out of Africa, the invention of weapons for big-game hunting, Eskimo adaptation to hunting sea mammals, humankind's eventual turn to agriculture—these can all be interpreted as responses to changes in opportunity cost, whether driven by environmental change, by human learning, or a combination of the two. A telling example of the influence of effort prices on prehistoric human choice is found in Lee's (1968) study of fifty-eight extant hunter-gatherer societies the world over. There is a strong correlation between a society's distance from the equator and the relative importance of

hunting over gathering in its diet. In the Arctic, the hunting of land and sea mammals predominates, whereas in the temperate latitudes up to 39° from the equator gathering is the more important economic activity.

Economic models of human development and change are often held suspect because they appear not to account for the richness of culture. But culture and institutions can be interpreted as providing the information system for transmitting the learning embodied in the unconscious response to opportunity cost. Thus hunter cultures use elaborate ceremony and ritual to communicate the value and significance of the chase and its technology of execution. Culture is the means of transmitting human capital from one generation to the next—of forming in the young an indelible impression of the hunt. The magnificent Cro-Magnon art preserved on the walls deep in the narrow crawl spaces of French and Spanish caves have been given this interpretation: "Imprinting enormous amounts of information in memory called for . . . the use of confined spaces, obstacles and difficult routes, and hidden images to heighten the natural strangeness of underground settings . . . piling special effect on special effect in an effort to ensure the preservation and transmission of the tribal encyclopedia" (Pfeiffer 1982, 132).

Another example of the hidden economic function of culture is the magical practice of the Naskapi Indians of Labrador, who, when the caribou were scarce and the tribe hungry, resorted to scapulimacy, a divination in which the shoulder blade bone of a caribou was heated by fire until it cracked. As cracks appeared they were interpreted by a diviner in terms of the local geography and caribou haunts—as trails, one of which the hunter should follow if he was to be successful. F. G. Speck (1935) reported having observed twelve successful hunts out of nineteen divinations, noting that the unsuccessful cases were always attributed to the failure of the diviner to read the scapula map correctly. All this is interpreted by Speck as showing the capacity of the Naskapi for belief in magic. But is scapulimacy functional? One function of course is to sharpen the hunter's concentration; another is to impress upon all the need for great dedication. But O. K. Moore's (1957) study of magical practices led him to the conclusion that they served immediate, practical, economic ends. The effect of Naskapi magic was to cause the hunter to choose a random route, steering him away from previously successful hunting routes and preventing the caribou from being sensitized to regularities in hunter behavior. This is of course precisely the normative argument for using noncooperative mixed strategies in certain games of conflict. What the Naskapi in effect seem to have discovered was that reading shoulder blades had survival value. "People are capable of formulating any number of strange ideas, not necessarily directed towards any particular end, but if they do have a practical application and are successful, they may persist. And if they persist long enough people will begin to believe in them" (Reader 1988: 139). If they are believed, I might add, they will be incorporated into educational rituals so that the tribal learning is not lost to each new generation.

3. *Prehistoric H. sapiens accumulated human capital.* Economic success as a hunter-gatherer required an endowment of human capital normally associated only with the agricultural and industrial revolutions: learning, knowledge transfer, skill in tool fabrication and design, and social organization. The aboriginal use of fire for game and plant management demonstrates that prehistoric humans possessed intricate knowledge of the phenology of trees, shrubs, and herbs and used fire to enhance the growth and flowering of certain food plants (huckleberry and hazel bushes, bear lilics, wild rice, for example) and to suppress the growth of competitors.[12] Effective game and wild plant management required people to know where, when, how, and with what frequency to burn. Aboriginals knew that the growing season for wild plants can be advanced by spring burns designed to warm the earth. They also knew that in dry weather fires should be ignited at the top of hills to prevent wild fires[13] but in damp conditions they should be set in depressions to avoid being extinguished. Moreover, the burning of underbrush aids the production of acorns by oak trees and attracts moose, deer, and other animals who feed on the tender new shoots that follow a burn.[14]

Humankind was a fire creature beginning with *H. erectus*, and fire "revolutionized human society and its relationship to the natural world" (Pyne 1991). Anthropogenic fire redefined or reformed food, dentition, facial muscles, tools (for example, wood spears could be fire-hardened, trunks could be fire-carved into dugout canoes), and the ecology of humankind's environments. The Australian aborigines were the "black lightening" that ignited Australia with their arrival some 40,000 years ago; they lived abundantly by fire stick farming: burning to increase access to roots and tubers, to recycle nutrients more quickly in dry regions, to increase grass and plant yield, to flush or kill game, and to increase plant food for a new cycle of game production.

The life of a hunter-gatherer is one of commitment to an intellectually and physically demanding activity requiring skill; technology; social organization; division of labor; knowledge of plant and animal behavior, of climate, seasons, and winds; the habit of close observation; inventiveness; problem solving; risk taking; and high motivation. These demands were selective in humankind's cultural and biological evolution and helped to develop the human capital and genetic equipment needed to create modern civilization. The aboriginal practice of awarding more wives to the most successful hunters would have favored the genetic selection of these traits.[15]

It was as a hunter-gatherer that humankind learned to learn: Young hunters needed to be imbued with knowledge of animal behavior and anatomy and with the habit of goal-oriented observation, needed to learn that ungulates often travel in an arc so that success could be increased by traversing the chord, and so on. Knowledge of animal behavior could substitute for weapon development. From knowledge of animal anatomy it was but a short step to curiosity about human anatomy, the discovery that we too are animals, and to the first practice of medicine.

4. *Property rights are probably of ancient origin.* Although humankind has made stone tools for at least 2.5 million years, the archeological record of property rights is more obscure. Although aboriginals everywhere have had sophisticated property rights and trading traditions, there is no direct evidence that prehistoric peoples maintained such traditions. But the similarities between the cultural materials of late-Pleistocene and aboriginal peoples suggest that such social traditions originated at least as early as the period 40,000–20,000 years B.P. Cultural materials (amber, seashells, stone tools) often occur hundreds of kilometers from their points of origin, indicating intergroup contacts over wide areas (Klein 1989, 376–378). No such evidence of social contact occurs before the late Pleistocene, when the archeological record shows a vast increase in property such as bows and arrows, atlatls, seed-grinding stones, boiling and storage vessels, kilns for firing clay, boats, houses, villages, animal-drawn sledges, and the domesticated wolf. New tools and techniques allowed new products of gathering and hunting to substitute for the loss of big game. Previously, gathering emphasized the seeds and plants that could be eaten while on the move. Now the seeds gathered were inedible without soaking, grinding, and boiling. This upsurge in personal paraphernalia implies more sedentary, less nomadic, hunting and gathering. Knowledge of the seasonal cycles of plants and animals, of the use of fire in resource management, of techniques of storing, drying, and preserving foods all combine to make life more sedentary. But with the accumulation of personal property and real estate would come more-complex property rights and contracting arrangements.[16]

George Dalton (1977) summarized the economic as well as the important political function of ceremonial exchanges in northwest America and in Melanesia; he found that such ceremonies as the potlatch, kula, moka, and abutu were, in substance, elaborate multilateral contracting mechanisms. The valuables exchanged (bracelets, pearl shells, cowries, young women) not only bought other commodities in ordinary exchange, but they also bought kinship ties with the exchange of daughters, military assistance if attacked, the right of refuge if homes and property had to be abandoned, and emergency assistance in the event of poor harvest, hunting, or fishing. They bought political stability in stateless societies and a property right environment that facilitated specialization and ordinary exchange. Property rights thus preceded the state. And property included not only private goods such as land, fishing sites, livestock, and cemetery plots but also public goods such as crests, names, dances, rituals, and trade routes that could be assigned to more than one individual or group.

How is it possible that property rights and exchange could exist prior to the advent of the state and of central enforcement? The answer is to be found in reciprocity, mutual dependence, and statelike forms of control achieved through broadened kinship ties and the outright purchase of political stability. If I grow beans and you grow corn, and we exchange our surpluses, we each have a stake in protecting our respective property rights. If either of us plays the game of "steal" rather than the game of "trade," this will end our prospect of maintaining a trading relationship tomorrow. Once humankind opted for less-nomadic forms of hunting and gathering, such reciprocal relationships would have been vastly more important. Transients always pose a more demanding problem of property right enforcement than those who are in more permanent contact with each other.[17] The conditions of reciprocity would have been powerfully present once the agricultural revolution came, but I want to suggest that they already existed in hunter-gatherer communities that were managing and harvesting from relatively fixed resource bases. Moreover, stateless societies did not have to rely entirely on voluntary forbearance based on the incentive support from reciprocal relationships. They also purchased political stability by paying tribute and by kinship exchange and "gift-exchange." (For an economic analysis of the Kula Ring see Landa 1983.)

Evidence for the existence of property rights and social contracting in stateless societies is incontrovertible. Robert Heizer (1955) notes that in North America the private ownership of fishing and hunting grounds, nut trees, and seed-gathering areas was common. Among the Karok (Kroeber and Barrett 1960), owning the right to fish a particular eddy or channel of a river was independent of who owned the land along the river, and the right was transferable by bequest or sale. Similarly, an individual would own sealing rights to a particular coastal rock. Peter Freuchen, who lived with the Greenland Eskimos at the turn of the last century, describes the social organization and trading behavior of these prehistoric hunting-fishing people. Among their social contracts was a simple incentive-compatible rule for allocating the skin among hunting team members when the prey was the dangerous polar bear: "The hunter who fixed his spear first in the bear gets the upper part. That is the finest part, for it includes the forelegs with the long mane hairs that are so much desired to border women's kamiks (boots) with" (Freuchen [1961] 1973, 53).

5. *Humankind was an intense user of the environment for self-interested ends.* Although today we associate environmental damage, including extinction, with the advent of industrial society and human population growth, it is probable that prehistoric humans had a comparable, or perhaps more severe impact, on their environment. This is because the species that have survived to the present represent the less vulnerable plants and animals. If Paul Martin is correct in his judgment that the wave of animal extinctions begin-

ning with the "invasion" of Australia 40,000 years B.P. and ending with the occupation of Madagascar and New Zealand were of anthropogenic origin, then the losses were of species that had inadequate defensive capabilities. The winnowing left the more stubbornly resistant species, able to survive all but major destruction of habitat. Major losses of hunted game animals in the prehistoric period can also help to account for the enculturation of self-serving conservationist principles in the myths, rituals, and beliefs of aboriginal societies. Thus the Choctaw had rules regulating the game that could be killed by one family. The Kaska trapped marten in a game area only every two or three years. The Iroquois and many other tribes spared the females of hunted species during the breeding season. The Yurok had "game laws"—whose violation would cause loss of "hunting luck." Many tribes believed that game was watched over by supernatural deities who would be angry if too many animals were killed or if they were merely wounded. (See Heizer 1955, 4–7, for these and many more examples.) Thus tribal property rights were conservationist.

A second source of ecological change induced by prehistorical peoples was their transportation of seeds in hunter-gatherer migrations throughout the world. The introduction of botanical exotics into new regions has often been noted by archaeologists, who have observed the association of various plants with campsites and dwellings. The wide distribution of wild squash, in particular, appears to be associated with humankind. Other plants whose patterns of incidence suggest that they were spread by early humans include mulberry, black walnut and buckeye trees, elderberry, nettle, scurvy grass, sweet flag, crabapple, cactus, and lotus (Heizer 1955, 12–13).

Finally, the human use of fire is thought to have had a profound effect on the ecology of the environment. Many authors who have studied patterns of land burning by primitive peoples have concluded that many of the world's great grasslands were produced by periodic burning (see Heizer 1955, 9–12; Lewis 1980). Where tree growth is favored by weather conditions, periodic burning will select for particular species. For example, the pine forests in southern New York and to the west have been attributed to Indian burning. Similarly, the disappearing grassland areas in northern Alberta are attributed to Canadian restrictions on traditional Indian burning (Lewis 1980, 76–77).[18]

6. *Long plateaus without change are punctuated with revolutionary leaps in biological and economic development.* There were essentially three prehistoric revolutions in the development of mankind prior to the agricultural revolution: bipedalism, the invention and development of tools, including fire, and the explosive accumulation of human capital by Cro-Magnon peoples. As I have already argued, bipedalism, which became adaptive somewhere in the period 10 to 5 million years ago, was probably a bioeconomic response to the cooler, dryer climate that reduced the proportion of forested lands in

Africa. Then sometime between 5 and 3 million years ago our protohuman ancestors discovered the value of stone tools, which by 2.5 million years B.P. were being fabricated by *H. habilis.* From the stone tool breakthrough down to about 40,000–30,000 years B.P., the record shows discrete improvement in tool use and fabrication (including fire) as *H. erectus* displaced *H. habilis,* followed by early *H. sapiens;* then the Neanderthals arrived, made their indelible mark, but disappeared some 30,000 years ago. Beginning sometime after 40,000 years B.P., the Cro-Magnon people produced an astonishing creative outburst—in tools, art, and hunting-gathering techniques (Pfeiffer 1982; White 1989; Marshak 1995). This acceleration in human capital formation and Cro-Magnon's rapid spread throughout all the major continents set the stage for the agricultural revolution. It did this partly by giving our immediate ancestors the knowledge of animals and seeds required by the agricultural way of life, but probably also by hastening the demise of the megafauna that were the favored game of the chase and thus tipping the opportunity cost balance in favor of tilling the soil.

What accounts for the sudden acceleration of human economic and cultural development after 40,000 years B.P.? The Cro-Magnons had already been firmly established in Africa for perhaps 60,000 years and had already begun their spread throughout the world. I believe the most likely cause is the emergence of language.[19] The ability to communicate effectively by the spoken word would make possible the accumulation and diffusion of knowledge on an unprecedented scale. The experience and knowledge of the elderly—at the time, these would be men and women only forty years of age—was a valued source of information. The necessity of preserving and drawing upon this human capital explains why older and incapacitated people were cared for, their value recognized by proper burial and enshrined in art. In aboriginal societies, the medicine man or woman was often a person handicapped from birth or crippled by injury. Thus Kokopelli, widely revered in the rock art of Mexico and of the Four Corners area of the southwest U.S., is depicted as a hunchbacked arthritic figure who is associated with paintings of corn, deer, goats, atlatls, and bison and who often carries or plays a flute. With the advent of spoken language the value of information relative to physical strength would have changed dramatically, and human society would have been highly motivated to preserve and transmit it to new generations. Based upon a reconstruction of the fossil evidence, it is thought by some that the Neanderthals had a vocal tract more like an ape than like that of the Cro-Magnon. If so, this might explain the extinction of Neanderthals and their failure to develop the tool, art, and hunting-gathering proficiency of competing Cro-Magnon peoples.

The affluence made possible by improvements in food-acquisition methods would have provided the released time necessary to give attention to language development and to the rituals, ceremony, and socializing that demand communication capacity. Big-game hunting placed new demands on planning, organization, coordination, and cooperation that depended on communication. It was the spoken word that allowed ideas and complex thought to be externalized. Memory, operated on by ritual, allowed knowledge to be preserved and, most important, accumulated. Writing, invented by 5000 years B.P. and appearing thereafter in many dispersed cultures, accelerated the human capacity to preserve and accumulate thought.[20] But by this time humankind's vast knowledge of seeds, eggs, and animals had already fomented the agricultural revolution, made all the more necessary by the disappearance of so many of the great game animals.

The Agricultural Revolution:
Reversion in America

In the Near East, beginning about 10,000 years ago, our ancestors abandoned the hunter-gatherer way of life that had served humankind so well over the vast stretch of at least 3 million years. The evidence appears in the form of several early Neolithic farming villages dated from 9500 to 9000 years B.P. (Zohary and Hopf 1988). Plant cultivation in this area appears to coincide closely with the domestication of animals. Sheep and goats were domesticated first, but cattle and pigs followed closely thereafter.[21] Domesticated plants consisted of only eight or nine species of local grains, such as wheat and barley, and the legumes (lentils, peas, and chickpeas). Sometime later bitter vetch and flax were added to the crops. About 3,000 years after the establishment of grain agriculture, various fruits—olive, grape, and fig—were cultivated. All these plants were domesticated forms of the wild varieties that were indigenous to the area.[22]

Subsequently plant cultivation appeared in Egypt, the Balkans, and the west Mediterranean 7000 years B.P., in central Europe and the Ukraine 6500 years B.P., and in Scandinavia about 5000 years B.P. Evidence for agriculture in New Guinea, where there were virtually no animals suitable for hunting, is dated 9000 years ago (Reader 1988).

In North America, the earliest evidence of agriculture is in Mexico, 10,000–9000 years B.P. From that point on, products were added slowly, one by one, over thousands of years, as if cultivation were a hobby used to supplement hunting and gathering. When the first Europeans arrived in the sixteenth century, there was great variability among the North American tribes in their dependence on agriculture versus hunting and gathering. In California, acorn gathering and hunting were important means of subsistence. In the Pacific Northwest, salmon fishing supplemented by gathering was paramount. On the Great Plains, many tribes, such as the Pawnee, Cheyenne, and Arapaho, had well-developed horticulture and pottery arts. The peaceful Pueblos of the Southwest grew cotton, corn, beans, tobacco, and squash.

The influence of opportunity cost on tribal choice of culture is well illustrated by the effect of the reintroduction of the horse to North America by the Spanish. The Spanish mustang—a docile and easily domesticated member of the *Equus* family—was a revolutionary innovation to the Plains Indians, causing many tribes to revert to the bison hunt as a permanent way of life. W. R. Wedel (1936) reported that the introduction of the horse caused the Pawnee to change from a sedentary tribe devoted to agriculture to one in which the chase and maize culture were equally important sources of sustenance. More dramatically, the Cheyenne and Arapaho abandoned their villages, agriculture, and pottery arts to become bison hunters (Wedel 1940; Strong 1940). Consequently, the fierce "fighting Cheyenne" known to the plains settlers were almost entirely a recent creature of the horse. Tribes such as the Apache, who were already subsisting on bison when the Spanish arrived, simply adapted the horse to their hunting culture.

Although Francisco de Coronado and other conquistadores lost or abandoned horses in the sixteenth century, it was not until the permanent colonization of New Mexico in the first half of the seventeenth century that peaceful Indians, forced to tend the Spaniards' horses, learned horsemanship. During this period, horses and knowledge of them were acquired by the Apache and other tribes, and by the 1650s the colonial settlements faced the formidable Apache, on horseback, whose raids became legendary. All the power of Spain in America failed to subdue them. Then out of the Rocky Mountain headwaters of the Arkansas River appeared a little-known tribe of hunter-gatherers who abandoned their homelands and took to the plains on horseback. They became great bison hunters and by 1725 had invaded the Apache lands of Colorado, Kansas, Oklahoma, and West Texas. Entire tribes of Apache who had been the scourge of the Spanish, disappeared. The invading Comanche exterminated the eastern tribes and drove the western tribes into Arizona and New Mexico. The Comanche were the greatest warriors ever to ride the high plains and plateaus of Texas. They were without peer on horseback, with men, women, and children skilled in the saddle. Their raiding parties ranged up to 1,000 miles across the Rio Grande deep into northern Mexico; their loot sometimes consisted of hundreds of horses in a single moonlight raid. They were known for their "boast that the warrior tribes permitted Spanish settlements to exist on the fringes of Comanche territory only to raise horses for them" (Fehrenbach 1983, 36). The Spanish were never again to muster any semblance of control of west Texas; nor were the white Americans able finally to control bison country until 1875 when the remnants of the fierce Comanche tribes finally surrendered at Fort Sill, and the bison, all but exterminated, were replaced by the longhorn steer. For a century and a half the history of the American West was a history of fear and terror of the Comanche, who, prior to the arrival of the mustang, had picked berries and dug roots while hunting miscellaneous game in the eastern Rockies—a threat to no one.

Genesis: A Folk Memory of
Conflict Between Two Cultures?

The remnants of our prehistoric past that reside in our cultural traditions today is well illustrated by a fascinating interpretation of Genesis as a myth of
conflict between the agricultural and hunter-gatherer ways of life, written
from the perspective of the latter (Hamblin 1987). According to this reconstruction, the Garden of Eden represents the economic affluence achieved
by humans as hunter-gatherers who lived abundantly on the plants, animals,
and fishes placed on earth by God for the benefit of humankind. Then Eve
broke the cultural command not to eat the fruit of the tree of knowledge.
But what "knowledge" was contained in this fruit? It was knowledge of the
reproductive cycles of seeds, eggs, and animals, which was the human capital
foundation of agriculture. And the woman, Eve, was the vehicle through
which Adam acquired this agricultural human capital. The interpretation
suggests a cultural bifurcation in which some hunter-gatherers were depart-
ing from their ancestral imperative and turning to agriculture. The punishment of Adam and Eve expresses a warning against this dangerous new direction: "Cursed is the ground for thy sake; in sorrow shalt thou eat of it.
... Thorns and thistles shall it bring forth to thee; and thou shalt eat the
herb of the field" (Gen. 3:17–18).

In translation, the biblical text suggests that Adam and Eve were placed in
the Garden to "till it and tend it" (Gen. 2:15), implying that they were
farmers. But the two verbs in Hebrew are "*eved*" and "*shamar,*" which more
appropriately can be translated "to serve" and "to guard." This suggests
"that humans were not to cultivate the Garden as farmers but to protect it as
servant guardians in the divine arboretum" (Beach and Pryor 1995, 40).

Eve bore two sons, who were split on the ancestral imperative: Cain became a tiller, and Abel was a herder of sheep. (Not quite a hunter-gatherer,
so the allegory here is weak, but Abel was a nomad nonetheless. Sheep herding does appear to be an intermediate step in the turn from hunting.) Cain
made offerings of the fruit of the ground to the Lord, and Abel offered the
first of his flock. Abel's offering was respected by God, but Cain's was not.
So Cain killed Abel, implying that the culture was in danger of losing the
skills of the hunter-gatherer, in which case there could be no turning back
from the world of thistles and thorns. "If you till the soil, it shall no longer
yield its strength to you" (Gen. 4:12). Then came the flood, all the game animals were in danger of extinction, and so on.[23]

Six generations after Adam and Eve, "Lamarch's wife Adah bears Jabal,
who 'was the ancestor of those who dwell in tents and amidst herds'" (Gen.
4:20). This is the first true nomadism depicted in the Bible. The implication
is that Abel had practiced sedentary herding near Cain's fields. Here again
the biblical account concurs with the anthropological reconstruction. True

nomadism, without a fixed home, developed after agriculture and sedentary herding (Beach and Pryor 1995, 42).

This allegorical interpretation is plausible in many ways. First, the timing is right. Second, the location is right. And third, the events described correlate with what is known about this period and place. The first evidence of agriculture dates from about 9500 years B.P. in the fertile crescent of the Tigris and Euphrates rivers. Surely this was not an unclimactic event after more than 5 million years of bipedalism, 2.5 million years of tool use, and a very successful adaptation to hunting and gathering. Moreover, the Sumerians invented and were using the first written cuneiform language 6000–5000 years B.P., a language that produced many epic poems that obviously influenced the Hebrew story of Genesis. The Sumerians had a cuneiform word for "Adam" that meant "settlement on the plain." They also had a word for "Eden" that meant "a fertile plain." Interestingly there was no word for "Eve," but their word "ti" had two meanings: "rib" and "to make live." The Hebrew scholars, not appreciating this dual meaning, concocted their story that God gave life to Adam's rib, thus creating the first woman. The Sumerian tablets, besides telling us of "Adam," "Eden," and the "lady of the rib," also tell us of a Great Flood and of their King Gil gamesh who went down to the Gulf in search of the Tree of Eternal Life. (Incidentally, he found it, but it was stolen from him by a serpent!) Moreover, it is known that there was a sudden warming trend 7000–6000 years B.P. shrinking the ice caps and raising the sea level. The Persian Gulf would have filled with water during this period, reaching its current level about 6000 years B.P. These considerations suggested to Juris Zarins (cited in Hamblin 1987) the hypothesis that the Garden of Eden was located at the upper end of the Persian Gulf, since the biblical text states that "a river went out of Eden to water the garden; and from thence it was parted, and became of four heads ... [the] Pison ... Gihon, Tigris [and] Euphrates" (Gen. 2:10–14). Of course the Tigris and Euphrates still flow, and the Pison and Gihon probably refer respectively to the Wadi Batin, a fossil river in Iraq, and the intermittently flowing Karun river in Iran.

Finis

The significance of prehistory to humankind, circa A.D. 2000, is that all we are today—our great cultural attainments and ever growing potential, our biological and human capital achievements—are a product of that prehistory. If there is much that is new in historical time it is because we have continued what began in prehistory. We have also had many millennia to accumulate the human capital made possible once our hunter-gatherer ancestors learned to learn. If we are a "kinder and gentler" species today than were our ancestors who slaughtered the great mammoth and bison on two continents, if we can care enough to launch a massive effort to save three great whales trapped in a hole in the Arctic ice, if we can debate reintroducing the timber wolf into Yellowstone Park, it is because we can now afford to do all these things and have learned to treasure the value of individual responsibility for preserving and managing natural resources.

But change has been episodic, not linear, as we have leaped from one long confining plateau to another less than a half-dozen times since we escaped—so improbably—our primate origins, which took 3 billion years of sporadic change to create. Through all these sweeping changes is discernible the blurred outline of continuity in humankind's development of the capacity to respond to effort prices, to create cheaper techniques and products as substitutes for dearer ones, and to accumulate and preserve knowledge, our most precious capital asset.

Notes

This article originally appeared as "Humankind in Prehistory: Economy, Ecology, and Institutions" in *The Political Economy of Customs and Culture: Informal Solutions to the Common Problem* (1993), edited by Terry L. Anderson and Randy T. Simmons. It is reprinted here with the permission of the publishers, Rowman and Littlefield.

I am indebted to Bob Heizer for first prevailing upon me to research and write on the economics of hunting and gathering when we were fellows together at the Center for Advanced Study in the Behavioral Sciences, 1971–1972; to Paul Martin for significant encouragement over the years as well as detailed criticism, comments, and corrections; to Robert Klein for helpful corrections; and to Adrienne Zihlman for references and comments leading to revisions in the second section. None of them can be held accountable for the difficulties facing an outside interpreter who must write without the intimate and important day-to-day operating knowledge of the sciences upon which this account is based. Finally, I acknowledge the comments of that master of economic prose, Robert Heilbroner, and many characteristically incisive comments from my friend Ed Ames.

1. This chapter is, and must be, a speculative extension of what we know from the paleoanthropological and biological records. This is because what we know about prehistoric humankind is interpreted from the artifacts and remains that our remote ancestors left behind and that have survived biodegradation, from backward extrapolation of what we know from the study of extant prehistorical societies during the last hundred years (Boas 1897), and from genetic differences between humans and other primates today. One of our most important characteristics as humans is the ability to pattern-search our data in order to make dumb facts speak and so increase our understanding. I make the case that economic principles help us to achieve this understanding. I refer to "natural," as distinct from "political," economy (Hirshleifer 1978), but, as will be seen, I think the outlines of "political" economy emerged in antiquity.

2. Nonhuman primates, such as baboons and chimpanzees, are known to prey on small vertebrates. There is also evidence of elementary forms of planning and cooper-

ation among chimpanzees in their predatory activities; they also transport materials to use as tools. Erik Trinkaus notes that "some level of predation as well as tool use is not unique to Hominidae. Much, if not all, of the evolution of these activities in the hominid lineage was therefore primarily a shift in emphasis rather than the introduction of completely novel behavioral patterns" (1986, 110–111).

3. Glaciation of the earth actually begins before the Pleistocene, about 14 million years B.P. in the middle Miocene. See Klein 1989, 29–35, for a summary of late Cenozoic Ice Age climate and its significance for humankind.

4. "Such a structure [the external nose] would have enabled members of *H. erectus* to retrieve moisture from exhaled air [which could be] used for humidifying the next breath without using additional body moisture. . . . Such a system would have been more efficient at conserving body fluids [which] would have been important for a diurnal primate exploiting resources in open country, especially in relatively arid regions" (Trinkaus 1986, 120). In fact it is possible that these people were capable of running prey to exhaustion (Trinkaus 1986, 128). Native American aboriginals had the capacity literally to run down a horse or deer by pacing the animal.

5. For a time as a child, I lived on a Kansas farm. My mother cooked on a wood cookstove in a house with no indoor (or outdoor) plumbing. Wood being a scarce source of fuel in Kansas, my mother used dried corncobs and "cow chips" for fuel in the cookstove.

6. Until very recently the woolly mammoth was thought to have become extinct in the period 12,000–10,000 B.P. Then it was discovered by radio carbon dating that the woolly mammoth had survived into the period 7,000–4,000 B.P. on the island of Wrangel off the northeast coast of Siberia between Alaska and Siberia. (See Vartanyan, Garutt, and Sher 1993). Teeth fossils show that this isolated subpopulation consisted of mammoth of normal size plus a dwarfed form that is believed to have been the result of selection occurring after Wrangel became isolated from Siberia because of the rising sea level. No evidence of human habitation appears during the period that the mammoth was adapting to this isolation.

7. In North America horse bones are among the most common Pleistocene fossils (Martin and Guilday 1967, 41–42).

8. Dwarfing may have provided a higher biomass growth rate, enabling the bison to overcome a high rate of Paleolithic harvesting of megafauna. "Human technology, including use of missile weapons, greatly reduced the counterattacking defensive advantages of larger size and emphasizes concealment and speed of flight. At this point of increased pressure of human predation, the genetically selected optimum body size of many forms declines sharply" (Edwards 1967, 149). Hammond (1961, 321) has noted that a considerable reduction in size has occurred since the beginning of the century in the major beef breeds of cattle. This is due to deliberate selection for early maturation in body proportions. Under appropriation, investment favors the smaller animals with a higher biomass growth rate. But under common property conditions, Paleolithic hunters (also the Hazda and Ache) selectively harvested the larger, slower-growing animals (Hawkes, O'Connell, and Jones 1991).

9. G. Caughley (1988) offers a population diffusion and growth model to account for the geographical and temporal distribution of radiocarbon dates at prehistoric sites (many of them moa bird kill sites) in New Zealand. According to this model, colonization began on the northeast coast of the South Island 1050–900 years B.P.

and diffused at an accelerating rate throughout New Zealand. Accordingly the population increased about 3 percent per year (doubling every twenty years), and sea elephants, sea lions, and about twenty-five species of birds became extinct. Earlier, similar models were used (see references in Caughley 1988) to structure hypotheses concerning the colonization of Australia more than 30,000 years B.P. and the colonization of North and South America about 11,000 years B.P.

10. Yet it has been estimated that a population of only 15,000 people in northern Eurasia would need to consume up to 60,000 horses or 10,000 bison per year (Vereshchagin and Baryshnikov 1984, 508).

11. Some African hunter-gatherer tribes, such as the Pygmies, have fared well because they depend on trade with their agricultural neighbors (Reader 1988, 155). But for the Kung it is the opposite; their neighbors have survived droughts and poor crops by joining the Kung in gathering mongongo nuts and other wild plants. During the third year of a drought phase the Kung consumed an average of 8.3 percent more calories and 55 percent more protein than the estimated daily recommended allowance for people of their stature and activity (Lee 1968; Lee and Devore 1976; Lee and Devore 1968). But see Hawkes and O'Connell 1981 for a critique of Lee's interpretation of the Kung data: Lee's foraging calculations do not include the time spent in processing food. Thus the mongongo nut requires considerable cracking/roasting time, which correspondingly reduces the net caloric yield per hour of labor.

12. A Karok woman stated: "They . . . burn the brush . . . so that good things will grow up. . . . Some kinds of trees are better when . . . burned off. . . . But some . . . disappear. . . . the Manzanita . . . does not come up when it is burned off. . . . They are careful lest the[se] trees burn" (Lewis 1973, 50–51).

13. As a Cree man explained in a wonderful merging of science with poetry: "See, you start a fire at the top of a meadow in the afternoon, when you feel the wind change, the way the cool air does at that time. This way the fire burns toward the low part of the meadow. . . . It's safe. You have to know the wind" (Lewis 1980, 82).

14. Modern experiments have tested the Amerindian policy of burning to improve game productivity. It's been found, for example, that deer in recently burned-over chaparral cover show marked increases in numbers and size and improvement in health (Biswell 1967, 81).

15. Among the Ache hunter-gatherers of eastern Paraguay, the most successful hunters devote more, not less, time to hunting than do less successful hunters. They also share disproportionately their surplus with people outside their family group. In return, they gain increased access to extramarital mates, producing illegitimate children and a higher survivorship of their offspring (Kaplan and Hill 1985; Hawkes 1990).

16. Of course we have no idea as to whether the early property rights systems were based on regimes of private property. By "property rights" I mean rules governing the actions of individuals. Aboriginals had concepts of both private and tribal property, and both probably originated in this early period with the great increase in individual (or group) possessions.

17. This is illustrated in Jonathan Hughes's (1982) account of the seasonal closing of the Alaska cannery where he worked in the summer of 1952. A half-Eskimo winter watchman was removing the locks and chains from various items of property. When

asked why, he stated that locks were not needed now that the Christians were gone. For a discussion of the role of "repeat business" in inducing cooperation in the absence of enforcement see Hirshleifer 1978. Also see Hawkes 1991 for a discussion of reciprocal altruism, or "delayed reciprocity," wherein those in close relationship share resources in return for future shares, and for a generally incisive analysis of "sharing" in the context of individual incentives and game theoretic interactions.

18. Lewis quotes the reminiscences of a Beaver Indian woman: "Why the bush is so thick is because they [Indians] stop burning. . . . From about five miles from here you could see straight prairie right to Childs Lake and that timber. Did you ever see them prairies? . . . It was really prairie, just prairie, you know; here and there you see little specks of woods, and if there were trees there, they were quite high" (1980, 76). The imposition of fire prevention policies for many prior decades led to the great Yellowstone Park holocaust of 1988. Similar policies imposed on the Australian Aborigines "resulted in the sporadic eruption of gigantic wild fires feeding on several years' accumulation of litter, causing leaf scorch heights of up to 20m, with the death of mature woodlands of [Cypress pine] which the policy was intended to protect" (Jones 1980, 125).

19. Linguists are split on the antiquity of language: Radicals suggest that the roots of spoken language could go back 100,000 years, while traditionalists accept an origin of at most 15,000 years B.P. (Ross 1991). Of course the date for the common ancestor of modern humankind may be closer to 50,000 years B.P. Richard Klein (1992) notes that this is suggested by the archeological evidence for a radical biologically based change in human behavior 50,000–40,000 years B.P. Under Klein's hypothesis the development of language would have been a later consequence of the biological change. I assume that the dates based on DNA studies are roughly correct and that we have to account for a much later occurrence of the cultural revolution. There are still other perspectives; for example, Sofeer (1990) argues that the biological and archaeological records are consistent with a sociocultural innovation that introduced biparental provisioning of the young, division of labor, and food sharing. But I would argue that these and all manner of other cultural innovations could have been made possible by the development of language.

20. An interesting hypothesis, supported by the archaeological evidence, argues that the precursor of Sumerian writing was a clay token accounting system, appearing 11,000 B.P., used to preserve records and to facilitate the exchange of property (Schmandt-Besserat 1978). Thus the first forms of written language may have been invented as an aid to memory and security in contracting for property (Sumerian exchange included land, animals, vessels, bread, beer, clothing, and furniture). Early symbols then evolved into Sumerian pictographic writing and ultimately into ideographic and phonetic writing.

21. It would appear that sheep domestication predates agriculture in this region: "Most authorities now agree that the first species to be domesticated in the Near East was the sheep, 10,500 years ago or so" (Fagan 1989, 265).

22. In virtually all aboriginal societies studied in the last century, hunting was a preoccupation of men and gathering was the province of women. It therefore would appear probable that the agricultural revolution was due to women's knowledge of seeds, herbs, and edible plants.

23. Ed Ames has pointed out to me that a sharper contrast between hunting and tilling is found in Gen. 25–27, where Esau was a hunter whose birthright was bought by Jacob, the farmer-herder.

References

Anderson, Atholl. 1989. *Prodigious Birds.* Cambridge: Cambridge University Press.

Balter, M. 1995. "Did *Homo erectus* Tame Fire First?" *Science,* 16 June, 1570.

Beach, E. F., and F. L. Pryor. 1995. "How Did Adam and Eve Make a Living?" *Bible Review* (April):38–42.

Biswell, H. H. 1967. "The Use of Fire in Wildland Management in California." In *Natural Resources Quality and Quantity,* eds. S. V. Ciriacy-Wantrup and J. J. Parsons, 71–86. Berkeley: University of California Press.

Boas, Franz. 1897. "The Social Organization and the Secret Societies of the Kwakiutl Indians." In *Report of the U.S. National Museum for 1895.* Washington, D.C.: GPO.

Caughley, G. 1988. "The Colonization of New Zealand by the Polynesians." *Journal of the Royal Society of New Zealand* 18:245–270.

Dalton, George. 1977. "Aboriginal Economies in Stateless Societies: Interaction Spheres." In *Exchange Systems in Pre-History,* eds. J. Erickson and T. Earle. New York: Academic Press.

Dewar, Robert E. 1984. "Extinctions in Madagascar." In *Quaternary Extinctions,* eds. P. S. Martin and R. G. Klein, 574–593. Tucson: University of Arizona Press.

Dorit, R. L., H. Akashi, and W. Gilbert. 1995. "Absence of Polymorphism at the ZFY Locus on the Human Y Chromosome." *Science,* 26 May, 1183–1185.

Edwards, W. E. 1967. "The Late-Pleistocene Extinction and Diminution in Size of Many Mammalian Species." In *Pleistocene Extinctions,* eds. P. S. Martin and H. E. Wright Jr. New Haven: Yale University Press.

Fagan, Brian M. 1989. *People of the Earth.* Boston: Scott, Faresman.

———. 1994. "Bison Hunters of the Northern Plains." *Archaeology* 47 (May/June):37–41.

Fehrenbach, T. R. 1983. *Lone Star.* New York: American Legacy Press.

Freuchen, Peter. [1961] 1973. *Book of the Eskimos.* New York: Fawcett Premier Books.

Frison, George C. 1986. "Prehistoric, Plains-Mountain, Large-Mammal, Communal Hunting Strategies." In *The Evolution of Human Hunting,* eds. M. H. Nitecki and D. V. Nitecki, 177–123. New York: Plenum Press.

Gould, Stephen J. 1988. "A Novel Notion of Neanderthal." *Natural History* 97 (June):16–21.

Hamblin, Dora J. 1987. "Has the Garden of Eden Been Located at Last?" *Smithsonian* 18 (May):127–135.

Hammond, J. 1961. "Growth in Size and Body Proportions in Farm Animals." In *Growth in Living Systems,* ed. M. X. Zarrow. New York: Basic Books.

Harris, J. W. K. 1983. "Cultural Beginnings: Plio-Pleistocene Archaeological Occurrences from the Afar, Ethiopia." *The African Archaeological Review* 1:3–31.

Hawkes, Kristen. 1990. "Showing Off: Tests on an Hypothesis About Men's Foraging Goals." *Ethology and Sociobiology* 12:29–54.

_____. 1991. "Sharing and Collective Action." Department of Anthropology, University of Utah.

Hawkes, Kristen, and James F. O'Connell. 1981. "Affluent Hunters? Some Comments in Light of the Alyawara Case." *American Anthropologist* 83:622–626.

Hawkes, Kristen, James F. O'Connell, and Nicholas B. Jones. 1991. "Hazda Hunting and Human Evolution." Department of Anthropology, University of Utah.

Haynes, C. Vance. 1964. "Fluted Projectile Points: There Age and Dispersion." *Science*, 19 June, 1408–1413.

_____. 1988. "The First Americans: Geofacts and Fancy." *Natural History* 97 (February):4–10.

Hedges, S. B., S. Kumar, K. Tamura, and M. Stoneking. 1992. "Technical Comments." *Science*, 7 February, 737–738.

Heizer, Robert F. 1955. *Primitive Man as an Ecologic Factor*. Kroeber Anthropologic Society Papers, no. 13. Berkeley: University of California Press.

Hirshleifer, Jack. 1978. "Natural Economy Versus Political Economy." *Journal of Social Biological Structures* 1:319–337.

Hoffman, J. F., W. R. Powers, and T. Goebel. 1993. "The Colonization of Beringia and the Peopling of the New World." *Science*, 1 January, 46–53.

Hughes, Jonathan R. T. 1982. "The Great Strike at Nushagak Station, 1951: Institutional Gridlock." *Journal of Economic History* 42 (March):1–20.

Jones, Rhys. 1980. "Hunters in the Australian Coastal Savanna." In *Ecology in Savanna Environments*, ed. D. R. Harris. New York: Academic Press.

Kaplan, Hillard, and Kim Hill. 1985. "Hunting Ability and Reproductive Success Among Male Ache Foragers: Preliminary Results." *Current Anthropology* 26 (February):131–133.

Klein, Richard G. 1989. *The Human Career*. Chicago: University of Chicago Press.

_____. 1992. "The Archeology of Modern Human Origins." *Evolutionary Anthropology* 1 (January).

Knecht, Heidi. 1994. "Late Ice Age Hunting Technology." *Scientific American* 271 (July):82–87.

Kroeber, A. L., and S. A. Barrett. 1960. "Fishing Among the Indians of Northwestern California." *Anthropological Records* 21, no. 1.

Landa, Janet. 1983. "The Enigma of the Kula Ring: Gift-Exchanges and Primitive Law and Order." *International Review of Law and Economics* 3:137–160.

Laporte, Leo F., and Adrienne L. Zihlman. 1983. "Plates, Climate, and Hominoid Evolution." *South African Journal of Science* 79 (March):96–110.

Lee, R. B. 1968. "What Hunters Do for a Living, or, How to Make Out on Scarce Resources." In *Man the Hunter*, eds. R. B. Lee and I. DeVore, 30–48. Chicago: Aldine.

Lee, R. B., and I. DeVore. 1968. *Man the Hunter*. Chicago: Aldine.

_____. 1976. *Kalahari Hunter Gatherers: Studies of the Kung Son and Their Neighbors*. Cambridge: Harvard University Press.

Lewis, Henry T. 1973. "Patterns of Indian Burning in California: Ecology and Ethnohistory." *Anthropology Papers*, no. 1. Ballview Press.

_____. 1980. "Indian Fires of Spring." *Natural History* 83 (January):76–83.

Marshak, Alexander. 1995. "Images of the Ice Age." *Archaeology* 48 (July/August):28–39.

Martin, P. S. 1967. "Prehistoric Overkill." In *Pleistocene Extinctions*, eds. P. S. Martin and H. E. Wright Jr., 75–120. New Haven: Yale University Press.

_____. 1984. "Prehistoric Overkill: The Global Model." In *Quaternary Extinctions*, eds. P. S. Martin and R. G. Klein, 354–403. Tucson: University of Arizona Press.

_____. 1990. "Who or What Destroyed Our Mammoths?" In *Megafauna and Man: Discovery of America's Heartland*, eds. L. D. Agenbroad, J. I. Mead, and L. W. Nelson. Flagstaff: Northern Arizona University.

Martin, P. S., and J. E. Guilday. 1967. "A Beastiary for Pleistocene Biologists." In *Pleistocene Extinctions*, eds. P. S. Martin and H. E. Wright Jr. New Haven: Yale University Press.

Mead, J. I., and D. J. Meltzer. 1984. "North American Late Quaternary Extinctions and the Radio Carbon Record." In *Quaternary Extinctions*, eds. P. S. Martin and R. G. Klein, 440–450. Tucson: University of Arizona Press.

Moore, O. K. 1957. "Divination: A New Perspective." *American Anthropology* 59:69–74.

O'Connell, James F., Kristen Hawkes, and Nicholas B. Jones. 1988. "Hazda Scavenging: Implications for Plio/Pleistocene Hominid Subsistence." *Current Anthropology* 29 (April):356–363.

Pfeiffer, John E. 1982. *The Creative Explosion*. Ithaca, N.Y.: Cornell University Press.

Pope, Geoffrey G. 1989. "Bamboo and Human Evolution." *Natural History* 98 (October):49–56.

Pyne, Stephen J. 1991. *Burning Bush: A Fire History of Australia*. New York: Henry Holt.

Reader, John. 1988. *Man on Earth*. New York: Harper and Row.

Ross, Philip E. 1991. "Hard Word." *Scientific American* 264 (April):138–147.

Sahlins, Marshall. 1972. *Stone Age Economics*. London: Tavistock.

Schmandt-Besserat, D. 1978. "The Earliest Precursor of Writing." *Scientific American* 238 (June):50–59.

Smith, Vernon L. 1975. "The Primitive Hunter Culture, Pleistocene Extinction and the Rise of Agriculture." *Journal of Political Economy* 83 (August):727–755.

Sofeer, Olga. 1990. "Before Beringia: Late Pleistocene Bio-Social Transformations and the Colonization of Northern Eurasia." Symposium on Chronostratigraphy in North Central East Asia and America. Novosibirsk.

Speck, F. G. 1935. *Naskapi: The Savage Hunters of the Labrador Peninsula*. Norman: University of Oklahoma Press.

Stringer, Christopher B. 1990. "The Emergence of Modern Humans." *Scientific American* 263 (December):98–104.

Strong, W. D. 1940. "From History to Prehistory in the Northern Great Plains." In *Essays in Historical Anthropology of North America*. Washington, D.C.: Smithsonian Institute.

Templeton, Alan R. 1992. "Technical Comments." *Science*, 7 February, 737.

Todd, Lawrence C. 1986. "Analysis of Kill-Butchery Bonebeds and Interpretation of Paleoindian Hunting." In *The Evolution of Human Hunting*, eds. M. H. Nitecki and D. V. Nitecki, 177–223. New York: Plenum Press.

Toth, N. 1985. "The Oldowan Reassessed: A Close Look at Early Stone Artifacts." *Journal of Archaeological Science* 12:101–120.

Trinkaus, E. 1986. "The Neanderthals and Modern Human Origins." *Annual Review of Anthropology* 15:193–218.

Trotter, Michael M., and Beverley McCulloch. 1984. "Moas, Men, and Middens." In *Quaternary Extinctions*, eds. P. S. Martin and R. G. Klein, 708–727. Tucson: University of Arizona Press.

Tyldesley, J. A. and P. Bahn. 1983. "Use of Plants in the European Paleolithic: A Review of the Evidence." *Quaternary Science Review* 2:53–81.

Valladas, H., J. L. Reyss, J. L. Joron, G. Valladas, O. Bar-Yosef, and B. Vandermeersch. 1988. "Thermoluminescence Dating of Mousterian 'Proto-Cro-Magnon' Remains from Israel and the Origin of Modern Man." *Nature* 331:614–616.

Vartanyan, S. L., V. E. Garutt, and A. V. Sher. 1993. "Holocene Dwarf Mammoths from Wrangel Island in the Siberian Arctic." *Nature* 362:337.

Vereshchagin, N. K. and G. F. Baryshnikov. 1984. "Quaternary Mammals in Extinctions in Northern Eurasia." In *Quaternary Extinctions*, eds. P. S. Martin and R. G. Klein, 483–516. Tucson: University of Arizona Press.

Vigilant, L., M. Stoneking, H. Harpending, K. Hawkes, and A. Wilson. 1991. "African Populations and the Evolution of Human Mitochondrial DNA." *Science*, 27 September, 1503–1507.

Vrba, E. S. 1985. "Ecological and Adaptive Changes Associated with Early Hominid Evolution." In *Ancestors: The Hard Evidence*, ed. E. Delson, 63–71. New York: Alan R. Liss.

Walker, A. C. 1984. "Extinction in Hominid Evolution." In *Extinctions*, ed. M. H. Nitecki, 119–152. Chicago: University of Chicago Press.

Wedel, W. R. 1936. *An Introduction to Pawnee Archeology*. Bureau of American Ethnology, bulletin 112. Washington, D.C.: Smithsonian Institute.

_____. 1940. *Culture Sequences in the Great Plains*. Washington, D.C.: Smithsonian Institute.

Wheat, J. B. 1967. "A Paleo-Indian Bison Kill." *Scientific American* 216 (January):44–51.

White, Randall. 1989. "Visual Thinking in the Ice Age." *Scientific American* 261 (July):92–99.

White, T. D., G. Suwa, and B. Asfaw. 1994. "*Australopithecus ramidus:* A New Species of Early Hominid from Aramis, Ethiopia." *Nature* 371:306–312.

Zihlman, Adrienne L. 1991. "The Emergence of Human Locomotion: The Evolutionary Background and Environmental Context." University of California, Santa Cruz. Forthcoming in *Human Origins*, vol. 1, ed. T. Nishida. Thirteenth Congress of the International Primatology Society.

Zihlman, Adrienne L., and B. A. Cohn. 1988. "The Adaptive Response of Human Skin to the Savanna." *Human Evolution* 3, no. 5:397–409.

Zohary, David, and Maria Hopf. 1988. *Domestication of Plants in the Old World*. Oxford: Oxford University Press.

2

The Mississippians and Economic Development Before European Colonization

LINDA BARRINGTON

Contrary to common perception, the precolonial indigenous societies north of the Rio Grande were not universally composed of hunters and gatherers prior to European contact. The planting of corn, squash, and grains for harvest was, in fact, prevalent across the continent, and even these sedentary agricultural practices did not represent the limit of precolonial indigenous development in what would become the United States and Canada. The archaeological and anthropological records show that prior to the arrival of European colonizers, within the sphere of what is known as the Mississippian civilization, there existed long-distance trade, specialization of labor for manufacture, urban population clusters, and a system of taxation or tribute that involved, in part, social hierarchy and coerced labor. Like many civilizations throughout time, the pre-Columbian Mississippian civilization developed in ways necessary to support denser population clusters. The implication of this development for the study of U.S. economic history is that the original colonies were not established on a blank slate.[1] It is reasonable to infer that, as in Meso-America and Andean America, the European colonizers of North America built their empires by utilizing existing trade routes, indigenous institutions, and regional specialization.

The influence of the Mississippian civilization—most visibly recognized by earthen mounds upon which wooden structures were built—reached from present-day Florida, north through the Ohio River Valley, and northwest as far as the Great Plains. (Henceforth this region of the continent will be re-

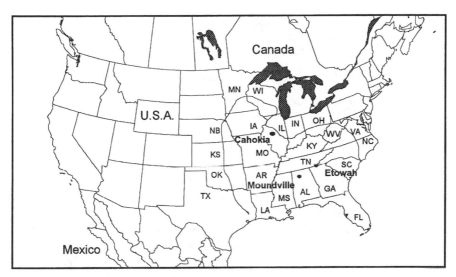

Map 2.1   *Mississippian Civilization, Southeastern North America, ca. A.D. 1400*

ferred to as southeastern North America. See Map 2.1.) Between A.D. 900–1400 the dominant population and mound center of the region was the Mississippian town of Cahokia, located in present-day southern Illinois. Cahokia supported the highest population density in southeastern North America prior to European colonization (Yerkes 1991, 49). It is estimated that at its apex, "downtown" Cahokia encompassed roughly three square miles (2,000 acres) and alone had a population of 15,000–38,000 people (Shaffer 1992, 53 and illustration 15). Other notably large Mississippian population clusters existed at Moundville and Etowah in the present-day states of Alabama and Georgia, respectively. Accompanying the higher population densities of the pre-Columbian Mississippian population clusters was trade in raw materials (for example, shells) and finished products (such as dried meats, stone sculptures, and blades). Long-distance trade routes linked the population clusters to each other and to the less densely populated hinterlands and periphery. Full-time skilled artisans were employed in "workshops" in and near the population clusters, demonstrating that the Mississippian economy benefited from specialization of labor. From both the archaeological record and eyewitness accounts by the first Spanish explorers, it is clear that there was also a high degree of stratification within Mississippian society. The elite controlled prestige goods and the labor of servants in both life and death. Elite burial sites have been found to contain valuables and sacrificial bodies. Eyewitness accounts by the early European explorers of southeastern North America tell of indigenous rulers' caches of furs, pearls, and metals and of the ability of these rulers to summon thousands of warriors or to give a human subject as a gift to the European parties.

Population Density and Development

To provide a framework for analyzing the archaeological evidence that has accumulated on the Mississippian civilization, it is useful to consider some theoretical ideas about the relationship between labor specialization, trade, and the emergence of population centers in early civilizations. In *Population and Technological Change* (1981) Ester Boserup analyzed how urban history has been propelled by population density and technological change. Boserup linked the rise of urban populations and interregional trade to technological and social advances and the creation of economic surplus. In primitive societies people produce only for their own consumption. Therefore the production of traded surplus—that is, production above subsistence—demonstrates development inasmuch as it requires technical and social change. In the Mississippian civilization, we see the simultaneous production of surplus food and manufactured goods and the existence of long-distance and local trade between food producers and craftspeople and the urban centers. An elite class is clearly distinguishable from the mass Mississippian population. The establishment of this elite class presumably provided such public services as social stability, conflict resolution, and public infrastructure—services necessary for the growth of population density.

According to Boserup, urban populations, by virtue of the higher population density, require food production to take place outside of the urban confines. Food can be imported from distant producers by establishing long-distance trade routes, or food can be produced locally on lands adjacent to the urban center. Importation of food means that the food producers must be producing surplus and that transportation networks exist to move the food from producer to consumer. Local food production, Boserup argued, means technological advances in agriculture must have taken place: "Unless they rely on imported food, densely populated areas must employ systems of intensive agriculture, such as annual cropping or multicropping" (1981, 15). And even locally produced food must be transported to consumers, albeit a shorter distance than that secured through trade.

It follows from Boserup's theory that the ability to produce enough food to support the dense population of Cahokia and other smaller Mississippian centers demonstrates substantial development in pre-Columbian southeastern North America. Archaeological evidence shows that large quantities of dried meat were produced as far away as present-day Iowa and were probably transported to Cahokia over long-distance trade routes (Tiffany 1991). Imports of dried meat would have provided the necessary protein for the Mississippian population center of Cahokia at its apex. As with early civilizations in general, pre-Columbian urban populations had to import meat because the land demands of animal husbandry were too great to be met within the urban confines. This constraint would have existed for the pre-colonial societies of the New World too. The large quantities of meat produced for trade reveals that an economy located on the periphery of the Mississippian civilization was able to produce well above subsistence by specializing in this product. Evidence of salt works and crafts-producing hamlets also reveals that there were communities specializing in non–food-producing activities, implying that Mississippian food producers needed to supply food in excess of their own families' needs. More intensive agricultural techniques were necessary to create the surplus that points to technological advance. Trade, both over long distances and between neighboring hamlets, farms, and urban population centers, implies that transportation of food into the urban center was occurring. The higher population densities of Cahokia and other Mississippian centers appear to correlate with the existence of a more intense food supply system that involved specialization of production and trade.

A similar correlation exists between population density and the creation of a social hierarchy. The greater the population density, the greater the need to maintain social order. According to Boserup, increases in population density mean heightened potential for conflict. As more people live within a smaller area and expanded trade brings together more diverse peoples, conflicts will multiply. Douglass North also argued that an increased potential for conflict accompanies population growth, but North attributed this phenomenon to the corresponding specialization of labor: "Conflict arises over the division of output (that is, income distribution) associated with the division of labor" (1981, 64). Whether because of the increased population density, diversity, or the greater division of labor, change in social structure was necessary in early civilizations to meet the risk and changing character of conflict. An elite class usually arose to provide the social organization necessary to resolve conflict born of increasing population size and density. Boserup suggested that "the fortifications and large temples in ancient towns are indications that military power and religious ceremony provided motivation for urban concentration. Such physical structures are also related to population size and density. . . . internal and external conflicts enhance the power of chiefs and military (and religious) leaders" (1981, 64). Although growing population density stimulates greater social stratification, the establishment of a more stratified society can also promote increases in population density. Through taxation or labor coercion, elites could direct resources to the public works projects necessary for feeding and keeping order among the urban population or preserving their own power or claims to authority. The record clearly identifies the existence of such an elite Mississippian class, who extracted tribute in both goods and coerced labor in order to support themselves and direct the construction of large public structures. And at mound centers, luxury goods were imported and consumed by the few.

The Mound Builders

The most visible evidence today of the advances made by the Mississippian civilization are the earthen mounds. These mounds rise in stunning animal and geometric forms across the central and southern United States. The quantity of known mounds and the scale of the largest are impressive. But by 1950 roughly 90 percent of the recorded mounds had been destroyed, and construction of highways and housing has continued to plow through and over the remaining 10 percent. Among the mounds still intact is Monks Mound near East St. Louis, Illinois. With an estimated volume of 22 million cubic feet, Monks Mound is 1,000 feet long and 700 feet wide, and it rises at its highest point 100 feet above the surrounding landscape (Fowler 1975). Monks Mound is surrounded by 120 smaller mounds, arranged in possibly eleven mound and plaza groupings that together comprise the site called "Cahokia." And within twenty-five kilometers of Cahokia lie another ten "town-and-mound centers" (Yerkes 1991, 49). Photo 2.1 provides an artist's rendition of Cahokia and Monk's Mound.

So impressive were the mounds that the pioneers discovered as the nation expanded westward that throughout the eighteenth and nineteenth centuries various theories arose attributing this architecture to races other than the American Indian. Such achievements seemed impossible for a people characterized as "savage." Viking explorers, the Lost Tribes of Israel, and even Welsh explorers who under Prince Madoc supposedly preceded Columbus to the New World were all hailed as the mounds' architects. Such theories allowed the ancestors of the now dominant European Americans, rather than the surviving American Indians, to take credit for the construction of these massive structures (Kennedy 1994, chap. 10). Today, three successive indigenous peoples are acknowledged as the mounds' architects. The last of these were the Mississippians (A.D. 900–1500), ancestrally linked to such present-day peoples as the Cherokee and Choctaw. These earthen structures required thousands of hours of labor to build. Such public works projects required considerable organization of resources and suggest a high degree of social and economic development.

The Economy:
Specialization of Production and Trade

What do we know about the economy and social structure of the Mississippian civilization? What social and economic stratification existed among those first contacted by the Spanish explorers? What goods were produced

Photo 2.1 *Artist's Representation of "Downtown" Cahokia.*
Painting by William R. Iseminger. Courtesy: Cahokia Mounds State Historic Site (Collinsville, IL).

locally, and what was imported? The answers to these questions provide evidence of precolonial long-distance trade and specialization of production.

In order to engage in trade, a society must produce quantities above subsistence. The archaeological record shows that Mississippian production of household (utilitarian) and nonhousehold (nonutilitarian or prestige) goods occurred on a level consistent with intra- and intercommunity trade. Specialized and surplus manufacture of shell objects, salt, meat, and stone implements is well documented in the Mississippian archaeological record. Throughout the region, the pattern of settlement was one of densely populated mound centers with hamlets dotting the surrounding areas. These hamlets appear to have been the sites of specialized manufacturing centers (Scarry 1992, 179; Lewis 1990, 44).

At its peak around A.D. 1250–1300, Cahokia was the center of Mississippian civilization. Population estimates for Cahokia range from 20,000 to 50,000 people (Gregg, cited in Tiffany 1991, 338). Found in the archaeological record of Cahokia are items produced from raw materials originating in areas as far away as the Gulf Coast and Great Lakes regions. The evidence suggests that the economy of Cahokia was characterized by substantial trade routes and division of labor in manufacturing and agriculture directed toward supporting the small class of elites.

Because of their resilient nature and universal usage, stone implements have left the best "hard" record of specialized production and trade. Nearby sites prove that the manufacture of stone products was undertaken by specialized artisans employed full time. During the Stirling phase (A.D. 1050–1150), stone hoes produced at Mill Creek, in present-day Illinois, were dispersed as far as Yazoo County in Mississippi and Moundville in Alabama (Brown, Kerber, and Winters 1990, 265). (See Map 2.2.) Although the transportation cost of exporting lithic products to customers downstream would have been lower, the archeological record shows that stone hoes from Mill Creek, Illinois, and elsewhere tended to flow upstream toward Cahokia and other smaller population centers. However, the distribution of these artifacts is not strictly correlated with estimated population densities. These stone implements provide evidence of a trade network expansive enough to support specialized distribution nodes. James Brown, Richard Kerber, and Howard Winters noted that sites located near the confluence of major rivers had a higher estimated per capita incidence of hoes, suggesting the existence of trade route nodes or entrepôts (1990, 269). Stockpiles of traded goods would have accumulated in entrepôts, and the citizens therein should have enjoyed relatively lower prices. The lower relative price of the traded good would increase consumption. The archaeological record discussed by Brown, Kerber, and Winters is consistent with this prediction: There is a higher per capita recovery of the traded relic in the tributary nodes than in surrounding areas.

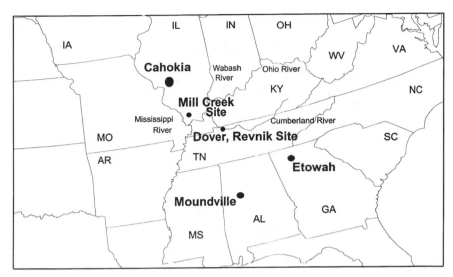

Map 2.2   *Location of Mill Creek, Illinois, and Revnik Sites*

Evidence of production for trade is also found in the Revnik sites of Dover County, Tennessee.[2] (See Map 2.2.) In his detailed study of the lithic industry in Dover County, Richard Gramly (1992) estimated that in its approximate twelve-year occupation, the Revnik site produced over 37,000 items—vastly more than the occupants could ever have used themselves. Not supporting more than ten persons, this site was probably home to a couple of craftspeople and their families. Given estimates of the production time for the stone implements produced at Revnik and given evidence that the occupants did not hunt for themselves, Gramly concluded that "full-time lithic craft specialization at the Revnik site is a fact" (1992, 88). The nearest mound sites of any size, and therefore the nearest possible entrepôts for Dover stone implements, were no closer than twelve to fifteen miles up and downstream. There is no reason to believe that Revnik is not representative of other, currently less-studied, manufacturing sites of the Mississippian civilization.

Excavated evidence also supports the existence of shell workshops in the hamlets of Cahokia's hinterland (Brown, Kerber, and Winters 1990, 270) as well as at the Ramey site within Cahokia proper (Gramly 1992, ix). Additionally, salt works were located near St. Mary, Missouri. Trade in biodegradable goods has also been suggested by surplus bone remains in sites like that in Iowa, coincidentally also named Mill Creek. (For approximate location see Map 2.3.) There, according to Joseph A. Tiffany (1991, 337), the archaeological records indicate an annual surplus production of over 392,000 kilograms of bison meat. Production of dried meat was technically feasible at Mill Creek, and such meat could have been easily transported

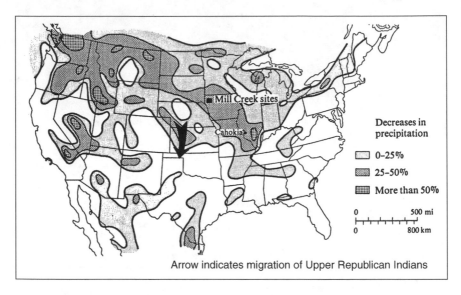

Arrow indicates migration of Upper Republican Indians

Map 2.3   *Fourteenth-Century Drought Estimates*
Source: Reid A. Bryson and Thomas J. Murray, Climates of Hunger: Mankind and the
World's Changing Weather *(Madison: University of Wisconsin Press, 1977). Reprinted
by permission of the University of Wisconsin Press.*

by a thirty-day river trip to Cahokia, where archaeological evidence suggests
that protein was in short supply for some proportion of the population. Oral
histories of peoples related to the Mill Creek settlement tell of ancestors
traveling long distances across water to receive shells "that were very numerous on that shore" (Tiffany 1991, 328). Thus consistency exists between the
oral histories and bone and shell records.

By piecing together evidence of many separate archaeological sites, we can
generalize that prior to Spanish conquest, Mississippian trade took place
along a "Lazy J pattern." The "stem" of the J pattern lies just above the
thirty-fifth parallel, from the Great Plains across the Midwest to Appalachia,
and the "hook" connects Georgia and Florida (Brown, Kerber, and Winters
1990, 263). One exception to this pattern was Moundville. Rising in power
in the fourteenth century, Moundville was located in west central Alabama.
Moundville was centered along a long-distance trade route stretching from
Memphis to the Gulf Coast (James A. Brown, cited in Brown, Kerber, and
Winters 1990). Map 2.4 identifies the locations of artifacts or materials imported to or exported from Moundville (Welch 1991, 188–189). The archaeological evidence suggests that the chiefdom in Moundville controlled
its craft manufacturing. Although stone was imported from outside
Moundville and stone celts were disbursed throughout the region, the

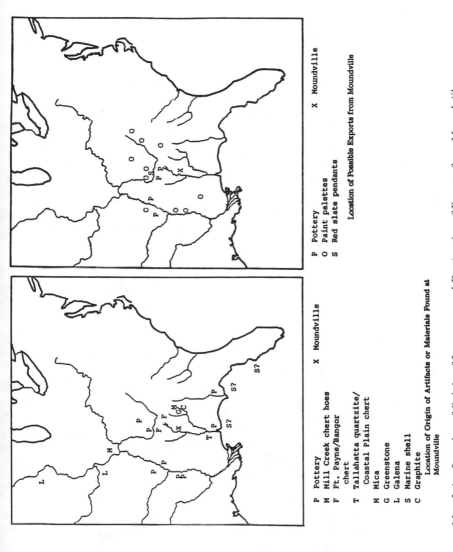

P   Pottery   X Moundville
O Paint palettes
S Red slate pendants

        Location of Possible Exports from Moundville

P   Pottery   X Moundville
H Mill Creek chert hoes
F Ft. Payne/Bangor
    chert
T Tallahatta quartzite/
    Coastal Plain chert
M Mica
G Greenstone
L Galena
S Marine shell
C Graphite
        Location of Origin of Artifacts or Materials Found at
        Moundville

Map 2.4   Location of Origin of Imports to and Destination of Exports from Moundville
Source: Paul D. Welch, Moundville's Economy (Tuscaloosa: University of Alabama Press, 1991). Used
by permission of the publisher.

skilled production of stone objects took place only within Moundville. "In general, Moundville was the only site [in the vicinity] where nonlocal raw materials of any kind were made into finished products" (Welch 1991, 176–177).

Meteorological history can also provide evidence of the importance of trade to the economy of the Mississippian population clusters. The simultaneous occurrence of Cahokia's decline and a major drought in its northern trade regions also suggest that Cahokia was dependent upon trading partners such as the Mill Creek, Iowa, community. Many consider long-distance trade to have been a necessary condition for political stability within the Mississippian civilization (Welch 1991, 191–195; Peebles, as quoted in Hudson, Smith, and DePratter 1990, 190–191; Stoltman 1991, 352). Without large quantities of food resulting from specialization of grain and meat production and foreign objects to denote elite status, a densely populated elite center such as Cahokia could not have sustained itself. Map 2.3 illustrates the areas affected by a drought that, Bryson and Murray (1977) claimed, decimated a large region of the Great Plains and Northwest. A drought as severe as that hypothesized by Bryson and Murray certainly would have greatly reduced or eliminated meat available for trade from Mill Creek, Iowa, as well as disrupted other ongoing trade in the region. It seems reasonable that Cahokia would not have been able to support itself if it were dependent on trade and if drought had affected both local and distant production centers.

Hierarchical Rule: Eyewitness Accounts

Europeans appear to have contacted Mississippian civilization after the major mound centers had already begun to decline from their apex in the thirteenth and fourteenth centuries. Archaeological evidence of the decline of Cahokia predates the first Spanish expeditions. Additionally, the paramount chiefdoms of Coosa (in modern Georgia) and Apafalaya (in modern Alabama) appear from the accounts of early Spanish expeditions not to have been located at the Mississippian mound sites of Moundville and Etowah (Hudson, Smith, and DePratter 1990, 188–189).

Despite this, eyewitness accounts by survivors of the de Soto, de Luna, and Pardo expeditions describe a still-vital hierarchical system with lesser tributary chiefs subjugated by regional paramount chiefs. One telling example is the report of the Quigaltam paramount chief's response to de Soto's request for tribute. In 1542 Hernando de Soto, strapped for supplies, sent a messenger to make such a request of the Quigaltam people of northern Mississippi. (Some believe the Quigaltam to be ancestors of the Natchez who were eighteenth-century inhabitants of this area.) Revealing his regional stature, the Quigaltam paramount chief responded:

> It is not my custom to visit any one, but rather all, of whom I have ever heard, have come to visit me, to serve and obey me, and pay me tribute, either voluntarily or by force. If you desire to see me, come where I am; . . . neither for you, nor for any man, will I set back one foot. (Theodore H. Lewis, as quoted in Shaffer 1992, 69–70)[3]

This chief's expectation that he be paid tribute is representative of the attitude among paramount chiefs encountered by the Spanish explorers. More than once the Spanish conquistadores were asked to assist paramount chiefs in collecting tribute from negligent tributary tribes.[4] And according to some, Juan Pardo was able to take over native tribute collection in 1560 (Smith and Hally 1992; Hudson, Smith, and DePratter 1990). Additionally, burden bearers and women frequently were given to the Spanish, and they went willingly. In another encounter, two indigenous subjects were offered to de Soto's party after the local ruler learned of de Soto's death. The two men were meant for sacrificial burial with de Soto's body. The ruler explained that it was customary "when any lord died, to kill some persons who should accompany and serve him on the way" (Theodore H. Lewis, quoted in Shaffer 1992, 66). The acquiescence of those provided as gifts and other corroborating evidence in eyewitness accounts suggest indigenous accep tance of hierarchical rule (Smith and Hally 1992, 103–105).

Wider Implications: New World Comparison

How does the Mississippian society compare to Aztec, Incan, and Mayan civilizations of Meso- and South America? The Aztec, Incan, and Mayan societies of Meso- and South America are uniformly classified as hierarchical statehoods (Sanders and Price 1968; Lockhart and Schwartz 1983). It is generally agreed among scholars that the Mississippian civilization was also a multitiered hierarchy. There is a disagreement, however, over whether Mississippian civilization had the characteristics necessary to classify it as a nation. Debate exists over the degree of complexity of the Mississippian civilization and whether Mississippian trade occurred under the control of the society's elite or through point-to-point contact (Stoltman 1991, 351–352). Note, however, that these disagreements are not over the existence of a powerful elite but, rather, over the degree and centralization of power held by the elite. That Mississippian civilization supported a well-defined hierarchy and was centered amid long-distance and intraregional trade routes is not contested (Armelagos and Hill 1990; Barker and Pauketat 1992; Brown, Kerber, and Winters 1990; Dye and Cox 1990; Griffin 1990; Welch 1991). Thus, with respect to social complexity, Mississippian civilization was closer in structure to the great empires of Meso- and South America than it was to the contemporary tribes of the Great Plains and northern North America. In fact, Lynda Shaffer made a direct comparison in noting that Cahokia's size compares favorably to that of the Toltec capital in Mexico (1992, 51).

What can be gained from a study of the economic history of this pre-Columbian civilization as it compares to the great pre-Columbian civilizations of Meso- and South America? Apart from revising the common perception that indigenous societies north of the Rio Grande were all subsistence hunters and gatherers, such a study suggests that European colonizers met with highly developed societies that may have influenced the subsequent economic development of the southern United States.

It has been argued for the cases of Latin America and the Caribbean that indigenous peoples were part of the factor endowments that influenced early European colonization of this region (Engerman and Sokoloff 1994). We know that hierarchical societies flourished among the Aztecs, Incas, and Mayans prior to Spanish conquest and that compared to colonial institutions along the North American eastern seaboard, early European colonial institutions of these regions favored limited, not open or egalitarian, access to economic resources. Stanley Engerman and Kenneth Sokoloff (1994) argued that for Meso- and South America, the similarity in precolonial and colonial coercive labor institutions was not coincidental. High population densities and a social history of hierarchical rule (in which tribute was a key feature) existed in the great Meso- and South American empires conquered by the Spanish. The indigenous institutions and endowments of labor made it easier for European colonizers to set up labor-intensive production, coercive labor systems, and a stratified economy that generated high imperial revenues because they could adapt the preexisting structures for their own purposes (Lockhart and Schwartz 1983). Given the apparent degree of stratification present in Mississippian civilization and the ensuing growth of slavery in the southern United States, one must ask to what degree the early indigenous institutions of southeastern North America influenced that region's later development.

Some notable differences remain between the Mississippian economic history and that of Meso- and South America. The Mississippian civilization of southeastern North America did share a history of precolonial hierarchical rule with the indigenous empires of Mexico and Peru, but its population density at the time of active colonization was much lower. Further, a more drastic reduction in population appears to have taken place between first contact and intense colonial activity. Even de Luna's (1559–1561) and Pardo's (1566–1568) expeditions to towns visited by de Soto just a few decades earlier found much smaller populations than the records of de Soto's (1539–1543) expedition describe. By the time of large, permanent European settlements, low native population densities in the southern United States meant that slaves were imported to exploit the economies of scale enabled by large plantations. The mass importation of slaves into what became the southern United States is a practice that more closely resembles the histories of the Caribbean and Brazil than Meso- and South America. In Meso- and South America, colonial powers clearly exploited indigenous labor through a tributelike system of coercion adapting the indigenous institution of tribute.

Attempts were made by Europeans to use indigenous peoples as slaves in the colonies of what would become the southern United States. Slave raids between neighboring indigenous communities were encouraged by colonial powers—at times with the explicit purpose of fanning intertribal animosities. The colonial government of South Carolina, for example, purchased Indian captives, reselling them to finance expeditions against the Spanish (Perdue 1979, chap. 2). Overall, however, the use of indigenous slaves by the colonial slave holders in southeastern North America failed.

The hierarchy of Mississippian society may not have been as multitiered as that of the Incan, Aztec, or Meso-American civilizations, but neither was it as egalitarian as either the Canadian fur-trading tribes or the tribes of the eastern seaboard, woodlands, and plains that survived into the eighteenth and nineteenth centuries. While the degree to which the Mississippian civilization influenced colonial institutions requires further analysis, we can conclude that, like the *encomenderos* of Latin America, the plantation owners of southern colonial America were not the first in the region to benefit from exploitative institutions restricting equal access to economic resources.

More work needs to be done before the role that precolonial institutions played in the economic development of the southern United States is clearly identified. For example, how much influence did the early Spanish colonization of the southern United States have on its later institutional development? To what degree, if any, did the indigenous hierarchical institutions descending from Mississippian culture affect those early Spanish and French institutions? How did Mississippian trade routes and goods compare with those of early European colonists of southeastern North America? Did continuing economic interaction between later European colonists and surviving indigenous peoples nurture lingering effects of the initial conditions at the time of conquest? Further investigation of the historical record, incorporating that of the indigenous civilizations, is needed to fully illuminate the factors affecting the course of economic development in the New World.

Conclusion

Although the economic history of the Mississippians may appear quite distant from the American revolution, it is part of the long economic history of southeastern North America. The organization of vast trade routes and the specialization of manufactures demonstrate substantial precolonial indigenous economic development. The story of the Mississippian economy is one of long-distance trade, production specialization, and social hierarchy. The Mississippians were not a "primitive" people, producing only for subsistence consumption. An artisan class produced the more skill-intensive goods such as flint blades, while others produced and transported the food to feed the artisans. The record of the importation of luxury goods consumed by the Mississippian urban elite demonstrates that that society was hierarchical. And eyewitness accounts from the first contact with Europeans confirm that the Mississippian elite exacted tribute in both goods and coerced labor.

The social hierarchy and degree of economic and urban development within the Mississippian civilization is thus at odds with the commonly held belief that all indigenous peoples north of the Rio Grande lived in egalitarian hunting and gathering communities prior to European contact. Urban clusters did exist within Mississippian civilization, providing the stimulus and labor force for substantial development. With the arrival of the colonizers from Europe, the influence that indigenous Americans had on the economic history of the region did not come to an end. Pre-Columbian nations molded the future economic development of the New World in more ways than just teaching the pilgrims to plant corn or increasing the cost of European land acquisition through diplomatic, litigious, and violent opposition to the expropriation of their land. New World institutions arose from the interaction between indigenous and colonial economic interests. Previously acquired wealth, varying population densities, and social hierarchies of indigenous peoples impacted the economic development of the region.

Notes

This chapter benefited greatly from the comments and suggestions of David Wishart, Kenneth Sokoloff, Margaret Levenstein, Stanley Engerman, and Alan Dye. Ellyn Artis and Arianne De Govia provided valuable research assistance.

1. Another work that postulates an important role for precolonial indigenous institutions in long-term American economic growth is Engerman and Sokoloff 1994.

2. Lithic production from Dover County, Tennessee, overtook that of Mill Creek, Illinois, sometime after A.D. 1200. This was despite the greater distance between Dover County and Cahokia. The growth of a subsequent production site farther from Cahokia, and hence more costly, is economically consistent with the exhaustion of the Mill Creek, Illinois, mines.

3. Reports by the Spanish conquistadores also claim that the dominant town in this region had more than 500 houses and the paramount chief had domain over some 30,000 warriors (Shaffer 1992, 69).

4. Marvin Smith and David Hally make an interesting comparison between the probable practice of Mississippian paramount chiefs visiting tributary villages to maintain allegiance and similar practices in aboriginal Hawaii (1992, 106).

References

Armelagos, George J., and M. Cassandra Hill. 1990. "An Evaluation of the Biocultural Consequences of the Mississippian Transformation." In *Towns and Temples Along the Mississippi*, eds. David Dye and Cheryl Cox. Tuscaloosa: University of Alabama Press.

Barker, Alex, and Timothy Pauketat, eds. 1992. "Lords of the Southeast: Social Inequality and the Native Elites of Southeastern North America." Archeological Papers of the American Anthropological Association, no. 3.

Boserup, Ester. 1981. *Population and Technological Change: A Study of Long-Term Trends.* Chicago: University of Chicago Press.

Brown, James, Richard Kerber, and Howard Winters. 1990. "Trade and the Evolution of Exchange Relations at the Beginning of the Mississippian Period." In *The Mississippian Emergence*, ed. Bruce Smith, 1–8. Washington, D.C.: Smithsonian Institution Press.

Bryson, Reid A., and Thomas J. Murray. 1977. *Climates of Hunger: Mankind and the World's Changing Weather.* Madison: University of Wisconsin Press.

Dye, David, and Cheryl Cox, eds. 1990. *Towns and Temples Along the Mississippi.* Tuscaloosa: University of Alabama Press.

Engerman, Stanley, and Kenneth Sokoloff. 1994. "Factor Endowments, Institutions, and Differential Paths of Growth Among New World Economies: A View from Economic Historians of the United States." National Bureau of Economic Research, Working paper series on Historical Factors in the Long Run, historical paper no. 66 (December).

Fowler, Melvin. 1975. "A Pre-Columbian Urban Center on the Mississippi." *Scientific American*, August, 92–101.

Gramly, Richard. 1992. *Prehistoric Lithic Industry at Dover, Tennessee.* Monographs in Archaeology. Buffalo, N.Y.: Persimmon Press.

Griffin, James B. 1990. "Comments on the Late Prehistoric Societies in the Southeast." In *Towns and Temples Along the Mississippi*, eds. David Dye and Cheryl Cox. Tuscaloosa: University of Alabama Press.

Hudson, Charles, Marvin Smith, and Chester DePratter. 1990. "The Hernando de Soto Expedition: From Mabila to the Mississippi River." In *Towns and Temples Along the Mississippi*, eds. David Dye and Cheryl Cox. Tuscaloosa: University of Alabama Press.

Kennedy, Roger G. 1994. *Hidden Cities: The Discovery and Loss of Ancient North American Civilization.* New York: Free Press.

Lewis, R. Barry. 1990. "The Late Prehistory of the Ohio-Mississippi Rivers Confluence Region, Kentucky and Missouri." In *Towns and Temples Along the Mississippi*, eds. David Dye and Cheryl Cox. Tuscaloosa: University of Alabama Press.

Lockhart, James, and Stuart B. Schwartz. 1983. *Early Latin America: A History of Colonial Spanish America.* Cambridge: Cambridge University Press.

North, Douglass. 1981. *Structure and Change in Economic History.* New York: W. W. Norton.

Perdue, Theda. 1979. *Slavery and the Evolution of Cherokee Society, 1540–1866.* Knoxville: University of Tennessee Press.

Sanders, William T., and Barbara J. Price. 1968. *Mesoamerica: The Evolution of a Civilization.* New York: Random.

Scarry, John. 1992. "Political Offices and Political Structure: Ethnohistoric and Ar-
chaeological Perspectives on the Native Lords of the Apalachee." In *Lords of the
Southeast,* eds. Alex Barker and Timothy Pauketat. Archeological Papers of the
American Anthropological Association, no. 3.

Shaffer, Lynda Norene. 1992. *Native Americans Before 1492.* Armonk, N.Y.: M. E.
Sharpe.

Smith, Marvin, and David Hally. 1992. "Chiefly Behavior: Evidence from Sixteenth
Century Spanish Accounts." In *Lords of the Southeast,* eds. Alex Barker and
Timothy Pauketat. Archeological Papers of the American Anthropological Associ-
ation, no. 3.

Stoltman, James B., ed. 1991. *New Perspectives on Cahokia: Views from the Periphery.*
Monographs in World Archaeology, no. 2. Madison, Wisc.: Prehistory Press.

Tiffany, Joseph A. 1991. "Modelling Mill Creek-Mississippian Interaction." In *New
Perspectives on Cahokia: Views from the Periphery,* ed. James B. Stoltman. Madison,
Wisc.: Prehistory Press.

Welch, Paul. 1991. *Moundville's Economy.* Tuscaloosa: University of Alabama Press.

Yerkes, Richard W. 1991. "Specialization in Shell Artifact Production at Cahokia." In
New Perspectives on Cahokia: Views from the Periphery, ed. James B. Stoltman.
Madison, Wisc.: Prehistory Press.

3

Institutional Change in the Indian Horse Culture

TERRY L. ANDERSON AND
STEVEN LACOMBE

Introduction

Institutions that governed American Indian society prior to European contact demonstrate how dynamic these premodern cultures were. Indeed, "long before Darwin and Wallace brought biological evolution to the attention of the world in 1858, observers of the American Indian had recognized that evolution occurs in cultures" (Farb 1968, 6). This evolution produced a variety of institutional arrangements as varied as any found in human history.

And just as Darwin's theory of evolution predicts that surviving species must adapt in response to ecological constraints, necessity was often the mother of institutional invention for American Indian tribes. All societies must find ways to adjust to changing resource endowments, but the evolution of culture and institutions was particularly important for those societies that

> lived at the margin of subsistence. In more developed societies, departures from optimality mean lower living standards and lower growth rates—luxuries these societies can afford. By contrast, in societies near the margin of subsistence, with populations under Malthusian control, such departures had harsher effects. . . . Unsound rights structures generally implied lower population size and, perhaps, the disappearance of the society. (Bailey 1992, 183)

Certainly not all North American Indians were living at the subsistence margin, but those that were had to adapt. If they could not or did not, they would either be conquered or starve. For those not living at subsistence levels, the ability to adapt to changing resource endowments still determined the extent to which they would prosper or stagnate.

Simply put, the theory of institutional change argues that people produce institutions just as they produce other goods and services in response to changes in costs and benefits. In his seminal article on the evolution of property rights, Harold Demsetz argued that "the emergence of new property takes place in response to the desires of the interacting persons for adjustment to new benefit-cost possibilities. . . . Property rights develop to internalize externalities when the gains of internalization become larger than the cost of internalization" (1967, 350). With some animal species like the beaver, increased scarcity made it economical for Indians to establish property institutions that encouraged a sustainable harvest. However, for other species, like the buffalo, the costs of establishing ownership rights were much higher, and therefore the prospect of preventing the tragedy of the commons less likely. The process of institutional change among the Plains Indians was gradual and continual, as described by Virginia Trenholm and Maurine Carley:

> While the Indians retained many of their legends and customs, they were receptive to their new environment and to the way of life of enemy tribes whose background was far different from their own. Resistance was lacking since Plains culture was not forced upon them, and the change was gradual, if never complete. In fact, these Basin aborigines were unaware that they were adjusting to their surroundings sufficiently to be called Plains Shoshonis. (1964, vii)

The purpose of this chapter is to explain how Plains Indian institutions and culture responded to the introduction of the horse. Hypotheses based on an economic theory of institutional change and tested in the context of the Indian horse culture illustrate the diversity of rights, customs, and property rights found among North American Plains Indians.

Institutional Change in Primitive Societies

Since Harold Demsetz first elucidated his theory of property rights, other economists have fleshed out and applied the theory. In keeping with Demsetz, Douglass North asserted that "institutions change, and fundamental changes in relative prices are the most important source of that change" because "relative price changes alter the incentives of individuals in human interaction" (1990, 84). Such heavy emphasis on relative prices may seem inappropriate for primitive societies, but Vernon Smith noted that even prehistoric humans were able "to adapt to changes in their environment by substituting new types of capital, labor and knowledge for old, and by fabricating new products when effort prices were altered by the environment or by new learning" (1993, 46).

Of course, tastes or ideology provide another potential source of institutional change, which has received more attention in the case of primitive societies. "Changing relative prices are filtered through preexisting mental constructs that shape our understanding of those price changes. Clearly ideas, and the way they take hold, play a role here" (North 1990, 85). In this process,

> cultural elements are in a continual process of interaction: new syntheses and combinations are constantly being produced. But whether or not the new combinations survive in a human group depends on whether or not they work in the existing cultural context. An invention or new combination can be successful only if all of the elements necessary for the recombination are present in the culture. (Farb 1968, 10)

It is important to emphasize that individuals are the producers of institutional change, particularly in the context of American Indians. Strong central political organizations were generally lacking among Indians prior to European contact.[1] Since institutions that support property rights are human constructs, their creation, development, and ruin hinge on individual decisions. This is not to say that collective action was absent in Indian institutional change. Especially as the horse increased the range of individuals and groups, collective influence increased as tribes began to interface with one another. As a consequence, conquest and discontinuous institutional change became more prevalent. Nonetheless, throughout the nineteenth century individual or small group adaptation remained paramount.

Until recently, with the notable exceptions of economists Demsetz (1967) and Posner (1980), explaining how and why primitive institutions change has been the "stuff" of which anthropology is made. The question of private ownership of land among aboriginals has fascinated anthropologists. "It has been one of the intellectual battlegrounds in the attempt to assess the 'true nature' of man unconstrained by the 'artificialities' of civilization" (Demsetz 1967, 351). Through this debate, anthropologists became keenly aware of institutional change. For example, Julian Steward observed that "band ownership of food territories obviously originated somewhere for good reasons. Its repeated occurrence among widely separated groups in different parts of the world suggests that under certain conditions it has developed very readily" (1941, 255). But anthropologists have tended to shun the explanatory power of economic models, contending that

> Primitive economy is different from market industrialism not in degree but in kind. The absence of machine technology, pervasive market organization, and all-purpose money, plus the fact that economic transactions cannot be understood apart from social obligation, create . . . a non-Euclidean universe to which Western economic theory cannot be fruitfully applied. (Dalton 1961, 20)

Recently, however, more economists have taken a keener interest in the evolution of aboriginal institutions and fruitfully applied their models. Richard Posner's theory of primitive society emphasizes that

> many of the distinctive institutions of primitive society, including gift giving and reciprocal exchange, customary prices, polygamy and bridesprice, the size of kinship groups, and the value placed on certain personality traits, such as generosity and touchiness, can be explained as adaptations to uncertainty or high information costs. (1980, 4)

To this list of distinctive features, we must add common property, which often typified Indian property institutions. Aboriginal circumstances that made common property institutions an optimal system

> generally included a small population when compared to a modern nation state, so that the enforcement of various behavioral norms through social pressure was much easier. For this and other technological reasons, optimal rights structures in aboriginal societies could include more common property and group enterprises and fewer disjoint individual rights (Bailey 1992, 184)

Five specific attributes of resources or technology are hypothesized to determine whether common property prevails over private property:

> (1) the low predictability of prey or plant location within the tribal territory; (2) the public-good aspect of information about the location of this kind of unpredictable food resource; (3) the high variance of the individual's success because of 1, 2, or other circumstances beyond the individual's control; (4) the superior productivity of group hunting techniques, such as driving prey into ambush or over a cliff; and (5) the safety from large predators, especially when bringing home the product of a successful trip. (Bailey 1992, 187)[2]

These attributes suggest a trade-off between the superior incentive effects inherent in private property and the advantages from scale economies captured through communal activities.[3] In a hunting and gathering society, low predictability of prey and plant locations explains why cooperation was a necessary condition for survival—a point that dovetails with Richard Posner's information cost theory. Similarly, what Martin Bailey calls the "public-good aspect of information" or what can be more appropriately understood as economies of scale in information collection encouraged coordination of searching because coordination would "produce better total results for the group than would an individual's solitary tracking" (Bailey 1992, 188). High variance of hunting and gathering success meant that individual efforts could result in starvation. And finally, just as the size of the firm in modern economies requires trading off the gains from scale economies against the costs of monitoring the activities on the assembly line, tribes had to consider the superior productivity of communal hunting efforts vis-à-vis the potential for shirking by individual members.

Essentially Bailey is trying to explain why and how aboriginal people interact with one another rather than living separately. Ronald Coase's (1937) seminal article "The Nature of the Firm" and Steven Cheung's (1983) later elaboration help us understand such interaction in the context of the economics of organizations by focusing on transaction costs. According to Coase and Cheung there are two types of costs that result from human interaction. The first are transaction costs associated with exchange in which each party to the exchange must measure and monitor performance by the other. The second transaction costs are the agency costs associated with collective organization (for example, the firm, the state, or the tribe) in which an individual or group is assigned the responsibility of coordinating interaction within the organization. In this case, members of the collective have an incentive to shirk to the extent that their share of the group's output is independent of their individual effort. It is here that agency costs arise. Armen Alchian and Harold Demsetz (1972) have pointed out that the modern firm overcomes this problem by making the owner of the firm a residual claimant, thus giving him a stake in monitoring inputs. In social groups, however, residual claimants are not always well identified, and certainly claims on the residual are not usually transferable; there is, nonetheless, a residual. The smaller the group and the nearer it is to subsistence, the greater the role that residual plays in encouraging efficient organization.

Given the transaction costs associated with either exchange or collective action, we might ask why individuals do not just avoid interaction all together. The simple answer is that there are gains from interaction as long as there are differential resource endowments (comparative advantage) or economies of scale.

In attempting to capture these gains from interaction, people have choices along a continuum that has at its extreme ends the options of producing separately and exchanging with others when the gains from exchange exceed the measuring and monitoring costs, or producing collectively when the gains from collective action (especially scale economies) exceed the agency costs. Along this continuum can be found the optimal size of collective unit by trading off the exchange costs that decline with increased collective action against the agency costs that rise (see Cheung 1983, 9–10).

Applying this methodology to the Indian horse culture reveals three factors that would condition the choice between disjoint individual activities and collective enterprises. First, scale economies in gathering information about the location of migratory species such as the buffalo and in hunting those buffalo would encourage coordinated hunting efforts. Second, communal organizations allowed a way for subsistence societies to share risk in the face of variability because of game location, weather, or other biological factors. Third, the gains from scale economies and risk sharing had to be traded off against the costs of collective organization.

The central hypothesis that follows from this framework is that if horses changed the production function for hunting by reducing scale economies and decreasing variability in the access to buffalo and by changing the relative value of hunting inputs, the optimal size of social organizations would decline.

Pre-Equestrian Organization

Prior to the arrival of the horse from Europe, Plains Indian tribes lived relatively sedentary lives, gathering plants and hunting mostly smaller game. Property rights generally centered around the "work-use-ownership" principle, which imbued rights to resources or objects to those persons who expended work on them and used them.

> Water, seed, and hunting areas, minerals and salt deposits, etc., were freely utilized by anyone. But once work had be done upon the products of natural resources (mixed labor with them) they became the property of the person or family doing the work. Willow groves could belong to anyone, but baskets made of willows belonged to their makers. Wild seeds could be gathered by anyone, but once harvested they belonged strictly to the family doing the task, even though they might be shared with other families. (Steward 1934, 253)

By contrast, the Owens Valley Pauite were distinctive for their band ownership of hunting and seed territories. Their population was comparatively dense, and they lived fairly stable and settled lives. Their land was fertile, providing conditions necessary for agriculture and thus enabling a more static lifestyle, usually organized in permanent villages. The result was a system of enforceable property rights supported by a degree of organized tribal control. Named, landowning bands lived under the direction of chiefs with well-defined authority. Band unity was reinforced by communal sweat houses and mourning ceremonies. Exploitation of the natural resources in a given area was exclusive, and trespass was punishable. Clearly competition for relatively scarce resources made it productive for individuals and families to absorb the costs incurred, defining rights to a territory in order to gain the benefits.

Because it involved significant economies of scale, hunting provided an exception to the "work-use-ownership" rule and to property rights such as those of the Owens Valley Pauite. Hunting activities brought the families together under the leadership of a hunting chief, whose job it was to organize the hunt and to minimize free-riding or shirking by members of the group. Among the Shoshone and the Hopi, rabbits, for example, "were hunted by a communal drive under the leadership of a secular rabbit chief. The officer was distinct from both the leader of the deer hunt and the antelope charmer" (Freed 1960, 351). The nets into which the rabbits were driven, however, were privately owned and maintained. "The catch of these large drives was usually divided equally among those who participated, but sometimes a larger share was offered to the hunt's organizer and leader or to the owners of the nets" (Fowler 1986, 82).

Before the advent of the horse, most Plains hunting of buffalo and other large game was pursued mainly in the summer as a communal exercise that brought together groups that were dispersed in smaller bands throughout the rest of the year. Pedestrian hunting required larger groups for driving herds of animals (sometimes with the aid of fire) into surrounds (semicircular arrangements of women interspersed with upended travois) or over cliffs known as jumps or piskuns. Men chased the animals, closed in on them, and finally killed them. The meat was carved up and distributed equally among all participants. A hunt leader coordinated activities by appointing guards "who prevented the disruption of the communal effort by attempts to hunt alone in advance of the village. These guards punished offenders through destruction of their property 'without the man or woman saying a word'" (Ewers 1969, 303).

When the Plains Indians did pursue large game animals like the buffalo, their social organization can be explained in terms of information costs, variance in hunting success, and scale economies. From the stories of millions of buffalo roaming the Great Plains, one might infer that information costs and variance in hunting success would be trivial problems. It is likely that the Great Plains may have been inhabited with somewhere between 30 million and 60 million buffalo in the eighteenth century, but this by no means should lead us to believe that the distribution was geographically or temporally even. Despite their large populations, the buffalo was a fugitive resource and often difficult to locate. In Alberta, John McDougall wrote in 1898 that as late as 1865 the plains and forests were "full of buffalo" and recounted one episode in which, from a hillock, he observed one dense herd filling a large plain ten miles across (1898, 95).

The estimates and accounts of millions of buffalo, however, are contradicted by other contemporary accounts. When numbers are mentioned in the historical record, they frequently suggest hundreds rather than thousands or millions of buffalo. One captain traveling through the Ohio valley in 1750 found that contrary to the claims that there were "vast herds" grazing there, his troop could only kill a score of them—he decried the "hyperbole and exaggeration" of his Canadian sources (quoted in Roe 1951, 339). Nicholas Cresswell journeyed to Kentucky in 1775 to hunt the promised "immense herds" but found none to kill; after some time he was rewarded with "a herd of two hundred odd," a number he found incredibly large

(Cresswell 1928, 86). John Filson pointed to the sighting of one herd of bison numbering "above one thousand" at the Blue Licks as evidence of "the amazing herds" that were "so numerous" (quoted in Hornaday 1889, 386).

The probable explanation for the contradiction between the estimate of 30 million to 60 million buffalo on the Plains and the scarcity in other accounts can be explained by the perennial unpredictability of location and migration. The account of Dr. Josiah Gregg on the Cimarron River country in 1831 captures the nature of this unpredictability:

> Not even a buffalo was now to be seen to relieve the dull monotony of the scene; although at some seasons (and particularly in the fall) these prairies are literally strewed with herds of this animal. Then, "thousands and tens of thousands" might at times be seen from this eminence. But the buffalo is a migratory animal, and even in the midst of the Prairies where they are generally so very abundant, we sometimes travel for days without seeing a single one. . . . Nevertheless, the number of buffalo upon the Prairies is still immense. But as they incline to migrate *en masse* from place to place, it sometimes happens that, for several days' travel together, not a single one is met with; but in other places, many thousands are often seen at one time. (1905: xx, 264)

The tendency of bison to be unevenly distributed about the plains was confirmed by McDougall: "There were millions of these cattle, and yet so big was the field that you might travel for days and weeks and not see one of them" (1898, 248).

The scattered nature of the herds might not be a problem if they followed systematic migrations routes, but predictability of migration routes is doubtful. The most common migration hypothesis is that bison emigrated from the north to the warmer south come winter.[4] But other accounts argue that the bison herds wintered in the wooded north (see McDougall 1911, 26; Simpson 1847, 1:92; McHugh 1972, 177). Despite the apparent lack of consensus on the compass directions, the various migratory hypotheses do share common elements: They suggest the bison sought shelter in the winter and followed fresh grass through the remaining seasons. The exact patterns of migration, however, varied according to the localized topography and climate,[5] making it very difficult to place much faith in the regularity of the bison's migratory patterns. Frank Gilbert Roe (1951, 393) discussed an anecdote from the early summer of 1823 noting that the Assiniboin found the bison so scarce in the Upper Red River that they had to move to Saskatchewan; the following month, Major Stephen H. Long witnessed a hunt returning from the Red River with 115 carts, each loaded with 800 pounds of meat, and personally saw "herds numbering thousands" at the upper confluences of the Red and Missouri rivers. George Catlin, who spent many years living with the Plains Indians documenting and painting their lifestyle, stated: "These animals are not migratory. They roam about and over vast tracts of country, from East to West and from West to East as often as from North to South" (quoted in McHugh 1972, 176). George Bird Grinnell called the bison "a wandering race, sometimes leaving a district and being long absent, and again returning and occupying it for a considerable period. What laws or impulses governed these movements we cannot know" (1970, 271).

There is no evidence to indicate that Indians took advantage of great north-south patterns of movement to set up killing stations as the herds passed; instead, they wandered, oftentimes irregularly and blindly (see McHugh 1972, 173–174). In fact, the Indians often seemed puzzled by the erratic bison movements. "Often, the rolling grassland around the Teton [Sioux] camp was thickly dotted with them; again not an animal was in sight. The Indians . . . believed that there was something supernatural back of it all. . . . Rituals were performed and prayers made that the buffalo be plentiful, and when they were scarce, the praying, singing, and rituals intensified" (Wissler 1966, 179). Such divine intervention would not have been needed if the bison performed like clockwork. Indeed, chancing upon a vulnerable herd of bison was such a stroke of good fortune that a group of Indians was unlikely to pass up the opportunity, even if stockpiles were overflowing.

Given the scattered and unpredictable nature of buffalo, Plains Indians hunters had to produce the best information they could about location in order to reduce variance of hunting success. Given their lack of transportation, it was not possible to follow the bison over vast territories. Instead, the Plains Indians formed into groups under the direction of a hunt chief. Grinnell describes the use of buffalo jumps:

> As spring opened, the buffalo would move down to the more flat prairie country away from the pis'kuns. Then the Blackfeet would also move away. As winter drew near, the buffalo would again move up close to the mountains, and the Indians, as food began to become scarce, would follow them toward the pis'kuns. In the last of the summer and early autumn, they always had runners out, looking for the buffalo, to find where they were, and which way they were moving. In the early autumn, all the pis'kuns were repaired and strengthened, so as to be in good order for winter. (1962, 234)

Piskuns in the northern Rocky Mountains show patterns of utilization in the late fall–early winter, midwinter, and late winter–early spring, with no representation of summer kills.[6] Tom McHugh paraphrased the philosophy as articulated by a Teton Sioux chief: "Buffalo were like cherries—they didn't stay around very long, so the tribes should take plenty whenever they had the chance" (1972, 75). When the Indians knew that the buffalo were nearby, they formed into their hunting groups and partook of the bounty; when the buffalo were not, the Indians dispersed. As Sarah Carter put it,

"Indian life on the prairie followed a pattern of concentration and dispersal that paralleled that of the buffalo" (1990, 27).

The unpredictability of the bison influenced Indian culture in many ways. All possessions within the tribe were adapted to best serve the nomadic lifestyle, by making them more compact, lightweight, and quickly collapsible (see McHugh 1972, 6). Tribes would break camp and follow the bison herds as often as necessary to sate their hunger and need for supplies (see Ewers 1955, 128). Plains tribes went out of their way to invent mechanisms to minimize the unpredictability of the bison flow. One strategy was to develop methods of preservation, such as jerking, pemmican, and caching, that would tide them over when fresh supplies were short. Another tactic was to share the risk with other tribes. For instance, the Pawnee and Omaha tribes struck a treaty guaranteeing reciprocal hunting privileges (McHugh 1972, 173). Not knowing where the herds might graze next, it behooved both tribes to secure reciprocal agreements so that if fortune should strike their neighbor, it would not mean famine for them.[7]

The economies of scale involved in pedestrian hunting techniques also dictated relatively large, communally organized social groups. Three general methods of hunting the bison prevailed in pre-equestrian times: the stalk, the surround, and the drive.

Pedestrian Stalk. The stalk provided the fewest scale economies of any of the pedestrian techniques and therefore allowed larger groups to disband.[8] This explains why the stalk was used most in winter when other techniques were ineffective and why winter hunting groups were smaller. The pedestrian stalk was most successful in winter because the bison were mired in deep snowdrifts (Ewers 1958, 84). After a warm day or two of thawing followed by nighttime refreezing, the snow surface might become hard enough to support a human on snowshoes but collapse under the buffalo's hooves. The disparity in ground speed would then be narrowed, as the Indians with snowshoes could dart across the snow surface to great advantage. Sometimes the buffalo could be run down and rendered so helpless that it might be killed with a dagger or spear (see Arthur 1975, 64; Hornaday 1889, 423). Even after the arrival of the horse, the pedestrian stalk remained a necessity in winter when deep snow might preclude the use of a horse (Denig 1930, 160).

Pedestrian Surround. The surround incorporated elements of both the stalk and the drive and therefore entailed scale economies and communal organization costs. One version of the surround consisted of a makeshift fence constructed by tying dog travois together. A group of swift-footed men would rouse the herd and drive it toward the fence, while others would stand alongside the drive route and close in behind the herd. When the surround was complete, the herd would run in a circle while hunters slaughtered them with arrows. A more spontaneous, though less successful, surround might do away with the fence altogether and merely use buffalo robes or waved arms to create the illusion of an obstacle. Though coordination could be costly and the setup time lengthy, the economies of scale made the pedestrian surround the technique of choice when terrain was suitable and buffalo were available.

Pedestrian Drive. The drive was truly the maximalist form of hunting. It promised the wholesale slaughter of an entire herd but at the greatest expense in planning, labor, coordination, and care. The drive involved corralling a herd of bison into a natural topographical pit or trap or into a permanent man-made pound. The most famous variant of the drive was the buffalo jump, where a herd was stampeded over a cliff. Unlike the pedestrian stalk, the successful drive had little chance of startling neighboring herds; the selected herd could be directed to the place to be killed. Thus many tribes could conduct drives all season long until bison availability became low (see Barsness 1985, 45–46).

One difficulty that the drive strategy posed was that at times it required drawing the herd over great distances to the specific location of the predesignated trap. Most jumps or traps were surrounded by a gathering area—often a basin or valley floor where herds of buffalo might collect. From this area, the herds would be slowly led into drive-lines made of stone, buffalo chips, or other available resources and laid out in a V shape with the apex at the trap. The herd was thus funneled toward the trap as Indians stood at the sidelines beating their robes to prevent the bison from testing the durability of the drive-lines. At the Vore Site, the drive-lines extended at least 2.5 miles to the west, and bison may have been driven a considerable distance before even arriving at the opening of the drive (Reher and Frison 1980, 8). Often the herd was led by a "runner" or "decoy"—an Indian who dressed like a buffalo and imitated its movements and calls. By bleating like a stray calf or attracting the curiosity of the herd in some fashion, the decoy could start the herd moving toward him and then ever closer to the drive lines.

> If the herds had been found grazing far from the pound, a herder, an aide to the decoyer, would have gone for them, ten, twenty, as far as fifty miles away, to work them toward the pound, again using smoke and available wind, or showing himself at strategic moments, or running at top speeds to turn the herd when necessary, or sitting for hours to wait for a "convenient season." At night he might nudge them along by slapping his robe on the ground to startle them into movement. When the herder had brought the herd close, the decoyer took over. (Barsness 1985, 44)

A group of persons walking behind a herd could direct a herd by cutting back and forth as need be (Barsness 1985, 37).

The drive was a laborious process requiring a great deal of time, patience, and "buffalo savvy." Though bison were considered most manageable in the fall, the drive was a difficult operation at all seasons. The slightest provocation might set the buffalo off in a stampede. The possibility of losing a herd at any time was high. The greatest danger occurred at the point just before the bison reached the edge of the cliff or the pound opening. If the lead animal was not sufficiently exhausted from the long drive or was not pushed forward by the press of stampeding bison behind, it might turn, leading the whole herd back with it (Schaeffer 1978, 247; Henry and Thompson 1965, 725). Success also depended on topographical features of the cliff and surrounding area.

Because both the surround or drive hunting techniques involved significant coordination costs and provided scale economies, they were only used by large groups with strong hunt chiefs.[9] In order for these techniques to be worth the organization costs, there had to be sufficient numbers of buffalo in the area. According to Charles Reher and George Frison, "There had to be hundreds or thousands of animals to allow a jumping season of any duration. During the first part of the Vore [bison jump] sequence, in the initial Little Ice Age, this occurred only about every 25 years" (1980, 137). Variations at the Vore buffalo jump suggest that threshold populations were more prevalent during the later 1600s and 1700s.[10]

> It may not be out of line to assume bands would integrate at a productive kill only once in five to ten years during the initial Little Ice Age (and less frequently prior to this). An increasing frequency of kill operations thus documents more regular and larger congregations of cultural groups, and eventually more elaborate social mechanisms to structure and institutionalize this integration. (Reher and Frison 1980, 59)

They further noted that the idea of a critical threshold suggests that "too few animals in a gathering area make cooperative kill ventures unfeasible" (45).[11] Since availability fluctuated throughout the seasons, bands aggregated and disaggregated in response to the bison supply.

Smaller groups would come together seasonally in groups of approximately 150 persons[12] to hunt bison.[13] According to John Ewers, "The cooperative hunt necessitated a band or village organization of 10 or preferably more lodges" (1969, 303). Barsness (1985, 38) claimed that 150 people may have been the optimal number of participants in a bison drive—about the size of a permanent band. When a group got larger than this, it would peaceably divide, apparently because the agency costs rose significantly (see Wissler 1966, 261).

Post-Equestrian Institutions

The horse has come. Almost overnight, it seems, he has captured the west; and by his coming the west has been awakened, transformed.

> *It was one of the most dramatic and one of the most momentous transfor-*
> *mations that ever took place in any land under the sun. The bare facts of the*
> *coming of the horse and the transformation thus wrought constitute the*
> *greatest animal epic ever enacted in the world.*
>
> —H. R. Sass, 1936

The horse proliferated northward from Mexico, passing from Indian tribe to tribe over a period from 1600 to 1740 (Roe 1955, 191). "A simple calculation reveals that southern tribes adopted the horse at an over 60 percent faster rate than did northern tribes. Stated differently, for the early epoch adoption was about *six times faster* than for the northern tribes" (Jacobsen and Eighmy 1980, 338).

During the eighteenth and nineteenth centuries, the horse changed the Indians' lives in many ways. Before the arrival of the horse, Indians were seminomadic, spending the greater part of the year living in communal earthen lodges cultivating fields of corn, beans, and squash. In the summer and fall months, they swapped their lodges for tepees that could be broken down and loaded on travois pulled by dogs, and they followed the buffalo, living on a diet of both meat and vegetables. The horse changed all of this by increasing mobility and reducing transportation costs:

> The immediate effect upon the Indians of the acquisition of a few Spanish horses by trade or theft was to discourage what little agricultural work they did, and cause them to rely upon the buffalo more than ever before. . . . With the horse they roamed for miles, encroached upon others' hunting grounds, went to war, and otherwise became marauders of the plains. (Wyman 1945, 70)

Indians changed their diet from one balanced between vegetables and meat to one dominated by buffalo. Moreover, they used the animals they killed much less intensively:

> The abundance of buffalo in the Blackfoot Country, the relative ease with which they could be killed by mounted hunters, the limited facilities of the average family for transporting meat surpluses, and the demands of the fur trade for buffalo robes encouraged the wasteful slaughter of these animals during the 19th century. . . . As early as 1754, Anthony Hendry observed that when buffalo were plentiful the "Archithinue" of the Saskatchewan Plains took only the tongues and other choice pieces, leaving the rest to the wolves. . . . These factors encouraged "Light butchering" and use of only the choice parts of the buffalo in good times. (Ewers 1969, 168–169)[14]
>
> By the same token, the horse increased the possibility of killing more selectively and prudently than with buffalo jumps. The equestrian chase encouraged the Indian to select the choicest buffalo from a herd because horses would tire and fall from the chase within a few minutes. Roe concluded: "So far from the equestrian era inaugurating mass slaughter, it seems to be more correct, historically, to suggest that the advent of the horse terminated it, or at least marked the beginning of the end" (1955, 358).[15]

The horse also changed the Indians' housing from earthen lodges or small tents to large tepees, now a symbol of Plains life. With added mobility, Indians needed housing that was transportable. In the "dog days," when canines were used for transportation, Indians used tepees, but they averaged approximately twelve feet in diameter. "Once the horse was introduced, the tepee became larger (the horse could carry the longer poles required of a larger tepee) and its territory expanded. The tepee spread so far because there was always a ready supply of buffalo skins for the cover and because it could be used in just about any terrain or climate" (Faegre 1979, 152). In fact, tepee rings on the Plains indicated that after the introduction of the horse, tepees eighteen to twenty-one feet in diameter were common.

The optimal size of socioeconomic groups and seasonal economic patterns shifted dramatically with adaptation to the horse culture. The mobility gains made possible by the horse immediately made the bison more available by virtue of increasing the proximity of the bison (even as the bison population declined): "With dogs, five or six miles had been a good day's journey; with the horse, ten, fifteen, or even twenty miles could be traversed" (Barsness 1985, 50). Before the advent of the horse, a tribe could scarcely move fifty miles in an entire season; whereas in equestrian days the same tribe could cover 500 (White 1979, 71–72; Wissler 1966, 289). The horse could also help minimize the need to move camp, as a permanent hub camp would be situated with temporary foraging parties sent out to gather meat (Barsness 1985, 50). The Nez Percé of Idaho suddenly found themselves able to undertake expeditions lasting several months or even several years ranging across the Rocky Mountains to partake of the numerous buffalo herds in the Yellowstone region (Lavender 1992, 22). Even when the horse could not make fresh meat available, it did allow the Indians to transport even more stored provisions as insurance against hard times (Ewers 1969, 304).

Acquisition of the horse reduced the scale economies in hunting, making it easier for bands to be independent of one another. On horseback, individuals could more easily track and kill game. Moreover, with greater individual ability to follow and harvest game, the need for communal insurance schemes declined.

> It was the chase on horseback that fully exploited the horse's ability to run faster than the swiftest buffalo. This new hunting technique was more efficient and adaptable than any method previously employed. Not only did it require a fraction of the time and energy but it was less dangerous and more certain of success than other methods. It could be employed by a single hunter or the men of an entire village. Within a few minutes a skilled hunter, mounted on a fleet, intelligent, buffalo horse could kill at close range enough buffalo to supply his family with meat for months. (Ewers 1969, 305)

Hence tribes were generally more dispersed after the introduction of the horse.

Dispersion was also required because the horse needed adequate pasturage and water, dictating more frequent changes of camp (Lowie 1982, 42). With a Blackfoot lodge averaging eight horses (Ewers 1955, 21) and a Cayuse lodge averaging fifteen to twenty horses (Farnham 1843, 82), it is clear that large bands could face acute grazing problems. Campsites always "had to be chosen with a view to adequate pasturage" (Carter 1990, 27).

If the horse eliminated economies of scale in hunting and hence the need for centralized hunting institutions, it increased the need for military institutions and their inherent scale economies. "It was . . . leisure time, the rise of the pony as a measure of wealth, and the infringement upon one another's buffalo range that was a cause of intertribal war" (Wyman 1945, 74). Increased mobility brought more conflict between tribes for larger hunting territories and more raids to steal horses. As a result, Plains Indians had to "construct new trade and military patterns to replace those that had collapsed" (Carter 1990, 35).

To organize for intertribal warfare, new, more centralized political structures evolved to capture the scale economies. Demitri Shimkin described this transition for the Eastern Shoshone: "With the acquisition of horses came . . . widespread raiding throughout the Plains, 1700–1780. In this period, it is certain that strong chiefly leadership and considerable protocol and sumptuary rights prevailed" (1986, 309). Prior to the horse, there was little intertribal warfare. For the Blackfoot—one of the fiercest Plains tribes—"traditions claim that the Shoshoni were their only enemies in pre-horse times" (Ewers 1969, 172). After the acquisition of the horse, however, there were few alliances, and intertribal warfare was common. "Throughout the century prior to 1885, peace between the Blackfoot tribes and their neighbors (other than Sarsi and Gros Ventres) was the exception, war the rule. Peaceful periods were brief interludes between hostilities" (Ewers 1969, 175).

The enhanced mobility meant that tribes would more frequently encounter one another and potentially fight over common herds of buffalo. The heightened danger of encroachment by other tribes, the greater dependence on the buffalo, and the ability to patrol and protect an area thanks to the horse made the declaration of private tribal hunting grounds ubiquitous. Tribes drew boundary lines and signed treaties to defend them; if no clear topographic features existed to delineate the boundary, boulders wrapped in buffalo hides were substituted (Barsness 1985, 53).

On the heels of intertribal warfare came conflicts with whites and an even greater demand for institutional change to accommodate warfare. During the nineteenth century institutions with strong tribal chiefs evolved for organizing warriors. In many cases tribes were totally unprepared for these political changes: "The institution of the band chief was novel and hence provided opportunity for influential personalities to assert themselves"; hence the horse and the accompanying warfare transformed the organization of Plains Indian tribes into political bonds that "interlocked in all directions.

... Previously independent villages, now traveling with horses, united into military bands under high commands" (Steward 1938, 248–249).[16]

Because the horse had such profound impacts on Indian life, it is not surprising that ownership of horses became a symbol of wealth and prestige. Horses were always considered personal property with full rights of inheritance and trade, but the number of horses owned by tribal members could mean the difference between survival and starvation or conquest. James Schultz remarked of the Blackfoot in the 1870s that "horses were the tribal wealth, and one who owned a large herd of them held a position only to be compared to that of our multi-millionaires. These were individuals who owned from one hundred to three and four hundred" (1907, 152). With property rights in horses more secure, as in the case of tribes that "lived west of the Rockies where they were relatively immune from horse raids of the Plains Indians and where winters were milder and forage more plentiful than on the northern Plains," groups became "noted for their attention to and skill in breeding horses" (Ewers 1969, 22).

It is interesting that the impact of the horse was uneven, radically altering some lifestyles and barely affecting others. Initially, horses were eaten by many tribes on the Great Plains. Indeed, rather than using the horse to obtain their food more readily, the Paiute Indians of the Great Basin used them as a source of nourishment (Farb 1968, 10: Driver and Massey 1957, 191). Some tribes never adapted sufficiently to utilize the horse to the fullest. For instance, the possession of the horse among the Northern Shoshone distinguished them from their cousins in the west. Trenholm and Carley state that "when an Indian acquired a horse (the emblem of Plains culture) he was considered a Shoshoni; if he found himself deprived of it, he was once again a Shoshoko (walker or digger). The Western Shoshonis (Shoshokos) were recognized as such because they lacked organized bands as well as horses before the arrival of the white man" (1964, 4).

Conclusion

It is clear from this brief history of the impact of horses that the American Plains Indians readily adapted to their physical, economic, and social environment by changing the institutions that governed human relations. Often institutional changes are marginal adaptations, but in the case of the horse, they were more discontinuous. Indeed, it is remarkable how complete and rapid the transformation to the horse culture was. Although the horse, tepee, and buffalo are accepted as symbols of the Indian life encountered by the first whites on the western frontier, they were all relatively new to Indians. Had the whites arrived a few decades earlier, they would have found less-nomadic groups ill-prepared to do battle. In fact, had the Indians not developed their military institutions in response to the demands of intertribal warfare brought on by the horse, it is unclear whether they could have resisted the onslaught of whites as long as they did.

Notes

This chapter is adapted from Terry Anderson's *From Sovereign Nations to Reservations* (San Francisco: Pacific Research Institute, 1995).

1. For further discussion see Anderson 1995 and Benson 1992.

2. Since the last point is more applicable in Africa, where predatory animals, especially large cats, are more likely to take the product of the hunt, it will be ignored here.

3. In the context of this discussion, the firm can be thought of as a communal institution, though the residual claimant is generally clearer than in the more traditional communal institutions. For a discussion of the firm in this context, see Alchian and Demsetz 1972.

4. For example, see Father Louis Hennepin, quoted in McHugh 1972, 174.

5. This appears to be the prevailing hypothesis among anthropologists and zoologists. See Johnson and Holliday 1980, 148–159; Davis and Wilson 1978, 198.

6. See Davis and Wilson 1978, 76–77. However, they argued (68–69) that the wintering in the valleys and foothills of the Rocky Mountains is accompanied by a summer migration to alpine and subalpine elevations, not to the eastern prairie lands as Grinnell would have it.

7. There is also a military rationale for this relationship, a rationale captured in Anderson and McChesney 1994. If the herds were to graze on Omaha land, the Pawnee would see little alternative to invading other than starvation. Thus the Omaha would realize a security advantage even if it meant surrendering some of their buffalo. One might wonder, however, whether such reciprocal arrangements would arise if one group were overwhelmingly more powerful than the other; a bison-deprived tribe would find a competitive advantage perhaps in simply invading other territory.

8. While the pedestrian stalk avoided some of the coordination costs of the communal hunt, it did have scale economies to the extent that, once disturbed, the buffalo herd would be scared off. At the same time, however, too many hunters on foot would be more likely to scare the herd before any were killed.

9. Of course, groups would try to economize on labor. The Crow, for example, burned incense along the drive-lines to repel escaping animals. This allowed the Crow to concentrate their personnel at the very end of the drive, where stones would be stacked higher and closer together to provide greater protection for the braves. Fire also could be used to direct the bison herds if the group was shorthanded.

10. During the 1500s and early 1600s, "apparently this density threshold was surpassed in the Vore area only about two or three times in a man's lifetime. During the later 1600s and the 1700s, buffalo populations may have supported almost continual cropping" (Reher and Frison 1980, 59).

11. "The Gros Ventre once ran three buffalo into a pound, but three is not then the critical number. . . . The Gros Ventre did not construct the pound and settle down for the winter because they saw three animals, but only when the presence of

numerous buffalo made it appear that a series of communal kills was feasible." Reher and Frison (1980, 45–46) speculate that the critical number for a successful jump or series of pounds is about 100 to 300 animals; however, repeated hazing of the animals will inevitably provoke some to flee the area. For several weeks of kills on a reliable basis, the gathering area would need to support "closer to 1000 than 500 animals," depending on the topography.

12. The literature generally does not differentiate the community size for Plains Indians from other North American groups. Jon White (1979, 76) gave the inclusive figure of 100 to 300 persons. But earlier in the book he wrote: "The most comfortable size of a band was usually felt to be about 100–150 persons, but it was often much smaller. When it began to swell in size, and approached the 200 mark, the problem of feeding it became serious, and the usual solution was fission" (55). Clark Wissler wrote: "An Indian community rarely consisted of more than a hundred persons of all ages" (1966, 261).

13. These congregations were not always for hunting. The Shoshoni organized in composite bands only to deter Blackfoot aggression; when Blackfoot power waned by 1850, the seasonal congregations ended (Madsen 1980, 24–25).

14. Also see Baden, Stroup, and Thurman 1981 for a discussion of Indian responses to relative prices.

15. Whether this actually decreased the overall rate of buffalo killing, however, is not clear. In fact, increased availability of bison would increase overall human carrying capacity and hence total human predation. The Indians are also known to have engaged in the killing of buffalo purely for fun. Roe himself noted the "wasteful slaughter" of bison by Cree young men in Saskatchewan in 1868 "despite the warnings and entreaties of the elders" (Cowie, cited in Roe 1955).

16. It should be noted that these warfare institutions evolved out of necessity and hence disappeared when the Indians were subjugated by the whites. "The office and its duties, having no precedence in native institution and concerning principally warfare negotiations with the white man, were limited in scope and duration. They survived too briefly to have won general respect and support. When the wars ceased the need for organization largely vanished and the chiefs lost authority" (Steward 1938, 249).

References

Alchian, Armen, and Harold Demsetz. 1972. "Production, Information Costs, and Efficiency." *American Economic Review* 62 (5):777–795.

Anderson, Terry L. 1995. *Sovereign Nations or Reservations? An Economic History of American Indians.* San Francisco: Pacific Research Institute.

Anderson, Terry L., and Fred S. McChesney. 1994. "Raid or Trade? An Economic Model of Indian-White Relations." *The Journal of Law and Economics* 37 (April):39–74.

Arthur, George W. 1975. "An Introduction to the Ecology of Early Historic Communal Bison Hunting Among the Northern Plains Indians." National Museum of Man Mercury Series, Archeological Survey of Canada, paper no. 37. Ottawa: National Museums of Canada.

Baden, John, Richard Stroup, and Walter A. Thurman. 1981. "Myths, Admonitions, and Rationality: The American Indian as a Resource Manager." *Economic Inquiry* 19 (1):132–143.

Bailey, Martin J. 1992. "Approximate Optimality of Aboriginal Property Rights." *The Journal of Law and Economics* 35 (April):183–198.

Barsness, Larry. 1985. *Heads, Hides, and Horns.* Fort Worth: Texas Christian University Press.

Benson, Bruce L. 1992. "Customary Indian Law: Two Case Studies." In *Property Rights and Indian Economies*, ed. Terry L. Anderson. Lanham, Md.: Rowman and Littlefield.

Carter, Sarah. 1990. *Lost Harvests: Prairie Indian Reserve Farmers and Government Policy.* Montreal and Kingston: Magill-Queens University Press.

Cheung, Steven N. S. 1983. "The Contractual Nature of the Firm." *The Journal of Law and Economics* 26 (April):1–22.

Coase, R. II. 1937. "The Nature of the Firm." *Economica* 4:386–405.

Cresswell, Nicholas. 1928. *The Journal of Nicholas Cresswell, 1774–1777.* Introduction by A. G. Bradley. New York: Dial Press.

Dalton, George. 1961. "Economic Theory and Primitive Society." *American Anthropologist* 63 (1):1–25.

Davis, Leslie B., and Michael Wilson. 1978. "Bison Procurement and Utilization: A Symposium." *Plains Anthropologist: Journal of the Plains Conference* 23 (November):v–xxiv.

Demsetz, Harold. 1967. "Toward a Theory of Property Rights." *American Economic Review* 57 (2):347–359.

Denig, Edwin T. 1930. "Indian Tribes of the Upper Missouri." In *46th Annual Report* (1928–1929), Bureau of American Ethnology, ed. J.N.B. Hewitt. Washington, D.C.: GPO.

Driver, Harold E., and William C. Massey. 1957. *Comparative Studies of North American Indians* 47, no. 2. Philadelphia: American Philosophical Society.

Ewers, John C. 1955. "The Horse in Blackfoot Indian Culture." Bureau of American Ethnology Bulletin, no. 159. Washington, D.C.: GPO.

_____. 1958. *The Blackfeet: Raiders on the Northwestern Plains.* Norman: University of Oklahoma Press.

_____. 1969. *The Horse in Blackfoot Indian Culture.* Washington, D.C.: Smithsonian Institution Press.

Faegre, Torvald. 1979. *Tents: Architecture of the Nomads.* Garden City, N.Y.: Anchor Press.

Farb, Peter. 1968. *Man's Rise to Civilization as Shown by the Indians of North America.* New York: Dutton.

Farnham, T. P. 1843. *Travels in the Great Western Prairies, the Anahuac and Rocky Mountains, and in the Oregon Territory.* New York: Greeley and McElrath.

Fowler, Catherine S. 1986. *Handbook of North American Indians.* Vol. 11: *Great Basin.* Washington, D.C.: Smithsonian Institution Press.

Freed, Stanley A. 1960. "Changing Washo Kinship." *Anthropological Records* 14 (6):349–418.

Gregg, Josiah. 1905. *The Commerce of the Prairies, 1831–39.* Early Western Travels, 1748–1846, series editor Reuben Gold Thwaites. Cleveland: A. H. Clark.

Grinnell, George Bird. 1962. *Blackfoot Lodge Tales.* Lincoln: University of Nebraska Press.

———. [1892] 1970. *The Last Buffalo.* New York: Arno Press. First published in *Scribner's Magazine* 12 (September 1892).

Henry, Alexander, and David Thompson. 1965. *New Light on the Early History of the Greater Northwest: The Manuscript Journals of Alexander Henry and David Thompson, 1799–1814.* 2 vols. Ed. Elliott Coues. Minneapolis: Ross and Haines.

Hornaday, William T. 1889. "The Extermination of the American Bison, with a Sketch of Its Discovery and Life History." Report of the U.S. National Museum, 1887. Part 2:367–548. Washington, D.C.: GPO.

Jacobsen, R. Brooke, and Jeffrey L. Eighmy. 1980. "A Mathematical Theory of Horse Adoption on the North American Plains." Part 1. *Plains Anthropologist: Journal of the Plains Conference* 25 (90):333–341.

Johnson, Eileen, and Vance T. Holliday. 1980. "A Plainview Kill/Butchering Locale on the Llano Estacado: The Lubbock Lake Site." *Plains Anthropologist: Journal of the Plains Conference* 25 (88):89–111.

Lavender, David Sievert. 1992. *Let Me Be Free: The Nez Perce Tragedy.* New York: Doubleday.

Lowie, Robert Harry. 1982. *Indians of the Plains.* Lincoln: University of Nebraska Press.

Madsen, Brigham D. 1980. *The Northern Shoshoni.* Caldwell, Idaho: Caxton Printers.

McDougall, John. 1898. *Pathfinding on Plain and Prairie.* Toronto: William Briggs.

———. 1911. *In the Days of the Red River Rebellion.* Toronto: William Briggs.

McHugh, Tom. 1972. *The Time of the Buffalo.* New York: Knopf.

North, Douglass C. 1990. *Institutions, Institutional Change, and Economic Performance.* Cambridge: Cambridge University Press.

Posner, Richard A. 1980. "A Theory of Primitive Society, with Special Reference to Primitive Law." *The Journal of Law and Economics* 23 (April):1–54.

Reher, Charles A., and George C. Frison. 1980. "The Vore Site, 48CK302, A Stratified Buffalo Jump in the Wyoming Black Hills." *Plains Anthropologist: Journal of the Plains Conference* 25 (88):121–153.

Roe, Frank Gilbert. 1951. *The North American Buffalo: A Critical Study of the Species in Its Wild State.* Toronto: University of Toronto Press.

———. 1955. *The Indian and the Horse.* Norman: University of Oklahoma Press.

Sass, H. R. 1936. "Hoofs on the Prairie." *Country Gentleman,* July.

Schaeffer, Claude E. 1978. "The Bison River of the Blackfoot Indians." *Plains Anthropologist: Journal of the Plains Conference* 23 (82, Part 2):243–248.

Schultz, James Willard. 1907. *My Life as an Indian.* Boston: Houghton Mifflin.

Shimkin, Demitri B. 1986. "Eastern Shoshone." *Handbook of North American Indians.* Vol. 11:308–335. Washington, D.C.: Smithsonian Institution Press.

Simpson, Sir George. 1847. *Narrative of a Journey Around the World in the Years 1841 and 1842.* 2 vols. London: H. Colburn.

Smith, Vernon L. 1993. "Humankind in Prehistory: Economy, Ecology, and Institutions." In *The Political Economy of Customs and Culture,* eds. Terry L. Anderson and Randy T. Simmons. Lanham, Md.: Rowman and Littlefield.

Steward, Julian H. 1934. "Ethnography of the Owens Valley Paiute." *American Archaeology and Ethnology* 33 (1):233–324.

_____. 1938. *Basin-Plateau Aboriginal Sociopolitical Groups.* Smithsonian Institution, Bureau of American Ethnology, bulletin 120. Washington, D.C.: GPO.

_____. 1941. "Cultural Element Distributions: XIII Nevada Shoshoni." *Anthropological Records* 4 (2):209–259.

Trenholm, Virginia Cole, and Maurine Carley. 1964. *The Shoshonis: Sentinels of the Rockies.* Norman: University of Oklahoma Press.

White, Jon Manchip. 1979. *Everyday Life of North American Indians.* New York: Indian Head Books.

Wissler, Clark. 1966. *Indians of the United States.* New York: Doubleday.

Wyman, Walker D. 1945. *The Wild Horse of the West.* Lincoln: University of Nebraska Press.

Part Two

Trade and Colonial Economies

Introduction

Intertwining Economies

KAREN CLAY

The chapters in this section examine eighteenth-century frontier trade between Native Americans and intermediaries. Native Americans brought furs and other animal skins to an intermediary, typically a merchant or a trading post, and received in return manufactured goods such as rifles, cloth, and axes. Voluntary exchange is presumed in economics to be mutually beneficial; otherwise it would not occur. This exchange, therefore, both moved the Native Americans to a higher level of utility and generated profit for the intermediaries. It also made use of the two parties' comparative advantages in production. Native Americans, for instance, were skilled hunters and maintained a locational advantage because they lived in the interior, closer to the animals. The strengths of the merchants and the firms that owned the trading posts, in contrast, lay in their ability to mediate in the market, which involved the purchase of goods suitable for sale at the posts and the acquisition, storage, and delivery of furs or skins to the market.

Frontier trade, unlike most of the trade in the bigger cities, took place between a producer and an intermediary. Native Americans active in the region around Hudson Bay and in South Carolina produced furs and skins through hunting and then took these to a merchant or a trading post where they exchanged them for goods. In cities, production and consumption were increasingly separate—individuals sold their goods or services on the market and then went to shops, emporiums, and general stores to make purchases from the available stocks of household goods, cloth, tools and hardware, alcohol, food, and spices. This separation was not as prevalent in the South, where many planters sold their produce—tobacco, indigo, or rice—through the merchants who supplied them with goods. The structure of trade differed from that of the frontier, however, because planters consigned rather than sold their produce to the merchants. Consignment meant that planters received the London market price, less commission and related costs, rather than the value of the goods in the local market.

The dominant mode of exchange was barter rather than the exchange of goods for money or a promise of future payment. Native Americans could have obtained specie in exchange for their pelts or skins but usually chose not to. Merchants and the managers of trading posts preferred this practice, since it was more profitable if the Native Americans took goods in trade. A frontier merchant or trading establishment might, depending on their relationship with the customers, also extend credit. Frontier merchants in Mexican California, for example, regularly allowed customers to buy goods on credit. Credit was also a feature of small-town trade even outside the frontier. The intermediaries' willingness to extend credit depended, not surprisingly, on whether they thought that they would be able to collect when the debt came due. This, in turn, depended on the existence of either an environment in which reputation was sufficiently important that individuals would repay their debts voluntarily or one in which courts could quickly and inexpensively enforce payment.

Trade around Hudson Bay and in South Carolina, like most frontier trade, was not competitive. Economists usually focus on competitive markets, in which there are many buyers and sellers. On the frontier, however, many Native Americans traded with just one or two intermediaries. These intermediaries offered Native Americans lower prices for furs or skins and charged them higher prices for goods than would have been the case in a competitive equilibrium. The extent to which these prices exceeded competitive prices depended on whether the intermediary was a monopolist or an oligopolist. In Chapter 4, Ann M. Carlos and Frank D. Lewis document the increase in the price of furs and the relative fall in the price of goods that occurred when the Hudson's Bay Company's monopoly was broken at York Factory. French entry into the market provided additional competition, which benefited the Native Americans who received higher prices for their furs. In Chapter 5, Edward Murphy discusses the fall in the value of deerskins that occurred after the British victory in the Seven Years War. This victory, by eliminating Spanish and French competition in the market for deerskins, gave the British monopoly power in the deerskin trade.

Furs and skins made their way from the frontier to port cities on the coast and from there to world markets for sale. Deerskins and beaver pelts were a subset of the staple items such as furs, rice, indigo, and tobacco exported from British North America. Exporters shipped the furs and skins east to European markets and later west to Chinese markets, where they commanded high prices as the raw material for hats and other luxury goods.

Trade near Hudson Bay and in South Carolina was part of a more general pattern of frontier expansion throughout North and South America during the colonial and postcolonial periods. A continual search for new sources of furs and skins for world markets drove this expansion. When traders reached the western coast of North America, for instance, they discovered that Native Americans and a small number of local trappers could supply both sea otter pelts and furs from inland animals such as beaver. When political disruption during the early nineteenth century limited the supply of cattle products from South America, traders, who through the fur trade were familiar with the cattle herds maintained by the Catholic missions, began to develop California as a source of hides and tallow.

Trade in furs and skins, like that in most goods traded internationally, was brokered by intermediaries. The merchants and firms who came into possession of the furs and skins at the port cities rarely traveled personally with their goods. Instead, they shipped them, often on consignment, to a merchant who operated in the desired market. Using other merchants as sales agents was efficient because it allowed the intermediary to diversify the risk of shipwreck or piracy by sending smaller shipments to several different ports. Further, it allowed him to make use of the other merchant's or firm's specialized knowledge of the local market. The fact that another merchant handled the sale of goods left open the possibility of mismanagement or fraud, and merchants sometimes employed family members in trade to reduce the risk of opportunistic behavior. Large firms such as the Hudson's Bay Company, however, bypassed this particular problem by maintaining employees on both sides of the ocean who supervised shipping from the frontier to Europe.

Unlike the sources of many of the other goods that British North America supplied to world markets, the wild animals whose furs and skins were desired were common property. Animals as well as timber, oil, and other natural resources can be depleted. Economists have found that private ownership of these assets leads to optimal use or harvesting. Cattle or sheep ranchers, for instance, usually sell only the increase in their herds and not the entire stock. Similarly, timber companies do not cut their entire stock of trees in a single year; instead, they harvest only a small fraction of the stock. If an asset is common property, however, then harvesting is rarely optimal. Fisheries are a good example of an asset that is common property. Since no one owns the fish, individuals have little if any incentive to preserve the stock of fish so there will be ample supplies in the future. Harvesting fish this season generates personal profit, whereas preservation generates profit for some unknown person the next season. These incentives have led to the drastic depletion of stocks of fish such as cod, sardines, and salmon.

Carlos and Lewis outline the reasons why beaver were common property and the implications of this for the beaver population. While the Hudson's Bay Company had a monopoly in the region, they had an incentive to conserve the beaver population. Despite the fact that beaver were common property, the managers of the trading posts could indirectly control the number of furs harvested in a given year through the price that they paid for furs. Lower prices induced less hunting. French competition in York Factory drove up prices, which benefited Native Americans in the short run. Ironically, this increase in prices also led to overharvesting and the eventual destruction of the beaver population. Although Murphy does not focus on this point, decreases in the size of the deer population as a result of competition may have been a reason why Native Americans in South Carolina began to switch from hunting to raising cotton in the early nineteenth century.

By examining Native Americans' economic activity, these chapters seek to understand two major puzzles in their economic history: Native Americans' failure to conserve the beaver stocks and their dispossession from tribal lands. The traditional historical explanations for these phenomena hinge on the irrationality of Native Americans and on the rise of the capitalist economy. Carlos and Lewis show that the decline of the beaver was a result not of irrationality but, rather, of overharvesting in response to the common pool problem. Competition in some areas prevented the Hudson's Bay Company from keeping prices at a level that would control overharvesting. Murphy brings to bear evidence on a number of empirical questions related to Native American dispossession in the Southeast. He finds that their terms of trade were eroding and that although Native American economic activity was sizable, deerskin exports were not as important as rice for the South Carolina economy. He focuses, in particular, on the fact that Native Americans responded rationally to economic incentives by producing more when prices were high, less when prices were low, and eventually abandoning hunting in favor of raising cotton.

4

Property Rights and Competition in the Depletion of the Beaver

Native Americans and the Hudson's Bay Company, 1700–1763

ANN M. CARLOS AND FRANK D. LEWIS

The trade in Canadian beaver was based on European demand. Furs were shipped from Hudson Bay or down the St. Lawrence River and across the Atlantic, eventually to be transformed into the high-fashion felt hats that remained popular in England and on the Continent for almost two centuries. The beaver was thus part of an interdependent trade that encompassed North America and Europe. What happened in the market for the final product, moreover, played back into the primary resource market, helping to shape Native American responses and determining the level of extraction of the resource. To point out the international nature of the Canadian fur trade is not new. In their seminal works, Harold Innis (1956) and E. E. Rich (1958) focused on the conduct and behavior of the European companies and on the geographical spread of the fur trade within North America. Although they acknowledged that many aspects of the trade were determined by Indian custom and practice, they gave the Indians a peripheral role. In contrast, much of the recent research treats Native Americans as central players rather than passive agents in the trade.[1] Clearly this is as it should be. After all, it was the Indians who hunted, trapped, and traded furs to the Europeans.

   With the increasing recognition of the Indians' role in the trade, an important issue has emerged. Historians have long known that the geographical expansion of the fur trade was related to depletion; but recently the questions have become why and to what extent did the Native peoples deplete the fur resource upon which much of their livelihood was based? In Carlos and Lewis 1993 we tried to address these issues by analyzing the extent, pattern, and determinants of beaver harvesting within the hinterlands of three Hudson's Bay Company trading posts during the period 1700 to 1763. We asked whether the observed patterns could be explained in terms of beaver population densities and the economic variables facing the Indians. Not surprisingly, we found that the introduction of a commercial trade led to a fall in beaver populations, an outcome that does not necessarily imply depletion,[2] but in two of the hinterlands—those served by Fort Albany and York Factory—there were serious declines in stocks caused by overharvesting, particularly in the latter part of the period.

Historians have been concerned with these and other depletions of fur-bearing animals by Indians. Calvin Martin (1978) specifically rejected economic factors and looked for an answer within Native American cultural and spiritual life. He claimed that "the mutually courteous relationship between man and animal" had broken down (1978, 19). Although Martin's analysis generated considerable debate, much of it revolved around the terms of his analysis (Krech 1981). Here we take a view that he specifically rejected and argue that issues relating to the ownership and control of the animal population were central to depletion. It is well known from the natural resource literature that in a world with common property rights and open access, there will tend to be overexploitation because it is in no one's interest to take a long-run perspective and conserve the resource (Berkes et al. 1989; Feeny 1995). The patterns of depletion in the Fort Albany and York Factory hinterlands argue that the Indians were operating under such a common property rights regime. But the Indians were not the only group involved in the trade; the Hudson's Bay Company and French traders purchased furs and sold them on the European market. Their relationship to each other was also crucial in determining the level of exploitation. In fact, overharvesting occurred only where there was competition between French and English traders and a high price in the European fur market.

We try to explain this and other aspects of the historical record in terms of the optimal strategies of the participants. For example, where the Hudson's Bay Company had a monopoly, its best policy, even in the face of rising fur prices in Europe, was to pay low prices to the Indians to ensure beaver stocks remained close to or above maximum sustained yield levels. In the presence of competition and rising prices in Europe, however, its optimal strategy was to raise prices to the Indians to prevent the French from capturing too much of the trade, despite the adverse effect on beaver stocks. Of course Native Americans did the actual trapping, so their reaction to rising fur prices was central to any overharvesting that occurred.

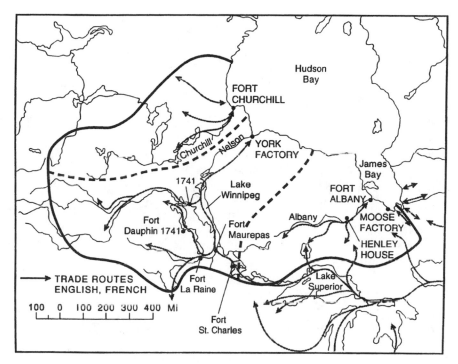

Map 4.1   *Hudson's Bay Company Trading Hinterlands: Fort Albany, York Factory, Fort Churchill*

Our treatment of depletion begins in the next section with a description of the trends in the beaver population in three Hudson's Bay Company hinterlands: those served by Fort Albany, York Factory, and Fort Churchill (see Map 4.1). To help explain these trends we review the nature of Native American property rights in regards to fur-bearing animals; then we analyze the profit-maximizing strategies of the Hudson's Bay Company in the presence and absence of French competition. Finally, we discuss the implications of our analysis in relation to what was happening in the European fur market.

The Estimated Beaver Population in the Hudson Bay Drainage Basin

Much of the fur trade literature to date has been qualitative, but the lack of quantitative analysis has not been occasioned by an absence of data. The Hudson's Bay Company preserved its trading post records and in Carlos and Lewis 1993 we used these records to determine trends in the beaver popula-

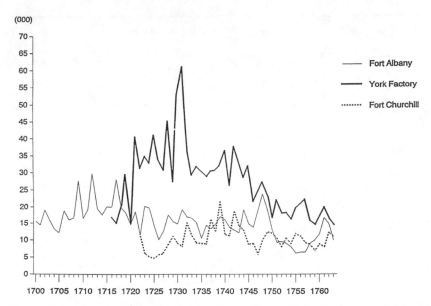

Figure 4.1   *Beaver Skins Traded at Fort Albany, York Factory, and Churchill Hinterlands, 1701/1716/1722–1763*

tion from 1700 to 1763. Each trading post reported annual returns on three categories of beaver pelts: whole parchment, half parchment, and coat. Whole parchment and coat pelts sold for the same price, whereas half-parchment pelts, which were from smaller animals or those trapped during the summer, sold for one-half that price.[3] By summing over the three categories, we obtained an estimate of the number of beaver killed by Indian trappers and traded to the Hudson's Bay Company (see Figure 4.1). These numbers provide the basis of our beaver population estimates for each of the hinterlands—Fort Albany, York Factory, and Fort Churchill.[4]

The Fort Albany hinterland was roughly 600,000 square kilometers and included an area within about 100 kilometers of the coast where the company faced no competition; however, this region, consisting of boreal forest, could only support low beaver densities. Further south, where the environment was more suitable and beaver densities were very much higher, the company faced the presence of French traders, especially after 1720. The increasing French presence influenced the magnitude of the English trade. From 1700 to 1720, returns from Fort Albany averaged 20,000 pelts, but with wide year-to-year fluctuations. After 1720 the number of beaver traded declined to an average of about 15,000. Returns remained fairly stable until the late 1740s, when there were some unusually large harvests. Following these years, however, the trade fell precipitously to about 6,000 pelts annually. Returns were low through the 1760s despite a modest recovery in the early part of the decade.

The York Factory hinterland, at nearly 1 million square kilometers, was roughly two-thirds greater than the area served by Fort Albany, but a larger proportion of this hinterland was boreal forest, implying again fewer beaver per square kilometer. Unlike Fort Albany, which faced French competition early in the eighteenth century, York Factory was protected by distance until the 1730s. In 1732 the French established Fort St. Charles on Lake of the Woods, and in 1734 they built Fort Maurepas at the mouth of the Red River (see Map 4.1). These posts, both located near the southeastern limit of the York Factory hinterland, provided some competition, but it was not until several years later and the building of four additional trading posts that large numbers of furs were diverted to Montreal. By 1755 the French accounted for 40 percent of the region's trade.

The pattern of beaver skins traded at York Factory from 1717 to 1763 not only reflects the increasing French competition but is also strongly suggestive of depletion. In the early years 1717–1730, returns were increasing but highly variable, consistent with an emerging trade; then in the 1730s the trade stabilized at about 30,000 furs annually. The first break in the pattern came in the early 1740s. The French built Fort La Raine in 1738 and three years later established two more posts, both in the heart of the York Factory hinterland. Surprisingly, given the greater competition, trade at York Factory increased substantially to an average of 34,000 furs over the period 1740–1743. Indeed, the 1742 return was the largest since the French had established any trade in the region. For the remainder of the 1740s the trade declined to under 30,000 furs, and even these smaller harvests could not be sustained. From 1750 to 1763, an average of 18,000 pelts were traded annually.

Fort Churchill was the farthest west and north and therefore was protected by distance from significant French competition. It served a large hinterland (500,000 square kilometers), but because of its northerly location, the region consisted mainly of boreal forest with its consequent low beaver densities. The volume of beaver skins traded in the early years was very low, about 5,000 pelts from 1723–1727, but as the Fort became established, trade increased. During the 1730s returns averaged 12,000 per year. There was a modest decline in the 1750s, but in the 1760s volume returned to the earlier levels. What distinguishes Fort Churchill from the other posts is the comparative stability, in the long run, of fur returns. The lack of French trading in the region almost certainly accounts for part of the difference in harvest patterns, but the absence of competition may also have influenced Hudson's Bay Company strategy in exploiting the beaver stocks.

To derive the beaver population in each region, we combined the trade data with a model of biological resource extraction.[5] We used data from the

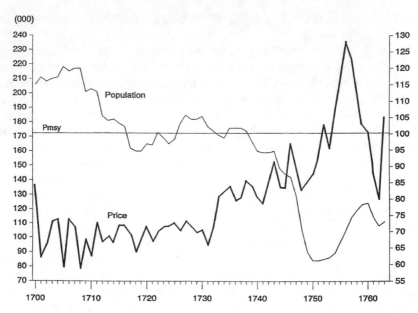

Figure 4.2   *Fur Prices and Simulated Beaver Population: Fort Albany, 1700–1763*

beaver ecology literature, including number of kits per litter and mortality in the absence of trapping, and recent Canadian provincial field reports on beaver densities. These allowed us to estimate natural growth rates of the beaver population in each hinterland and, in conjunction with the trade data, to simulate the population and derive the biomass consistent with a maximum sustained yield (Carlos and Lewis 1993).

According to our simulation, the beaver population in the Fort Albany hinterland declined over the period 1700 to 1717, which is the expected pattern for a resource that has not yet been fully exploited; but by 1717 the beaver population appeared to have reached an equilibrium (see Figure 4.2). For the next twenty years the stock remained at levels roughly consistent with maximum sustained yield management. In the 1740s, however, a combination of greater French competition and unabated trading by the Hudson's Bay Company began to deplete the stock. This was especially true of the period 1747–1749, when Fort Albany received an average of 20,500 pelts, which was a larger harvest than in any of the preceding twenty years. These harvests, in particular, devastated the beaver colonies, reducing the stock to about half maximum sustained yield levels.

The simulated beaver population in the York Factory region is described in Figure 4.3. From an assumed population of 275,000 in 1716, we have the population declining to about 240,000 in the 1730s, which is roughly equal

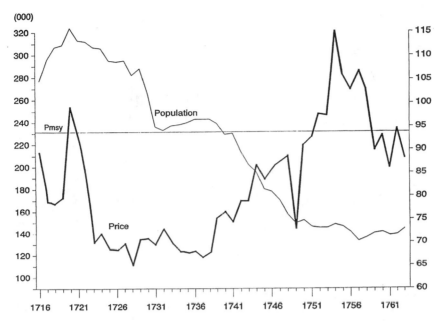

Figure 4.3   *Fur Prices and Simulated Beaver Population: York Factory, 1716–1763*

to the population consistent with maximum sustained yield management. The falling population during this period, although partly a consequence of some very large harvests, does not indicate overharvesting of the stock. It simply represents the usual pattern observed when a resource has previously been underexploited. With the increase in French competition starting in 1738, however, the beaver population became severely depleted. This was not simply because the French were taking more furs from the region. The number of furs traded to the Hudson's Bay Company also increased. According to our simulation, the beaver population during the 1740s declined to just above 60 percent of the level consistent with a maximum sustained yield, and these low levels persisted through the 1750s, although there was a modest recovery in the early 1760s.

Unlike Fort Albany and York Factory, the third post—Fort Churchill—was too far west and north to face significant competition from the French. The simulated beaver population in the Fort Churchill hinterland was much more stable than beaver stocks at the other trading posts (see Figure 4.4). From 1722 to 1742, population fell from an assumed 84,000 to the maximum sustained yield level of 70,000.[6] Although declining somewhat below that level for a few years, population climbed back. This is in direct contrast to the behavior of population in the Fort Albany and York Factory hinter-

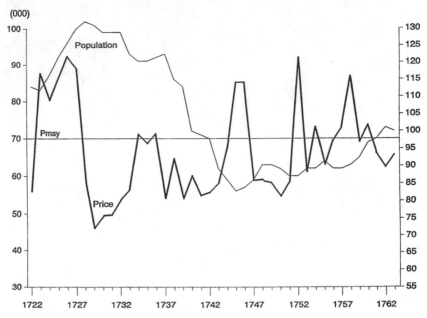

Figure 4.4   *Fur Prices and Simulated Beaver Population: Fort Churchill, 1722–1763*

lands. The lack of a French trade was almost certainly a direct factor in explaining the stability, but, in addition, the fact that the Hudson's Bay Company had a monopoly in the region led it to adopt a strategy that discouraged depletion.

Because the hunting and trapping was done by Native Americans, the
Hudson's Bay Company could only influence the size of the beaver harvest
indirectly by adjusting fur prices at the posts. We have estimated, from company records, the prices paid to Indians. Throughout the period 1700 to
1763, prices were based on the company's official standard, which remained
constant over time and was roughly the same across posts. The actual price
received by the Indians, however, rarely equaled that standard because post
managers were encouraged to increase their net returns by offering the Indians less in terms of trade goods. When this variance occurred, managers
recorded the difference as an "overplus" in the accounts.[7] At the same time,
the ceremonial nature of the trading process required that managers provide
gifts to the Indians. These gifts were expenses additional to the value of
goods traded directly for furs. When the overplus exceeded expenses, Indians received less than the official standard for their furs, and when the re-
verse was true, they received more. Because both the overplus and the expenses are reported in the annual accounts of each post, it is possible to
derive a price series for each area.

As is evident in Figures 4.2, 4.3, and 4.4, there is a connection between the prices the Indians received for their furs and the size of the beaver stocks. In the Fort Albany region, we estimate that from 1717 to 1730, when there was almost no change in fur prices, the beaver population was stable or rising; whereas from the 1730s to the early 1750s, when fur prices increased by 40 percent, the beaver population declined by 50 percent. This negative relationship between fur prices and beaver stocks can also be observed in the York Factory data. In that region, the simulated population fell from an average of 242,000 in the 1730s to 146,000 in the period 1751–1755, while fur prices at the trading post were raised from 0.7 to 1.0 of Made Beavers. Equally suggestive is the evidence from Fort Churchill. In that region, we estimate that the beaver population remained fairly stable after the early 1740s. Although there is a slight upward trend in the price series, prices are consistent with that stability.

The effect of a rising price at the trading post on the number of beaver harvested depends crucially on how Native Americans responded. We assume that their trapping effort was positively affected, since they returned to that effort. Others, such as Arthur J. Ray (1974), have argued that Indians reduced trapping in the face of rising prices.[8] This behavior, however, seems inconsistent with the fact that trapping was just one of a number of productive Indian activities; moreover, it does not conform with the positive short-run relationship that we observe between prices and the number of beaver traded. Using a wide range of effort elasticities, we found that price increases in the 1730s and 1740s accounted for much, perhaps all, of the estimated decline in the beaver population in the Fort Albany and York Factory regions (Carlos and Lewis 1993).

This analysis takes us some distance toward explaining the pattern and extent of depletion, but it does not really tell us why the prices paid at the posts were rising, other than to suggest English-French competition was somehow involved; neither does it explain the reaction of Native Americans to the price changes. We now try to understand more fully the nature of these relationships: first, by considering the forces that shaped Native American reactions to price, and second, by examining how the Hudson's Bay Company responded to changes in the English fur market and how those responses were influenced by the degree of French competition.

From Utrecht to Paris:
Implications for Native Property Rights

The Hudson's Bay Company was established in 1670, becoming yet another player in the world fur market.[9] Its first forty years were stormy, as competition with the French became an extension of the ongoing European conflict. Each side periodically captured its rival's posts in an effort to gain the upper hand, but with the Treaty of Utrecht in 1713, the Hudson Bay basin was declared British territory, temporarily bringing an end to military actions. The French were now caught between the English posts on Hudson Bay and English activity along the Hudson River in the east. This created a tension that led to political alliances with various Indian tribes. Indeed, it was the rivalry, not just between the Europeans but also among the tribes who traded with them, that was so damaging to the beaver stocks.

But was overharvesting inevitable? The answer to this question depends in part on who had access to the resource and what the structure of property rights was.[10] Depletion tends to take place in an environment of open access where it is in no one's interest to conserve the resource. By contrast, private ownership, through its ability to control access, allows an individual to reap the benefit of any conservation measures. Although the issue is usually set up starkly in terms of open access versus private property, a communal system can also lead to conservation (Feeny et al. 1990). Of course, for any system to be effective, the rights of the individual or the community have to be specified and enforced, and this may require the evolution of social and cultural institutions that can respond to changing market and ecological conditions.

Harold Demsetz (1967) has argued that the commercial fur trade gave Indians an incentive to move to a more clearly specified structure of property rights, since the new market for beaver increased not just the current value of each animal but also the value of the beaver stock in the future. But Native groups would restrict hunting only if they had rights to those future animals. Private property was not required, but it was necessary at least that a specified area come under the control of some single group. In fact, despite some statements to the contrary, there appears to have been no social or cultural reasons preventing Native Americans from establishing such a communal system of property rights.

Appealing to the work of Eleanor Leacock, Demsetz (1967) pointed to the Montagnais, in Labrador, who introduced land tenure arrangements in response to changes in the value of the underlying resource. And William Cronon, quoting fur trader Joseph Chadwick, described how in the eighteenth century, Maine Indians divided their land into inheritable hunting territories: "Their hunting ground and streams were all parcelled out to certain families, time out of mind [in the distant past]" (1983, 105). There is also the example of the Plains Cree, who, in the nineteenth century, closed access to the buffalo herds in order to preserve the stock. As John Milloy put it: "A sealed country was not only an attempt to harbour a dwindling resource, but also a policy to deal with that resource as a now-valuable commercial commodity" (1991, 66). If, as this evidence suggests, Native Americans were able to adapt their property rights structures to preserve and conserve the resource base, the question of Indian depletion of the beaver becomes even more puzzling.

John McManus (1972) may have part of the answer. He has argued that the ability of a tribe to establish private property was attenuated by what he calls the "Good Samaritan" principle in Indian culture. Survival came first, and given the precarious nature of the food base this meant that at any time individuals were permitted to enter another's territory to hunt for food. Such a policy made implementing a system of purely individual property rights much more difficult, but it did not rule out a community-based system. At issue here is the cost of introducing such a framework in relation to the future benefits. Unfortunately, the commercial fur trade, which did create a benefit to private property, also had effects that raised the cost of establishing such property rights.

Trade with rival Europeans was a source of tension among the tribes of the St. Lawrence and Great Lakes basin, and warfare was common: "Originally conducted primarily for reasons of prestige, revenge, and religion, warfare gradually changed in purpose and increased in intensity after European contact" (Harris 1987, plate 35). The result of this conflict was the breakup and dispersion of many tribes. In the mid-seventeenth century, the Iroquois confederacy first scattered the Huron tribes, then the Petun, the Nipissing, and the Neutral. Fearing the Iroquois, many other groups fled west and north into Algonquian and Nipissing territory. In the late 1660s the French burned a number of Mohawk villages and forced a peace on the Iroquois confederacy, but by the 1680s war broke out again as the Iroquois, Mohawk, and Mahican were aided by the English (Harris 1987, plate 38). Although a formal peace was again imposed, the dispersal of tribes continued. In 1700, for example, the resumption of hostilities by the Dakota caused much of the native population to move toward the lower Great Lakes, changing once again the pattern of contact between English and French traders. This pattern of conflict continued through the 1720s and 1730s. For the next fifteen years there was calm, but then English and French traders became involved in the Seven Years War, usually referred to in the American theater as the French and Indian Wars. Once again there was turmoil in the interior of the country with its attendant migration of Native groups. The Treaty of Paris restored peace in 1763, brought the cession of New France to Britain, and ended a significant French military presence in North America.

Thus the hundred years prior to 1763 saw the forced and voluntary migration of Native groups in the St. Lawrence, Great Lakes, and Hudson Bay basins. These migrations, moreover, were not into vacant lands but, rather, into regions occupied by groups already involved with the fur trade. The result was not only a mixing of cultures and languages, and sometimes further conflict, but also an environment in which property rights to the stock of fur-bearing animals was blurred or nonexistent. It was in this climate that depletion of beaver stocks took place; for even though it would have been in the

Indians' interest to conserve, no one group had the security of tenure necessary to make this the optimal strategy. Conservation on the part of any group
probably meant reducing current consumption and enhancing the future
consumption of a rival. Indeed, it was only after 1763 that Native Americans
were in a position to establish more-secure rights to the beaver resource.

The ability to form new tenure arrangements in response to a commercial
fur trade was further exacerbated by the demographic collapse and disease
consequent on Native American contact with Europeans. Territorial rights
and responsibilities within Native society tended to be vested in the person
of the sachem, that is, the symbolic leader, of the group. It was he, as
William Cronon (1983) pointed out, who arranged agreements both within
the village and with other communities. This social structure was brought
under severe pressure as a result of the waves of epidemics following the arrival of the Europeans. The loss of large numbers of people led to social upheaval as some communities were wiped out and others had to make new
political alliances. While this demographic collapse was appalling in its own
right, the disorganization and disintegration of communities greatly increased the cost of introducing a new property rights structure. As a secondary effect, the turmoil allowed those with ambition the opportunity to
increase their political power, but doing so required the accumulation of
trade goods for distribution among supporters. Trade goods could be used
to gain allies (Cronon 1983, 93–96). The inducement was to harvest at a
high rate.[11] Thus the new political and social reality made it difficult to establish the property rights that might have stabilized the harvest and con-
served the resource for the future.

Instead, conflict, migration, social divisions, and the "Good Samaritan"
principle together combined to produce a regime in which Indians could
place little value on the future stock of the animals they hunted. Native
Americans were forced to operate under open access, a system that was not
in their long-run interest. But despite this, the animal populations might still
have been maintained. The European traders, especially the Hudson's Bay
Company, could control the harvests and therefore the animal stocks
through the price they paid to the Indians for furs. So even though the Indians may have regarded the animals as common property, depletion was not
inevitable and, indeed, did not always occur, as we demonstrated in the case
of Fort Churchill. But a full analysis of these issues requires that we turn
from the Indian trappers to the policies of the Europeans.

Optimal Pricing Policies of
the Hudson's Bay Company

The Hudson's Bay Company did not harvest beaver directly; it purchased
furs from the Indians. The company's only control over the harvest was

through what it offered the Indians for their furs in terms of trade goods, or possibly through its decision not to purchase certain furs, such as smaller pelts or pelts of animals trapped during the summer.[12] Naturally, the level of the harvest was of serious concern to the Hudson's Bay Company, since its revenue stream was related to the long-term viability of the beaver stock. How the company translated this concern into policy is what we explore next.

Basically, we assume that the company followed a pricing strategy that maximized the present value of the stream of profits at each trading post. The present value of the stream of profits depended on the available biomass (the stock of beaver) and the actual harvest. The harvest, in turn, was affected by both the biomass and the level of effort expended by the Indians. The direction of causation, moreover, went both ways, since the harvest affected the future size of the biomass. The general solution to the problem of maximizing long-run profits turns out to be one in which the natural growth of the beaver population is closely related to the discount rate and the price of furs in Europe. Crucial as well is the nature of the market. The Hudson's Bay Company's optimal pricing policy differed markedly depending on whether it had a monopoly in a region or was forced to compete with the French.

In the monopoly case, the company's profit each period was simply the difference between the revenue it received in Europe for the total fur harvest and what it paid to the Indians, less trading and transport expenses (Carlos and Lewis 1996). In this case, even in the face of very high prices in Europe, the smallest biomass consistent with long-run profit maximization was one in which the slope of the natural growth function of beaver equaled the discount rate, in other words, a biomass just below the maximum sustained yield level. This biomass is consistent with only one size of harvest, implying that once the beaver population approached the optimum, changes in the European price should have had little effect on the price received by the Indians. The monopoly solution shows that even in the absence of private property rights among the Indians, depletion was not inevitable. Indeed, it was in the interest of the Hudson's Bay Company through its pricing policy at the posts to maintain the animal stock at levels close to or above the biological optimum.

However, in two of the hinterlands, those served by Fort Albany and York Factory, the French were trading actively during at least part of the period. This competition affected the Hudson's Bay Company's pricing strategy in two ways (Carlos and Lewis 1996): First, it reduced the benefit to the company of preserving the stock of beaver, since part of the gain would be lost to the French. More important, it encouraged the company to raise prices at the posts in order to reduce the share of the trade going to the French. French inland penetration of the market depended on the difference between the price of furs in Europe and the price being paid to the Indians. In the absence of a price response from the Hudson's Bay Company, a rising price in Europe meant the French would capture a larger share of the trade.

On the other hand, if the company did respond by raising prices at its posts, the outcome would be increased harvests in short run but lower beaver stocks in the longer term. The Hudson's Bay Company's optimal response, not surprisingly, involved a compromise between the objectives of market share and the beaver stock. It meant raising fur prices to the extent that some depletion occurred and some market share was lost.

Hudson's Bay Company Pricing Policy and the European Fur Market

Whatever level of competition the Hudson's Bay Company faced, ultimately it was the fur market in Europe that determined prices at the bay. And it is to that market that we now turn. With the start of operations in 1670, the Hudson's Bay Company began importing furs into England. Although this was a new venture for the joint-stock company, the larger European fur market was already well developed. Supplies had been coming from New France, the American colonies, northern Europe, and Russia (Lawson 1943). What the Hudson's Bay Company had to offer this market was a supply of top-quality beaver pelts. All fur was classified as either fancy or staple. Fancy furs were those demanded for the beauty and luster of the pelts, which were then fashioned into garments. Staple furs were demanded for their wool, which could be transformed into felt for use by the hatting industry.

Beaver was the best of the staple furs. Its pelt has a double coating of hair: short, soft, barbed hair close to the skin, protected by longer, stiffer, smoother hair called guard hair. Only the short hair can be felted, and one production problem is to separate it from the guard hairs and the pelt. By the last quarter of the seventeenth century the Russian technology for combing pelts was known in England.[13] Separation of the two types of hairs also occurred when the Indians wore the beaver pelts as clothing. Over the course of a year the pelt would become greasier and more pliable, and eventually the guard hairs fell out. This type of pelt was known as *castor gras*, or coat beaver, to differentiate it from a freshly caught pelt, which was known as *castor sec*, or parchment beaver. A third category of beaver pelt, cub, was *castor sec* but from smaller or inferior animals.

A price series for parchment, coat, and cub beaver sold in England is given in Table 4.1. These prices are based on fur sales to individual purchasers as reported in the company's *Fur Price Book* continuously from 1735 and erratically in the *Grand Journal* prior to that date. Along with the date of each sale, the company also indicated whether the furs had been "damaged." Our price series are restricted to nondamaged skins. Unfortunately, we could not find fur prices for individual types of pelts covering the decade from 1726–1736, but the *Minute Books*, although less complete, give a good idea of the price trend in the missing years.

TABLE 4.1   Price of Beaver Pelts in Britain, 1713–1763 (shillings per skin)

Year	Parchment	Coat	Average[a]	Year	Parchment	Coat	Average[a]
1713	5.21	4.62	5.03	1739	8.51	7.11	8.05
1714	5.24	7.86	5.66	1740	8.44	6.66	7.88
1715	4.88		5.49	1741	8.30	6.83	7.84
1716	4.68	8.81	5.16	1742	7.72	6.41	7.36
1717	5.29	8.37	5.65	1743	8.98	6.74	8.27
1718	4.77	7.81	5.22	1744	9.18	6.61	8.52
1719	5.30	6.86	5.51	1745	9.76	6.08	8.76
1720	5.31	6.05	5.38	1746	12.73	7.18	10.88
1721	5.27	5.79	5.29	1747	10.68	6.99	9.50
1722	4.55	4.97	4.55	1748	9.27	6.22	8.44
1723	8.54	5.56	7.84	1749	11.27	6.49	9.77
1724	7.47	5.97	7.17	1750	17.11	8.42	14.00
1725	5.82	6.62	5.88	1751	14.31	10.42	12.90
1726	5.41	7.49	5.83	1752	12.94	10.18	11.84
1727			7.22	1753	10.71	11.97	10.87
1728			8.13	1754	12.19	12.68	12.08
1729			9.56	1755	12.05	12.04	11.99
1730			8.71	1756	13.46	12.02	12.84
1731			6.27	1757	12.59	11.60	12.17
1732			7.12	1758	13.07	11.32	12.49
1733			8.07	1759	15.99		14.68
1734			7.39	1760	13.37	13.06	13.22
1735			8.33	1761	10.94	13.03	11.36
1736	8.72	7.07	8.38	1762	13.17	16.33	13.83
1737	7.94	6.46	7.50	1763	16.33	17.56	16.34
1738	8.95	6.47	8.32				

[a]A weighted average of the prices of parchment, coat, and cub beaver. Weights are based on the trade in these types of furs at Fort Albany (basing the average on York Factory or Fort Churchill gives similar values). The prices of coat and parchment beaver were generally close and were about double the price of cub beaver. Prices of the individual types of pelts are not available for the years 1727 to 1735. Prices in the table are averages based on the company's *Minute Books*. A complete listing of prices and output weights for the three posts is available from the authors.

Source: Hudson's Bay Company Archives (microfilm copy), *Post Records*, MG20B (Public Archives of Canada, Ottawa).

Over the entire period there seem to have been three price episodes: 1713–1725, 1725–1745, and 1745–1763. The years from 1713 to 1725 were ones of stability, with prices generally between five and six shillings per pelt. In the late 1720s prices jumped to the range seven to nine shillings; then, starting in 1746, parchment rose to over twelve shillings and stayed high to the end of our period. These price increases were driven by rising demand. Exports of beaver hats nearly tripled between 1720 and 1750, and there was a similar increase in the export of felt hats made with a combination of beaver and other pelts (Lawson 1943, appendix 1).

The impact of the rising price of furs in Europe on the Hudson's Bay Company's North American activities fits well with the implications of our analysis. At Fort Albany, a post that had faced French competition since 1700, prices paid for furs remained low as long as the fur market in Europe was weak, but once the price in England began to rise there was a quick response in the form of higher prices to the Indians (see Figure 4.2). From 1731 to 1733 the price index jumped from 66 to 81, and eventually peaked in 1756 at 128. The experience at York Factory was slightly different, in that the Hudson's Bay Company reacted by raising prices at the post only after 1738, the year the French began setting up trading posts in the interior of the region (see Figure 4.3). The delay of seven years in comparison to Fort Albany is further evidence that it was competition that moved the company from a pricing strategy that preserved the beaver stock to one that led to depletion. The price at Fort Churchill provides additional support for this view. Fort Churchill was too isolated to face competition, and there the price changes in the European market had almost no impact on the price Indians received.

Conclusion

There has been considerable debate on why and to what extent the Indians depleted the stock of beaver. We examined how Native American social organization and the relationships between the European and North American markets helped determine the level of harvesting and resource depletion. Three factors seem to have played especially important roles: competition between the French and the Hudson's Bay Company, the rising demand for furs in Europe, and the inability of Native American groups to generate a communally based or closed access property rights system. The evidence from Fort Churchill, where the Hudson's Bay Company had a monopoly and beaver stocks were maintained, suggests that beaver were not overexploited where there was no French competition. And the early evidence from Fort Albany suggests that even in the presence of competition beaver stocks were strong as long as fur prices in Europe remained low. Beginning in the late 1730s, however, fur prices in Europe rose, and the French were trading in both the Fort Albany and York Factory hinterlands. The Hudson's Bay Company, unwilling to abandon most of the market to the French, raised prices at its trading posts. The result was serious depletion.

Central to this story is the reaction of Native Americans to higher fur prices. They responded with increased harvests despite the adverse effect on the beaver population. But why did the Indians not take a longer-run perspective and control their activities? Demsetz (1967) has argued that in the face of a commercial fur trade, tribes had an incentive to adopt a property rights structure that would lead to conservation. McManus (1972) countered by pointing out that Indian custom regarding the right to hunt for food and other aspects of their "Good Samaritan" principle mitigated against the emergence of strong property rights in fur-bearing animals.

It was, however, not just the strength of Indian custom that prevented the various tribes from acquiring sole ownership. Other factors also increased the cost of establishing property rights to the beaver. The Treaty of Utrecht gave the lands around Hudson Bay to the English, thus making the Hudson's Bay Company's trading posts physically secure, but there continued to be hostility between French and English traders. The raiding and conflict played out among the various Indian groups, with some siding with the French and others with the English: "War displaced populations, reduced numbers, forced people to adjust to different environments, and mingled cultures" (Harris 1987, 89). In short, the physical environment in which the Indians were operating was not conducive to private property rights. From the perspective of the Indians, the beaver remained an open access resource for which high prices led to high harvesting rates. In the regions served by Fort Albany and York Factory, this lack of Native property rights, along with competition between the French and the Hudson's Bay Company and a strong fur market in Europe, combined to produce the severe depletion that has been such an important theme in the fur trade literature.

Notes

This chapter is an adaptation of Carlos and Lewis, 1993. Reprinted with permission of Cambridge University Press.

1. For a list of references and a brief discussion of the literature, see Rea 1991, topic 6.

2. We interpret depletion as a fall in population below the maximum sustained yield level, which is the population that allows the largest annual harvest on a sustained basis.

3. All trades at the posts were denominated in the company's unit of account, the Made Beaver. A coat or parchment pelt sold for one Made Beaver. Other types of furs sold for different prices. For example, marten were receiving one-third Made Beavers. Prices of all trade goods were also stipulated in the same unit of account, a four-foot gun, for example, commanding eleven Made Beavers.

4. For a complete discussion of the hinterlands and the beaver densities they could support, see Carlos and Lewis 1993.

5. We assume the standard quadratic relationship between the growth of the biomass and its size: $F(X) = aX - bX^2$, where X is the biomass and $F(X)$ is the change in the biomass. Growth is at a maximum where $dF(X)/dX$ is zero. This is the biomass that provides the maximum yield on a sustained basis. Assuming a plausible discount rate of say, 5 percent (.05), it follows that, where $dF(X)/dX$ equals the discount rate, the biomass will be below but close to the maximum sustained yield level.

6. Note that the scale for beaver population for each of the three hinterlands is different in each case. Using the York Factory scale for Fort Churchill would have made population movements almost indiscernible.

7. For a discussion of company standards, see Ray 1974, 61–70.

8. The assumption here is that Native Americans were interested only in generating a particular level of income. In a world of rising prices, that income could be earned by trading fewer beaver pelts.

9. The Hudson's Bay Company has been in continuous operation from 1670 until the present. In 1954 the company archives were moved from London to Winnipeg, Manitoba.

10. David Feeny describes the various categories of ownership: open access, communal property, private property, and state property (Feeny 1995, 5).

11. The Hudson's Bay Company policy of creating trading captains would also have tended to undermine the existing political structure.

12. This latter method of restricting the harvest was used only infrequently and never during periods of competition with other European traders (Carlos and Lewis 1993).

13. Prior to this, felters could either export the pelts to Russia and reimport the wool or shave the pelt to obtain the wool, but this rendered the remaining skin useless to furriers.

References

Berkes, Fikret, David Feeny, Bonnie J. McCay, and James M. Acheson. 1989. "The Benefits of the Commons" *Nature,* July, 91–93.

Carlos, Ann M., and Frank D. Lewis. 1993. "Indians, the Beaver, and the Bay: The Economics of Depletion in the Lands of the Hudson's Bay Company, 1700–1763." *Journal of Economic History* 53 (September):465–494.

_____. 1995. "Strategic Pricing in the Fur Trade: The Hudson's Bay Company, 1700–1763." In *Wildlife in the Marketplace,* eds. Terry Anderson and P. J. Hill, 61–89. Rowman and Littlefield.

_____. 1996. "Property Rights, Competition and Depletion in the Eighteenth-Century Canadian Fur Trade: The Role of the European Market." Working paper, Department of Economics, Queen's University, Kingston, Ontario.

Cronon, William. 1983. *Changes in the Land: Indians, Colonists, and the Ecology of New England.* New York: Hill and Wang.

Demsetz, Harold. 1967. "Toward a Theory of Property Rights." *American Economic Review, Papers and Proceedings* 57 (May): 347–359.

Feeny, David. 1995. "The Coevolution of Property Rights Regimes for Land, Man, and Forests in Thailand, 1790–1990." Working paper, Department of Economics, McMaster University, Hamilton, Ontario.

Feeny, David, Fikret Berkes, Bonnie J. McCay, and James M. Acheson. 1990. "The Tragedy of the Commons: Twenty-Two Years Later." *Human Ecology* 18 (March):1–19.

Harris, R. Cole, ed. 1987. *Historical Atlas of Canada.* Vol. 1. Toronto: University of Toronto Press.

Hudson's Bay Company Archives (microfilm copy) 1956. *Post Records*, MG20B; *Grand Journal*, MG20A; *Fur Price Book*, MG20A; *Minute Book*, MG20A. Public Archives of Canada, Ottawa.

Innis, Harold. 1956. *The Fur Trade in Canada*. Rev. ed. Toronto: University of Toronto Press.

Krech, Shepherd III, ed. 1981. *Indians, Animals, and the Fur Trade: A Critique of Keepers of the Game*. Athens: University of Georgia Press.

Lawson, Murray G. 1943. *Fur: A Study in English Mercantilism, 1700–1775*. Toronto: University of Toronto Press.

Martin, Calvin. 1978. *Keepers of the Game: Indian-Animal Relationships and the Fur Trade*. Berkeley: University of California Press.

McManus, John. 1972. "An Economic Analysis of Indian Behavior in the North American Fur Trade." *Journal of Economic History* 32 (March):36–53.

Milloy, John. 1991. "'Our Country': The Significance of the Buffalo Resource for a Plains Cree Sense of Territory." In *Aboriginal Resource Use in Canada: Historical and Legal Aspects*, eds. Kerry Abel and Jean Friesen, 51–70. Winnipeg: University of Manitoba Press.

Ray, Arthur J. 1974. *Indians in the Fur Trade: Their Role as Trappers, Hunters, and Middlemen in the Lands Southwest of Hudson Bay, 1660–1870*. Toronto: University of Toronto Press.

Rea, K. J. 1991. *A Guide to Canadian Economic History*. Toronto: Canadian Scholars' Press.

Rich, E. E. 1955. "Russia and the Colonial Fur Trade." *Economic History Review* 7 (April):307–328.

_____. 1958. *The History of the Hudson's Bay Company, 1670–1870*. 2 vols. London: Hudson's Bay Record Society.

5

The Eighteenth-Century Southeastern American Indian Economy

Subsistence Versus Trade and Growth

EDWARD MURPHY

Since their Stone Age ancestors migrated from Asia to North America, American Indian men had hunted deer and other fauna for food and materials. With the arrival of Europeans, they began to sell the excess hides and pelts. By the 1700s Indians in the Southeast had developed a brisk trade in hides with Charleston and New Orleans. Although an increasing number of Indians were adopting agriculture at this time, the hunters remained more numerous. Was this persistence of hunting evidence that Indians clung to Stone Age lifestyles that were inherently less efficient despite price incentives to go into agriculture? Or was hunting a profitable commercial enterprise that departed from subsistence practices? Indian histories maintain seemingly contradictory positions: On the one hand, they suggest that Indians did not have a profit motive; on the other hand, they demonstrate that the hunting market was competitive and commercial.

Even historians who believe that the southeastern deerskin trade was an exchange economy believe that Indians sought to avoid the price system. Characterizations of the Indians both as disdainful traditionalists and as shrewd market negotiators can be found within single works. Daniel Usner noted that Indian societies were somewhat protected from the price system because "insistence by tribal leaders that prices be fixed, commerce regulated, and gifts granted often coincided with the needs of colonial governments and thereby buffered Indian societies from the commercial revolution" (1988). Yet these same Indians did not seek fixed prices when they sold their goods, as Usner further explained: "Rivalry between the British and the French empires was responsible for chronic tension in a zone of overlap between colonial regions, which Choctaws and upper Creeks effectively used to their advantage by trading with both sides and bargaining for better exchange rates" (1988).

In fairness to Usner, these two positions are not mutually exclusive. Societies always contain elements that cling to tradition and elements that seek change. People seek fixed prices when the terms of trade are sliding against them and seek flexible prices when the terms of trade are moving in their favor. Is the eighteenth-century hunter an example of resistance to change or an example of adaptation? Prior to removal, did the hunter represent the Stone Age subsistence traditionalists or the modernizing market entrepreneurs? This chapter tries to estimate the extent to which the eighteenth-century southeastern Indian economy was a market economy.

Charleston Deerskin Trade Volume

The deerskin trade in the Southeast was a poor cousin to the beaver pelt trade around the Great Lakes. However, the soft leather of deerskins was ideally suited for gloves, leather straps, book bindings, and other soft leather goods. The French traded for the deerskins from New Orleans and the Spanish from their possessions in Florida. Originally, the British entered the trade through the Chesapeake region. Although the trade never reached the value of the beaver trade, the production of deerskins became intense throughout the Southeast.

The British ports in the Chesapeake region traded goods to the local Occonochee tribe, who then acted as middlemen for the tribes deeper in the interior. The middleman position became valuable enough to the Occonochee that they killed the first English trader to visit the interior tribes on his own (Rothrock 1929). The founding of Charleston eventually ended the Occonochee's position. This section attempts to determine the size of the trade for which the Occonochee were willing to kill and to assesses how that trade compared with other South Carolina export trades.

The volume of the Native American trade for deerskins can be measured from the South Carolina tax records because hides were taxed by weight when exported (Crane [1929] 1956). The tax collections were recorded twice each year in the colonial tax ledger. The quantity in pounds of deerskins produced each year can be calculated using the tax rate and the value of taxes collected.

Table 5.1 presents the weight in pounds of deerskins exported per year from South Carolina between 1736 and 1768. The tax revenues are recorded in pounds sterling. The cured skins weighed on average two pounds each (Crane [1929] 1956). This suggests that 100,000 to 150,000

TABLE 5.1   Yearly Volume of Deerskin Exports (in pounds)

Year	Lbs. Deerskins	Year	Lbs. Deerskins
1736	200,720	1752	220,960
1737	215,520	1753	258,160
1738	221,920	1754	270,240
1739	252,000	1755	294,320
1740	197,120	1756	314,640
1741	170,400	1757	223,360
1742	185,280	1758	325,360
1743	314,400	1759	138,240
1744	180,960	1760	237,920
1745	376,160	1761	123,120
1746	323,920	1762	165,040
1747	262,080	1763	328,480
1748	368,080	1764	252,080
1749	256,400	1765	213,840
1750	226,240	1766	230,960
1751	270,560	1767	148,960

Source: Calculated from *Records of the Public Treasurer of South Carolina, 1725–1776* (South Carolina Archives, SCARM3/1, Ledger B).

hides were exported in a typical year. This figure does not include the lesser-quality deerskins that were traded within the other colonies or those used domestically among the Indians.

The Indians were the primary producers in one of North America's most valuable export industries in the eighteenth century. Combined with the northern beaver trade, the animal hide industry generated the fourth-highest export earnings in the British North American colonies on the eve of the American Revolution. The top ten colonial exports by value in 1770 are presented in Table 5.2. By the late eighteenth century the Indians had supplemented this valuable export industry with other cash-earning activities.

The Indians produced other goods besides deerskins. Men sold their labor as guides, pack bearers, and rowers to frontiersmen. They also bred horses for sale; the Choctaw, for example, sold ponies to colonists and to other Indians (Adair [1776] 1966). The Choctaw also sold a variety of foodstuffs, trading vegetables, chickens, and hogs as far away as Mobile, Alabama (Usner 1988). Although the total value of these activities is unknown, it is unlikely that they could match the deerskin trade.

Yet as valuable as the southeastern Indian trade in hides was, it was eclipsed by the rival agricultural interests in Virginia and the Carolinas. Two of the three commodities ahead of fur and deerskin exports in Table 5.2 were southern agricultural staples: tobacco and rice. Although deerskin ex-

TABLE 5.2   Value of Articles Exported from British Continental Colonies, 1770, the Top Ten Commodities (in pounds sterling)

Article	Value
Tobacco	906,638
Bread and flour	504,553
Rice	340,693
Furs and deerskins	149,246
Indigo	131,467
Wheat	131,467
Whale oil	85,013
Beef and pork	66,035
Staves and heading	61,619
Horses	60,228

Source: U.S. Bureau of the Census, *Historical Statistics of the United States: Colonial Times to 1970,* Bicentennial Edition (Washington, D.C.: GPO, 1975).

ports in 1749 exceeded the combined value of indigo, cattle, and pork, the value of rice alone was triple the value of deerskins (Crane [1929] 1956).

Production of deerskins grew into the middle of the eighteenth century. Average production rose from 54,000 hides in the 1699–1715 period (Crane [1929] 1956) to 175,000 in 1745. The fact that the deerskin trade was large in volume, high in value, and growing over time does not tell us by itself that Indian hunters were responding to the market instead of clinging to Stone Age ways. Price information would help solve another piece of that puzzle.

Real Price Changes for Deerskins

In 1812 the United States dropped the price paid to Indians for deerskins from $0.20 to $0.17. Usner (1985) claims this price drop caused the Indians to switch from hunting to cotton growing on the southeastern frontier. Cotton production does, indeed, take off after 1812; however, focusing on the change in the nominal price paid for deerskins in 1812 ignores the role of the real deerskin price drop that occurred sometime before 1807.

Although we might be able to track the prices charged by various middlemen, it is very difficult to determine the price received by Indians in their villages. The prices in the early nineteenth century are known because the United States set up frontier trading factories that kept daily records. An index constructed from the *Records of the Office of Indian Trade, Choctaw Factory Day Books* shows that relative prices were turning against the hunters well before 1812.

TABLE 5.3   Purchasing Power of Deerskins Relative to Price of Goods Bought by Indians

Commodity	1762–1765	1807	% Change
Axe	4.0	5.0	25
Flannel, yd.	1.5	2.0	33
Looking glass	1.5	19.5	600
Gun	14.0	69.5 (rifle)	300
Tin kettle	4.0	5.0	25

Source: Calculated from *Records of the Office of Indian Trade, Choctaw Factory Daybooks* (National Archives, RG75, microfilm T-500).

Table 5.3 presents the results of constructing a Paasche price index. An index of this kind uses a fixed basket of goods using trade weights in the end period. Inflation or deflation is calculated by comparing the period of interest to the cost of the basket if the prices of a previous period had prevailed. Inflation or deflation is understated by this index. The records of the trading office were used to construct a basket of goods in 1807. Although the prices paid by the Indians themselves is difficult to find for most periods, it is available for 1762–1765 because the colony of South Carolina listed the barter values of goods charged by its traders.

The index reveals that the terms of trade were turning against the hunters in the late eighteenth century. Using the 1807 basket of goods as a standard, we can see that the real price that Indians received for their deerskins had dropped. Indians could purchase no more than four-fifths as many axes, flannel shirts, and tin kettles for the same quantity of deerskins. Unfortunately, the index does not tell us the path prices took between 1765 and 1807. There may have been substantial variation in any intervening decade, but ultimately the price had dropped considerably by 1807. The price reduction in 1812 continued this trend.

The 1812 price drop is the continuation of a previously established trend. The price received by Indians before 1760 is not available. However, prices of the colonial deerskin exports can be calculated for selected years between 1715 and 1770. Assuming that the changes in the price Indians received varied directly with changes in colonial export prices, the direction of change can be measured. Table 5.4 presents the prices of colonial deerskin exports in 1715, 1748, and 1770. Deerskin export prices rose between 1715 and 1748 but fell from 1748 to 1770. The price fell again between 1770 and 1807 as shown in Table 5.3. Then the price dropped once more in 1812, when the United States changed deerskin prices at its trading factories from $0.20 to $0.17.

The price trend suggests that Indians received the highest real price for deerskins in the mid-eighteenth century. Table 5.1 shows that this was also

TABLE 5.4   Colonial Deerskin Export Price, 1715–1770

	Lbs. Skins	Value	Nominal Price	% Change	Avg. Price Index	Avg. Real Change	Real Change Skins
1715	242,000	10,000	0.04		58		
1748	368,080	36,000	0.09	137	76	33%	104%
1770	800,000	57,750	0.07	–26	80	5%	–31%

Source: Calculated from U.S. Bureau of the Census, *Statistical History of the United States: From Colonial Times to the Present* (Washington, D.C.: GPO, 1976), and *Records of the Office of Indian Trade, Choctaw Factory Daybooks* (National Archives, RG75, microfilm T-500).

the period of peak production. As prices rose up until the 1740s, Indians responded to changes in relative prices by increasing hunting production; then when prices dropped in the late 1700s, they switched to alternative activities.

Although a number of market factors caused the price decline, a political change also influenced deerskin prices. Prior to 1763 the Cherokee, Creek, and Choctaw Indians had been able to trade with Britain, Spain, or France in the Southeast. British victory in the Seven Years War gave the British a monopoly position in the regulation of the deerskin trade. Although Choctaw chief Tomatly Mingo and other Indians wanted the deerskin trade to continue after the war at the same exchange rates (Usner 1988), the above calculations show that real prices and output dropped. This is consistent with the British being monopsony buyers, reducing purchases in order to lower prices. The next section examines the value of Indian trade from the perspective of British colonials.

Value of Indian Trade Taxes to Colonial Governments

British traders and the taxes they paid both helped and hurt Indian-colonial relations. Traders were accused of peddling alcohol to the Indians and cheating them. Yet the value of the trade and the taxes provided the British crown with an incentive to slow colonial expansion and protect the Indians. According to W. Jacobs, "Fur trading interests combined with imperial officers in giving inland tribes a delay in White occupation of the frontier" (1988).

How important was the Indian trade to colonial officials? South Carolina officials believed the trade was crucial to the survival of the colony between 1687 and 1736 (Crane [1929] 1956). South Carolina officials praised the aggregate level of deerskin tax revenues, but they did not compare it to other tax sources. Table 5.5 presents the means and standard deviations of South Carolina's tax sources from 1736 to 1768.

TABLE 5.5   Mean and Standard Deviation of South Carolina Tax Sources,
1736–1768

	Slaves	Deer	Sundry	Other	Total
Mean	7764.7	1563.6	10,144.4	3744.8	23,217.6
STD	8216.7	546.5	5,870.3	2867.0	10,641.0

Source: Calculated from *Records of the Public Treasurer of South Carolina, 1725–1776* (South Carolina Archives, SCARM3/1, ledger B).

The tax on deerskins brought in less than 10 percent of South Carolina's tax revenues. The stoppage of slave imports during wartime in the 1740s was more influential on South Carolina tax revenues than growth of deerskin export revenue. So although the deerskin trade was large and valuable, it is hard to argue that the total level of tax revenues it generated was its chief source of protection for Indian-colonial relations.

In addition to the total taxes generated by a revenue source, public administrators had also to consider the dependability of the tax source. While the deerskin trade was not the primary source of South Carolina's revenues, the standard deviations reveal that it was the most stable in relation to its mean. In other words, the duty on deerskin exports was a more dependable tax source for the colony even though it provided less revenues on average than other sources.

Value of Indian Trade to British Traders

In addition to the duty on deerskin exports, British colonies sold trading licenses. In order to protect the Indians from fraud and abuse, colonial officials allowed only those traders with licenses to trade with the Indians. To the extent that licenses were enforceable, they restricted the market and created rents. These licenses can be used to estimate the value of these rents to colonial traders.

Traders were required to pay a yearly fee and place a substantial deposit. The total cost of the license per year is the annual fee plus the interest foregone on the deposit. If a trader planned to be in the business indefinitely by training his children, then the capitalized value of the license is the present value of the stream of payments of the fee and the foregone interest.

The yearly fee was 8 pounds sterling, and the deposit was 100 pounds. The interest rate before 1781 was approximately 6 percent (Rothenberg 1985). As shown in the calculation of the price index, the overall price level did not show a clear trend. If expected inflation was therefore 0 percent, then the capitalized value of each trading license was 233 pounds. The journals of the South Carolina treasurers list thirty trading licenses sold in 1721.

The colonial documents of the legislature list an additional thirty sold. The total value of the licenses was 13,980 pounds in the limit. The figure drops to 11,500 if the traders' time horizons drop to twenty years. The traders were willing to pay half of South Carolina's one-year tax bill for the right to trade with the Indians.

Indian Per Capita Export Revenues

Although the volume of the Indian trade was high and the colonials were willing to expend resources to participate in it, it might still have been a subsistence economy on a per person level. The traditional explanation of Indian demise says that Indians lost sovereignty to their land because their subsistence economy came into conflict with a capitalist one (Gibson 1988). It is not currently possible to calculate per capita incomes prior to the Cherokee census in the 1820s. However, it is possible to estimate per capita export revenues from tax and trading house records. The per capita earnings help distinguish between subsistence production and surplus production.

As a point of comparison, New York in 1750 had a population of 76,000. The world price of New York's exports was 48,000 pounds sterling. New York exported 0.6 pounds per capita. The southeastern Indian population was approximately 54,000 (Lebergott 1984), and they exported 187,250 pounds sterling worth of deerskins just through Charleston. At 3.5 pounds sterling per person, southeastern Indians' export earnings compare very favorably with the economy of the Middle Colonies in the middle of the eighteenth century.

But as the terms of trade turned against deerskins and the Indians turned to alternative production, the deerskin trade provided substantially less per capita export revenues. In 1807 dollars, southeastern Indians exported $2 per capita in 1748. Although the figures for the entire region are not yet available for 1807, there is an estimate of the Choctaw's per capita deerskin exports in that year. Table 5.6 presents the exports through the Choctaw trading house in 1807 when the Choctaw had a population of about 8,000. The Choctaw earned $1 per capita from animal hide exports; the U.S. average was $9 per capita for all exports. As noted above, the Choctaw began selling ponies, chickens, and other goods.

Conclusions and Limitations

These estimates of the size and value of the deerskin trade in the Southeast suggest that the Indians were involved in a large commercial hunting market by the eighteenth century. Until the 1740s their production rose as the relative price of deerskins rose and their production fell afterward when the real price fell. When the market was at its peak in the middle of the eighteenth

TABLE 5.6   Choctaw Trade with U.S. Factory, 1807

Commodity	Dollar Value
Deerskins	7,042.40
Beaver fur	234.75
Otter skin	327.00
Fox skin	265.00
Raccoon	244.37
Cat skin	139.50
Bear skin	60.00
Tallow	12.50
Bees wax	14.00
Total	8,539.52

Source: *Records of the Office of Indian Trade, Choctaw Factory Daybooks* (National Archives, RG75, microfilm T-500).

century, the deerskin trade provided export earnings rivaling the economy of the Middle Colonies. In the late eighteenth century, continual price drops steered the Indians into alternative production. These estimates, however, are based on figures from Charleston and do not take into account exports through Mobile, Pensacola, and New Orleans. Therefore, these numbers underestimate the total value of the trade.

References

Adair, James. [1776] 1966. *A History of the American Indians.* New York: Argonaut Press.

Crane, Verner. [1929] 1956. *The Southeastern Frontier.* Ann Arbor: University of Michigan Press.

Gibson, A. 1988. "Indian Land Transfers." In *Handbook of American Indians.* Vol. 4. Washington, D.C.: Smithsonian Institution.

Jacobs, W. 1988. "British Indian Policies to 1783." In *Handbook of American Indians.* Vol. 4. Washington, D.C.: Smithsonian Institution.

Lebergott, Stanley. 1984. "The Destruction of the Indians." In *The Americans: An Economic Record.* New York: Norton.

Records of the Office of Indian Trade, Choctaw Factory Daybooks. National Archives, RG75, microfilm T-500.

Records of the Public Treasurer of South Carolina, 1725–1776. South Carolina Archives, SCARM3/1, ledger B.

Rothenberg, Winifred. 1985. "The Emergence of a Capital Market in Rural Massachusetts, 1730–1838." *Journal of Economic History* (December):781–808.

Rothrock, M. 1929. "Carolina Traders Among the Overhill Cherokees, 1690–1760." East Tennessee Historical Society Publication, no. 1:3–18.

U.S. Bureau of the Census. 1976. *Historical Statistics of the United States: From Colonial Times to the Present.* Washington, D.C.: GPO.

Usner, Daniel. 1985. "American Indians on the Cotton Frontier: Changing Economic Relations with Citizens and Slaves in the Mississippi Territory." *Journal of American History* 72, no. 2 (September).

———. 1988. "Economic Relations in the Southeast Until 1783." In *Handbook of American Indians.* Vol. 4. Washington, D.C.: Smithsonian Institution.

Part Three

Westward Expansion

Introduction

The Economic Historian's Use and Sources of Data

JAMES W. OBERLY

Economic historians work in the long and distinguished tradition of the social sciences, where the task of the researcher is to pose verifiable hypotheses based on theory, to gather data for testing, and then to determine if the results are adequately explained by the theory. What makes economic history such an interesting scholarly practice is precisely its mix of intellectual curiosity based on theorizing and its investigative curiosity based on digging for historical sources for data. Unlike the social scientist who studies the present and has recourse to direct observations and surveys of living people, the economic historian has to scramble to find whatever sources are in the archives, knowing full well that people in the past did not leave oral or written accounts just to satisfy the curiosity of future scholars.

The ethnoeconomic historian working on how American Indians and Native Hawaiians have produced, consumed, and traded must work under unusual constraints. On the one hand, officials of the westward-expanding United States devoted a great deal of time to investigating and reporting on almost every aspect of American Indian society, including economic relations. On the other hand, there is a dearth of sources created by American Indians or Native Hawaiians about how they viewed their own economies. The challenge for the economic historian, therefore, is to make judicious use of reports and documents created by the conquering and occupying U.S. power.

The three chapters in Part 3 feature work by scholars who use different data sources to help make sense of the diverse American Indian past from different places and times. David M. Wishart has read carefully in the policy debates of the 1830s about the level of so-called civilization among the Cherokee and others of the Five Civilized Nations. He observes that historians in the twentieth century are divided on the issue, as were contemporaries of President Jackson's Indian removal policy. Wishart makes careful use of economists' understanding of the terms "subsistence" and "surplus" as a way of thinking about the issue. He then offers a fresh analysis of the special census of the Cherokee taken in 1835. The federal decennial census is probably the most heavily used primary source among U.S. historians, and Wishart shows how a study of the questions asked by census marshals of Cherokee households in 1835 can help answer important historical questions today.

The policy of Indian removal in the U.S. South is so central to the study of the Jacksonian era that it sometimes obscures the history of other Indian nations that managed to hold on to at least portions of their ancestral land without being removed. The Lake Superior Ojibwa that James W. Oberly studies are an example of such a people; they entered into a series of treaties with the United States, exchanging a vast territory in return for guaranteed reservations and the reserved right of off-reservation hunting, fishing, and gathering rights. Oberly is interested in tying this history of treaties to demographic questions about mortality, morbidity, and fertility among the Ojibwa. He uses a number of data sources, including reports by Bureau of Indian Affairs agents, military enlistment records, and Indian census records.

The pan-Indian cultural renaissance of the late twentieth century has been inspired in large part by the tribes of the Great Plains, and there remains in the minds of both Indians and non-Indians alike a fascination with the nineteenth-century wars between the U.S. Army and their Indian opponents, whom observers called the world's "finest light cavalry." Economists Terry L. Anderson and Fred S. McChesney ask a fundamental historical question: Why did the level of violence and conflict escalate in the second half of the nineteenth century? They offer a public choice model for theorizing about the level of conflict, and then provide data taken from U.S. Army records about why warfare seemingly became a primary choice for solving disputes.

6

Could the Cherokee Have Survived in the Southeast?

DAVID M. WISHART

Transformations in Cherokee Social, Political, and Economic Systems Before 1835

Regular contacts between Europeans and the Cherokee began after 1650. Until that time, the Cherokee population totaled about 20,000 and occupied some sixty independent towns located in five regions. These were the Lower Towns set in South Carolina's western foothills along the Keowee River, the Valley Towns across the first range of the Appalachians on the upper part of the Hiwassee River, the Middle Settlements situated due east of the Valley Towns along the Little Tennessee River, the Out Towns northeast of the Valley Towns, and seven Overhill Towns along the upper branches of the Little Tennessee. Although the total area occupied by the Cherokee in the mid-seventeenth century was only about 150 miles long and 40 to 50 miles wide, a sense of cohesiveness was absent. Cherokee life was town centered and in fact three dialects were spoken in these regions, suggesting little interaction among the groups of towns.[1]

The civil structure in these towns was based upon kinship ties that enforced a blood law via a matrilineal clan structure. The Cherokee law of blood meant that the death of a clan member at the hands of another clan had to be paid for in blood, and not necessarily that of the perpetrator of the original offense.[2] The matrilineal clan structure meant that children belonged to their mother's clan. In fact, the matrilineal uncle was more important as a mentor and protector to his sister's children than was the children's father.[3]

The Cherokee economic base consisted of subsistence agriculture supplemented by fishing and hunting in the Appalachians. Agricultural plots were typically located adjacent to towns in fertile bottomland soils. Town councils probably divided common fields between households, and the actual cultivation was done communally.[4] Relative plenty probably existed. These communities were able to support a leisure class of chiefs (one for peacetime and one for war), warriors, myth tellers, conjurers, and ball players.[5] Food security was ensured through the maintenance of communal grain storage systems.[6] Ritualized sharing functioned to minimize the rate of household failure.[7]

The Cherokee economy and social structure experienced two distinct transformations after contact with Europeans had become more or less continuous in the late seventeenth century. The first of these was a transformation from hunting, gathering, and subsistence agriculture to commodity trade and mercenary activities with Europeans (mainly the British) based on barter, cash, and credit terms. British traders along the Carolina coast sought captive Indians from the interior to be sold as slaves on the sugar plantations in the Caribbean and on tobacco plantations to the north. Cherokee Indians were among those captured by coastal tribes to be exchanged for guns from the British. In 1693 headmen from Cherokee towns went to Charleston, South Carolina, to guarantee peace and to secure their own trade relationship with the British colonists.[8] The Cherokee began a lucrative trade in deerskins with the British to acquire firearms to bolster their defense against hostile neighboring tribes. From 1699 to 1715 the number of deerskins shipped from Charleston averaged 54,000 per year. Most of these came from the Cherokee because of the high quality of the hides taken from deer killed in the Appalachian mountains.[9] Over time, Cherokee communities appear to have allowed traders to circulate quite freely, despite attempts by the South Carolina colonial government to regulate the trade.[10] Intermarriage between these traders and Cherokee women was relatively common. These intermarried couples tended to settle near Cherokee towns, building houses, barns, and stores. Their offspring were imbued with European attitudes toward enterprise and the accumulation of property. However, tribal law held that the property that passed to mixed-blood children through inheritance was part of the Cherokee Nation's holdings.[11]

The Cherokee came under intense pressure during the mid-eighteenth century. A smallpox epidemic that may have killed as many as 10,000 Cherokee in 1738 was followed by a war with the adjacent Creek Nation in the 1750s, another war with the British in the 1760s, and the American Revolution, in which the Cherokee sided with the British. All of these contributed to a relative decline in their numbers and holdings.[12] During the American Revolution nearly all the Cherokee towns were destroyed by the Continental Army. At the war's end, most of the Cherokee population was situated in the area surrounding present-day Chattanooga, Tennessee.[13]

Clearly, the Cherokee existed in a state of flux during the mid-eighteenth century. The end of the American Revolution found their population signifi-

TABLE 6.1   Property Holdings for the Cherokee Nation, 1810 and 1820

	1810	*1820*
Negro slaves	113	1,277
Cattle	19,500	22,000
Horses	6,100	7,600
Hogs	19,600	46,000
Sheep	1,037	2,500
Grist mills	13	31
Saw mills	3	10
Saltpeter works	3	—
Wagons	30	172
Plows	480	2,943
Spinning wheels	1,600	2,488
Looms	467	762
Blacksmith shops	—	62
Cotton machines	—	8
Ferries	—	18
Schools	—	18

Source: Rennard Strickland, *Fire and the Spirits: Cherokee Law from the Clan to the Court* (Norman: University of Oklahoma Press, 1975), Theda Perdue, "Cherokee Planters: The Development of Plantation Slavery Before Removal," in *The Cherokee Indian Nation,* ed. Duane H. King (Knoxville: University of Tennessee Press, 1979), 114.

cantly reduced and impoverished. The deerskin trade had dried up substantially. The end of nearly thirty years of continual warfare had brought to a halt a lucrative trade in prisoners of war who could be exchanged for guns, ammunition, household utensils, and agricultural implements.[14] The Cherokee Nation had made a transition from agriculture to hunting, trade, and mercenary activity during the early and mid-eighteenth century and needed to make the transition back to agriculture in the late eighteenth century if they were to survive. George Washington initiated efforts by the United States to foster agricultural development in the Cherokee Nation during the early national period, thus marking the beginning of the second transformation in the Cherokee economic, political, and social structures. Washington appointed Benjamin Hawkins to be superintendent of the Indian tribes south of the Ohio River. Hawkins, his successor Return J. Meigs, and later in the 1820s Thomas McKenney all had considerable success introducing white methods of agriculture to the Cherokee.[15] Property accumulated rapidly in the Cherokee Nation, as shown in Table 6.1. The figures show considerable capital accumulation for the Cherokee in the first decades of the nineteenth century. Of particular note are the statistics on Cherokee slaveholdings. By 1835 slaveholders constituted less than 8 percent of Cherokee households but were responsible for operating the largest and most productive farms. For example, in 1835 slaveholders farmed on average seventy-five acres with an average output of 1,040 bushels of corn per year, whereas nonslaveholding families farmed on average eleven acres with an average output of 141 bushels of corn.[16] In Cherokee society, just as in the neighboring white community, slaveholders rose to become the dominant class during the early nineteenth century. Most slaveholding families were mixed-blood. In 1835, 17 percent of the Cherokee claimed white ancestry, whereas among slaveholders' families 78 percent claimed white ancestral links. In the same year, 39 percent of slaveholders' families could read English, whereas 13 percent could read Cherokee. However, among nonslaveholders, only 4 percent could read English whereas 18 percent could read Cherokee.[17]

The policy toward Indians initiated by George Washington and maintained through John Quincy Adams's administration up to 1828 can be described conveniently as promoting assimilation. The feeling was that as white methods of agriculture were transmitted to Indians they would give up their traditional practices and their claims to status as separate political entities. However, in the case of the Cherokee, the adoption of white agricultural methods was paralleled by the introduction of a more formal political structure. For example, in 1817 the Cherokee National Council Assembly passed the first written legislation for the Cherokee Nation, establishing a police force for investigating crimes, adjudicating criminal cases, and administering punishment. The same national assembly centralized Cherokee government under a standing committee with thirteen members elected for two-year terms to function in executive, legislative, and judicial roles. In 1820 a separate judicial branch was created. A republican form of government was formally adopted by the Cherokee in 1828 with the creation of a written constitution modeled after the U.S. Constitution. As Cherokee economic and political institutions developed, cash became substitutable for blood in compensation for harmful acts.[18] The Cherokee legal structure expanded to cover matters of private and communal ownership of land; monopoly control of roads, turnpikes, and ferries; inheritance; regulation of hired labor; control over the slave population; borrowing and lending; livestock management; and contractual relations. Instead of being assimilated by the neighboring white community, the Cherokee were building an economy and institutions that would allow them to function independently as a political entity.[19]

During the 1820s, as white settlers pushed westward and as the cotton economy expanded into the fertile river valleys of the Southeast, political pressure built for the removal of the Cherokee and other southeastern tribes to the trans-Mississippi West. Andrew Jackson ran for president in 1828 on a pro-removal platform favored by the southern and western states. Congress passed an Indian removal bill in 1830 that cleared the way for the Jackson administration to negotiate terms of removal with the southeastern tribes.[20] In 1835 the Treaty of New Echota, which established the terms for the Cherokee removal to Oklahoma, was approved by a small minority of the Cherokee Nation.[21] The political debate over the Cherokee removal was particularly heated. However, proponents of removal ultimately prevailed, and the Cherokee were forcibly evicted from their homes in the Southeast in 1838 by the U.S. Army under the direction of General Winfield Scott. The Cherokee removal is commonly referred to as the Trail of Tears. Though estimates vary widely, most historians agree that some 4,000 Cherokee lost their lives on the trek westward from the Southeast to Oklahoma.[22]

The Cherokee removal is uniquely suited for examination by economic historians because a remarkably complete set of demographic and economic data exists for the Cherokee in the year 1835. The federal government conducted a census of the Cherokee that year in order to catalog their holdings in the Southeast. Furthermore, the issue of Cherokee economic progress figured prominently in the political debate over the Cherokee removal. In the pages that follow, I will explain the significance of the statistical record to the debate over the Cherokee removal and then examine economic data found in the 1835 census to look for evidence of surplus production by Eastern Cherokee households. First, I describe the stated purpose of the census and the categories of information recorded in it. I then present a comparative analysis of summary statistics for the sections of Tennessee, Alabama, North Carolina, and Georgia that comprised the Eastern Cherokee Nation as well as statistics on literacy and skill levels among the Cherokee for each state. In the following section, I use the census results to evaluate the extent of surplus Cherokee agricultural production and to calculate a lower bound estimate for the percentage of households attaining at least subsistence levels of food production. I also estimate aggregate surplus production. I conclude with observations relating the results of the analysis presented in this chapter to the debate over Cherokee economic progress and the removal policy. The answer to the question, "Could the Cherokee have survived in the Southeast?," turns out to be quite complex and hinges on both political and economic factors.

The Significance of the Statistical Record to the Cherokee Removal Debate

There were two distinct opinions expressed during the 1830s about the appropriateness of removal, opinions based on different assessments of Cherokee economic progress. For example, the pro-removal camp led by President Andrew Jackson bemoaned the lack of economic progress among the southeastern Indians, the Cherokee included. Jackson argued in his first annual message to Congress that the Indians had no right to "tracts of country on which they have neither dwelt nor made improvements, merely because they have seen them from the mountain or passed them in the chase"; he also felt that their inability to adopt white agricultural methods quickly would doom them to "weakness and decay" with "the fate of the Mohegan, the Narragansett, and the Delaware . . . fast overtaking the Choctaw, the Cherokee, and the Creek."[23] Jackson elaborated on these views in a talk given to a Cherokee delegation visiting Washington in 1835 to protest the provisions of an early draft of the Treaty of New Echota, which ultimately set the terms for Cherokee removal. Jackson maintained: "The game has disappeared among you, and you must depend upon agriculture, and the mechanic arts for support. And, yet, a large portion of your people have acquired little or no property which can be useful to them. How, under these circumstances, can you live in the country you now occupy?"[24]

Jackson and his followers promoted the belief that removal to the trans-Mississippi West was a humanitarian policy essential for Cherokee survival. Jackson's remarks reflect a tone that was set by Lewis Cass, the secretary of war during Jackson's second administration. Cass had written a piece titled "Removal of the Indians" that appeared anonymously in the 1830 volume of *The North American Review*. Cass, then governor of Michigan, wrote at some length specifically about economic progress among the Cherokee. He argued:

> That individuals among the Cherokees have acquired property, and with it more enlarged views and juster notions of the value of our institutions, and the unprofitableness of their own, we have little doubt. . . . But, we believe, the great body of the people are in a state of helpless and hopeless poverty. With the same improvidence and habitual indolence which mark the northern Indians, they have less game for subsistence, and less peltry for sale. We doubt whether there is, upon the face of the globe, a more wretched race than the Cherokees as well as the other southern tribes, present.[25]

In stark contrast, opponents of removal pointed to the significant progress that had been made by the Cherokee in adopting white agricultural practices. For example, the Reverend Samuel Worcester, a missionary who had lived with the Cherokee since 1826, wrote in a letter to the Reverend E. S. Ely, an advocate of removal who edited *The Philadelphian*, that "the mass of the Cherokee people have built them houses and cultivated lands with their own hands" and that furthermore, "there may be a few families among the mountains, who depend mostly on the chase for support, but I know not of one."[26] Worcester continued this optimistic tone in another letter written to William Shorey Coodey, a member of a Cherokee delegation to Washington in 1830: "The land is cultivated with very different degrees of industry; but I believe that few fail of an adequate supply of food. The ground is uniformly cultivated by means of the plough, and not, as formerly, by the hoe only."[27]

A surprising degree of disagreement about Cherokee economic progress prior to their removal westward exists in today's literature. For example, the Jacksonian case that the Cherokee, along with the rest of the American Indians, were doomed to a technologically inevitable destruction because of the high per capita land requirement associated with a hunter-gatherer existence has recently been advanced by Stanley Lebergott, who put the pre-1825 per capita land requirement for the Cherokee at 1,900 acres.[28] Arguing along similar lines, prominent modern historians of Jacksonian Indian policy such as Robert V. Remini and Francis Paul Prucha have characterized Jackson's policies as motivated by humanitarian concerns. Remini wrote in his chapter on Indian removal that Jackson left the White House "believing that he had saved the Indians from inevitable doom. And, indeed, he had."[29] Prucha maintained that

> Jackson was genuinely concerned for the well-being of the Indians and for their civilization. Although his critics would scoff at the idea of placing him on the roll of the humanitarians, his assertions—both public and private—add up to a consistent belief that the Indians were capable of accepting white civilization, the hope that they would eventually do so, and repeated efforts to take measures that make the change possible and even speed it along.[30]

A contrasting view is presented by Theda Perdue and Donald L. Shadburn, who have described in great detail the use of African slaves in Cherokee agriculture and the growth of a planter class among the Cherokee.[31] The adoption of white agricultural techniques suggests both a degree of assimilation into white culture and a significant reduction in the per capita land requirement for the Cherokee. Douglas Hurt's 1987 volume on American Indian agriculture also describes qualitative aspects of Eastern Cherokee agriculture that leave the reader with the impression that average Cherokee households and members of other southeastern tribes were proficient farmers.[32] However, little in the way of statistical evidence is mustered to support this view.

The dearth of Cherokee economic data in the published literature is surprising given the detailed statistics that were collected by the federal government in the process of removal. The *Census of the Eastern Cherokee Indians,* 1835, is the most comprehensive statistical record available covering property holdings and economic activity by household for an Indian population in the antebellum period.[33] In fact the 1835 census includes agricultural statistics for Cherokee farmers that were not collected systematically for white farmers until the 1840 *Schedules of Mines, Agriculture, Commerce, and Manufacturing,* and then only for countywide aggregates. Moreover, by using the statistical information contained in the Cherokee census it is possible to gain insight into the extent of Cherokee economic progress. In particular, an important question relevant to the removal debate that can be addressed through an examination of the 1835 census is what percentage of Cherokee households were producing food surpluses in 1835.

William G. McLoughlin carefully examined the 1835 census in a 1977 article (with Walter H. Conser) and in his 1986 work *Cherokee Renascence in the New Republic*. McLoughlin and Conser gave a detailed examination and interpretation of the census data focused on the way racial characteristics of households and communities are related to the distribution of skills and assets inside the nation. Their analysis portrayed a "bourgeois socioeconomic structure" with "not only an expanding Cherokee bourgeoisie but also a growing planter or upperclass gentry who lived very much on the same scale and with the same values and style of life as the surrounding white planter class."[34] McLoughlin's 1986 work emphasizes a high degree of stratification in the Cherokee social structure, which had a small elite of planters, a somewhat larger group of yeoman farmers, and a large class of impoverished subsistence farmers.[35] McLoughlin's and Conser's work is based on a typed version of the 1835 census that was prepared "under the direction of Acting Secretary of Interior J.D.C. Atkins in 1897." This typescript covers 2,637 of the 2,669 households included in the original manuscript.[36]

McLoughlin and Conser posed an interesting question when they considered the relative sizes of social classes in the Eastern Cherokee population, but they did not reach firm conclusions about the relative sizes of the social classes for the Eastern Cherokee prior to removal. If a bourgeois Cherokee household is defined simply as one that produces surpluses, thus creating a source for investment, then based on data from the original manuscript of the 1835 census, it is possible to calculate a lower bound for the percentage of households that achieved surplus production and to estimate the magnitude of household surplus or deficit production. A lower bound for aggregate surplus production for the Eastern Cherokee can also be estimated. Lower bound calculations bias the number computed downward. If one has structured a computation in such a way as to arrive at the smallest possible number and it still turns out to be large, then a stronger case is made for the true figure being quite large. By comparing household production with subsistence requirements in a way that generates lower bound estimates, more definitive statements can be made about the number and percentage of households that could have achieved something like bourgeois status in the Eastern Cherokee population. Thus the debate over Cherokee economic progress prior to removal can be resolved using the census data and statistical methods.

The Census of the Eastern Cherokee Indians, 1835

Major Benjamin F. Currey was the acting Indian agent at the Cherokee Agency East and the superintendent of Cherokee removal in charge of conducting the 1835 census. Currey stated (albeit not clearly) that the purpose of the census was to be fully possessed of a knowledge of their number, the number of each man's houses, the number of his farms, with the quantity of land under cultivation, the proportions of tillable land, the mineral resources and water privileges of the country, etc., [that] the commissioners would be able to fix a true estimate upon the value of the country in case the whole title does not approve of the gross sum fixed upon already.[37]

Major Currey submitted the completed census to the commissioner of Indian affairs on February 27, 1836.[38]

The 1835 census records household-by-household data on thirteen demographic categories, nine agricultural categories, and nine categories of physical capital and skills. Demographic information includes the number of Cherokee per household grouped by sex and by age (above and below age eighteen for males, above and below sixteen for females). The Cherokee are also categorized by racial mix, with columns for half-breeds, quadroons, full-bloods, mixed Catawba, mixed Spaniards, and mixed Africans. The number of African slaves held by households is recorded by sex. The census shows no evidence of the use of Indian slaves by the Cherokee. Whites connected by marriage are also listed.

Agricultural data include the number of farms, the total number of acres cultivated, bushels of corn raised and sold, bushels of wheat raised and sold, gross income from corn sales, bushels of corn purchased, and cash outlays for corn purchases. A serious drawback of the census as a source of agricultural data is that crops other than wheat and corn and the amount of livestock held per household are omitted. Also, it is not clear what defines a farm for those households with more than one farm listed.

Physical capital counted (but, unfortunately, not valued) in the census includes the number of houses, mills, and ferryboats per household. Skills possessed by household members are listed in six categories: farmers over age eighteen, mechanics over age eighteen, weavers, spinners (listed as "spinsters" in the manuscript), readers of English, and readers of Cherokee per household.

Summary Statistics from the
Census of the Eastern Cherokee Indians, 1835

The statistics presented in Table 6.2 calculated from the population of Eastern Cherokee households reflect the situation experienced by the average Cherokee household in each state just prior to removal. Note that the number of observations for each variable changes because statistics were calculated only for those households with nonzero values reported for specific variables. Production measures are listed per household rather than per farm,

TABLE 6.2 Summary Statistics

Variable	Tennessee		Alabama		N. Carolina		Georgia		Totals	
	Mean	N	Mean	N	Mean	N	Mean	N	Mean	N
Males under 18	2.12	314	2.15	172	2.01	472	2.19	1,033	2.13	1,991
Males over 18	1.61	356	1.59	220	1.50	600	1.72	1,259	1.64	2,435
Females under 16	2.18	305	1.91	172	1.91	435	2.11	1,024	2.06	1,936
Females over 16	1.60	389	1.63	228	1.56	617	1.80	1,309	1.70	2,543
Cherokee	5.96	424	5.80	245	5.61	650	6.63	1,350	6.20	2,669
Male slaves	5.76	42	4.15	34	1.20	10	4.79	76	4.69	162
Female slaves	4.33	55	4.27	37	1.92	12	4.55	89	4.27	193
Total slaves	8.42	57	7.48	40	2.33	15	8.01	96	7.61	208
Whites married	1.01	77	1.00	27	1.00	10	1.00	67	1.01	181
Cultivated acres	27.05	399	36.17	198	10.96	628	15.19	1,271	17.69	2,496
Houses	4.44	408	2.78	214	1.53	635	3.71	1,289	3.20	2,546
Bushels wheat cultivated	35.43	28	95.00	2	0.00	0	43.55	29	41.44	59
Bushels wheat sold	18.78	9	0.00	0	0.00	0	20.76	17	20.08	26
Bushels corn cultivated	380.54	366	477.92	189	126.45	622	222.80	1201	242.17	2,378
Bushels corn sold	129.61	209	454.52	31	93.38	63	103.08	513	122.47	816
Corn income	57.75	209	234.90	31	46.62	63	63.18	440	67.41	743
Bushes of corn purchased	59.31	150	34.18	34	108.00	2	19.42	119	41.27	305
Grain expenditure	21.89	150	16.62	34	54.00	2	10.11	119	16.9	305
Readers of English	2.34	169	2.07	92	1.97	31	2.12	179	2.18	471
Readers of Cherokee	1.97	242	2.28	139	1.77	313	1.92	715	1.93	1409

Note: The column headed *N* lists the number of households for which observations were taken for each variable. A handful of observations on some variables in the census were recorded with half units. These were rounded up to the nearest integer in the data entry process.

Source: U.S. National Archives, Microcopy no. T-496, Census Roll, 1835, of the Cherokee Indians East of the Mississippi and Index to the Roll, Records of the Bureau of Indian Affairs, Record Group 75, Washington, D.C.

since it is not clear how a farm is defined in the manuscript and the focus of interest in this study is household production.

Household sizes were roughly similar—from six to seven Cherokee members—throughout the Eastern Cherokee Nation. The average number of acres cultivated per household varied from eleven in North Carolina to thirty-six in Alabama. Corn output per household averaged 126 bushels in North Carolina, 223 bushels in Georgia, 381 bushels in Tennessee, and 478 bushels in Alabama. Average corn sales per household making a sale were $46 in North Carolina, $58 in Tennessee, $63 in Georgia, and $235 in Alabama. The percentage of households that sold corn was 10 in North Car-

TABLE 6.3   Cherokee Literacy by State

	Percent of Households		Percent of Population	
	Cherokee	English	Cherokee	English
Tennessee	57.1	39.9	18.9	15.6
Alabama	56.7	37.6	22.3	13.4
North Carolina	48.1	4.7	15.2	1.7
Georgia	53.0	13.2	15.3	4.2
Overall	52.8	17.6	16.4	6.2

Note: These figures are computed from Table 6.2. The first two columns give the percentage of households with at least one literate member. The second pair of columns gives the literacy rate as a percentage of the total Cherokee population.

olina, 13 in Alabama, 38 in Georgia, and 50 in Tennessee. Rates of slave ownership were highest in Alabama and Tennessee, with some 16 percent of households owning an average of seven to eight slaves in Alabama and 12.5 percent of Tennessee households owning an average of eight to nine slaves.

For the Eastern Cherokee Nation as a whole, only 173 out of 2,669 households, or 6.5 percent, had no acreage in cultivation. The average cultivated acreage was slightly less than eighteen for all households engaged in farming. Some 89 percent of households produced a corn crop. The average annual harvest per household was 242 bushels. Almost 31 percent of households sold some corn, the average amount sold being 122 bushels. Approximately 8 percent of Cherokee households owned slaves, with an average of seven to eight slaves each.

Literacy rates varied little between states for the Cherokee language. However, a big difference in English literacy shows up when Tennessee and Alabama are compared to North Carolina and Georgia. Literacy rates are shown in more detail in Table 6.3. The proportion of households with at least one member literate in English was 39.9 percent in Tennessee and 37.6 percent in Alabama, as contrasted with 4.7 percent in North Carolina and 13.2 percent in Georgia. On the other hand, over half of the households in every state except North Carolina (where the figure was 48 percent) had at least one member who was literate in Cherokee.

Data for physical and human capital among the Eastern Cherokee Indians are presented in Table 6.4. The number of houses far exceeds the number of households for all four states, and the number of farms is greater than the number of households for every state but Tennessee. Apparently, households frequently made investments in land clearing in different locations, perhaps to better ensure a successful crop or to take advantage of differences in soil and growing conditions. Weavers and spinners were found in most households. Tennessee and Georgia are notable for the large number of ferryboats owned by Cherokees and for the number of mechanics.

TABLE 6.4   Cherokee Physical and Human Capital Statistics by State

	Tennessee	Alabama	North Carolina	Georgia
Houses	1,803	596	978	4,801
Farms	412	262	714	1,667
Grain mills	8	2	6	9
Ferryboats	45	9	0	13
Farmers over 18	581	327	822	1,933
Mechanics over 18	209	9	13	100
Weavers	547	159	325	1,410
Spinners	863	274	721	2,202

Source: U.S. National Archives, Microcopy no. T-496, Census Roll, 1835, of the Cherokee Indians East of the Mississippi and Index to the Roll, Records of the Bureau of Indian Affairs, Record Group 75, Washington, D.C.

Estimating the Extent of Surplus Agricultural Production for the Eastern Cherokee Indians

Data from the 1835 census can be used to test the competing views regarding the ability of Cherokee households to produce their own subsistence. The data are well suited to the calculation of a lower bound for the percentage of households that achieved at least subsistence levels of output because Cherokee agriculture is known to have been fairly diversified. It is widely accepted that many other crops besides corn and wheat, in addition to substantial herds of livestock, were raised by the Cherokee.

For example, McLoughlin and Conser cite an 1828 census taken by the editors of the Cherokee newspaper, *The Phoenix*, that lists 22,405 black cattle, 7,628 horses, 38,517 swine, and 2,912 sheep.[39] Citing contemporary accounts of Cherokee agriculture, Perdue notes that the Cherokee cultivated "corn, gourds, melons, cucumbers, squash, cymlins [cymlings], beans, and a 'red pease'" (perhaps kidney beans) during the colonial period.[40] Writing about agriculture practiced during the mid-eighteenth century, Hurt maintains that pumpkins, sunflowers, cabbage, potatoes, peaches, leeks, and garlic were grown in addition to the crops noted above.[41] McLoughlin cites Cherokee accounts of their agricultural practice in 1826 that refer to production of wheat, rye, oats, sweet potatoes, apples, butter, and cheese and to widespread cotton cultivation, mostly for domestic use.[42] A mixture of cornmeal and boiled beans baked as a bread was a traditional staple of the Cherokee.[43] This undoubtedly nutritious but bland fare was supplemented with hunting and fishing activities by Cherokee in the mountainous regions of North Carolina.[44] Douglas C. Wilms refers to peach orchards in Georgia during the 1830s so extensive that the surplus peaches that were not dried for winter consumption were fed to hogs. Wilms also notes involvement by

Georgia Cherokee in the hog trade, with Cherokee providing both hogs for market and corn for feed to hogs that were driven through Georgia for sale on plantations.[45]

Given this evidence of diversification in food production, a plausible lower bound percentage of self-sufficient households can be estimated by comparing the size of households' corn crops with an appropriate threshold level of corn output for self-sufficiency. If the corn crop alone was large enough to provide for the subsistence of a household (including slaves and intermarried whites), then almost certainly, given diversification in production, the household produced some surplus food. Thus the percentage of households producing above the threshold would be a lower bound for the percentage achieving at least self-sufficiency. Following David Weiman's work on production by upcountry farmers in Floyd County (which was part of the Cherokee Nation) and Dekalb County in Georgia in 1859, I have chosen twenty bushels of corn per consumer equivalent as an appropriate threshold for calculating a lower bound for self-sufficiency for Cherokee farmers.[46] Using methods similar to Weiman's, I calculated consumer equivalents per household by summing the adult populations of both sexes, the slave population, the whites by marriage, 0.5 times the females under sixteen, and 0.5 times the males under eighteen. The amount of corn potentially available for human consumption can be computed by taking 95 percent of the corn output per household, to allow 5 percent of the corn produced to be used for seed. All these calculations can be done based on the figures presented in Table 6.2.

Lower bound estimates for the percentage of households that achieved self-sufficient levels of corn production and the magnitude of surplus corn production are presented by state and for the Cherokee Nation as a whole in Table 6.5. These results show that for Tennessee and Alabama, at a minimum, 74 percent of the households that produced any corn produced surpluses. When non–corn producing households are included, the percentages producing above the threshold fall to 63.7 percent for Tennessee and 59.1 percent for Alabama. Somewhat lower percentages of households exceed the lower bound threshold in North Carolina and Georgia. At least 48.4 percent of North Carolina households and 52.1 percent of Georgia households that produced any corn were producing surpluses. When non–corn producing households are included for these states, the percentages fall to 46.1 percent for North Carolina and 46.4 percent for Georgia. Overall, 56.5 percent of households that produced corn in the Cherokee Nation produced above the lower bound threshold, and just over half of all households exceeded the threshold. The last column of Table 6.5 records the magnitude of surplus corn production by state and for the Cherokee Nation as a whole. This surplus represents a minimum estimate because it is calculated based on the lower bound threshold for self-sufficiency of twenty bushels per consumer

TABLE 6.5 Percentage of Households Achieving Self-Sufficiency in Corn Production and Magnitude of Surplus Corn Production

	All Households (%)	Corn-Producing Households (%)	Surplus Corn (bushels)
Tennessee	63.7 (270)	74.0	86,224
Alabama	59.1 (145)	76.7	59,367
North Carolina	46.1 (300)	48.4	18,916
Georgia	46.4 (626)	52.1	106,419
Cherokee Nation	50.3 (1341)	56.5	270,758

Note: These figures are computed from Tables 6.2 and 6.6. The figure in parentheses below the percentage figures for all households is the number of households producing surpluses.

equivalent. The aggregate corn requirement for subsistence is twenty bushels per consumer equivalent times the number of consumer equivalents. Corn that is potentially available for human consumption is 95 percent of the total corn output, thus allowing for seed requirements. Surplus corn is the difference between these figures. The surplus varies from a high figure of 106,419 bushels in Georgia to a low of 18,916 bushels in North Carolina. The aggregate surplus is recorded at 270,758 bushels. This aggregate surplus could have been used for livestock production, for redistribution to households that were unable to produce adequate amounts of food, for sale in the market in order to earn a cash income, and for insurance against future crop failures.

A more detailed picture of the distribution of Cherokee corn output per consumer equivalent is presented by state and for the Cherokee Nation as a whole in Table 6.6. These data support the percentage calculations that appear in Table 6.5. The first column in Table 6.6 shows categories for bushels of corn available for consumption per consumer equivalent; the columns N and % show the number of households and the percentage of the total number of households represented, respectively. The category 0–9.9 excludes those households that were recorded as having raised no corn from the calculation.

These data are striking in that a substantial percentage of Cherokee households fall below the twenty bushel per consumer equivalent threshold for self-sufficiency. However, for several reasons, the Jacksonian conclusion regarding the high level of misery in these households may not always be war-

TABLE 6.6 Distribution of Cherokee Corn Output per Consumer Equivalent by State in 1835 (number and percentage of households)

bu/CE	Tennessee		Alabama		N. Carolina		Georgia		Cherokee Nation	
	N	%	N	%	N	%	N	%	N	%
0–.9	110	26.0	73	29.8	158	24.3	493	36.5	834	31.2
1–9.9	52	12.3	17	6.9	130	20.0	344	25.5	543	20.3
10–19.9	43	10.2	27	11.0	192	29.5	231	17.1	493	18.5
20–29.9	36	8.5	28	11.4	110	16.9	158	11.7	332	12.4
30–49.9	71	16.8	45	18.4	118	18.2	208	15.4	442	16.6
50–69.9	49	11.6	17	6.9	29	4.5	87	6.4	182	6.8
70–99.9	46	10.9	19	7.7	23	3.5	84	6.2	172	6.4
100–149.9	27	6.4	18	7.3	13	2.0	54	4.0	112	4.2
> 150	41	9.7	18	7.3	7	1.1	35	2.6	101	3.8

Note: Consumer equivalents per household were calculated by summing the adult populations of both sexes, the slave population, the whites by marriage, half the females under sixteen, and half the males under eighteen. Corn available for human consumption was computed by taking 95 percent of corn output for the household, thus allowing 5 percent for seed. These methods follow those used by David F. Weiman, "Farmers and the Market in Antebellum America: A View from the Georgia Upcountry," *The Journal of Economic History* 47 (September 1987):627–647.

Source: U.S. National Archives, Microcopy no. T-496, Census Roll, 1835, of the Cherokee Indians East of the Mississippi and Index to the Roll, Records of the Bureau of Indian Affairs, Record Group 75. Washington, D.C.

ranted. First, the twenty bushel per consumer equivalent is a stringent lower bound threshold to employ in this analysis. Since Floyd County, Georgia, was one of the counties that Weiman included in his 1987 study of up-country Georgia farmers and was also a part of the Eastern Cherokee Nation prior to removal, it seems reasonable that in 1835 many Cherokee farmers would have experienced conditions similar to those experienced by white farmers in Weiman's 1859 sample of Floyd County.[47] After all, most of the Cherokees in the Southeast in 1835 were up-country farmers. Weiman uses twenty corn equivalent bushels per consumer equivalent and thirty-six corn equivalent bushels per consumer equivalent as the lowest and highest thresholds for self-sufficiency in his analysis.[48] The more detailed statistics listed in the 1860 *Census of Agriculture* allowed Weiman to convert noncorn food crops to corn equivalent bushels in his calculations of the percentage of farms that were self-sufficient in foodstuffs. For example, tenant farmers in Floyd County, the least diversified farmers in Weiman's sample, produced noncorn food crops that accounted for 1.32 times as many corn equivalent bushels than corn itself.[49] If one assumes that on average Cherokee farmers were as diversified as white tenant farmers in Floyd County in 1859, then a Cherokee household just achieving the threshold of twenty bushels of corn per consumer equivalent would also produce 1.32 times 20, or some 26.4 corn equivalent bushels of noncorn food crops, for a total of 46.4 corn equivalent bushels per consumer equivalent. Thus, assuming diversification in Eastern Cherokee agriculture that is on par with white tenants in the same region some fifteen years later, the twenty corn equivalent bushels per consumer equivalent threshold greatly exceeds Weiman's highest threshold of thirty-six corn equivalent bushels per consumer equivalent.[50]

Since tenant farmers would have been under pressure to specialize in crops for sale in the market in order to generate cash income to pay rent, it seems reasonable that Cherokee farmers, who did not experience such pressure, would have been inclined to push diversification further in order to ensure against specific crop failures. Put differently, if Cherokee farmers achieved levels of diversification as limited as those achieved by white tenant farmers, then ten bushels per consumer equivalent of corn production would have been accompanied by 13.2 bushels per consumer equivalent of noncorn food crops that would put all of the 493 households in the 10–19.9 bushels per consumer equivalent category listed in Table 6.6 over the twenty bushel per consumer equivalent threshold. If these households are included among those achieving self-sufficiency, the percentage of all households achieving self-sufficiency becomes 68.7, and the percentage of corn-producing households achieving self-sufficiency becomes 77.2. Indeed, these percentages could be interpreted as conservative upper bound estimates for the share of Cherokee households that achieved at least self-sufficient levels of production.

Clearly, the analysis presented here hinges on the assumption of extensive diversification in Cherokee agricultural practice. Unfortunately, direct statistical evidence of diversification appears to be nonexistent.[51] However, it is possible to strengthen the anecdotal case for diversification with statistical analysis of data on corn production, wheat production, and cultivated acres listed in the 1835 census. The fact that corn yields per acre (total bushels of corn produced divided by total cultivated acres) computed from data in Table 6.2 are low suggests diversification. These yields range from a high of 13.8 bushels per cultivated acre for Georgia to a low of 11.4 bushels per cultivated acre for North Carolina and an average for the entire population of 13 bushels per cultivated acre. The national average yield for corn in 1840 was 25 bushels per acre.[52] Wilms cites corn yields from the year 1914 of thirty to forty bushels per acre with little or no fertilizer in the northwestern portion of what had been Cherokee Georgia.[53] Even if Cherokee farmers were only half as efficient as white farmers in Floyd County in 1914, the calculated yields should have been in the twenty bushels per acre range.

In fact, the data presented in Table 6.7 show that Cherokee corn yields measured per capita rather than per acre were in the same range as those for southern up-country whites in the antebellum period. The Eastern Cherokee corn output per capita figure of 31.44 bushels in 1835 even exceeds the figures reported by Lewis C. Gray[54] for white Virginia farmers in 1850. A complete comparison of Cherokee and white farming practice in the region under study is beyond the scope of this study. However, a spot comparison of Floyd County Cherokee farmers with white farmers in Floyd and Dekalb Counties in 1840 shows that the Floyd County whites produced significantly more than the Cherokee per capita, who produced roughly the same amount as Dekalb County whites per capita. Dekalb County is an interesting county to compare with Floyd County in 1835 and 1840 because Weiman found that farmers in Floyd County were producing greater surpluses and were better integrated into markets for their surplus produce than farmers in Dekalb County on the eve of the Civil War. Weiman attributes this differential performance to differences in natural endowments and internal infrastructure development between the two counties.[55] However, based on per capita corn production statistics from 1840, it appears that Floyd County farmers were well ahead of Dekalb County farmers just two years after the Cherokee removal in 1838. These data suggest that white Floyd County farmers may have experienced systematic gains from taking over Cherokee investments in farm capital compared to the situation faced by nearby farmers in Dekalb County, who may have been faced with significant farmmaking costs. A comparative study of the Cherokee data from 1835 with countywide data from 1840 for white farm production on former Cherokee land and white production on adjacent non-Cherokee land could shed greater light on the extent of gains for white farmers who moved onto Cherokee land relative to white farmers who did not.

A second reason to discount the Jacksonian contention that the Cherokee were unable to procure a living from the resources available to them in the

TABLE 6.7   Corn Output in Selected Regions of the Southeast in 1840, 1850 and for the Cherokee in 1835 (bushels per capita)

Region or Group	Output
Valley of Virginia	21.37
Valley of East Tennessee	49.41
Middle Tennessee	65.26
Kentucky Blue Grass region	82.66
Virginia mountains	26.97
Kentucky mountains	39.07
Cumberland plateau	42.16
Northwest Georgia	41.89
Floyd County Georgia in 1840	55.06
Dekalb County Georgia in 1840	27.99
Tennessee Cherokees in 1835	45.15
Alabama Cherokees in 1835	51.70
N. Carolina Cherokees in 1835	21.31
Georgia Cherokees in 1835	27.34
Floyd County Cherokees in 1835	30.85
Eastern Cherokees in 1835	31.44

Note: Cherokee output per capita is computed from data in Table 6.2 by dividing total corn output by the total population including slaves and whites by marriage. White output per capita for Dekalb County and Floyd County, Georgia in 1840 is computed by dividing total corn output in these counties by total population. Other figures for 1850 are listed in Lewis C. Gray, *History of Agriculture in the Southern United States to 1860* (Gloucester, Mass.: Peter Smith, 1958).

Sources: U.S. National Archives, Microcopy no. T-496, Census Roll, 1835, of the Cherokee Indians East of the Mississippi and Index to the Roll, Records of the Bureau of Indian Affairs, Record Group 75, Washington, D.C.; Lewis C. Gray, *History of Agriculture in the Southern United States to 1860* (Gloucester, Mass.: Peter Smith, 1958), 876; *Schedules of Mines, Agriculture, Commerce, and Manufacturing,* Records for Dekalb County and Floyd County, Georgia, 1840; *Manuscript Census,* Dekalb County and Floyd County, Georgia.

Southeast is that many of these households depended on other human and physical capital to make a living. Evidence to support this assertion is presented in Table 6.8, which shows that among the 406 households listed with two or fewer acres in cultivation, 98.8 percent had at least one member with some skill or owned physical capital of some type.

Third, the demographic characteristics of the 173 households with no acres under cultivation suggest that a significant number were made up of aged Cherokee. Approximately 21 percent of these households consisted of a single adult male, a single adult female, or an adult couple with no children. Five of these households had members who were all below age eighteen for males and sixteen for females, forming another smaller class of de-

TABLE 6.8 Distribution of Skills Held by Households with Two or Fewer Cultivated Acres

Skill	Tennessee	Alabama	N. Carolina	Georgia
	(N = 50)	(N = 52)	(N = 61)	(N = 243)
Mill owner	1 (1)	1 (1)	0	0
Ferryboats	10 (3)	4 (3)	0	0
Mechanics	14 (9)	1 (1)	0	21 (20)
Weavers	38 (32)	27 (27)	10 (9)	170 (137)
Spinners	65 (43)	45 (41)	65 (45)	290 (184)
Farmers	45 (36)	42 (37)	60 (50)	253 (180)
No skills	(3)	(3)	(1)	(26)

Note: The *N* listed below the states refers to the number of households with two or fewer cultivated acres. The first number listed in each column is the number of people with the skill (except for the mills and ferryboat lines for which the number is the actual number of mills and boats). The figure in parentheses is the number of households with such capital or skill.

Source: U.S. National Archives, Microcopy no. T-496, Census Roll, 1835, of the Cherokee Indians East of the Mississippi and Index to the Roll, Records of the Bureau of Indian Affairs, Record Group 75, Washington, D.C.

pendents. The largest group of households with no acres under cultivation consisted of adults living with children. As a percentage of the total number of households in each state, these zero-acre households with adults and children are 4.7 percent in Tennessee, 12.6 percent in Alabama, 2.6 percent in North Carolina, and 4 percent in Georgia. Alabama's concentration of larger Cherokee farms could have afforded employment opportunities to those with no acreage of their own. Many of these families may have hired out their labor to nearby farms.

Finally, it is possible that household production is the wrong unit of measure by which to judge Cherokee economic performance relative to subsistence, especially for the North Carolina households.[56] Anthropological evidence for the North Carolina Cherokee suggests that town-centered, communal, aboriginal forms of production were operative well into the second half of the nineteenth century. These towns and their production systems were called the *gadugi* and operated under the direction of a benevolent community chief. Production was split between private plots and, in some cases, community fields, with communal labor employed throughout. Sharing of the output was ritualized in the *gadugi*. It would have been possible for a household to produce less than a subsistence amount of food on its private plot yet still earn a livelihood in the context of the *gadugi*.[57] Clearly, a communal system of labor organization could cause the *gadugi* to be noticeably less inclined toward surplus production than private farmsteads. Once subsistence was produced by the *gadugi*, labor probably ceased.

Taken together, the evidence presented in the foregoing discussion points to a large majority of Cherokee households that either were farm producers at levels well in excess of subsistence or were procuring a living some other way with other types of human or physical capital. Many of the households with no visible means of support were probably made up of aged and orphaned Cherokee. The extent of surplus production across Cherokee households is surprising given the widely accepted view of extreme Cherokee social stratification. As McLoughlin stated, this view polarizes the Cherokee into an elite of "a small group of well-to-do, influential merchant-traders, large planters, slave-owning farmers, and entrepreneurs, . . . a somewhat larger group of farmers and herdsmen who mixed small-scale farming with another enterprise . . . and by far the largest class, . . . the small farmers who barely made enough to live on."[58] Mary Young maintained this view in a recent article stating that "most Cherokees were self-sufficient hillbilly farmers."[59] To be sure, the results presented here indicate that there were many farmers who perhaps resembled hillbillies and produced at or below the margin of subsistence. However, at a minimum, the calculations also point to a clear majority of households producing surpluses in Tennessee and Alabama and just under 50 percent doing so in North Carolina and Georgia. Contrary to McLoughlin's and Young's conclusions, the largest class of Cherokee consisted of households producing more than enough to live on.

Conclusion

With at least half of Cherokee households producing substantial surpluses, advocates for the Cherokee removal were on shaky ground when they used economic arguments to justify imposing the costs of a forced migration on a developing economy as a humanitarian policy. Perhaps Jackson and other supporters of Indian removal were in fact motivated by feelings of benevolence toward the Indians, and perhaps the large numbers of Cherokee who were undoubtedly poor caused them to overlook the larger number of Cherokee households producing substantial surpluses. There is no doubt that supporters of removal claimed to have weighed the evidence for Cherokee progress carefully against evidence of increasing misery. For example, Cass wrote:

> We are as unwilling to underrate, as we should be to overrate, the progress made by these Indians in civilization and improvement. . . . We hope that our opinion upon this subject may be erroneous. But we have melancholy forebodings. That a few principal men, who can secure favorable cotton lands, and cultivate them with slaves, will be comfortable and satisfied, we may well believe. . . . But to form just conceptions of the spirit and objects of these efforts, we must look at their practical operation on the community. It is here, if the facts

which have been stated to us are correct, and of which we have no doubt, that they will be found wanting.[60]

Did supporters of the Cherokee removal deliberately understate the extent of economic progress in the Eastern Cherokee Nation? The political end of instituting a general policy of Indian removal was certainly well served by understating the size of the surplus-producing class of Cherokee. Moreover, the practical effect of removal was the transfer of rents in the form of improved acreage capable of surplus production to white farmers. A thorough analysis of the political economy of the Cherokee removal might find that the policy was a politically pragmatic transfer of wealth from Cherokee households to white farmers, even if the supporters of removal believed at the time that it was a humanitarian policy toward an indigenous population.

Could the Cherokee have survived in the Southeast after 1835? From a purely economic standpoint, almost certainly they could have. However, from a political standpoint it is less clear. Cherokee property rights were anything but secure in the Southeast in the 1830s. The federal government was hardly inclined to defend the property rights of an Indian nation against the depredations of white settlers and their state governments in this period. Under these circumstances, there was little choice for the Cherokee but to endure the cost of a forced migration to Oklahoma and to begin the task of establishing new communities in a very different setting.

Notes

I thank a series of undergraduate research assistants for their help reading microfilm and entering data. They are Jamie Shilling, Brian Mauser, Stanley Zikhali, David Hart, Mark Johnson, Jeff Miller, Anne Lindman, and Sherri West. I also thank Louis Cain, Thomas T. Taylor, Richard Sullivan, Larry Neal, Jeremy Atack, Thomas Ulen, Lee Alston, Joan Orr, and Douglas Wilms for numerous comments on earlier drafts. I am indebted to participants at Economic History Workshops at the University of Illinois, Urbana-Champaign, and at Miami University, Oxford, Ohio, and to participants at the Economic History Seminar at Columbia University, who have contributed many useful suggestions. Of course, remaining errors are my own. This research was supported in part by a grant from the Wittenberg University Faculty Research Fund Board. Portions of this chapter are taken from the article "Evidence of Surplus Production in the Cherokee Nation Prior to Removal," which appeared in *The Journal of Economic History* 55, no. 1 (March 1995): 120–138. Reprinted with permission of Cambridge University Press.

1. John Phillip Reid, *A Better Kind of Hatchet: Law, Trade, and Diplomacy in the Cherokee Nation During the Early Years of European Contact* (University Park: Pennsylvania State University Press, 1976), 2.

2. John Phillip Reid, *A Law of Blood: The Primitive Law of the Cherokee Nation* (New York: New York University Press, 1970), 75.

3. Ibid., 39–41.

4. Reid, *A Better Kind of Hatchet*, 5.

5. Reid, *A Law of Blood*, 129.

6. Ibid., 139.

7. Ibid., 129.

8. Reid, *A Better Kind of Hatchet*, 29.

9. Ibid., 34–36.

10. Ibid., 125.

11. Theda Perdue, "Cherokee Planters: The Development of Plantation Slavery Before Removal," in *The Cherokee Indian Nation,* ed. Duane H. King (Knoxville: University of Tennessee Press, 1979), 112.

12. Rennard Strickland, *Fire and the Spirits: Cherokee Law from the Clan to the Court* (Norman: University of Oklahoma Press, 1975), 32; Betty Anderson Smith, "Distribution of Eighteenth-Century Cherokee Settlements," in King, *The Cherokee Indian Nation,* 49–50.

13. Smith, "Distribution," 48–50.

14. Theda Perdue, *Slavery and the Evolution of Cherokee Society, 1540–1866* (Knoxville: University of Tennessee Press, 1979), 53.

15. Ibid., 53–54; Ronald N. Satz, *American Indian Policy in the Jacksonian Era* (Lincoln: University of Nebraska Press, 1975), 9–63.

16. Perdue, "Cherokee Planters," 118.

17. Ibid., 117.

18. Strickland, *Fire and the Spirits*, 54–62; V. Richard Persico Jr., "Early Nineteenth-Century Cherokee Political Organization," in King, *The Cherokee Indian Nation,* 93.

19. Strickland, *Fire and the Spirits*, 74.

20. Perdue, "Cherokee Planters," 62.

21. Charles J. Kappler, *Indian Treaties, 1778–1883* (New York: Interland Publishing, 1973), 439–449.

22. Strickland, *Fire and the Spirits*, 8.

23. Satz, *American Indian Policy*, 19.

24. Robert V. Remini, *Andrew Jackson and the Course of American Democracy, 1833–1845* (New York: Harper and Row, 1984), 298.

25. Lewis Cass, "Removal of the Indians," *The North American Review*, 30 (January 1830):71.

26. Letter from the Reverend Samuel A. Worcester to the Reverend E. S. Ely, editor of *The Philadelphian*, March 10, 1830, in Jack Frederick Kilpatrick and Anna Gritts Kilpatrick, eds., *New Echota Letters: Contributions of Samuel A. Worcester to the Cherokee Phoenix* (Dallas: Southern Methodist University Press, 1968), 75.

27. Letter from the Reverend Samuel A. Worcester to William Shorey Coodey, March 15, 1830, in Kilpatrick and Kilpatrick, *New Echota Letters,* 79.

28. Stanley Lebergott, *The Americans: An Economic Record* (New York: Norton, 1984), 16.

29. Remini, *Andrew Jackson and the Course of American Democracy,* 314.

30. Francis Paul Prucha, "Andrew Jackson's Indian Policy: A Reassessment," *Journal of American History*, 66 (December 1969):533–534.

31. For detailed accounts of plantation agriculture practiced by the Cherokee, see Perdue, *Slavery and the Evolution of Cherokee Society*, and Donald L. Shadburn, *Cherokee Planters in Georgia: 1832–1838* (Roswell, Ga.: W. H. Wolfe, 1990).

32. R. Douglas Hurt, *Indian Agriculture in America: Prehistory to the Present* (Lawrence: University Press of Kansas, 1987), 32–33, 68, 91, 98–99.

33. The census is available on microfilm from the U.S. National Archives, Microcopy no. T-496, Census Roll, 1835, of the Cherokee Indians East of the Mississippi and Index to the Roll, Records of the Bureau of Indian Affairs, Record Group 75, Washington, D.C.

34. William G. McLoughlin and Walter H. Conser Jr., "The Cherokees in Transition: A Statistical Analysis of the Federal Cherokee Census of 1835," *The Journal of American History*, 64 (December 1977):697.

35. William G. McLoughlin, *Cherokee Renascence in the New Republic* (Princeton: Princeton University Press, 1986), 327.

36. McLoughlin and Conser, "The Cherokees in Transition," 680, 683. My analysis of the microcopy of the original manuscript showed there to be 2,669 households.

37. George Nixon, "Records Relating to Native American Research: The Five Civilized Tribes," in *The Source: A Guidebook of American Genealogy*, eds. Arlene Eakle and Johni Cerny (Salt Lake City: Ancestry Publishing Company, 1984), 535.

38. Ibid., 535.

39. McLoughlin and Conser, The Cherokees in Transition," 681, table 1.

40. Perdue, *Slavery and the Evolution of Cherokee Society*, 15.

41. Hurt, *Indian Agriculture in America*, 32. See also Raymond D. Fogelson and Paul Kutsche, "Cherokee Economic Cooperatives: The Gadugi," in *Symposium on Cherokee and Iroquois Culture*, eds. William N. Fenton and John Gulick (Washington, D.C.: GPO, 1961), 95.

42. McLoughlin, *Cherokee Renascence in the New Republic*, 301.

43. John R. Finger, *The Eastern Band of Cherokees, 1819–1900* (Knoxville: University of Tennessee Press, 1984), 62.

44. Ibid., 62.

45. Douglas C. Wilms, "Cherokee Indian Land Use in Georgia, 1800–1838" (Ph.D. diss., University of Georgia, Athens, 1973), 113, 139.

46. David F. Weiman, "Farmers and the Market in Antebellum America: A View from the Georgia Upcountry," *The Journal of Economic History* 47 (September 1987):627–647.

47. Ibid., 630.

48. Ibid., 635.

49. Ibid., 633, table 1.

50. Weiman's lowest threshold of twenty bushels per consumer equivalent is assumed by Roger Ransom and Richard Sutch; see Roger Ransom and Richard Sutch, *One Kind of Freedom: The Economic Consequences of Emancipation* (Cambridge: Cambridge University Press, 1977), 251–252. Weiman's highest threshold of thirty-six bushels per consumer equivalent is based on estimates by Robert Gallman; see Weiman, "Farmers and the Market in Antebellum America," 635, note 29.

51. Conversations with Douglas Wilms and Joan Orr, Archivist, Museum of the Cherokee Indian, Cherokee, North Carolina.

52. *Historical Statistics of the U.S.*, p. 500.

53. Wilms, "Cherokee Indian Land Use in Georgia," 61.

54. Lewis C. Gray, *History of Agriculture in the Southern United States to 1860* (Gloucester, Mass.: Peter Smith, 1958).

55. Weiman, "Farmers and the Market in Antebellum America," 627.

56. I thank Professor Jennifer Roback for pointing out this possibility to me.

57. Fogelson and Kutsche, "Cherokee Economic Cooperatives," 94–95.

58. McLoughlin, *Cherokee Renascence in the New Republic,* 327.

59. Mary Young, "The Exercise of Sovereignty in Cherokee Georgia," *Journal of the Early Republic,* 10 (Spring 1990): 46.

60. Cass, "Removal of the Indians," 71–72.

References

Cass, Lewis. 1830. "Removal of the Indians." *The North American Review* 30 (January):62–120.

Finger, John R. 1984. *The Eastern Band of Cherokees, 1819–1900.* Knoxville: University of Tennessee Press.

Fogelson, Raymond D., and Paul Kutsche. 1961. "Cherokee Economic Cooperatives: The Gadugi." In *Symposium on Cherokee and Iroquois Culture,* eds. William N. Fenton and John Gulick, 87–123. Washington, D.C.: GPO.

Gray, Lewis C. 1958. *History of Agriculture in the Southern United States to 1860.* Gloucester, Mass.: Peter Smith.

Hurt, R. Douglas. 1987. *Indian Agriculture in America: Prehistory to the Present.* Lawrence: University Press of Kansas.

Kappler, Charles J. 1973. *Indian Treaties, 1778–1883.* New York: Interland Publishing.

Kilpatrick, Jack Frederick, and Anna Gritts Kilpatrick, eds. 1968. *New Echota Letters: Contributions of Samuel A. Worcester to the Cherokee Phoenix.* Dallas: Southern Methodist University Press.

Lebergott, Stanley. 1984. *The Americans: An Economic Record.* New York: Norton.

Manuscript Census. 1840. Dekalb County and Floyd County, Georgia.

McLoughlin, William G. 1986. *Cherokee Renascence in the New Republic.* Princeton: Princeton University Press.

McLoughlin, William G., and Walter H. Conser Jr. 1977. "The Cherokees in Transition: A Statistical Analysis of the Federal Cherokee Census of 1835." *The Journal of American History* 64 (December):678–703.

Nixon, George. 1984. "Records Relating to Native American Research: The Five Civilized Tribes." In *The Source: A Guidebook of American Genealogy,* eds. Arlene Eakle and Johni Cerny, 553–557. Salt Lake City: Ancestry Publishing Company.

Perdue, Theda. 1979a. "Cherokee Planters: The Development of Plantation Slavery Before Removal." In *The Cherokee Indian Nation,* ed. Duane H. King, 110–128. Knoxville: University of Tennessee Press.

_____. 1979b. *Slavery and the Evolution of Cherokee Society, 1540–1866.* Knoxville: University of Tennessee Press.

Persico, V. Richard, Jr. 1979. "Early Nineteenth-Century Cherokee Political Organization." In *The Cherokee Indian Nation*, ed. Duane H. King, 92–109. Knoxville: University of Tennessee Press.

Prucha, Francis Paul. 1969. "Andrew Jackson's Indian Policy: A Reassessment." *Journal of American History* 66 (December):527–539.

Ransom, Roger, and Richard Sutch. 1977. *One Kind of Freedom: The Economic Consequences of Emancipation*. Cambridge: Cambridge University Press.

Reid, John Phillip. 1970. *A Law of Blood: The Primitive Law of the Cherokee Nation*. New York: New York University Press.

_____. 1976. *A Better Kind of Hatchet: Law, Trade, and Diplomacy in the Cherokee Nation During the Early Years of European Contact*. University Park: Pennsylvania State University Press.

Remini, Robert V. 1984. *Andrew Jackson and the Course of American Democracy, 1833–1845*. New York: Harper and Row.

Satz, Ronald N. 1975. *American Indian Policy in the Jacksonian Era*. Lincoln: University of Nebraska Press.

Schedules of Mines, Agriculture, Commerce, and Manufacturing. 1840. Records for Dekalb County and Floyd County, Georgia.

Shadburn, Donald L. 1990. *Cherokee Planters in Georgia: 1832–1838*. Roswell, Ga.: W. H. Wolfe.

Smith, Betty Anderson. 1979. "Distribution of Eighteenth-Century Cherokee Settlements." In *The Cherokee Indian Nation*, ed. Duane H. King, 46–60. Knoxville: University of Tennessee Press.

Strickland, Rennard. 1975. *Fire and the Spirits: Cherokee Law from the Clan to the Court*. Norman: University of Oklahoma Press.

U.S. National Archives, Microcopy no. T-496, Census Roll, 1835, of the Cherokee Indians East of the Mississippi and Index to the Roll, Records of the Bureau of Indian Affairs, Record Group 75, Washington, D.C.

Weiman, David F. 1987. "Farmers and the Market in Antebellum America: A View from the Georgia Upcountry." *The Journal of Economic History* 47 (September):627–647.

Wilms, Douglas C. 1973. "Cherokee Indian Land Use in Georgia, 1800–1838." Ph.D. diss., University of Georgia, Athens.

Young, Mary. 1990. "The Exercise of Sovereignty in Cherokee Georgia." *Journal of the Early Republic* 10 (Spring):43–63.

7

Land, Population, Prices, and the Regulation of Natural Resources

The Lake Superior Ojibwa, 1790–1920

JAMES W. OBERLY

This chapter sketches part of the history of the Lake Superior Ojibwa and links their past to two of the great ongoing scholarly enterprises in North American historical demography: the work of Robert Fogel (1986) and his associates, which gives an account of the mortality decline in the entire population of North America and explains its timing, and Russell Thornton's (1987) narrative of the decline and rebound of the Native American population over the four centuries from 1500 to 1900. In particular, this chapter will look at the role of diet and nutrition among the Lake Superior Ojibwa (also known as "Chippewa") people of Wisconsin and attempt to make some connections to the larger history of the tribe's experience with treaties and land cessions, economic change, and demographic change.

This chapter provides a broad overview of Ojibwa demographic history using what data are available. Records are lacking for basic vital statistics until the end of the nineteenth century. Only sketchy estimates of population levels exist before the U.S. Bureau of Indian Affairs began an annual census in 1885. It is possible, however, to use the writings of federal Indian agents and missionaries to get some sense of epidemic diseases that hit the Ojibwa. In addition, it is possible to use the same types of records studied by Fogel (1986) to compare the Ojibwa and their diet to that of other Americans in the mid-nineteenth century.

Fogel (1986) found that mortality rates in what would become the United States dropped throughout the first three-quarters of the eighteenth

century as the populations became longer-lived, but the economic dislocation of the Revolutionary War and its aftermath caused an increase in the
death rate until about the year 1850. Since the mid-nineteenth century,
death rates in the United States have steadily declined. This change preceded
not only new medical techniques but even simple public health measures.
Therefore, Fogel attributed much of the decline in mortality to improved
nutrition among the population as a whole—particularly improved nutrition
for infants and children. He made these generalizations from a broad sam-
pling of heights of largely male populations at different times and places.

Thornton (1987) concerned himself with charting what he called the decline and nadir of the American Indian population to the end of the nineteenth century. He gave four reasons for the continuing population drop,
which he and other scholars have pointed out was ongoing from the sixteenth century: disease, warfare, removal and relocation, and the "destruction of tribal ways of life." Thornton estimated that the Native American
population in what is now the lower forty-eight states was about 600,000 in
1800, dropping to just 250,000 by 1900.

At first glance, the mortality history of the United States and Canada, as
well as western Europe, seems to run at a countertrend to that of the Native
American population: Clearly, the eighteenth century was no golden age for
American Indian people; nor did their life expectancy increase by 1850.
However, the gradual decline in American Indian population after 1850 may
have paralleled the earlier European and North American cases in that its explanation may be a drop in nutritional standards. This chapter will investigate such a possibility by looking at the diet of the Ojibwa, particularly their
intake of fish and game, as well as other traditional foods. One of the working hypotheses of this chapter is that the Ojibwa suffered demographically as
their traditional diet based on hunting, gathering, and fishing was curtailed
by a combination of federal pressure, state encroachment on Ojibwa treaty
rights, and the environmental transformation of their homeland.

In addition to linking the population history of the Ojibwa to that of the
rest of Indian country and to North America, I would like to outline in this
chapter a tentative periodization scheme of the Ojibwa economy. Indeed,
the historical challenge is to connect the demographic and economic histories of the tribe in a careful manner and to make that new history a part of
the better known story of Ojibwa culture (Landes 1937; Densmore 1929).

It is, of course, arbitrary on the part of the historian to try to impose a set
of chronological subdivisions on the century-plus between the end of the
American Revolution and the beginning of World War I that saw the last
great epidemic sweep through the Lake Superior region. Throughout this
time span, the various Ojibwa bands consistently sought to maintain their established nonmarket subsistence patterns based on hunting, fishing, making
maple sugar, and gathering wild rice, fruits, berries, and other plants. Yet dis-

tinct changes occurred in the ways in which the Ojibwa encountered the market for goods and its ancillary instruments of cash and credit. Four such periods stand out, with the middle two being the main focus for this chapter.

First, the decades from the end of the American Revolution through the 1830s were characterized by Ojibwa involvement in the fur trade, primarily with British traders. Before the War of 1812, this trade was carried on by the Northwest Company and the XY Company within U.S. territory as it was recognized by the 1783 Treaty of Paris. After the War of 1812, the trading center for the Ojibwa was relocated to Manitoulin Island in Georgian Bay, and it remained there for at least another two decades.

From the signing of the first land cession treaty in 1837 through the last annuity payment in 1874, we can discern a second subperiod of getting and spending—this time based on the annual payment of federal annuities in goods and cash.

A third period of the Ojibwa economic history overlapped the end of the annuity years and continued into the early twentieth century. During those years the U.S. government allotted the reservation land base and also contracted with lumbering firms for stumpage rights on reservation land.

Finally, after 1910, many of the Ojibwa had been reduced to living as an increasingly landless, rural proletariat in an area stripped of its once expansive forests. Whereas the nineteenth century saw the Ojibwa bringing wildlife and land into the market as commodities, the twentieth century has witnessed their large-scale movement into the market as labor. In large part, this shift to the marketing of labor involved the relocation of Ojibwa from the Lake Superior region to urban areas; but even those men who stayed behind hired out as woodsmen, tourist guides, powwow dancers, and migrant farm workers, while many women became involved in producing handicrafts. This economy, which has dominated the twentieth century, is only now being challenged by the enormous revenue realized from gaming operations in recent years. The new casino riches, based as much on sovereignty as were the old annuity payments, may very well constitute a new period of Ojibwa economic history.

Ojibwa Population and Resource Utilization

The Ojibwa probably came to the waters around Sault Ste. Marie sometime in the fifteenth or sixteenth century. Their earlier home was the lower St. Lawrence River downriver from the early French settlements at Quebec and Montreal. The Ojibwa say that they received a message from a special shell (called a *megis*) with instructions to move westward to the end of the water, or in geographical terms, up the rivers and lakes to Lake Superior. The Ojibwa established settlements around Sault Ste. Marie and around the Straits of Mackinac. On the western part of Lake Superior the principal

Ojibwa settlement was at Madeline Island, or as the French called it for the peninsula that sticks up into Lake Superior and shields Chequamequon Bay, La Pointe (Warren 1885, 79–80; Danziger 1978, 7).

The Ojibwa of Madeline Island were the ancestors of today's Lake Superior Ojibwa, as well as of the Mississippi Ojibwa. The Madeline Island settlement first started sending hunting parties out at the start of the eighteenth century, and some of those parties established permanent settlements south of Lake Superior. In most instances, the new settlements were located on inland lakes where the fishing was particularly good or where wild rice and wild berries flourished. Among the new settlements were villages at Lac Courtes Oreilles, at Lac du Flambeau, at Lac Vieux Desert at the headwaters of the Wisconsin and Chippewa rivers, at Fond du Lac near present day Duluth, and along the Namekagon and St. Croix rivers, which led down to the Mississippi. The Ojibwa at the new settlements continued for many decades to return each summer to Madeline Island for religious and political reasons, but by the end of the eighteenth century the settlements had clearly evolved into autonomous bands (Warren 1885, 80–82).

The Ojibwa bands pursued a seasonal hunting and gathering economy that featured a few major commodities and over 100 minor ones. In the early spring the Ojibwa concentrated on making maple sugar. Later in the spring the bands devoted their attention to catching fish that came close to the shores for spawning in the inland lakes. During the summer the Ojibwa spent considerable time gathering berries and over 100 medicinal plants, as well as tending garden plots in which they raised a few staple crops. In the early fall came ricing time, as the ponds and sloughs ripened with the grain of the wild rice plant. Later in the fall the Ojibwa hunted deer and other large animals, making full use of the meat, hide, and hooves. During the long winter the men trapped fur-bearing animals, sought whatever deer could be found, and fished through the ice (Tanner 1987, 21; Densmore 1929, 37–43; Vennum 1988; White 1991).

This economy was devoted for the most part to obtaining food, with supplementary effort devoted to the fur trade with other Indians or Europeans. Writers earlier in this century paid so much attention to the European-Indian fur trade that, as Tanner wrote, "Indian people appear to have been exclusively concerned with fur-bearing animals." Instead, she properly notes that "Indians continued to procure food in traditional ways, and that the pressures of Euro-American contact had the effect of intensifying" the search for foodstuffs. Tanner wrote:

> It was not until the destruction of the environmental resources base in the twentieth century that these traditional subsistence patterns were substantially modified. Lumbering, draining of lakes and bogs, and over-hunting and fishing by an expanding non-Indian population brought an end to the subsistence pat-

terns that had proved equal to the cycles of nature and the immense social changes of the fur trade era. (1987, 23)

The Ojibwa flourished by extending their control over territory, particularly territory that was rich in the resources they sought: fish, rice, deer, berries, sugar maple trees, and medicinal plants. In effect, they substituted gains in geographical space for gains in labor productivity as a way to improve their output; the richer the territory they controlled, the less labor they had to devote to maintaining a target subsistence level. Thus control over richer resources allowed the Ojibwa greater leisure, or to be more accurate, lowered the risk of hardship or even famine in any given year (Satz 1991, 97–98; Warren 1885, 155–193).

By the time of the mid-nineteenth-century treaties, observers began to produce good written accounts of the diet and economy of the Lake Superior Ojibwa (Armstrong 1972). It is interesting to note that under the terms of the 1837 treaty, the United States paid for the services of three black-smiths for the tribe and that one of the principal tasks for the smiths was to forge fishing spears and traps. Albert Bushnell, the Indian agent at La Pointe, despaired of ever converting his wards into agriculturalists when he wrote in 1840 that the Ojibwa "subsist at present by hunting, fishing, and on the wild rice found in the lakes and rivers" (U.S. Bureau of Indian Affairs 1824–1881: Daniel Bushnell to Comm. Indian Affairs, Sept. 30, 1840; Satz 1991, 155). Further east, a few years later, one of the surveyors on the Owen expedition of 1847 wrote that the Indians at Lac du Flambeau "raise excellent potatoes, better, indeed, than are usually grown, with all the aids of cultivation, in the valley of the Ohio," but, he added, "their principal dependence for food is upon the lake, which yields them a plentiful supply of fine fish" (Owen 1852, 280–281).

The hunting and fishing economy, supplemented by annual treaty annuity payments, continued through 1874. The agent at La Pointe reported in July 1863 that the "Indians had all left on their Summer hunt," and in October he requested a winter "furlough" to Connecticut from the Indian Office in Washington because the Ojibwa "usually go on their hunting trips about the first of Nov. and there is usually but little business requiring the presence of the Agent during the Winter" (U.S. Bureau of Indian Affairs 1824–1881: L. E. Webb to Comm. Indian Affairs, Oct. 20, 1863).

Albert Ellis, author of *Northern Wisconsin—Its Capacities and Its Wants* (1852), strongly favored Indian removal of the Menominee and Ojibwa from Wisconsin; this constituted the chief "want" alluded to in his title. Still, he carefully studied how the Ojibwa had made use of the land around the inland lakes south of Lake Superior, an area he called the "Lake Region":

The natives, with the sagacity of their race, made these little seas their resting places, having their villages both for summer and winter on their borders, while a large district south of them has only been used for hunting grounds. The early traveller, whether penetrating from Lake Superior, or from the lower Wisconsin and Mississippi, has always found inhabitants in the Lake Region. (1852, 16)

Ojibwa Diet and Nutrition in the Treaty Era

In 1843 the Reverend Alfred Brunson, then newly appointed as Indian Office agent to the Lake Superior Ojibwa, submitted a lengthy memorandum to the secretary of war concerning the recently negotiated 1842 treaty. As part of his government duties, Brunson wrote a paragraph that set out his estimates about the quantity and price of Ojibwa output:

> The annual value of the furs are estimated by the traders at $25,000. There are about 1000 families, who make upon an average 300 pounds of sugar per an. worth at 10 cts per pound [totaling] 30,000. The same No. of families average 25 bushels of rice at $1 [totaling] 25,000 The materials of which they make their canoes, which are as essential to them as a wagon or plow to a farmer, are estimated at $10 per an. To each family 1000 [totaling] 10,000. The fish & game they subsist upon, are worth to them or could not be supplied by other provisions for less value that $100. To each family of four persons amounting to 100,000. This makes the annual produce of their country worth $190,000. (U.S. Bureau of Indian Affairs 1824–1881: Alfred Brunson to Secty. of War, Jan. 8, 1843)

Modern research has focused much attention on Brunson's letter. A study of federal annuity payments under treaties negotiated by the United States and the Ojibwa in 1837 and 1842 shows that when Brunson wrote his letter, there were about 3,100 Lake Superior Ojibwa in what is today Wisconsin, another 900 or so in Michigan's Upper Peninsula, and about 4,000 so-called Mississippi Band Ojibwa in what is now eastern and northern Minnesota. The Mississippi Band, for administrative purposes, were under the agency of a different Indian Office employee. The price, quantity, and population data in Brunson's letter permit one to make some gross estimates about the Ojibwa economy. The per capita income, in 1843 dollars, was $45 ($190,000 divided by 4,000 population); by comparison, the national income per capita estimates for 1839 is estimated to have been about $63.

It is also possible to translate Brunson's price and quantity estimates of the 1843 Ojibwa economy into a sketch of the tribal diet, as shown in Tables 7.1 and 7.2. Table 7.1 presents a diet rich in protein from venison because written accounts from the nineteenth century stress the importance of deer hunting to the so-called inland bands at Lac Courtes Oreilles and at Lac du Flambeau. As might be expected, Table 7.2 shows the lakeshore bands around Chequamequon Bay in Lake Superior having a higher protein intake from lake fish. The caloric and protein intake is remarkably high, but be-

TABLE 7.1 Estimated Cost of the Inland Bands' Protein Sources in 1859
(in 1843 dollars)

Measurement	Salt Pork Diet	Whitefish		Venison
1859 Eau Claire retail (cents/lb.)	7	12		6
Annual consumption (in lbs.)	1,200	912.5		1,825
Annual cost (in 1859 $)	84.00	109.50		109.50
Annual cost (in 1843 $)	65.33	84.32		84.32
Total protein cost (1843 $)	65.33	—	168.64	—

Note: Excludes small-mammal component of diet; inland bands include Lac Courte Oreilles, Lac du Flambeau, Mole Lake, and St. Croix.

Sources: Beverly Smith, "Dietary Requirements of Historic Wisconsin Chippewa," unpublished paper, Great Lakes Indian Fish and Wildlife Commission, 1991; *Eau Claire Free Press,* February 2, 1859; U.S. Commerce Department, *Historical Statistics of the United States from Colonial Times to 1975* (Washington, D.C.: GPO, 1976), 208–209.

TABLE 7.2 Estimated Cost of the Lakeshore Bands' Protein Sources in 1859
(in 1843 dollars)

Measurement	Salt Pork Diet	Whitefish		Venison
1859 Eau Claire retail (cents/lb.)	7	12		6
Annual consumption (in lbs.)	1,200	1,714		365
Annual cost (in 1859 $)	84.00	208.08		21.90
Annual cost (in 1843 $)	65.33	160.22		16.86
Total protein cost (1843 $)	65.33	—	177.08	—

Note: Excludes small-mammal component of diet; lakeshore bands include Bad River and Red Cliff.

Sources: Beverly Smith, "Dietary Requirements of Historic Wisconsin Chippewa," unpublished paper, Great Lakes Indian Fish and Wildlife Commission, 1991; *Eau Claire Free Press,* February 2, 1859; U.S. Commerce Department, *Historical Statistics of the United States from Colonial Times to 1975* (Washington, D.C.: GPO, 1976), 208–209.

TABLE 7.3   Estimated 1843 Diet of the Inland Bands (family of four)

Category	Venison	Fish	Wild Rice	Maple Sugar	Other	Total
Lbs.	3.60	1.82	4.36	0.82	1.82	12.42
Calories	2214	1749	7025	1303	484	12,775
Protein (g.)	433	138	279	—	16	866
Thiamin (mg.)	2.82	0.22	4.41	—	0.61	7.86
Riboflavin (mg.)	9.35	0.16	12.52	—	0.56	22.59
Niacin (mg.)	134.53	5.82	121.44	—	6.07	269.86
Vitamin C (mg.)	—	—	—	—	92.21	92.21[a]
Calcium (g.)	0.57	0.83	0.28	—	0.12	1.11
Iron (mg.)	35.58	0.84	83.34	—	4.94	165.33

[a]Does not meet USDA minimum recommended daily allowance for a family of four.

Note: Excludes small-mammal component of diet; inland bands include Lac Courte Oreilles, Lac du Flambeau, Mole Lake, and St. Croix.

Source: Beverly Smith, "Dietary Requirements of Historic Wisconsin Chippewa," unpublished paper, Great Lakes Indian Fish and Wildlife Commission, 1991.

cause much of the caloric intake was based on wild rice production, it may be assumed that some food was used for trade purposes, as recorded in much of the ethnohistorical literature (Vennum 1988).

Table 7.3 shows a breakdown of this 1843 diet by nutritional need. As can be seen, in all but a few areas the diet more than satisfied the nutritional requirements of the Ojibwa people by modern USDA standards. The deficiencies might very well have been satisfied by the gathering of berries, greens, and herbs, which was supervised by women and which Brunson may have overlooked. In sum, there is good reason to believe that the diet and nutrition of the Ojibwa during the fur trade and through the treaty era was a healthy one. That does not mean that every Ojibwa averaged 3,000 calories a day every day of the year. The accounts of observers are filled with stories of lean years, even crisis years, when food was very scarce (Tanner 1830).

The fishing, hunting, and gathering economy did not disappear, of course, immediately after the Ojibwa signed their land cession treaties with the United States. Of the elements mentioned by Brunson, only the fur trade was under threat during the treaty era, and that not because of Euro-American encroachment but because of the depletion of the wildlife. To a remarkable extent, the cash and goods paid out under the treaty terms replaced the cash and goods derived from the fur trade, as shown in Table 7.4. Was this evidence of shrewd bargaining, either by the Ojibwa who knew their needs or by U.S. negotiators who anticipated those needs in advance? The treaty journals—the record of speeches, give-and-take, and bargaining

TABLE 7.4   Comparison of Annual Estimated Fur Trade Revenues and Annuity
Payments to the Lake Superior Ojibwa

Type of Payment	Revenue (in current $)	Population	Per Capita (in current $)
1843 Brunson estimate of fur trade	25,000	4,000	6.25
1837 treaty annuity in cash and goods (term = 1837–1857)	31,000	8,000	3.88
1842 treaty annuity in cash and goods (term = 1842–1862)	25,000	8,000	3.13
1854 treaty annuity in cash and goods (term = 1854–1874)	13,000	4,000	3.25

Sources: U.S. Bureau of Indian Affairs, "Letters Received from the La Pointe
Agency," National Archives, RG75, Micro Series 234, 1824–1881: Brunson letter;
Ronald S. Satz, *Chippewa Treaty Rights: The Reserved Rights of Wisconsin's Chippewa
Indians in Historical Perspective* (Marison: Wisconsin Academy of Sciences, Arts,
and Letters, 1991), 155–184.

behind the formal treaty—is most revealing for the 1837 U.S.-Ojibwan
treaty. The U.S. negotiator came to "St. Peter" (now St. Paul, Minnesota)
with an annuity offer, and the Ojibwa countered with a proposal to lease the
pinelands for sixty years—about the amount of time the Indians thought
would be sufficient for whites to cut the timber they sought. The United
States refused that Ojibwa offer, which turned out to be quite prescient
about the time needed to log the pineries. The compromise ultimately
reached was for the United States to gain permanent title to the land but for
the Ojibwa to reserve hunting, fishing, and gathering usufructuary rights to
the ceded territory. That arrangement was repeated in the 1842 treaty. The
1854 treaty created reservations out of land whose Indian title had already
been relinquished. (See Map 7.1.) The reserved rights in the ceded territory
were not interfered with by the United States or the State of Wisconsin until
1864, when Wisconsin first sought to regulate Ojibwa hunting and trapping.
From then on, until stopped by a federal court in the 1980s, Wisconsin interpreted the 1854 treaty as having extinguished the off-reservation rights
(Satz 1991).

Ojibwa Population History in Context

The broad outline of population decline that Thornton proposed for all Native Americans within U.S. borders does describe the population history of

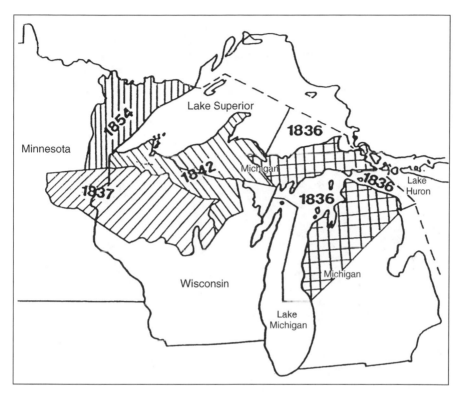

Map 7.1 *Treaty Ceded Areas*

the Lake Superior Ojibwa. Figure 7.1 presents a record of ethnohistorical observations about the Wisconsin bands of Lake Superior Ojibwa population at different times in the nineteenth and twentieth centuries. The figure shows the population holding steady during the mid-nineteenth century, declining to Thornton's "nadir" point around 1900, and then dramatically rebounding in the twentieth century.

In the absence of good mortality statistics for most of the nineteenth century, I have used the absolute population level as an indicator of increasing or decreasing mortality. As Thornton noted, the much-studied demographic transition to a regime of low birth and death rates never quite applied to American Indians. The 1890 census did conduct a special count of Indian country, and for that year alone in the nineteenth century we have reliable vital statistics, summarized in Table 7.5. The crude birthrate was very high by Wisconsin standards of the day, at 51.7 per 1,000 population. The death rate was also high, at 28.6 per 1,000 population. The gap between those two measures in a population that seemed to be declining was

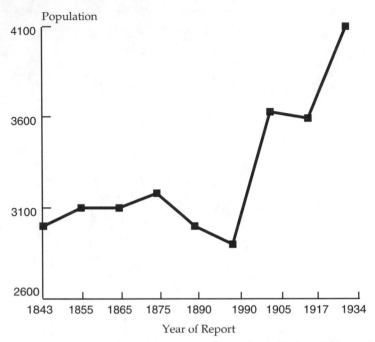

Figure 7.1 *Estimated Population of the Lake Superior Ojibwa, 1843–1934 (settlements at Lac Courtes Oreilles, Lac du Flambeau, Bad River, and Red Cliff)*

not because of net out-migration but, rather, because the Indian agent at La Pointe apparently did not count infant deaths in the mortality figures: Out of a total of 152 births, he counted only 72 children alive who were under one year of age in 1890. In short, it appears that in 1890 the Ojibwa population among Wisconsin's Lake Superior bands was on the decline because of a fearful infant mortality that negated much of the population gains that could have been expected from a very high birthrate (U.S. Bureau of the Census 1890).

Was the population so unhealthy earlier in the century when the economy was firmly rooted in hunting, fishing, and gathering? We lack the mortality figures to be certain. Fogel's work with the muster rolls of white and black volunteers in the Union Army is useful here for comparing the heights of recruits to those of the Ojibwa in the same era. My initial research strategy was to replicate Fogel's search of muster rolls for similar height information on Ojibwa volunteers. Unfortunately, the one unit among Wisconsin volunteer regiments that contained numerous Ojibwa does not have the height information recorded. As a substitute, I used the height data that was noted for Menominee Indian volunteers in Company K of both the Seventeenth and Thirty-Seventh Wisconsin Volunteers. The

TABLE 7.5   Vital Statistics for Wisconsin Bands of Lake Superior Ojibwa, 1890
(Lac Courte Oreilles, Lac du Flambeau, Bad River, and Red Cliff)

Population	2,889
Births	152
Crude birthrate	51.7
Deaths	83
Crude death rate	28.6
Surviving infants under one year of age	72

Source: U.S. Bureau of the Census, *Special Census for Indians Taxed and Not Taxed* (Washington, D.C.: GPO, 1890).

Menominee are an Algonquian-speaking tribal people whose territory abutted that of the Ojibwa; indeed, their name translated from Algonquian means "People of the Wild Rice," or as the French called them in the eighteenth century, the "Folles Avoines." The ethnohistorical evidence available suggests that the Menominee pursued an economy of hunting, gathering, and trading, similar to the Ojibwa until at least the mid-1850s, when they lost most of their once formidable 9-million-acre land base and retreated northward to a much smaller reservation.

The Civil War comparisons are of particular interest to the case of the Ojibwa because of the chronology involved. Brunson made his estimates about the levels of hunting, fishing, and gathering in 1842, or about the time that the Menominee cohort of Civil War soldiers were infants and toddlers. Put another way, the adult stature of the Menominee Indians in the Union Army reflects the dietary patterns of the Ojibwa that Brunson observed in his capacity as Indian agent at La Pointe.

Table 7.6 presents the data comparing the average heights of three racial groups in the Union Army: Fogel's sample of 8,500 black soldiers; a subsample of 3,000 Wisconsin white volunteers from his larger sample of 39,000 soldiers; and the Menominee of Company K, Thirty-Seventh Wisconsin Volunteers. The table shows that the black volunteers and the Menominee were almost identical in height and also that the distribution of heights within the samples was similar. The white volunteers serving in Wisconsin units were about a third of an inch taller on average than the Menominee; in turn, the Menominee, who had been raised on a diet of venison, fish, wild rice, and maple sugar similar to the diet of the Lake Superior Ojibwa, were on average more than a half-inch taller than the black soldiers. When compared to other nineteenth-century populations that Fogel studied, the average height of the adult male Menominee (171 centimeters—see Figure 7.2) was well within the normal range and shows no evidence that the Native Americans suffered any protein or calorie deficiency.

What caused the Ojibwa population decline at the end of the nineteenth century? Of the four reasons Thornton gave for the decline of Native American

TABLE 7.6   Average Heights of Three Volunteer Groups in the Union Army
(southern blacks, Wisconsin whites, and Menominee Indians)

Group	N	Mean (inches)	Standard Deviation
Southern blacks	8,154	66.63	2.63
Wisconsin whites	3,063	67.50	2.57
Menominee Indians	56	67.20	2.68

   Source: ICPSR Studies 9425 and 9426; Wisconsin Adjutant General, "Muster
Rolls of Volunteer Regiments," State Historical Society of Wisconsin, 1861–1865.

populations in the nineteenth century, we may quickly dismiss two when talking about the Ojibwa: war and removals. The Ojibwa only went to war with
the United States once during the century, and in that instance (the War of
1812), the tribe was the victor, defeating the United States in battles at the
Straits of Mackinac. The Jacksonian policy of Indian removal was not applied
to the Ojibwa, or at least not successfully. There was an aborted attempt in
1849–1850 to move the Lake Superior Ojibwa from Wisconsin and Michigan
west to Minnesota, and though frightful in terms of human suffering, the removal attempt was not repeated (Satz 1991). This leaves two causes of population decline to be investigated: disease and "destruction of tribal ways of life."

   Helen Hornbeck Tanner's *Atlas of Great Lakes Indian History* (1987) cata-
logs some of the epidemics to hit the western Great Lakes in the nineteenth
century, concentrating particularly on smallpox and cholera outbreaks. The
former disease was particularly virulent among the Ojibwa in the first half of
the century, but except for an outbreak of smallpox in 1869–1870, that great
killer of Native peoples seems to have been tamed by the time of the Civil War.
Cholera introduced from Europe was quite lethal to the Ojibwa in the pan-
demics of 1832 and 1849, but it was also fatal to many in the Euro-American
population. Matching smallpox epidemics to the history of the Ojibwa population cannot explain their continued decline up to 1900. In this respect, the
Ojibwa lagged at least a century behind the Europeans, who, according to
Fogel, had largely overcome smallpox and like diseases in the eighteenth century, only to face a new set of diseases in the nineteenth century that were
closely linked to diet and nutrition. The great killer among the Ojibwa after
the Civil War era was tuberculosis, a disease that Fogel classified with those
that have a "definite" susceptibility to being reduced by good nutrition.

The Assault on Ojibwa Tribal Culture
After the Civil War

By 1900—the low point for population of the Wisconsin bands among the
Lake Superior Ojibwa—a number of economic, political, and environmental

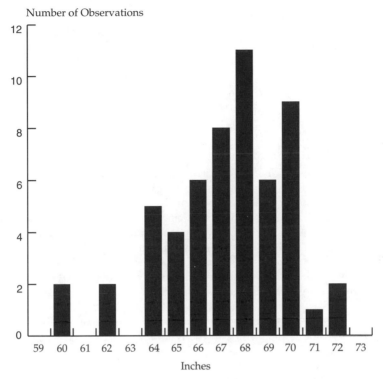

Number of Observations

Inches

Figure 7.2   *Heights of Menominee Indian Volunteers in the Union Army*

changes had altered their diet and nutrition. During the fifty years between the end of the Civil War and the onset of World War I, the Lake Superior region pineries were extensively logged. This did give employment and income to Indian people on the reservations, either directly from logging jobs or indirectly from trade. However, at the same time, the reservations themselves were divided up for allotment, and the tribal members in many cases quickly lost their individual landholdings. In addition, as the pine trees were cut, the environment changed dramatically. Stream flows ran differently because of new dams and changed water flows in the northern uplands. Limnologists think that this may have caused fish populations and wild rice propagation to decline in ways that have not fully been charted. The deer population, on the other hand, apparently thrived after the dense forest was leveled.

The 1890s and the first decade of the twentieth century was also the time when the federal government's Indian Office (today the Bureau of Indian Affairs) and the State of Wisconsin's Conservation Department put enormous pressure on the Ojibwa to give up their hunting, fishing, and gathering economy. Off-reservation rights to hunt, fish, and gather—protected by treaty—were stripped by the state legislature and by state courts in the late nineteenth century. In sum, the Ojibwa were a people vulnerable to adverse changes in their environment caused by massive logging just at the time that the federal and state governments cooperated on a policy of forced acculturation.

The modern historian of the Ojibwa of Michigan, Wisconsin, and Minnesota—Edmund Danziger—described the health effects on the people of the tumultuous 1890s:

> Just as intensive acculturation on the reservation changed the old Chippewa economy "from a food-gathering to a money-gathering" system, as anthropologist Robert Ritzenthaler put it, it also modified their standard of living. Thousands of woodland hunters and their families abandoned traditional seminomadic ways and lived on the tracts assigned to various bands. By the late 1890s, the portable birch-bark wigwams gave way to one-room log or frame cabins. Nearly a thousand such dwellings dotted the reserves, and each housed one to three families. Tubercular red men, coughing away in smoke-filled rooms, must have doubted the virtues of reservation life. (1978)

In every sense then, the period around 1900 was a nadir for the Lake Superior Ojibwa. Their renaissance in the twentieth century is therefore all the more remarkable.

References

Primary Sources

Armstrong, Benjamin. 1972. "Reminiscences of Life Among the Chippewa." *Wisconsin Magazine of History* 55:175–196, 287–309; 56:37–58.
Ellis, Albert G. 1852. *Northern Wisconsin—Its Capacities and Its Wants.* Madison: Transactions of the Wisconsin State Agricultural Society.
Owen, David Dale. 1852. *Report of a Geological Survey of Wisconsin, Iowa, and Minnesota.* Philadelphia: Lippincott.
Tanner, John. 1830. *A Narrative of the Captivity and Adventures of John Tanner During Thirty Years' Residence Among the Indians in the Interior of North America.* New York.
U.S. Bureau of the Census. 1890. *Special Census for Indians Taxed and Not Taxed.* Washington, D.C.: GPO.
U.S. Bureau of Indian Affairs. 1824–1881. "Letters Received from the La Pointe Agency." National Archives, RG75, Micro Series 234.

Secondary Sources

Danziger, Edmund Jefferson, Jr. 1978. *The Chippewas of Lake Superior.* Norman: University of Oklahoma Press.
Densmore, Frances. 1929. *Chippewa Customs.* Washington, D.C.: GPO.

Fogel, Robert William. 1986. "Nutrition and the Decline in Mortality Since 1700: Some Preliminary Findings." In *Long-Term Factors in American Economic Growth*, eds. Stanley Engerman and Robert Gallman. Chicago: University of Chicago Press.

Landes, Ruth. 1937. *Ojibwa Sociology*. New York: Columbia University Press.

Satz, Ronald S. 1991. *Chippewa Treaty Rights: The Reserved Rights of Wisconsin's Chippewa Indians in Historical Perspective*. Madison: Wisconsin Academy of Sciences, Arts, and Letters.

Tanner, Helen Hornbeck. 1987. *Atlas of Great Lakes Indian History*. Norman: University of Oklahoma Press.

Thornton, Russell. 1987. *American Indian Holocaust and Survival: A Population History Since 1492*. Norman: University of Oklahoma Press.

Vennum, Thomas. 1988. *Wild Rice and the Ojibwa People*. St. Paul: Minnesota Historical Society.

Warren, William. 1885. *History of the Ojibwa People*. St. Paul: Minnesota Historical Society.

White, Richard. 1991. *The Middle Ground: Indians, Empires, and Republics in the Great Lakes Region, 1650–1815*. New York: Cambridge University Press.

8

The Political Economy of Indian Wars

TERRY L. ANDERSON AND
FRED S. MCCHESNEY

Most Americans today view the story of Indian-white relations through a late-nineteenth-century lens. From this perspective, whites are intruders using military strength to take Indian lands and leaving the defeated Indians with nothing but useless tracts known today as reservations. This perspective of white acquisition of Indian resources by conquest has been the theme of many a western movie and historical best-seller. In the words of the late economic historian, J.R.T. Hughes, "From beginning to end primary title was deemed to come by right of conquest, Indian title being inferior in the views of the crown and the settlers" (1976, 35). Another historian characterized the conventional tale as one long episode of "'massacre,' 'extermination,' and 'annihilation,' both 'utter' and 'complete,'" recounted "with overtones of racism, genocide, and other shibboleths" (Russell 1973, 42). Certainly the final episodes in Indian-white relations, including Custer's Last Stand, Chief Joseph's attempted escape to Canada, and the tragedy at Wounded Knee, fit the scenario.

This version of Indian-white relations, however, misses the fact that the period from the first contact between the two groups until about 1850 was one of relative peace and harmony. The first Pilgrim Thanksgiving illustrates the peaceful and mutually beneficial relations between the two groups. Even on the western frontier, fur traders were hardly in a position to take from the Indians, and both sides partook of the gains from trade. Thus the story of Indian-white relations is more accurately seen as a gradual deterioration from peaceful to bellicose.

This deterioration has been attributed to changes in whites' ideologies or attitudes toward Indian property rights. Seventeenth-century Europeans supposedly believed that their land claims were "unjustified and illegal if the prior right of the Indian were not recognized. Full title was in the Indian . . . from whom alone a valid title could be derived" (Washburn 1971, 41). But by the end of the nineteenth century the prevailing attitude had allegedly become that of Teddy Roosevelt: "The settler and pioneer have at bottom had justice on their side; this great continent could not have been kept as nothing but a game preserve for squalid savages" (1889, 90).

The purpose of this chapter is to provide an alternative, political economy (public choice) explanation for the deterioration in Indian-white relations during the nineteenth century. This model picks up a theme suggested by Jack Hirshleifer in his presidential address to the Western Economic Association, in which he contrasted "the way of Coase with the way of Machiavelli." In the Coasian world, "people will never pass up an opportunity to cooperate by means of mutually advantageous exchange." But according to Machiavelli, "It is not gold, but good soldiers that ensure success . . . for it is impossible that good soldiers should not be able to procure gold." From this perspective, Hirshleifer offers two propositions: (1) "Cooperation, with a few obvious exceptions, occurs only in the shadow of conflict," and (2) "when people cooperate, it is generally a conspiracy for aggression against others (or at least, is a response to such aggression)" (Hirshleifer 1994, 3–4). This shadow also falls over Indian-white relations. In resolving conflicts over land claims, both sides had a choice. They could follow the Coasian way and peacefully exchange, thereby enhancing total welfare, or they could follow the Machiavellian way and fight, imposing deadweight welfare losses overall. That they switched from the former to the latter suggests a deterioration in the gains from trade relative to the net gains from warfare.

The political economy model that we present in the next section draws from two seemingly unrelated strains in the economics literature: One concerns the evolution of property rights and the other analyzes potential litigants' decisions to settle or go to trial. From this model we derive a series of testable implications regarding Indian-white relations in nineteenth-century America. We then, in the following section, present qualitative evidence and statistical tests of the model. The perspective throughout is positive, not normative: It does not seek to justify the choice of war, just to explain it.

An Economic Model of Negotiation Versus Taking

John Umbeck's (1981) article on the choice between contract and violence provides a useful starting point. According to his theory, no distribution of rights is stable if anyone has less than he can obtain by forcefully taking from others. Focusing on the California gold camps, Umbeck hypothesized that lands would be redistributed from existing miners to newcomers because the marginal value of a unit of gold land would be higher to the latter. His conclusion that "the total amount of homogeneous mining land [would] always be divided evenly among the competing miners" followed from four assumptions: (1) Miners had identical gold production functions; (2) claimants were equal in their abilities to use violence; (3) claimants had only their human capital to draw upon; and (4) negotiation costs were zero (Umbeck 1981, 43).

Though "might makes rights" in Umbeck's model, it does not necessarily follow that violence will dominate human interaction. Indeed, though nearly all residents of frontier communities were armed and capable of using force, actual violence was rare.[1] This conclusion is not surprising in light of Umbeck's assumptions. Identical production functions meant that no one had a differential incentive to put more effort into fighting. Equal abilities to use force and restrictions on the capital endowment that could be drawn upon for fighting meant that neither party had a greater likelihood of winning the fight. And finally, in a world of zero (or relatively low) negotiation costs, gains from trade could be captured without cost, thus avoiding the negative-sum game of war.

Once these assumptions are relaxed, however, Machiavellian outcomes can occur, as in the case of litigation. Robert D. Cooter and Daniel L. Rubinfeld (1989) summarize the nature of the decision to litigate disputes by considering three stages of a legal dispute: harm, assertion of a legal claim, and then either bargaining (and maybe settlement) or litigation (when no settlement is reached). Analytically, these phases apply to choices made between trade and war. Each phase has its analogue in the history of Indian-white relations.[2]

Harm

"When the white and red races met on the American frontier there occurred innumerable violations of the personal and property rights of one group by members of the other" (Prucha 1962, 188). Europeans' title to land was traced back to their respective sovereigns under a property rights system that made no provision for Indian ownership. To Indians, Europeans were merely trespassers, intruders who had no right to the land they claimed. The trespass obviously was costly to Indians if the resource was scarce. But even if not scarce among Indians themselves, land had exchange value if it could be sold or traded to whites for European goods.[3] In any case, to initiate the possibility of exchange, Indians would have to assert credible claims to what Europeans wanted.

Assertion of Claims

Once whites had trespassed upon Indian territory, two factors would determine whether Indians asserted claims to the disputed resources. First, asserting a claim depends on the expected loss from a continuing trespass relative to the cost of asserting the claim. The expected loss depends on the value of the disputed resource, and the cost of assertion will be a function of the costs of ending the dispute by negotiation or by fighting, as described below.

Second, asserting a claim requires a credible ability to fight. Even if negotiation is one's aim, there can be no contract if the other side has the physical ability simply to take at no important cost. Only in the cases where Indian rights were valuable enough to defend (that is, where Indians had sufficient military power to make a credible threat) would bargaining and exchange occur following whites' trespass. Given the vast amount of land held by Indians on first contact with Europeans and the relatively small amount initially desired by Europeans, it would be surprising for Indians to assert any claim against trespass at first. However, as the century progressed and the relative mass of land held and demanded by the two sides shifted, it would be more likely for Indians to defend against trespass as a prelude to either treaty or war.

Negotiating or Fighting

Once harm is imposed and a credible claim asserted, disputants must choose between bargaining or fighting, that is, between the Coasian way and the Machiavellian way. The interests of the two parties will diverge insofar as one party's gain is the other's loss. But their interests will converge as they search for the lowest cost method of settling their dispute.

Here, the Cooter and Rubinfeld model differs from the Umbeck model and provides an explanation for the shift from peaceful negotiations to warfare between Indians and whites. Under the Umbeck assumptions, the negative-sum solution of warfare will never result because negotiation costs are low, both sides have accurate information about the expected gains and losses from war, and they understand the relevant probability distributions associated with winning and losing. In this world, no violence would ever occur, though superior force would alter the terms of trade in any negotiation.

The Umbeck assumptions must be relaxed according to the four following criteria in order to model accurately the nineteenth-century world of Indians and whites:

1. Identical Production Functions.   Obviously Indians and whites did not place equal values on the lands in dispute. Especially on the Plains, where buffalo roamed over vast areas, Indians valued their hunting territories. In this setting the marginal value of an acre of land was quite low. On the other hand, whites generally were interested in more intensive agriculture, making their marginal value much higher. The differential values are even more dramatic in the case of gold-bearing lands. Given these differentials, we would expect more controversy over control of specific parcels of land and a differential willingness on both sides either to negotiate or fight over the land.

2. Fighting Endowments. Umbeck assumed that each individual had equal fighting abilities and that each could only use his personal endowment of human capital. Both of these assumptions are unrealistic in the case of Indian-white relations. Military technologies differed: Indians relied extensively on bows and arrows, whereas whites primarily used guns. Moreover, following Hirshleifer's second proposition noted above, unlike disputes between individuals, warfare between groups of people requires collective action. Consequently the analogy between contracts to settle litigation and treaties to avoid warfare breaks down. Individuals make settlement contracts or litigate on their own behalf; war is waged on behalf of entire groups in a public choice setting, and treaties are made by subsets of representatives from each group. A settlement contract must make all individuals better off, whereas litigation leaves them worse off; the same is not necessarily true of treaties and warfare.

One difference between individual contracting and collective treaty making is that treaties often create a prisoner's dilemma; that is, even if the total benefits from a treaty exceed its total costs for both sides, any particular individual may find it in his interest to violate the treaty terms.

> The individuals within the collectivities [to be bound by a treaty] may or may not have given their consent to arrangements entered into by their governments and may or may not benefit from the treaty provisions. . . . A monarch, for example, may make promises that impose significant costs on his own people. The monarch may not be able to obtain the needed cooperation from the populace. (Roback 1992, 7)

This prisoner's dilemma problem associated with treaty enforcement reduces the likelihood of negotiated outcomes and increases the likelihood of war.

Similarly, coalition costs can affect the decision to negotiate or fight in a collective setting. Coalition costs are typically unimportant in the individual contractual setting. But because war ordinarily is not undertaken by individuals or small groups, the calculus must include the cost of amassing military forces. Whites used two principal arrangements to fight Indians: part-time militia made up of local citizens and the standing national army of full-time professionals. Use of a full-time, professional army raises the fixed costs but lowers the marginal costs of warfare and so increases its likelihood.[4]

Finally, attempts to predict peace or war must recognize that these decisions are made by government officials (in the case of whites) and tribal leaders (for Indians). Just as dispute resolution by judicial trial is a "negative-sum game for the disputants, grafted onto collective choice by an impartial court" (Cooter and Rubinfeld 1989, 1071), war is a negative-sum game grafted onto a collective choice made by politicians and bureaucrats (including military personnel).

Rational avoidance of negative-sum situations presumes that the persons deciding between negotiation (settlement) and violence (litigation) bear the relevant costs. Where political decisions are made, however, individuals or coalitions can benefit themselves by shifting the costs of war to others, meaning that the relevant political actors may undervalue the cost of fighting. In other words, warfare that is negative sum overall may be value enhancing for influential persons or groups. If so, raiding will become more common relative to trading, for political reasons.[5]

In this respect, the existence of a standing national army is important. When settlers decide to encroach on Indian territory and a local citizen militia provides the military force, the congruence between the gains from trespass and the potential costs of fighting is relatively high. However, if a small group can call on a standing army composed mostly of outsiders and compensated from general tax receipts, the congruence between gains and costs is lost. The incentive increases for "political" wars, whereby wealth is created for one group at the expense of another. As Thomas Jefferson noted: "The U.S. finds an Indian war too serious a thing, to risk incurring one merely to gratify a few intruders with settlements which are to cost the other inhabitants of the U.S. a thousand times their value in taxes for carrying on the war they produce" (quoted in Prucha 1962, 139).

Moreover, a standing army creates a class of professional soldiers whose personal welfare increases with warfare, even if fighting is a negative-sum act for the population as a whole. For military bureaucrats (typically the highest-ranking soldiers), warfare increases budgets. War means potential distinction for soldiers in the field, more promotions, and simply relief from boredom. Particularly when the army has political influence, a full-time fighting force will increase the number of disputes resolved violently.

3. Information Costs. Information costs are crucial in the warfare calculus but are ignored by Umbeck because he assumes that everyone has an equal ability to use force and that each knows how much force the other will use. In this world, outcomes are known so there is no reason to expend resources in wasteful warfare.

Uncertainty, however, is a major factor in warfare, especially if it produces differential expectations about outcomes. Intuitively, fighting would be more likely to follow whites' trespass when Indians were more optimistic than whites about the outcome of fighting. Suppose, for example, that whites have developed better weapons (for example, repeating rifles). Before Indians have experienced the effects of whites' greater firepower, they might overestimate their likelihood of prevailing in battle. Faulty information about numbers of Indian braves or white troops likewise would alter decisions to negotiate or fight. Because, ceteris paribus, the potential for differential expectations decreases with repeat dealings, we would expect warfare to predominate over negotiation when parties are unfamiliar with one another. This explains the typical empirical finding in the literature on rates of settlement versus litigation (where there is generally good information about precedent) that "ten disputes settle out of court for every one that is tried" (Cooter and Rubinfeld 1989, 1070). At least among judiciable disputes, negotiation is the rule; fighting is the exception.

4. Negotiation Costs. Even with differential information and therefore different probabilities assigned to winning and losing a war, the likelihood of fighting is a positive function of negotiation costs. These include the cost of defining and enforcing property rights. As property rights become less clear and other transaction costs rise, the costs of negotiation will grow relative to the cost of fighting, and violence will become a more attractive alternative. In Indian-white negotiations, several transaction costs are potentially important.

The most obvious obstacles to negotiation over resources are differences in language and customs between Indians and whites. Differences in language and custom, particularly in the use of written contracts, were a major impediment to the peaceful resolution of disputes. "The [treaty] system contained major flaws. . . . Chiefs who signed treaties did not always understand what they had agreed to. 'Boone came out and got them to sign a paper,' recalled the Arapaho Little Raven, 'but they did not know what it meant.' Often such misunderstanding had no more sinister explanation than simply a bad interpreter" (Utley 1984, 43–44).

Also important would be the nature of property rights held by Indians relative to those desired by whites. Whites might earnestly seek to negotiate for peaceful acquisition of resources. But purchasing rights requires that someone be able to sell them. If a tribe had a system of well-defined rights recognized among themselves and other tribes, Indians indeed had something of value to sell, and negotiation with whites was then feasible. On the other hand, immigrants would find negotiation very costly where nomadic tribes hunted over large territories, where no tribe had recognized rights to exclude others, and where rights to the fruits of the land—bison—were governed solely by the rule of first possession. Indians then had nothing to offer in any negotiation, and whites could only obtain rights in the ways Indians themselves did—by conquest.

These problems would be further complicated by restrictions on alienability. Even Indian tribes with well-specified property rights among themselves often had restrictions on transferability. Rights that cannot be exchanged within a culture or across cultures naturally raise negotiation costs, reduce the surplus from negotiation, and increase the probability of war.

This political economy model of warfare has implications in five main areas.

1. Zone of Controversy.   Disputes over resources predictably will not occur at the first point of contact between whites and Indians. Nor will disputes continue to the point where all resources are owned by one group or the other. The zone of controversy is bounded at both ends. Thus the history of two contending groups' relations would not necessarily be one long saga of warfare, much less "extermination" or "annihilation."

Within the zone of controversy, negotiated outcomes will predominate over violent ones only if certain conditions hold. Decisions to rely on negative-sum solutions to disputes can be traced to some "contract failure" in the negotiation process. Putative explanations of increased violence based on ideology are neither helpful nor necessary. In the negotiation-warfare context of greatest interest here, several likely "failures" can be identified a priori.

2. Informational Asymmetry.   More disputes will degenerate into violence, ceteris paribus, if the two sides have differential expectations about likely outcomes of fighting. Different expectations may be due to differences in information.

3. Military Technology.   A likely source of information asymmetry is the development of new weapons by one side. New weapons may cause hostilities if the other side is not well-informed about their impact.

4. Property Rights.   For trade to occur, property rights must be well-specified and divestible, and agreements must be enforceable. Otherwise, increased transaction costs will reduce the surplus from negotiation and increase the likelihood of conflict. Agricultural tribes had property rights specified in ways that made negotiation less costly. Conversely, nomadic tribes relied more on the rule of capture, with land rights specified over large hunting territories. Hence dispute settlement with these tribes would be more costly and so entail greater use of force. Moreover, as opposing groups encounter agency-cost problems in enforcing agreements, incentives to trade property rights decline and the likelihood of fighting increases.

5. Standing Army Versus Militia.   A standing army lowers the incremental costs of assembling fighting coalitions, decreasing the marginal costs of war and shrinking the surplus from negotiation. The rise of a standing army also creates political incentives that increase the likelihood of fighting to resolve disputes. For example, a career army creates individual incentives among some military personnel to fight. A national army also means that well-organized groups can diffuse the cost of fighting over the larger tax-paying populace.

Empirical Evidence

Zone of Controversy

The theory predicts that initially Indians would not view land as worth fighting to protect. And indeed, there is evidence that Indians at first were prepared to accede to whites' assertion of land claims. As Robert Utley describes conditions on the Great Plains until about the time of the Mexican War, it was not worthwhile for the Indians to stop white intrusions, although whites' behavior was "sometimes reprehensible. . . . Neither race posed much of a threat to the other, and on the whole they got along fairly well" (1967, 59).

Within the zone of controversy, negotiated outcomes predictably will outnumber those resolved by conflict, as violence is a negative-sum proposition. Jennifer Roback summarizes Indian-white relations in colonial times: "Europeans generally acknowledged that the Indians retained possessory rights to their lands. More importantly, the English recognized the advantage of being on friendly terms with the Indians. Trade with the Indians, especially the fur trade, was profitable. War was costly" (1992, 11).

The legal doctrine that guided U.S. policy toward Indians in the late eighteenth and early nineteenth centuries "recognized the Indians' right to use and occupy land. Under this title, the United States is liable to pay the tribe when it decides to extinguish the Indian use and occupancy" (Kickingbird and Ducheneaus 1973, 7). Perhaps the most thorough legal scholar of Indian property rights, Felix Cohen, referred to this early period as one of "fair dealing" (1947, 46). By 1947, he estimated, some $800 million had been paid for Indian lands, and paying "$800,000,000 for a principle is not a common occurrence in the world's history."

The hypothesis that negotiations would have predominated over warfare in the early years of Indian-white relations can be tested with the data on the number of battles and treaties between Indians and whites shown in Table 8.1. Until 1830 fighting was comparatively rare and treaties frequent,[6] but the use of violence to settle disputes was increasing throughout the nineteenth century. Ultimately warfare became the principal way of resolving controversy, and in fact Congress voted in 1871 not to ratify any more Indian treaties.

Informational Asymmetries

This shift from negotiation to warfare can be explained, in part, by informational asymmetries that arose increasingly as interaction moved onto the Great Plains. Since western Indians were more nomadic, it was more difficult for whites to communicate with the disparate bands, let alone the entire tribe. Hence Indians often had little idea who the whites were, what they

TABLE 8.1   Indian-White Battles and Treaties, 1790–1897

Year	No. of Battles	No. of Treaties
1790–1799	7	10
1800–1809	0	30
1810–1819	33	35
1820–1829	1	51
1830–1839	63	84
1840–1849	53	18
1850–1859	190	58
1860–1869	786	61
1870–1879	530	0
1880–1889	131	0
1890–1897	13	0

Source: Anderson and McChesney (1994).

wanted, or how they fought. On the white side, the different landscape and climate on the Plains resulted in Indian warfare tactics that were different from what whites farther to the east had encountered.

In fact, one side's faulty information seems to have been an important factor in just about all the bloody fighting in the West. The Plains Indians "greatly favored the decoy tactic" (Utley 1984, 105), sending forth a small party to encounter a white detachment (seemingly by mistake) and then running from it to lure pursuing whites into a trap where many more Indian warriors lay hidden. Thus in the notorious Fetterman Massacre in 1866, eighty-one bluecoats were enticed into combat with some 2,000 Sioux and wiped out. General George Armstrong Custer's apparent foolhardiness in attacking over 3,000 Sioux and Cheyenne with just a few hundred men at the Little Bighorn in 1876 simply reflects his ignorance of the true number of Indians opposing him.[7]

Changing Technology

Superior military technology is often alleged to be a major factor in white domination of Indians. However, although Indian and white war technologies were often different, it is not obvious that one side or the other had systematically better technology. In the early years, Indians' bows and arrows were a match for whites' muskets. Even in later years when whites' technology improved markedly with fast-loading rifles and repeating rifles, the differential closed rapidly. Indians usually were able to obtain new weapons (from both private traders and even the reservation agents of the Bureau of Indian Affairs) almost as soon as they were available to whites. Moreover, as Custer's troops discovered, white technology was not always superior and certainly was not enough to guarantee success against large numbers. General William Tecumseh Sherman stated that "fifty Indians could checkmate three thousand troops" (quoted in Debo 1989, 221). Frontier army officers often called the horse warriors the "finest light cavalry in the world," and historians have repeated the judgment ever since (Utley 1967, 7). Even when U.S. troops finally caught up with Chief Joseph's Nez Percé—starving, frozen, and exhausted from their long flight—the battle lasted for several days before the Indians surrendered.

The real issue, however, was not whether whites had superior technology but whether Indians might sometimes have been unduly optimistic about winning when information about new weapons was unavailable. For example, in the case of the Wagon Box Fight in 1867, Sioux losses were extraordinarily heavy. "One chief placed them at 1,137, and called the battle a 'medicine fight'—meaning that the soldiers had had supernatural help. What the soldiers had were new Springfield breech-loading rifles and plenty of ammunition, while the Indians were using the old muzzle-loaders" (Chapel 1961, 259).

The importance of changing white technology can be tested by examining the ratio of whites to Indians killed in battle over time. Systematic technological improvements by one side or the other would have an ambiguous effect on the absolute number of deaths.[8] But better white technology should decrease the ratio of white to Indian deaths in those battles that did occur. The data, however, indicate that there was no significant change in the ratio of white to Indian battle deaths over time.[9] Thus, measured by the ratio of deaths, the hypothesis that technological change was a significant factor in the increasing recourse to war over time is not corroborated.

Property Rights and Negotiation Cost Problems

The costs of negotiated exchange decline when one party has well-defined, divisible property rights in the resources demanded by another. If whites believed Indians had exclusive control of a piece of land and had the authority to trade it, negotiation was possible. Conversely, when whites discovered that Indians did not have exclusive control and could not transfer land, they had little alternative but to raid.

In this regard, there were important differences between Indian tribes east and west of the Mississippi. East of the Mississippi, where agriculture was the principal commercial activity, private property was well established:

> The Creek town is typical of the economic and social life of the populous tribes of the Southeast. . . . each family gathered the produce of its own plot and placed it in its own storehouse. Each also contributed voluntarily to a public store which was kept in a large building in the field and was used under the di-

rection of the town chief for public needs. The Cherokee town had a similar economic, social, and political organization. (Debo 1989, 13–14)

Indian institutions west of the Mississippi were different, however, because the European introduction of the horse increased the yield available from the vast herds of bison. Many of the great nomadic hunting and warrior tribes of the West were initially sedentary and agricultural tribes who abandoned farming and moved to the Plains for the hunting:

As life on the Plains became more inviting with the use of horses, more tribes moved out there, the Sioux and Cheyennes and Arapahos from the east, the Comanches and Kiowas from the west. Some abandoned their agriculture entirely and based their economy on the buffalo herds—"We lost the corn," say the Cheyennes. Others like the Osages maintained their fixed residences, where they planted their crops, rode out to the Plains for their supply of meat, and returned to harvest their corn and settle down for the winter. (Debo 1989, 15)

For the nomadic tribes, land and the resources on it were a vast commons, with only usufructuary rights by possession recognized.

All the natives . . . venerated their homeland and looked upon it with a keen sense of possession. It was a group possession, however, recognizing the right of all to partake of its bounty. No individual could "own" any part of it to the exclusion of others. Use privileges might be granted or sold, but sale of the land itself was a concept foreign to the Indian mind. (Utley 1984, 8–9)

One would predict, therefore, that whites desiring resources used by western nomadic tribes would simply take them more often than they would take resources owned by eastern agricultural tribes.

The model applied here is also applicable to Indians' fighting among themselves. In the West, white migration did not intrude on a stable system of aboriginal rights recognized by Indians themselves "but rather broke over a congeries of scattered groups that had been fighting one another for generations and would continue to fight one another to the day of their final conquest by the whites" (Utley 1984, 11). A principal source of the continuous warfare among Indian tribes was the fact that major hunting grounds overlapped. Likewise, the belief that white migration generally dislodged Indians from centuries-old ancestral lands is inaccurate. The horse and the gun had arrived in the West well before major white incursions and had greatly altered the configuration of land use and possession among Indian tribes. As one Sioux chief declared to his white conquerors, "You have split my land and I don't like it. These lands once belonged to the Kiowas and the Crows, but we whipped these nations out of them, and in this we did what the white men do when they want the lands of Indians" (quoted in Utley 1984, 61).

Finally, much Indian-white violence can be traced to agency costs that made negotiated outcomes unenforceable. Most treaty violations were committed "not by the leaders of the United States or of the Indian tribes but rather by members of these groups who could not be controlled by the leadership, or more accurately, who could be controlled only at extremely high cost" (Roback 1992, 5). On the Indians' side, chiefs almost never constrained individual warriors. The Nez Percé warrior was typical:

> [He] accorded his loyalty and allegiance first to his family, then to his band, and finally to his tribe, but rarely beyond. . . . The autonomous bands looked to chiefs and headmen who counseled but did not command. . . . [Warriors] obeyed or disobeyed as personal inclination dictated, and combat usually took the form of an explosion of personal encounters rather than a collision of organized units. (Utley 1984, 7–8)

And furthermore, "chiefs rarely represented their people as fully as white officials assumed, nor could they enforce compliance if the people did not want to comply" (Utley 1984, 44).

On the white side, similar problems abounded. Treaties signed in good faith by white politicians proved to be unenforceable, as individual whites violated them with impunity. The problem lay with the national government's inability to defend local property rights against local white citizens—a difficulty described as "a massive principal-agent problem" (Roback 1992, 19). Government employees were notoriously faithless agents, frequently depriving tribes of the consideration due them under treaties.[10] Reservation Indians frequently viewed the raiding of local white settlements not as a treaty violation but as self-help in the face of whites' breach of contract in failing to deliver monetary and in-kind payments promised under treaties.

Standing Army Versus Militia

Throughout the nineteenth century, whites substituted full-time, professional soldiers for local militias in fighting Indians. In the first years of the new republic, the former English system was maintained: "Individual colonies, and more often the frontiersmen themselves, had to protect the frontier" (Beers 1975, 173).

Maintaining a standing army, as opposed to raising a militia, predictably would increase the number of battles, as noted above. Once the fixed costs of raising troops is incurred, the marginal cost of fighting is relatively low, increasing the incentive to fight rather than negotiate.

The rise of a standing army not only lowered the cost of fighting, but it also gave local citizens valuable army contracts. Not surprisingly, therefore, "citizens were happy to call on the regular army to do the shooting, especially as federal troops required supplies bought locally. This factor often caused citizens to holler loudly before they were hurt" (Russell 1973, 47). The fact that fighting meant increased federal revenues in a frontier area was often noted by politicians at the time (see Utley 1967, 14–17).

A standing army also meant full-time officers and, behind them, military bureaucrats whose careers and budgets were advanced by fighting. This latter phenomenon was particularly important during the nineteenth century. Following both the Mexican and Civil Wars, the size of the peacetime army had to shrink. This was acceptable to most enlisted men, who were volunteers. But reduced troop strength was of considerable concern to career officers.

The solution for postwar soldiers came principally from the "Indian problem."

> Protection of the frontier population and travel routes from hostile Indians placed the largest demand on the Army. . . . For [the latter half of the nineteenth century], the U.S. Army would find its primary mission and its main reason for existence in the requirements of the westward movement beyond the Mississippi. (Utley 1967, 2–3)

Civil War officers retained their brevet ranks and pay as long as they were fighting Indians. For enlisted men as well as officers, an absence of war meant ennui and lost chances for advancement.

> It was dismal, frustrating duty. Boredom, low pay, coarse food and shabby quarters, harsh discipline and cruel punishment, constant labor of an unmilitary character, field service marked by heat and cold, rain and snow, mud and dust, hunger and thirst, deadening fatigue—these were to be expected. But they were unaccompanied by the prospect of meaningful combat and the opportunity for distinction that ordinarily make the terms of military life more endurable. (Utley 1967, 110–111)

The antidote was battle.

Statistical evidence provides additional support for the hypothesis that the rise of a standing army would cause an increase in the number of battles with Indians. During the nineteenth century the army grew principally through two wars. In 1845 the U.S. Army totaled 8,509 officers and enlisted men. With the onset of the Mexican War (1846–1848), however, the army grew almost sixfold to 47,319. It never returned to prewar size, numbering over 16,000 in 1860. Growth during the Civil War (1861–1865) was phenomenal: The Union Army totaled over 1 million men in 1865. Again, it never returned to its prewar level, its size fluctuating between 25,000 and 30,000 men in the 1870s and 1880s.

If having a standing army increases the incentive to fight, one would expect the number of Indian battles to have risen after both the Mexican and the Civil Wars. And that, in fact, happened. For the period 1790 to 1900,

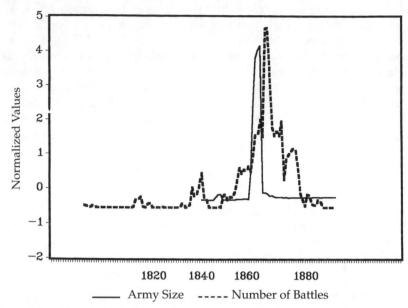

Figure 8.1   *Size of U.S. Standing Army and Number of Indian Battles*

Figure 8.1 shows the size of the army and number of battles (in normalized form).[11] Because the standing army was so much smaller during the Mexican War, the number of Indian battles initially declined as troops were called to fight in the Mexican War. It was after the war, when troops were available in great numbers, that there was an upsurge in fighting with Indians. In the case of the Civil War, the great spurt in army size starting in 1861 coincided with an increase in Indian battles. The army grew so large (in part as a result of the first military draft) that more men were stationed on the frontier than before. The increase in the number of battles is even more dramatic after the war, however, as the army's attention shifted westward.

Conclusion

In the case of Indian-white relations there is little doubt that Hirshleifer is correct; "cooperation, with a few obvious exceptions, occurs only in the shadow of conflict" (1994, 3). During the first half of the nineteenth century the two cultures struck a balance wherein negotiation predominated over warfare. "The middle ground arose because, although neither side could muster enough force to make their opposites conform, neither side could do without the other" (Thomas et al. 1993, 246). While Indians and whites were living a relatively peaceful coexistence, however, Indian nations were at war with one another. The arrival of the horse from the south gave the Apache and Comanche first access to the new form of transportation and superior military strength. Until the other tribes recognized the superiority that the horse afforded its owners or until they got their own horses, there was little peace. Because the horse also turned sedentary tribes into nomads pursuing buffalo, conflict between Indian nations not unlike that between Indians and whites was inevitable. More research on such conflicts is likely to confirm the power of political economy models in explaining the interface between the Coasian and Machiavellian worlds.

Notes

This chapter is an adaptation of Anderson 1994, where readers will find a fuller treatment of the subject discussed here. Reprinted with permission of *The Journal of Law and Economics*.

1. See also Anderson and Hill 1979; McGrath 1984; and Russell 1973 for similar conclusions.

2. It is assumed initially that collective decisions regarding Indian-white disputes were made within each group to maximize total group welfare; public choice matters involving special-interest decisions were introduced later.

3. Indians might give the land to whites to establish their colonies if the subsequent gains from trade in goods and services other than land were expected to be sufficiently great.

4. War's gains and losses depend in part on the other side's ability to organize. With zero transaction costs, military coalitions can form instantaneously, and there will be no differential in the gains to either side from forming a coalition. With positive organization costs, however, there will be higher gains from using violence for the side with lower costs.

5. This implication has parallels in the settlement-litigation literature: Litigation will be chosen more frequently when court costs can be shifted from one party to another.

6. The true extent of both fighting and negotiation are understated in Table 8.1 because the table includes only battles with government forces (militia, army) and only agreements with the U.S. government.

7. For a discussion of the unusually faulty information given Custer as to the Indians' strength, see Connell 1988, 263–264.

8. Better technology would make whites more eager to fight, but Indians would become less eager. Indians would simply concede greater numbers of land appropriations by whites without fighting or accept worse terms of trade in negotiation. Thus the effect of better technology on the total amount of warfare is unpredictable, a priori.

9. Data on deaths per battle are available for the period 1850 to 1891. Dividing the data set in half shows that the ratio falls from 2.34 in the first half of the period to 0.519 in the second half. The difference, however, is not statistically significant ($t =$

0.96). Even when one outlier in the second period is removed, causing the ratio to fall to 0.396, the difference is not significant ($t = 1.03$). The outlier is 1876, when Custer's Last Stand made the ratio 2.5, over six times above the mean for the other years.

10. "An insidious by-product of the treaty system was the annuity system—the practice of paying for land with cash dispensed in annual installments over a period of years. It was a system highly vulnerable to abuse by politically well-connected traders, who sat at disbursing tables each year to collect real or fictional debts run up during the year by the Indians" (Utley 1984, 45). The potential for skimming payments owed to Indians made positions as government Indian agents valuable in the late nineteenth century, and they were frequently allocated by political pressure and corruption.

11. The values are normalized, of course, to present a common scale of measurement. The extraordinary size of the army during the Civil War and the extraordinary number of Indian battles thereafter cause the extent of change in army size during the Mexican War and battles thereafter to appear insignificant. Both were, in fact, quite significant relative to the periods immediately before and after. Regression analysis presented in the longer version of our paper shows that army growth during both the Mexican and Civil Wars, independent of one another, had significant effects on the number of battles with Indians afterwards, all else equal. Naturally, since army growth was much greater during the Civil War, the size of the postwar effect on Indian battles was greater than that for the Mexican War. It is interesting, too, that estimates of the effect of a given year's battles on next year's army size show no significant impact. In other words, army size this year affects the number of battles next year, but not vice versa.

References

Anderson, Terry. 1994. "Raid or Trade? An Economic Model of Indian-White Relations." *Journal of Law and Economics* 36 (April):39–74.

Anderson, Terry L., and Peter J. Hill. 1979. "The *Not* So Wild, Wild West." *Journal of Libertarian Studies* 3:9–29.

Beers, Henry P. 1975. *The Military Frontier, 1815–46.* Philadelphia: Porcupine Press.

Chapel, Charles E. 1961. *Guns of the Old West.* New York: Coward-McCann.

Cohen, Felix. 1947. "Original Indian Title." *Minnesota Law Review* 32:28–59.

Connell, Evan S. 1988. *Cavalier in Buckskin.* Norman: University of Oklahoma Press.

Cooter, Robert D., and Daniel L. Rubinfeld. 1989. "Economic Analysis of Legal Disputes and Their Resolution." *Journal of Economic Literature* 27:1067–1097.

Debo, Angie. 1989. *A History of the Indians of the United States.* Norman: University of Oklahoma Press.

Hirshleifer, Jack. 1994. "The Dark Side of the Force." *Economic Inquiry* 32 (January):1–10.

Hughes, Jonathan R.T. 1976. *Social Control in the Colonial Economy.* Charlottesville: University Press of Virginia.

Kickingbird, Kirke, and Karen Ducheneaus. 1973. *One Hundred Million Acres.* New York: Macmillan.

McGrath, Roger D. 1984. *Gunfighters, Highwaymen, and Vigilantes: Violence on the Frontier.* Berkeley: University of California Press.

Prucha, Francis Paul. 1962. *American Indian Policy in the Formative Years: The Indian Trade and Intercourse Acts, 1790–1834.* Cambridge: Harvard University Press.

Roback, Jennifer. 1992. "Exchange, Sovereignty, and Indian-Anglo Relations." In *Property Rights and Indian Economies,* ed. Terry L. Anderson, 5–26. Lanham, Md.: Rowman and Littlefield.

Roosevelt, Theodore. 1889. *The Winning of the West.* Vol. 1. New York: G. P. Putnam's Sons.

Russell, Don. 1973. "How Many Indians Were Killed?" *American West,* July, 42–63.

Thomas, David Hurst, Jay Miller, Richard White, Peter Nabokov, and Philip J. Deloria. 1993. *The Native Americans: An Illustrated History.* Atlanta: Turner.

Umbeck, John. 1981. "Might Makes Rights: A Theory of the Formation and Initial Distribution of Property Rights." *Economic Inquiry* 19 (January).

Utley, Robert M. 1967. *Frontiersmen in Blue: The United States Army and the Indian, 1848–1865.* Lincoln: University of Nebraska Press.

———. 1984. *The Indian Frontier of the American West, 1846–1890.* Albuquerque: New Mexico Press.

Washburn, Wilcomb E. 1971. *Red Man's Land/White Man's Law.* New York: Charles Scribner's Sons.

Part Four

Twentieth-Century Federalism

Introduction

The Political Economy and
History of Allotment

LEONARD A. CARLSON

Part 4 contains two selections: a chapter on federal Indian policy in the twentieth century and a chapter on Native Hawaiians. Both look at the relationship of native peoples to federal agencies charged with helping them. The federal government has played a very important role in the lives of Native peoples in the twentieth century, but as with other forms of federal intervention in the economy (see, for example, Atack and Passell 1994, chap. 23), federal involvement began much earlier. Chapter 9, by Leonard A. Carlson, looks at federal programs that between 1900 and 1930 built irrigation projects on several reservations in the West. Chapter 10, by Sumner J. La Croix and Louis A. Rose, analyzes an important program that has provided land and housing for Native Hawaiians since 1921.

Both chapters use methodologies influenced by recent work in economics that stress the role of organized interest groups (including the regulatory agencies themselves) in setting policy.[1] This view contrasts to the public interest view of federal legislation, which assumes that the government and its agencies will act in the public interest. These two chapters both find that although Native peoples did benefit from the programs studied, there were many wasteful elements and that non-Native special interests were often major beneficiaries of the programs. A key issue left for the reader to decide is what policies might have worked better, given the actual historical conditions and knowledge of the participants.

There are interesting similarities and differences between the Hawaiian Home Lands Program and programs to irrigate Indian reservations and promote farming by Indians. By the twentieth century, Native Hawaiians were integrated into the larger economy of the Hawaiian Islands. Although, of course, at one time all people in Hawaii were ethnically Native Hawaiian, disease and immigration had tipped the balance so that in the nineteenth century Hawaiians had become a minority in the islands. Once Hawaii was annexed by the United States, Native Hawaiians were simply a large but poor ethnic group with roughly the same legal rights as any other group. Many Native Hawaiians worked as agricultural laborers or in unskilled urban jobs, and few commoners owned any land. Beginning in 1921 the federal government established the Hawaiian Home Lands (HHL) Program to try to assist Native Hawaiians to once again become farmers. Rose and La Croix discuss the fact that the program failed in part because the land that was made available for Native Hawaiian farmers was marginal at best. The HHL Program then changed its focus to try to help Native Hawaiians purchase homes. The program succeeded to a degree, although, for reasons that La Croix and Rose analyze, the program has been inefficient and inequitable.

In contrast, American Indians at the turn of the century often lived in relatively arid, remote locations but retained title to large amounts of land. The goal of federal programs for Indians was to encourage them to learn to use the resources they already owned in new ways. In the first three decades of the twentieth century, the federal government tried to help Indian tribes use their resources more effectively by building irrigation projects on several major reservations. Carlson discusses the fact that many of these projects finally served more white farmers than Indian farmers and shows that, as in Hawaii, they were very wasteful. Nonetheless, as with the Hawaiian Home Lands Program, Indians also received some benefits.

As a background for their study of the Hawaiian Home Lands Program, La Croix and Rose provide a detailed summary of the history of Native Hawaiians from first contact with Europeans in 1778 to the present. Carlson looks at the irrigation programs on Indian reservations, which were part of a larger program to promote farming by Indians. To put this in context, a brief survey of federal Indian policy follows, emphasizing federal programs to promote farming.

The Federal Government and Native Americans, 1880–1940

Since the annexation of Hawaii by the United States in 1898, Native Hawaiians have been citizens who vote and hold property just as do other citizens of Hawaii. At the same time, many Indians are members of tribes as well as U.S. citizens; some tribal governments have their own court systems and some state laws do not apply on reservation lands. Indeed, a number of tribal Indians were not made citizens until special legislation was passed by Congress in 1924.

The origins of the special status of Indian tribes goes back to the beginnings of the republic. The Constitution grants the federal government power "to regulate commerce with the foreign nations, and among the several States, *and with the Indian tribes*" (emphasis added). This simple statement has evolved so that the federal government has had a direct legal relationship with Indian tribes. A second source of this relationship was the practice of negotiating treaties with tribes. Soon after the United States gained independence from Britain, Congress decided to continue the British practice of recognizing the rights of Indian tribes to the territory they occupied. Although the government could acquire land from tribes through treaties or just wars, Indians still had recognized rights, and settlers could not purchase land directly from tribes. Chief Justice John Marshall wrote in the case of *Worcester v. Georgia* (1832) that the Cherokee Nation was "a distinct community, in which the laws of Georgia can have no force" (Prucha 1984, 77). In this ruling, Marshall affirmed the right of the federal government rather than the states to regulate intercourse with Indian tribes. Despite their success in court, the Cherokee were forced a few years later to leave Georgia along the "trail of tears" (see David M. Wishart, Chapter 6 in this volume).

The removal of the Cherokee was part of a larger policy of moving Indians westward. Until the 1840s the federal government negotiated treaties (sometimes by coercion) to move most (but not all) eastern tribes to lands in the West as a way of opening land for white settlement and to allow Indians time to adjust to the influx of white settlers. This system set a boundary between Indian tribes and white settlement, and in principle, whites were to stay east of the line and Indians would stay to the west in "Indian country."

This Indian frontier was completely breached in the late 1840s with the acquisition of new lands in the West and the massive movement of white settlers into California and Oregon to farm or mine for gold. To protect Indians while still opening land to numerous settlers pushing westward, the federal government induced tribes to sign new treaties in which they ceded all or part of their lands in return for some land "reserved" for their exclusive use.[2] Typically these treaties gave a tribe a defined territory and future goods in return for surrendering title to other tribal lands.[3]

Once Indians were settled on a reservation, the federal government assumed the role of guardian of Indian property and Indian welfare on the reservation. Federal agents distributed promised goods and supervised educational programs. The reservations often lacked sufficient resources for tribes to continue their traditional ways of supporting themselves. For example, the destruction of the buffalo herds in the 1870s and 1880s eliminated the major food resource of Plains tribes and ended that way of life. Consequently, one task of the federal agents was to teach Indians new ways of supporting themselves. Congress also expected agents to push Indians to assimilate into mainstream society. Farming was seen as the ideal means by which Indians could gain a new livelihood and almost magically become assimilated into white society. This work was made more difficult because of limited resources and widespread corruption. In addition, Indians often resisted heavy-handed programs to change their way of life.

The latter part of the nineteenth century saw renewed pressure to open still more Indian lands to outside settlement. In 1890 the total Indian population of the continental United States was less than 250,000, and the total area of reservations in 1887 was roughly 138 million acres (about two-and-one-half times the size of the state of Georgia). Although much Indian land was relatively arid, it seemed to land-hungry westerners that Indians had more land than they could ever use. At the same time, an active reform movement in the East sought to assimilate Indians into mainstream society by promoting agriculture. This influential group was made up of Protestant religious reformers, educators, and government officials. Congress tried to satisfy both westerners and reformers by passing the General Allotment Act, or Dawes Act, of 1887.

The humanitarian reformers who pushed for the passage of the Dawes Act believed that dividing reservations into privately owned farms would break the hold of the chiefs over individual Indians, encourage Indians to become farmers, and hasten the assimilation of Indians into white culture. This belief was based largely on an inaccurate model of Indian societies that was popular among social scientists in the 1880s. The law passed with little opposition, since it also allowed white farmers to purchase unallotted lands (called surplus land).

Under the Dawes Act, reservations were to be divided into 160-acre farms called allotments. Each family's land was placed in trust for a twenty-five-year period to prevent Indians from being defrauded of their land; but this also meant that the land could not be sold or mortgaged without government permission. The Dawes Act gave the president the authority to survey reservations when he thought it was appropriate. Individuals who refused allotments could have one assigned to them. Before 1903 a tribe had to consent to have surplus lands opened for settlement. After that date, the courts ruled that the federal government could sell surplus lands without a tribe's consent and hold the receipts in trust for members of the tribe.

After 1887 most Indian reservations were allotted under terms of the Dawes Act, but some tribes, especially in Oklahoma, received land allotted under special legislation. Reservations in desirable farming areas were allotted first, whereas reservations in remote or arid locations were sometimes never allotted. Thus a number of tribes in the Southwest and elsewhere were never allotted. Most reservations were allotted between 1887 and 1910, but allotment work continued until 1934.[4]

Congress saw allotment as the key to all other programs, and it remained at the center of federal Indian policy until 1934. In all, over 41 million acres were allotted to Indians under a variety of laws and treaties. One consequence was that that the land base of Indian tribes declined from 138 million acres in 1887 to 34,287,336 acres in 1934, including additions to some reservations in the Southwest. Moreover, another 17.8 million acres of land allotted to individuals was still under federal supervision. Allotments no longer supervised by the federal government had either been sold or the owners no longer had restrictions on their land.

The stated goal of federal Indian policy in these years was to make Indians self-sufficient and encourage their assimilation through the development of agriculture. By this standard, federal policies clearly failed. The number of Indian farmers and ranchers declined from 1900 to 1930, as did the amount of land farmed by Indians. There were many reasons that Indians, like Hawaiians, did not succeed as farmers. Many historians emphasize that Indians had little experience with commercial farming, or indeed any farming. Further, as farms became larger and more mechanized, farming in the twentieth century became an increasingly difficult endeavor for small farmers with little capital. The allotment policy itself was a part of the problem. Perversely, the restrictions placed on Indian allotments and the opening of the reservations often made it more attractive for an Indian to sell or lease land rather than farm it (Carlson 1981, chaps. 4–6). Indeed, Indian farming actually declined after reservations were allotted. Selling land was not necessarily harmful to Indians, but in many cases the sales were without Indian consent and were ultimately a bad idea. Allotment also often left tribes with a fragmented and diminished base that was inadequate for a growing population.

The decline in farming was unfortunate because many Indians continued to live in rural areas where agriculture was often the main opportunity for employment. In 1900 reformers had been optimistic that Indians would assimilate into white society and succeed economically, eliminating the need for the BIA. By the 1920s there was a growing belief that Indian policy had done a poor job of aiding Indians and protecting their rights and that reform was needed to address the poverty and poor health conditions on many reservations.

There were a variety of possible solutions. Moderate reform began in the late 1920s, and this might have continued. However, the Great Depression of 1929–1933 and the election of Franklin Roosevelt meant that more radical change was possible. Roosevelt named John Collier, a longtime critic of Indian policy, to be commissioner of Indian Affairs. Collier in turn proposed a radical change in Indian policy. The program designed by Collier was passed in 1934 as the Indian Reorganization Act (IRA) (also known as the Wheeler-Howard Act). The IRA ended allotment, placed most tribal land and allotted trust land under federal supervision, and created a way for tribes to establish legally constituted tribal governments to manage their affairs. In sharp contrast to earlier policymakers, Collier, who had worked with the Pueblo Indians in New Mexico, hoped to use tribes to promote group development.

Despite the rhetoric and good intentions, federal policy in this period has been criticized for again trying to impose a common policy on diverse groups. While many Indians supported these reforms, others have found them less satisfactory, sometimes for conflicting reasons. Some who opposed Collier's reforms felt that the "Indian New Deal" kept too much power in the BIA; others wanted to continue older, more individualistic policies. Still others complained that the tribal governments created by the Indian New Deal failed to recognize traditional tribal leaders.

In practice the actual workings of tribal governments were often not as Collier envisioned. Collier assumed that tribal governments would reflect the existing tribal traditions and values. But on a number of reservations, there was no common culture, and traditional institutions had disappeared, especially where there was more than one tribe occupying the same land. On other reservations, a number of collective action problems have arisen, including rent seeking and wasteful competition between different factions. However, despite problems and unintended consequences, tribal governments continue to play an important role on reservations, and some have been successful in promoting economic progress for tribal members. Like allotment, the reforms of the 1930s continue to have an influence on the institutions and laws governing Indians today.

Policy from 1940 to the Present

The period from 1940 to the present has seen further developments in Indian policy and in the economic position of Indians. The policy of promoting tribal governments begun by Collier was challenged in the late 1940s and 1950s. In that period, Congress tried once again to reduce the power of tribes and to encourage Indians to leave reservations and move to cities. Most notable was the policy know as termination. Termination was the name for the policy of ending the special status of tribes and turning Indians over to the local state and county services. Although only two major tribes were terminated in this way, the fear of a loss of federal services and tribal sovereignty made this one of the most disliked policies of all. The 1970s saw yet another reversal, with a movement toward greater tribal autonomy and a pledge by President Richard Nixon to end termination. Today, Indians are citizens of the United States, but recent court decisions and legislation have given tribal governments more authority than at any time this century. The total Indian population as measured by the census has risen from 265,683 persons counted as Indians in 1910, 95 percent of whom lived in rural areas, to 1.965 million[5] in 1990, 1.1 million of whom live in urban areas, although many maintain ties to reservations. The single best reference on Indian policy in the twentieth century is Prucha 1984.

Notes

1. The application of economic reasoning to the political process is known as public choice or rational choice.

2. This is the origin of the term "reservation."

3. Not all tribes had a clear title to any land. Later in the nineteenth century some reservations were created by executive order when the president authorized setting aside lands for a tribe or tribes from the public domain.

4. See Carlson 1981, chaps. 2 and 3 for a discussion of the political economy of allotment.

5. This includes all persons who identified themselves as Indian, Eskimo, or Aleut, including mixed-blood individuals.

Bibliography

Atack, Jeremy, and Peter Passell. 1994. *A New Economic View of American History.* 2nd ed. New York: Norton.

Carlson, Leonard A. 1981. *Indians, Bureaucrats, and Land: The Dawes Act and the Decline of Indian Farming.* Westport, Conn.: Greenwood Press.

Prucha, Francis Paul. 1984. *The Great Father.* Abridged ed. Lincoln: University of Nebraska Press.

9

The Economics and Politics of Irrigation Projects on Indian Reservations, 1900–1940

LEONARD A. CARLSON

In the West water resources are critical for the development of agriculture, and many Indian reservations are in areas with less than 20 inches of rainfall annually. Thus many Indians live on reservations where farming is difficult without irrigation. In order to carry out the mandate from Congress to turn Indians into farmers, the Bureau of Indian Affairs (BIA)[1] in the late nineteenth century began a series of irrigation projects on a number of Indian reservations in the West. One reason Congress emphasized programs to help Indians learn to farm was that agriculture was seen as the best available occupation on many reservations. Also, members of Congress and reformers in the 1880s and later had a strong, almost religious faith that teaching Indians to farm and assigning land to them individually was the best way to assimilate them into white society. A desire to hasten the transformation of Indians from hunters into farmers prompted Congress in 1887 to authorize the allotment of Indian reservations into 160-acre farms (with a restricted title).

However, despite the stated goal of promoting farming, Indian farming declined in the twentieth century (Carlson 1981a, 1981b). Irrigation projects also typically failed to yield as many benefits for Indians as expected. The failure of Indian irrigation projects is thus just one example of the broader failure of Indian policy to assist in the economic development of Indian reservations. In this chapter I model the behavior of the BIA in order to understand the performance of irrigation projects on Indian reservations and, more broadly, to understand Indians' relationship with the federal government.[2]

The reasons that the BIA's irrigation policy worked badly for Indians are interesting in their own right. But this subject also touches the broader issue of the relationship of Indian tribes to the federal government. The Constitution grants the federal government the authority "to regulate commerce with foreign nations, and among the several States, and with the Indian tribes." As a result, the federal government has had the leading role in dealing with Indian tribes, since tribes deal directly with the federal government and not the states. The ongoing nature of the relationship between Indians and the federal government also shows up in the budget. For example, the *Historical Statistics of the United States, 1789–1945* lists six categories of expenditure in the first federal budget, for 1789–1791 (U.S. Bureau of the Census 1949, 301). One category included a small expenditure for Indians, and every federal budget since has contained appropriations for Indian affairs. It is necessary to grasp this complicated relationship to understand the history of Indians in the United States since 1789.

The evidence indicates that many Indian irrigation programs were often inefficient and badly administered. I propose three interrelated but distinct reasons that federal irrigation policy was so inept. In the first place, the political coalitions required to pass legislation were such that Indian policy also inevitably served the interests of well-organized, non-Indian interest groups in addition to Indians. Second, there was a monitoring problem. Irrigation projects were scattered throughout the western states, and Congress or officials in Washington, D.C., could only measure imperfectly what was happening with each project. This inevitably led to a waste of resources (the principal-agent problem). Third, the way in which institutions in Indian country were adapted was such that many were not well suited to the task at hand and were inherently wasteful (the "panda's thumb principle").

Federal Irrigation Programs on Indian Reservations to 1930

Congress first appropriated funds for an irrigation project on an Indian reservation in 1867 and made regular annual appropriations for irrigation projects on Indian reservations after 1893. Before 1902 no one had questioned the right of the BIA to claim all the water needed to develop resources on Indian reservations. This changed when Congress created a rival claimant for western water when it passed the National Reclamation Act of 1902 (Newlands Act). The act established a new agency, the Bureau of Reclamation, to build dams and develop water resources in the West. But if the Bureau of Reclamation built a dam upstream from an Indian reservation it could divert water needed to develop Indian lands. Thus two agencies under the secretary of the interior were at times competing for control of the same resource. Conflicts inevitably arose, since the constituency served by the Bureau of Reclamation were often white farmers, not Indians. One strategy pursued by the BIA to protect Indian water rights was to construct irrigation projects, which established for Indians a right to water under the doctrine of prior appropriation and beneficial use.

Yet there were examples of cooperation between the agencies. The advantage for the BIA of cooperation was that the Bureau of Reclamation had more engineers with training and experience in building irrigation systems than did the BIA. In 1907 the BIA agreed to let the Bureau of Reclamation construct irrigation facilities on the Fort Pack, Flathead, and Blackfoot reservations in Montana and the Pima and Fort Yuma reservations in Arizona. The Bureau of Reclamation would retain control of these projects until 1924 (McDonnell 1991, 74). For the Bureau of Reclamation these projects meant additional funds to develop new projects and access to more sites suitable for irrigation (Pisani 1986, 168).

Another set of issues involved who would pay for the projects. Under the National Reclamation Act, landowners on a project were (at least in principle) expected to pay fees that would repay all construction and maintenance costs of projects. This implies that farmers and ranchers were receiving a substantial subsidy, since these costs did not include interest charges. In practice, however, the subsidy was much greater than the interest charges, since the federal government typically did not collect as much money as expected (Mayhew and Delworth Gardner, 1994). Over time, as the costs of the projects mounted and revenues lagged behind expenditures, members of Congress tried to collect more fees from the projects. This inevitably affected Indians as well. Originally, Congress appropriated funds for irrigation projects on Indian reservations without repayment provisions. In 1914 Congress amended the law governing Indian irrigation projects so that Indians were also liable for construction and maintenance costs past, present, and future. According to the new law, the government would now prorate the cost among individual Indians whose land was actually irrigated. This legislation, on first blush, appeared to put Indians on the same basis as other water users and would make the projects self-funding. In practice, however, this change made Indian tribes liable for accrued charges from earlier projects, even where tribes had not approved the projects and the federal government had agreed to fund the project. Reformers in the 1920s were especially critical of the provisions that retroactively made tribes liable for accrued charges for projects built without tribal consent.

Ironically, the problems of Indian irrigation worsened in the 1920s when Congress lost faith in the Bureau of Reclamation. By then it was clear to members of Congress that on many projects fees collected from water users would never come close to repaying construction costs. Members of Congress from the East were reluctant to fund more projects and demanded that the Bureau of Reclamation act vigorously to collect outstanding obligations. Projects on Indian reservations were also tarred with the same brush, and it became hard for the BIA to get Congress to authorize new projects (Pisani 1986, 172). BIA officials tried to appease congressional critics by collecting as much revenue as possible from the their projects, even if this meant encouraging Indians to lease their lands to whites. In the end, however, very little revenue was ever actually collected from Indian projects.

The criticism of irrigation projects in the 1920s coincided with increased criticism of all aspects federal Indian policy. New groups of reformers, including the General Federation of Women's Clubs and its representative, John Collier, publicly criticized the BIA for its poor record in protecting Indian interests. Collier was especially effective in rallying opposition to the Bursum Bill, which would have settled land claims in New Mexico in a way unfavorable to the interests of the Pueblo Indians. Collier and the American Indian Defense Association, another group of activists, also criticized other aspects of BIA programs in the 1920s. The issues they cited included the poor state of Indian health care, the loss of Indian lands after allotment, and the failure to protect the interests of those Indians in Oklahoma (especially members of the Osage tribe) who had received large oil royalty payments. One result of this campaign was that the secretary of the interior, Hubert Work, requested that an independent agency, the Institute of Government Research (which later became part of the Brookings Institution), investigate the quality of BIA programs (Prucha 1990, 808). The result was the influential Meriam Report, which was based on research done in 1926 and was published in 1928 (Meriam 1928).[3]

The study team was headed by Lewis Meriam, a permanent staff member of the institute, and it surveyed all aspects of Indian programs in the federal government, not just irrigation projects. Because the study team lacked the expertise to evaluate irrigation projects, their published report recommended that Congress authorize a technical evaluation of such projects. Nonetheless, the Meriam team was highly critical of irrigation projects. First, the Meriam Report criticized the requirement that tribes repay the government for projects for which tribes had not been consulted. Second, the report asserted that some projects were not economically sound; that is, they did not satisfy some sort of cost-benefit criterion. Third, even on the projects that were economically viable, the report team complained that the BIA agent did too little to help Indians actually use the irrigated land and too often encouraged Indians to lease their land to white farmers.

The call for a technical evaluation of Indian irrigation projects led to a survey of Indian irrigation in 1927 by government engineers Porter J. Preston and Charles Engle. Although their report received little attention at the time, it is the most authoritative examination of Indian irrigation projects done in the first four decades of the twentieth century. I discuss the findings of this report extensively in what follows.

Modeling the Administration of Indian Policy

The first set of issues to consider is the political issues that led to the origins of Indian policy. The legal basis for the BIA's control over the lives and property of Indians was that it was protecting Indian interests. Older historical works tend to accept this idea that the federal government was a benevolent guardian of Indians.[4] I think this is a reasonable place to start an investigation of Indian policy, since this was the legal basis for the extraordinary powers that the federal government had over the lives and freedoms of Indians. This is of course very similar to what Richard Posner (1974) called the "public interest view" of regulation.

One implication of a public interest view is that the BIA should have tried to carry out the statutory and other goals set for it by Congress in a way that served its mandate and the interests of Indians. With respect to irrigation projects, Congress mandated three objectives for the BIA: to protect Indian water rights, to make the projects self funding, and to encourage Indians to farm their own land.

The goal of protecting Indian water rights led the BIA to lease Indian land to whites where Indians were not yet ready to use the water themselves. The BIA was trying to guarantee Indian water rights through "prior appropriation and beneficial use." Under the law of most western states, unlike under common law, the first user of water has a right to water relative to later users. After 1908, however, Indians had another basis on which to make a legal claim to water. In 1908, in the case of *Winters v. United States*, the Supreme Court held that in creating Indian reservations, Congress had guaranteed Indians a right to "sufficient" water, even where they were not currently using the water. Modern critics of the BIA complain that the BIA did not aggressively use this decision to protect Indian water rights earlier (see McCool 1987). To be fair to the BIA, however, in the first two decades after the *Winters* decision, no one knew exactly how much protection this gave Indians.[5] However, if an Indian had leased his or her land to a white tenant who irrigated the land, the right of the Indian family to a certain amount of water was protected by the principle of prior appropriation. Hence it is understandable why the BIA might have used the doctrine of prior appropriation to try to protect Indian water rights.

The problem was that the first and second goals (utilizing the land on the irrigation projects to establish Indian water rights and generate revenue) were in conflict with the third goal (encouraging Indians to be farmers). The easiest way to be sure that someone farmed the irrigated land on a project was to lease it to white farmers, who had more capital, both physical and human, than did Indians. But as I have argued extensively elsewhere, the leasing of land by Indians often encouraged a *decline* in farming by Indians. Since the BIA wanted Indians to farm their own land, encouraging them to lease their land to whites was contradictory. The size of the allotments also proved to be a difficulty. Irrigated farming is a skill- and capital-intensive activity. Indian families were typically allotted more land than they could use. This was wasteful, since some of the funds used to irrigate Indian lands might have been better used to aid Indian farmers (by offering loans or training) rather than to irrigate lands Indians could not use and that many families simply leased to non-Indians.

In the end, few modern scholars find credible the view that the BIA was simply trying its best to act as a disinterested guardian. A number of recent works by historians and legal scholars have emphasized shifts in federal policy from pro-Indian (anti-assimilationist policies) to anti-Indian (pro-assimilationist policies) and back again (see, for example, Fixico 1986). The assumption is that the shifts in policy are largely ideological battles over perceptions of what is "the right thing to do" and that people with bad ideas win part of the time. A problem with such an analysis is that it does not lend itself to empirical testing. Nor does it explain the persistent problems in Indian administration, regardless of the stated goals of policy. A more promising approach in my view has drawn on the rent seeking/public choice approach to policymaking. Although relatively new in the study of Indian history, a number of studies have recently applied versions of public choice models to Indian policy (see Carlson 1981a, 1983; McChesney 1992; Alston and Spiller 1992). Outside of economics, scholars have used "iron triangle" and other forms of interest group analysis that have some similarities to a rent seeking approach.[6]

My model of Indian policy starts with four major interest groups. These are (1) Congress at large, (2) white farmers and ranchers who wished to use subsidized water on Indian reservations, (3) Indians living on the affected reservations, and (4) the BIA bureaucracy itself. These groups had different costs of organizing and different objectives, and my conclusion is that the contradictions found in Indian policy in part reflect trade-offs between these groups. In what follows I look at each group in turn.

The first group is Congress at large. Congress had final authority, subject to presidential veto, for passing enabling legislation that governed Indian policy. Further, since Congress controls the budget of the BIA, congressional committees had a great deal of influence over the day-to-day administration of Indian affairs. Most members of Congress, however, had little direct interest in what happened on reservations. Thus I model members of Congress from districts outside Indian country as having three objectives. First, they wanted to avoid spending too much on Indian programs. Second, they wanted to treat Indians "fairly." Fair is a subjective concept, of course. In this case it probably meant that Congress wanted to treat Indians like whites as long as the special needs of Indians would somehow be taken care of. Congress might also want to implement any currently popular humanitarian agenda about Indians. Third, members of Congress were probably willing to trade votes on Indian policy with members from the West in return for other votes favorable to their own constituents. Apart from this logrolling, altruism or paternalism toward Indians was relatively low-cost for members of Congress from areas outside Indian country. As a result Congress often set vague goals that were hard to implement and monitor and were subject to popular whim. The most important legislation of the period, the Dawes Act, carries the name of its sponsor, Henry Dawes, the senior senator from Massachusetts. Even though there were no reservations in Massachusetts, Dawes's role as advocate of the agenda of Indian reform groups made him popular with reformers, many of whom lived in Boston. The need to mobilize reform sentiment also explains why reformers in the nineteenth and twentieth centuries expended resources to influence public opinion. For example, Collier and the General Federation of Women's Clubs worked to get articles critical of Indian policy published in popular magazines of the 1920s.

The second interest group was white farmers who lived near Indian reservations and the members of Congress who represented them. These farmers often wanted to acquire Indian land and receive subsidized water. Public choice theory shows how such small groups will organize to influence policy and capture rents, since organizing costs are low relative to the potential benefits. Such groups were already mobilized to influence the policies of the larger Bureau of Reclamation.

The means that these groups had to assert their claims was really twofold. The first was through their representatives in Congress. Members of Congress from the West had a very direct interest in the outcome of Indian policy. Astute leaders of the BIA, such as Commissioner Francis E. Luepp in the first part of the twentieth century, clearly acknowledged the need to satisfy the interests of members of Congress from the West in order to advance the goals of the agency. A second way that farmers and ranchers could shape local Indian policy was to influence agents in the field. These agents were subject to imperfect controls from the bureaucrats in Washington and had a fair amount of independent authority. Agents in the field might have identified more with the interests of the white community than with Indians. Further, it was sometimes simply easier to authorize the leasing of land to white farmers than to work with Indians in helping them to farm their own land.

The third and perhaps weakest group in this period was the Indian tribes. Tribal lands were subject to BIA supervision, and in many cases individual Indians could only sell or lease their land with the consent of the BIA. This greatly limited the ability of many tribes to direct their own economic activities. In addition, Indians typically did not have much influence with local legislators. This was true for a number of reasons. For one thing, before 1924 not all Indians were citizens, and in some states (notably Arizona and New Mexico) Indians could not vote in state elections until 1948. They were, in any case, a small minority in most districts. Further, Indian tribes had only limited authority. Treaties could be overridden by Congress without the consent of the tribe, as illustrated by the 1903 Supreme Court case of *Lone Wolf v. Hitchcock*. Indeed, there was no well-established way for Indians to express their views. In negotiating with the BIA, Indians on many reservations were represented by ad hoc councils formed by the agent. Nonetheless, in some instances, the BIA needed consent from tribal representatives to undertake some actions, and this gave Indians a voice in BIA decisions. Additionally, when the popular press dramatized a particularly newsworthy example of what appeared to be an injustice toward an Indian tribe, it could rally public opinion and influence Congress at large.

The final interest group is bureaucrats within the Bureau of Indian Affairs, who sought to advance their careers subject to the imperfect monitoring provided by Congress. Many officials in the BIA were undoubtedly interested in advancing their own careers. This is not to say that career employees were strictly indifferent to the interests of Indians but, rather, that most had a multitude of goals. There were probably more opportunities for advancement if the BIA budgets increased. Fred McChesney (1992), for example, concluded that each major shift in Indian policy in this period led to increased budgets for the BIA. For example, when the BIA shifted from a policy of allotment and the privatization of Indian lands to a policy of working through Indian tribes and ending allotment, BIA budgets rose. Thus, as a way of advancing their own careers, officials in the BIA would have an interest in trying to influence how Congress set policy.

Once a project was authorized, monitoring BIA programs became a major problem. Since the BIA agents in the field could only be monitored very imperfectly by Congress or officials in Washington, it is not surprising that BIA agents focused on clearly visible objectives, such as promoting use of irrigation lands by white farmers. This is an example of the principal-agent problem. For example, a program to teach Indians to farm might take years to achieve noticeable results. By the time Indians learned to farm, the BIA employees who helped teach Indians to farm would have moved on to a new assignment and someone else would receive the credit. Thus an agent would have incentives to maximize use of the land by non-Indians rather than painstakingly nurture Indian farming.

These two sets of explanations—interest group politics and monitoring problems—are powerful, but they miss part of the story. Simply put, the missing piece is why the administration of irrigation policy was so wasteful from anyone's point of view. In a world of scarce resources, it always makes sense to economize. Thus it is always better to have an efficient institution to distribute the benefits of federal programs to different groups, rather than to simply dissipate the resources, unless an inefficient institution is the only option available.

Paul David (1992) concluded that new institutions are often adaptations of previously existing forms to serve new purposes. The result is institutions that are "serviceable, but inelegant." The reason that existing institutions are adapted to new uses is that institutions are embedded in a system with network externalities and learning effects. David used the metaphor of the "panda's thumb," based on biologist Stephen Gould's (1980) metaphor for evolution.[7] According to David, "the 'panda's thumb' metaphor offers institutional economics the paradigm of a serviceable, but inelegant, resultant of a path dependent process of evolutionary improvisation, a structure whose obvious limitations stem from its remote accidental origins" (1992, 22).

Here I use the "panda's thumb" metaphor in a somewhat different way. Congress passed laws for Indians on the premise that Indian tribes and Indian peoples need special institutions and laws to protect their interests. In order to do this, Congress almost inevitably adapted existing institutions to serve a new purpose, since Indians are a small minority interacting with the rest of society. Thus laws governing Indians had to be consistent with laws governing whites, while at the same time trying to serve a special purpose. It is also probably cheaper to use existing institutions for which legal opinions are already well established.[8] The result is that Indian policy is littered with institutions that are "contrivances." One example is the awkward and wasteful form of land tenure given to Indians by the General Allotment Act. Another is the special water rights of Indians recognized by the Winters Doctrine, with which courts have struggled for years to reconcile non-Indian water rights.

The case of *Winters v. United States* (1908) concerned water rights on the Fort Belknap Indian Reservation in Montana. The Fort Belknap Reservation was established by treaty in 1888 with members of the Assiniboin and Gros Ventre tribes. When white settlers diverted water from the Milk River feeding the reservation, the Bureau of Indian Affairs got an injunction to stop the settlers. The settlers then appealed to the Supreme Court. The Court ruled in favor of the government and the Indians. The Court concluded that when it established the reservation, the federal government had intended for the Indians to have sufficient water from the Milk River to use reservation lands. Thus Indians had a "reserved right" to water that was different from the rights to water covering other citizens. It was not clear from the Supreme Court's wording, however, how much water Indians had a right to or whether the federal government or the Indians had reserved the water (see Hundley 1985). Indeed, it is still not clear eighty-five years later how

much water Indians can claim under the Winters Doctrine. Thus Rodney
Smith (1992) argued that it is often better for Indian tribes to reach an
agreement with the surrounding community than to take the case to court
when there is a dispute over who has a right to water. Litigation can take
many years, the outcome is uncertain, and litigation often creates hostility
between the Indians and the surrounding community. This issue demonstrates the "panda's thumb" principle because it establishes Indian water
rights on top of an existing principle of prior appropriation. Starting from
scratch, a more efficient institution might have been devised to give Indians
a clearer claim to their water.

Similarly, the nature of irrigation projects on Indian reservations was influenced by the structure of the relationship of the BIA to the Bureau of Reclamation. Thus projects reflect these interrelationships rather than indicate an
attempt simply to serve the interests of Indians.

Testing the Model

The models I have sketched out above lead to a testable implication. If the
BIA were simply carrying out its legal mandate of protecting the interests of
Indians and carrying out the directives of Congress, the predictions that follow are straightforward. BIA policies should have generated larger benefits
for Indians than for other groups, and wasteful activities should not have
persisted. Clearly, the BIA officials might make mistakes, but if a policy was
wasteful or failed to promote Indians interests, it should have been changed
once the mistake was recognized. If, however, the model of interest groups
jockeying for benefits plus a waste factor due to the contrived nature of Indian institutions is correct, the prediction is that a large share of the resources would go to non-Indians and clearly wasteful projects would continue for many years.

The data to test these competing views are taken in part from the already-
mentioned report on Indian irrigation projects prepared by engineers Porter
J. Preston and Charles A. Engle. Secretary of the Interior Hubert Work authorized the survey in 1927. Between March and September 1927, Preston
(an engineer for the Bureau of Reclamation) and Engle (the supervising engineer for the Bureau of Indian Affairs) visited the largest irrigation projects
in the West; this included 91 percent of all irrigated land on Indian reservations (Preston and Engle 1930, 2210–2211, 2218–2219). The timing of the
study is also useful because it comes just before the major shift in Indian policy marked by the Indian Reorganization Act, the Wheeler-Howard Act of
1934.

I classify the projects visited by Preston and Engle into three groups: those
where most of the irrigated land was used by whites; those where the land

was mostly farmed by Indians; and those where there was little evidence that anyone benefited. The use of land can be seen in Table 9.1.

From an interest group perspective, the easiest projects to understand are those where most of the land was cultivated by white farmers and ranchers. White farmers and ranchers had already organized to capture rents from Bureau of Reclamation projects (Mayhew and Gardner 1994; Rucker and Fishback 1983). The BIA was interested in showing Congress that it was helping Indians, but it is also easy to see why BIA officials would want to show Congress that it was helping white farmers as well. If white farmers felt that their interests were served by Indian irrigation projects, it would be easier to gain the support of local members of Congress for Indian programs. Leasing the lands to whites also meant that someone used project lands, which helped placate members of Congress concerned with waste.

The largest Indian irrigation projects were on the Yakima Reservation in Washington. By 1927 the BIA had spent $3,698,994 on irrigation programs at Yakima. In that year, Indians farmed 6,250 acres out of 89,000 irrigated acres on the reservation, with the rest farmed by white lessors or owners. Who benefited from this project? White farmers benefited in using subsidized irrigated lands. Irrigation project officials benefited from the collection of fees from water users and from being able to demonstrate to Congress that project lands were used productively. Indians also benefited from the voluntary lease or sale of their lands to whites.

But this is not necessarily what Indians might have wanted nor what a guardian interested in the interests of Indian should have done. James Fitch (1974) concluded that the Yakima were far better equipped to be ranchers or dry farmers than to farm irrigated lands. Thus, although the Yakima benefited from the project, the BIA might have better served their interests by letting the land be used for grazing and dry farming or, at least, by building smaller irrigation projects. Indeed, according to Preston and Engle, lease payments made to the Yakima were sufficiently large that the Yakima could engage in casual day labor and refrain from agriculture altogether (1930, 2655–2656). If the goal of federal policymakers was to encourage the Yakima to farm their own land, the policy of irrigating the Yakima Reservation was at best a limited success.

The leading historian of Indian policy, Francis Prucha, reached a similar conclusion. According to Prucha,

> It became increasingly clear throughout the 1920's that irrigation projects were authorized for Indian reservations not with the primary intent of aiding the Indian to advance toward self-sufficiency, but to develop the arid west for the benefit of white interests. And, in fact, the whites were the ones who most profited from irrigation. (1984, 894)

TABLE 9.1 Status of Ownership of Project Lands as of June 30, 1927

Projects	Ownership of Lands Under Ultimate Irrigable Area			Ownership of Land Under Constructed Ditches			Indian Owned Land	Indian Owned Land, Leased	White Owned Land	Total Irrigated
	Indian	White	Total	Indian	White	Total				
Wapato–Yakima Reservation	80,200	39,800	120,000	61,000	39,000	100,000	4,661	38,862	34,415	77,938
Toppenish–Simcoe–Yakima Reservation	16,000	2,000	18,000	5,000	1,000	6,000	395	621	605	1,621
Satus–Yakima Reservation	4,290	710	5,000	4,290	710	5,000	854	2,902	710	4,556
Ahtanum–Yakima Reservation	35,200	4,800	40,000	6,566	4,000	10,566	340	3,054	1,585	4,979
Colville	6,500	1,500	8,000	3,300	200	3,500	216	238	29	483
Klamath	6,464	3,136	9,600	6,464	3,136	9,600	1,262	786	2,694	4,742
San Carlos–Pima Reservation	50,000	50,000	100,000	12,000	33,500	45,500	12,000	—	—	12,000
Colorado River	104,000	—	104,000	6,000	—	6,000	2,500	3,118	—	5,618
Southern Ute	14,579	2,621	17,200	14,579	2,621	17,200	3,181	1,373	1,949	6,503
Uintah	60,010	27,531	87,591	60,000	27,581	87,581	15,243	24,819	18,228	58,290
Fort Hall	44,203[a]	15,979	60,182	34,533	15,797	50,330	7,338	6,408	13,309	27,055
Wind River	58,986	19,514	78,500	41,108	15,343	56,451	6,697	1,944	12,855	21,491
Blackfoot	60,017	20,483	80,500	7,736	13,601	21,337	44	3,981	3,124	7,149
Fort Peck	45,044	2,763	47,807	20,031	2,763	22,794	1,503	1,034	—	2,537
Flathead	23,737[b]	88,763	112,500	88,765	23,735	112,500	452	1,836	32,153	34,441
Fort Balknap	24,206	1,079	25,285	14,975	2,000	16,975	9,803	1,884	838	12,525
Crow	43,163	13,000	56,163	43,000	13,000	56,000	2,703	14,281	5,908	22,892
Walker River	10,255	25	10,280	3,580	20	3,600	1,803	—	20	1,823
Miscellaneous (estimated)	449,413	20,000	469,413	51,123	10,000	61,123	46,199	6,171	3,005	55,375
Total	1,136,267	313,754	1,450,021	484,050	208,007	692,057	117,189	113,402	131,427	362,018

[a]2,641 acres of this area homestead.
[b]44,000 acres of this area homestead.
Source: Porter J. Preston and Charles A. Engle, "Report of the Advisors on Irrigation on Indian Reservations," in *Survey of Conditions of the Indians in the United States: Hearings Before a Subcommittee of the Committee of Indian Affairs*, U.S. Senate, 2nd sess., pt. 6:2224.

As shown in Table 9.1, it is easy to see why Prucha reached such a pessimistic conclusion. Out of a total of 362,018 acres of irrigated land on Indian reservations, only 117,189 acres were farmed by Indians. A total of 113,402 acres were farmed by whites leasing Indian lands, and 131,427 acres were used by white owners. If the goal was to promote Indian farming, other programs might have served Indians better.

In general, allotment of Indian lands created an incentive to sell or lease land. The biggest reason cited by Preston and Engle (1930) for the failure of Indians to use more of their land was the awkward form of land tenure created by allotment. Irrigated land required expensive labor and capital-intensive techniques in order to justify the irrigation charges. Indians were typically allotted forty or more acres under the Dawes Act when they could effectively farm only ten.[9] Once the land was allotted to Indian families, the engineers planning the project would try to make the project big enough so that all Indian land was irrigated, whether or not it was farmed by Indians. In order to put this irrigated land into cultivation to recover construction costs and to protect Indian water rights, it was necessary to sell or lease some of the land to white farmers. Thus even a conscientious agent trying to safeguard Indian interests might encourage the lease or sale of land to whites. Preston and Engle (1930) reported that the sale and lease of irrigated land were associated with a decline in Indian farming. This is consistent with what happened on reservations without irrigation projects (see Carlson 1981a, chap. 4–6; 1981b).

A related problem was that often the BIA did little to train Indians to farm irrigated lands. Preston and Engle complained that

> with a peculiar idea of economy, we expend some millions of dollars in building an irrigation plant to enable Indians to support themselves by farming, and employ a man called a "farmer," but who, in reality, is a chore boy or field clerk at a salary of $1500 a year, to instruct the Indians on how to use this intricate and complicated plant. (1930, 221)

Teaching Indians to farm was a long-term objective that yielded few immediate benefits that an agent could point out to superiors. In addition, such programs were not in the interest of white farmers. Why would an agent want to go to excessive lengths to help Indians to farm when white farmers were so readily available? By and large, many did not bother.

It does not follow, of course, that the only way that Indians could benefit from the irrigation projects was to farm the land themselves. Insofar as the increased price that Indians received for leased or sold land was greater than the amount they paid for the projects, they benefited. The taxpayers may have lost, but Indians would have received a net benefit. This was probably the case, since Indians, in the end, never paid that much to the federal government for the irrigation projects on the reservations. As reported in Table 9.2, on the large projects visited by the Preston-Engle team Indians

TABLE 9.2   Costs, Collections, and Assessments as of June 30, 1927

Projects	Total Ultimate Irrigable Area	Total Estimated Cost When Completed	Total Construction Cost to June 30, 1927	Per Acre Cost of Construction Based on Total Area Irrigable and Costs as of June 30, 1927	Total Construction Repayment Assessments
Wapato–Yakima Reservation	120,000	5,149,595.00	3,291,318.00	$32.91	$764,728.55
Toppenish-Simcoe– Yakima Reservation	18,000	1,893,803.00	143,823.30	23.97	—
Satus–Yakima Reservation	40,000	2,136,025.00	169,611.11	16.05	—
Ahtanum–Yakima Reservation	5,000	368,495.00	94,241.54	18.85	4,865.90
Colville	8,000	258,377.00	54,377.19	15.53	23,429.00
Klamath	9,600	499,994.00	219,994.23	22.91	42,213.65
San Carlos–Pima Reservation	100,000	7,111,156.00	3,635,674.07	79.90	—
Colorado River	104,000	7,850,700.00	615,699.74	102.67	137,349.00
Southern Ute	17,200	233,911.00	206,911.40	12.02	66,478.95
Uintah	87,591	1,521,896.00	913,896.86	10.43	1,522.88
Fort Hall	60,000	1,927,189.00	1,767,186.52	35.11	73,938.27
Wind River	78,500	2,614,187.00	1,451,429.70	25.71	168,957.29
Blackfoot	80,500	3,361,062.00	1,094,653.89	51.30	64,008.93
Fort Peck	47,807	803,876.00	803,876.82	35.26	56,760.64
Flathead	112,500	7,692,715.00	5,177,715.32	46.02	312,684.41
Fort Belknap	25,285	667,864.00	345,864.76	20.37	—
Crow	56,163	2,593,648.00	1,978,934.99	35.33	450,357.27
Walker River	10,280	547,352.00	137,352.64	38.15	—
Toung River			132,817.50	—	—
Miscellaneous (estimated)	489,595	8,782,410.64	4,905,400.04	—	1,835,128.10
Total	1,450,021	56,014,255.64	27,140,782.62	—	4,002,422.84

[a]6 percent penalty on delinquent assessments

[b]7 percent penalty on delinquent assessments

Source: Porter J. Preston, and Charles A. Engle, "Report of the Advisors on Irrigation on Indian Reservations," in Survey of Conditions of the Indians in the United States: Hearings Before a Subcommittee of the Committee of Indian Affairs, U.S. Senate, 2nd sess., pt. 6:2225.

Total Construction Repayment Collections	Total Operation and Maintenance Cost to June 30, 1927	Per Acre Operation and Maintenance Based on Total Irrigable Area and Costs as of June 30, 1927	Total Operation and Maintenance Assessments to June 30, 1927	Total Operation and Maintenance Collection to June 30, 1927	Unpaid per Acre Operation and Maintenance Costs on Irrigable Area
$737,098.59	$1,136,240.04	$11.36	$1,051,223.37	$1,045,611.99	$0.90
—	19,298.39	3.22	1,756.75	1,756.75	2.92
—	14,705.90	1.39	5,687.16	5,867.16	.85
833.60	74,115.80	14.82	70,405.04	69,002.11	1.00
12.50	34,279.56	9.79	2,196.79	874.52	9.54
6,157.20	65,998.00	6.87	20,356.50	6,686.56	6.18
—	85,929.16	1.89	—	—	1.89
14,341.06	408,355.25	68.06	96,197.66	95,309.31	52.18
498.42	92,450.70	5.38	7.441.15	4,725.23	5.10
1,522.88	1,023,744.94	11.69	346,503.38	274,901.96	5.49[a]
73,620.90	814,761.05	16.18	336,301.70	332,279.03	9.59[a]
12,802.01	798,339.12	14.14	470,800.76	119,676.30	12.02[b]
14,412.73	256,380.17	12.01	80,162.37	59,769.52	9.21[a]
5,904.98	137,152.35	6.02	14,202.46	12,196.96	5.48
74,788.90	774,855.56	6.89	413,609.74	316,404.95	4.08[a]
—	241,928.42	14.25	3,049.05	1,479.35	14.17[b]
4,789.46	1,011,284.58	18.06	596,096.02	249,241.12	13.61[b]
—	64,808.94	18.00	—	—	18.00
—	29,410.92	—	—	—	29.41
32,776.56	1,743,104.25	—	50,000.00	42,528.51	—
979,559.79	8,827,143.10	—	3,566,498.90	2,638,311.33	—

paid only $979,560 of the $27,140,783 cost of all the projects. Out of the $8,827,143 spent for operation and maintenance, Indians paid only $2,638,311. Thus it is likely that some Indians benefited—although not as much as modern critics of Indian policy would have liked.

There is more to the story, however, than a cozy relationship between the BIA and white landowners with some modest benefits to Indians—at the expense of taxpayers, of course. On a second class of projects, Indians farmed all or almost all of the land. These reservations were so far from markets that white farmers or ranchers did not want to buy or lease the land. It appears likely that the BIA built these projects knowing that most of the benefits from the project would go to the Indians living there, not to white farmers. Of course, those whites who built and administered the projects also benefited. Many of these were smaller projects targeted to the needs of Indians. Indeed, Indians farmed 46,199 acres out of 55,375 acres on the projects deemed too small for Preston and Engle to visit. Other examples of projects that largely benefited Indian land users include the Walker River project and the Carson Sinks allotments in Nevada. Indians also benefited from the jobs created by the building and maintenance of irrigation projects. Sometimes job creation was seen by the BIA as the primary benefit to Indians (Pisani 1986, 171).

Finally, there is a third class of projects that are notable because they were simply so wasteful that *no one* benefited very much. In the extreme, Preston and Engle (1930) recommended the closure of three of the projects they visited. In their opinion, there was simply too little water to justify further expenditure to develop those three projects. This is not to say that no one benefited. Administrators, builders, Indian workers, or someone must have benefited, or the BIA would never have built them. One of the three projects, Tongue River, had already been shut down by the mutual consent of the BIA and Indians living there at the time of Preston and Engle's visit in 1927. However, the other two projects that they recommended for closure, Blackfoot and Fort Peck, continued to operate (McCool 1987, 141). Several other projects also appear to have been marginal at best. For example, on the Colville Reservation only 483 acres were farmed in 1927, 216 by Indians, 238 by whites leasing Indian lands, and 29 acres by whites on land that they owned. The Preston-Engle team did not recommend that the Colville project be ended; but they did state that there was too little water for the size of the existing project, and they recommended that no further work be done until there was a demonstrated reason for expansion. They also concluded that the benefits of the project had been overstated in earlier reports by BIA officials.

Even where there was enough water, agents were willing to justify extending irrigation projects farther than was sensible from an engineering or economic sense. According to the Preston-Engle report:

Particularly, there is a tendency on the part of some of the irrigation employees to extend "irrigation works" over areas of land where there is no need for them, and apparently without regard to whether or not there is a water supply for such land. . . . These so called irrigation works sometimes consist of the mere skeleton—a furrow or a ditch—but they justify a request for increased appropriations "for extending the irrigation system to the lands of Indians who are anxious to farm," and after extensions are made, they form a justification for increased appropriations for operation and maintenance. (1930, 2316)

There is also a tendency to overstate how well Indian farmers were doing. Preston and Engle noted that

the Bureau of Indian Affairs tended to reward its agents if each successive report showed an improvement in the conditions described in the preceding report. Thus, the teacher feels it is in his interest to report an increase in the interest of Indian children to schoolwork, the farmers desire to show an increase in farm operations of Indian farmers and the physician is anxious to show an improvement in health conditions. (1930, 2316)

Indeed, one agent is reported to have said that "the Indian office expects a lot of hot air about the farming of Indians and it's up to us to give it to them, or they will put employees in here who will give it to them" (Preston and Engle 1930, 2316).

The "tests" of the competing hypotheses just presented are informal, but the evidence is consistent with the hypothesis that irrigation policy was shaped by competing interest groups rather than solely to protect the interests of Indians. The fact that relatively worthless projects continued and land on projects was tied up in a form of land tenure that made it difficult for *anyone* to use are a consequence of the adapted nature of the institutions. Thus I think that looking at Indian irrigation policy in light of both interest groups and institutions imperfectly adapted to a new use best fits the data.

Tribal Government, the Reform of Indian Policy in the 1930s, and the Panda's Thumb

The election of Franklin Roosevelt in 1932 was followed by major changes in the structure of Indian programs and the institutions governing Indian country and illustrates the adapted nature of many federal Indian programs. Criticism of Indian policy in the 1920s and the obvious problems faced by Indians had led to an increasingly active Indian reform movement and a feeling in Congress that changes were needed. The Meriam Report and the Preston-Engle Report were products of this agitation. The most serious attempts to implement the proposals put forward in the Meriam Report occurred during the Hoover administration and were carried out by two

Quaker reformers, Charles Rhoads and Henry Scattergood. However, the changes carried out by these reformers were within the existing institutional framework. Such moderate reform did not satisfy critics of Indian programs such as John Collier.

It is possible that this incremental approach to reform might have continued if it had not been interrupted by the Great Depression of 1929–1933 and the election of Franklin Roosevelt. In this period of crisis Roosevelt and Congress were willing to try a variety of new approaches to government. Some reforms instituted in Roosevelt's New Deal program were based on reform programs advocated by special interest groups in the 1920s. This was true of Indian policy as well. Roosevelt knew very little about Indian affairs, but he named John Collier, the most prominent critic of Indian policy, to be commissioner of Indian affairs in 1933. Collier was ready and willing to propose legislation that would fundamentally change how the government treated reservations.

The centerpiece of Collier's reform program was the Indian Reorganization Act (IRA) of 1934, also known as the Wheeler-Howard Act. The Wheeler-Howard Act embodied Collier's desire to preserve Indian cultures and to recognize Indian tribes as continuing political entities. Two provisions of the act bear on the issues discussed here: the end of allotment and the establishment of tribal governments. Collier was critical of allotment and saw that it ceased after 1934. Originally, he proposed to return allotted land to tribes. However, in the face of protests by Indian landholders, he let individuals who had received allotments prior to 1934 continue to hold title to their land, subject to restrictions. The Wheeler-Howard Act also created a mechanism for the BIA to establish and recognize tribal governments. The BIA held elections on each reservation to approve the provisions of the Indian Reorganization Act. Indians living on reservations that voted to approve the IRA were then assisted in drafting a tribal constitution. Although each constitution was different, most of these documents followed a very similar pattern. Each established a tribal council elected for two-year terms and an elected tribal chair to administer reservation affairs. Collier was an effective publicist for his ideas, and the tribal governments created by the IRA were hailed as an important step toward bringing representative democracy to Indian reservations. Recently, a number of studies have pointed out the weaknesses of the IRA and problems with the type of tribal governments created under the IRA.

Indian tribal governments are an example of an institution created to solve a set of problems by borrowing from existing ideas. We often speak of tribes as ratifying agreements with the federal government and, up until the mid-1870s, this was the case. This arrangement assumes that tribes had recognized leaders and councils with which government agents could negotiate. But in the late nineteenth and early twentieth centuries, some of these tribal institutions were deliberately weakened: The Curtis Act of 1898, for example, had abolished tribal laws and courts in the Indian Territory (Prucha 1984, 748). In other cases, a central tribal government never existed.

This absence of a recognized governing body led to some of the failures in Indian policy. For example, in the 1920s an obvious failure of irrigation policy was that Indians had so little input into the decision to build irrigation projects. If some form of widely recognized tribal government were in place, the agent could ask that body to vote its approval. On the Yakima Reservation, an ad hoc council of "head chiefs, head men, and sub-chiefs" was created to fill this institutional gap (Fitch 1974, 119). Similarly, the BIA established an elected council on the Navajo Reservation in 1923 in order to approve oil leases on tribal lands (Libecap and Johnson 1980). This policy of establishing tribal governments represented a marked change from the earlier policy of trying to eliminate tribal governments as a way to hasten assimilation. Yet this ad hoc form of government had obvious limitations in a bureaucratic and legalistic world. For one thing, decisions made by such a tribal government might be subject to challenge in non-Indian courts.

Once it was recognized that (1) Indian reservations and Indian nations were going to continue to exist and be a vehicle for the distribution of federal services and (2) Indians would have to be consulted in the distribution of these services, it was clear that there needed to be some kind of legally recognized body with whom the bureaucracy in Washington could negotiate. The tribal councils created by the IRA were not intended to simply rubber-stamp decisions already made in Washington, although this occurred in some cases. Rather, they filled a necessary legal and bureaucratic void by giving the courts and federal government a legally recognized institution with which to interact.

Tribal governments were not simply a consequence of the Indian Reorganization Act. In the elections held after the adoption of the IRA, 77 tribes voted to reject participation in the IRA and 181 voted to participate. Tribes that voted to exempt themselves from the IRA did not have tribal constitutions. Yet these tribes—which included the most populous Indian nation, the Navajo—have had to establish tribal councils and tribal governments that are virtually indistinguishable from those of tribes that ratified the IRA. Indians living on a reservation need a legally recognized body to broker their relationship with the federal government. The federal bureaucracy in turn needs a legally recognizable body on each reservation to help it deliver its services.

The legal structure of tribal governments thus functions as a representative democracy. This is a familiar, legitimate form of government in the U.S. system, and an elected council is a legally recognized body with which the bureaucracy can negotiate. There is also an existing body of law governing existing legislative bodies, such as city councils, and adapting a well-established form removes the need to create a new body of law.

It is not hard to see why such organizations are often inefficient in developing reservation resources. Their structure was created to ratify agreements with the federal government, not to engage in the day-to-day management of reservation resources or to write contracts with outside corporations. The two-year terms of tribal council members can sometimes lead to a complete change of policy every two years and can make it hard to pursue long-run economic development plans. Therefore, tribal government is "serviceable, but inelegant, resultant of a path dependent process of evolutionary improvisation, a structure whose obvious limitations stem from its remote accidental origins" (David 1992, 22). In other words, tribal councils are the panda's thumb of Indian country.

If this argument is correct, would it have been better to simply borrow traditional Indian institutions? In some cases, perhaps. But the problem turns out to be a very complicated one. Collier, in fact, had envisioned the creation of tribal governments that drew on existing Indian institutions. But for many Indian peoples the relevant political and social units were families or bands, not the tribe as a whole (Prucha 1984, 1010). Indeed, as Martin Bailey (1992) pointed out, the economic organizations created by Indians and other preliterate groups can be seen as sensible solutions to economic problems balancing the needs of group cooperation, risk sharing, and individual activity. There is no reason that the institutions developed to solve the problems of a preliterate society would exactly correspond to the needs of the federal bureaucracy. In addition, some Indians did not recognize older tribal institutions anyway. This was often true of the children of mixed Indian and white ancestry. Further, in many cases older institutions had largely atrophied or disappeared after the loss of aboriginal lifestyles.[10] Another problem was that on a number of reservations more than one tribe shared the reservation, so there were simply no common institutions. All of these factors suggest the difficulty of adapting Indian institutions to the needs of a modern bureaucracy.

The political nature of tribal governments has created opportunities for internal squabbles and rent seeking behavior by members of tribes. In some cases, the result has been waste of scarce reservations resources (see, for example, Anderson 1995, 150–152). Tribal governments since 1934 have had to assume the duties of modern sovereign governments with their own court systems, corporations for developing reservation resources, and intermediaries in dealing with the BIA and the federal courts. It is not surprising that some tribal governments failed to do all of these things well. The task is a difficult one. Recently, there is room for optimism. Joseph Kalt and Stephen Cornell (1994) and Terry Anderson (1995, 152–158) cited a number of cases where tribes have been able to assert their property rights and effectively manage reservation economic development.

What about irrigation? Did the existence of tribal government and the end of allotment greatly change the development of irrigation resources on Indian reservations? This is a question that I am still researching, but my preliminary reading of the evidence is that the 1930s brought relatively few changes. The 1932 law brought a welcome relief from the need to try to pay off federal irrigation projects during a period of extremely low agricultural prices. The big change was that only one major new irrigation project was authorized in the 1930s (McCool 1987, 141). It is hard to say whether the change in tribal government made white interests less inclined to support irrigation projects, whether the 1930s were simply not a good time to propose new projects, or whether there were simply no appropriate sites left undeveloped.

No major changes occurred in how Indians used existing lands. On the Yakima Reservation, for example, the amount of irrigated land farmed by Indians did not increase in the 1930s. Indeed, James Fitch (1974) reported that by the 1970s Indian farmers produced less relative to white farmers than they had in 1919. Similarly, Ronald Trosper (1974) found no change in the percentage of Indian-owned irrigated lands in the 1930s at Flathead in Montana.

Conclusion

Indian irrigation policy, like other programs to aid Indians, has been a mixed blessing at best. Although there have been some benefits for Indians, there has also been waste and a transfer of resources to bureaucrats and non-Indian ranchers and farmers. In designing a program to build irrigation projects on Indian reservations, Congress necessarily adapted laws designed for other purposes and responded to a variety of organized interest groups. The resultant institution was not necessarily well suited to the task at hand. Given such "contrivances" I draw several conclusions: (1) Bureaucratic entrepreneurs within the BIA appear to have tried to build as many projects as possible in order to justify bigger budgets and promotions. Indeed, most large reservations in the regions with less than 20 inches of rainfall annually were the site of major projects. (2) It suited the interests of BIA agents to have allies and to have the land used. At those locations where white farmers and ranchers were in a position to enter the reservation, white farmers owned or leased most irrigated land. This may have served the interests of Indians in protecting their water rights and giving them higher lease incomes, but the biggest beneficiaries may have been non-Indians. (3) Nonetheless, in areas where there was little interest by whites, Indian farmers did use most of the project lands. (4) Few of the projects appear to have been justified by any sort of cost-benefit criteria and, like other reclamation projects of the period, there were transfers from the general tax base to western water users. Some projects appear to have benefited no one very much. But someone must have benefited from even the most poorly designed projects.

Notes

Special thanks are due to Linda Barrington for organizing the seminar at Barnard College and Columbia University that gave rise to this chapter. Thanks also to Paul Rubin for helpful comments, Professor Francis Paul Prucha for suggesting that I investigate the Preston-Engle Report, and Paul David for permission to cite his unpublished paper. I have also benefited from the comments of participants in a special session of the Columbia University Seminar on Economic History, "Furthering Research into the Past: Current Research on the Economic History of Native Americans," May 6 and 7, 1994; the Emory University Economics Workshop and the Cliometric Society session at the Allied Social Sciences Association (ASSA) meetings, January 1995; and the Triangle Universities Economic History Workshop, Chapel Hill, N.C. Thanks also to Paul Rhode, Bob Carpenter, and Rohini Somanathan for helpful suggestions and to Heiwei Chen for research assistance. None of them is responsible for errors here, of course.

1. Although the agency charged with Indian affairs was known in the 1920s as the Office of Indian Affairs, to avoid confusion I use the modern designation, the Bureau of Indian Affairs, or BIA.

2. Four books include some discussion of irrigation policy on Indian reservations. The finest work on the history of federal Indian policy is Francis Paul Prucha's *The Great Father: The United States Government and the American Indians* (1984). Janet A. McDonnell's *The Dispossession of the American Indians, 1887–1934* (1991) has an excellent chapter on irrigation programs in this period. Daniel McCool's *Command of the Waters* (1987) looks at all aspects of Indian water policy in the twentieth century from the perspective of a political scientist. Michael Lawson's *Dammed Indians: The Pick-Sloan Plan and Missouri River Sioux* (1982) considers a different set of issues, including the impact of Army Corps of Engineers flood-control projects on the various Sioux tribes.

3. Properly, the report is Lewis Meriam et al., *The Problem of Indian Administration* (Baltimore: Johns Hopkins University Press, 1928). Henceforth it will be referred to as the Meriam Report.

4. A good example by a longtime employee of the BIA is Kinney (1937).

5. Indeed, water law in the West was still in flux, and the older common law principle of riparian rights was still recognized in some states (Pisani 1986).

6. This analysis of white and bureaucratic interests in determining Indian policy is very similar, in some ways, to the iron triangle analysis used by political scientist Daniel McCool in his study of Indian irrigation policy. There are, however, some important differences. "Iron triangle" is a term used to describe three interrelated interest groups. These interest groups are a constituency in the public at large, a group in Congress that represents that constituency, and, finally, the agency that best serves that constituency and must, in turn, go to Congress to have its budget approved. Where effective, this iron triangle of constituents, committees in Congress, and a bureaucratic agency can serve each other's interests and thereby promote larger budgets

and larger amounts of resources that benefit all three groups (McCool 1987). McCool, however, was primarily interested in distribution questions. In particular, he wanted to know why the iron triangle formed by the BIA, Indians, and the heads of the relevant committees in Congress is weaker and less effective at gaining access to the resources of the federal government than competing iron triangles formed by white farmers and ranchers, their representatives in Congress, and the Bureau of Reclamation.

7. The panda has evolved a crude sixth "finger" out of its wrist bone. This serves as an "inelegant" thumb, allowing the panda to eat bamboo.

8. Thanks to Paul Rubin for pointing this out.

9. The normal allotment was eighty acres per person (160 acres per family), but allotments of irrigated land were smaller, typically forty acres.

10. Thanks to Martin Bailey for pointing this out.

Bibliography

Alston, Lee J., and Spiller, Pablo T. 1992. "A Congressional Theory of Indian Property Rights: The Cherokee Outlet." In *Property Rights, Constitutions, and Indian Economies*, ed. Terry L. Anderson, 85–104. Lanham, Md.: Rowman and Littlefield.

Anderson, Terry L. 1995. *Sovereign Nations or Reservations? An Economic History of American Indians*. Lanham, Md.: Pacific Research Institute.

Bailey, Martin J. 1992. "Approximate Optimality of Aboriginal Property Rights." *Journal of Law and Economics* 35:183–198.

Carlson, Leonard A. 1981a. *Indians, Bureaucrats, and Land: The Dawes Act and the Decline of Indian Farming*. Westport, Conn.: Greenwood Press.

_____. 1981b. "Land Allotment and the Decline of American Indian Farming." *Explorations in Economic History* 18, no. 1 (April):128–154.

_____. 1983. "Federal Policy and Indian Land: Economic Interests and the Sale of Indian Allotted Land, 1900–1934." *Agricultural History* 52, no. 1 (January):33–45.

David, Paul A. 1992. "Why Are Institutions the Carriers of History." Working paper presented to Stanford Institute for Theoretical Economics.

Fitch, James B. 1974. "Economic Development in a Minority Enclave: The Case of the Yakima Indian Nation, Washington." Ph.D. diss., Stanford University, Stanford, Calif.

Fixico, Ronald. 1986. *Termination and Relocation: Federal Indian Policy, 1945–1960*. Albuquerque: University of New Mexico Press.

Gould, Stephen Jay. 1980. *The Panda's Thumb: More Reflections on Natural History*. New York: Norton.

Hundley, Norris, Jr. 1985. "The *Winters* Decision and Indian Water Rights: A Mystery Reexamined." In *Plains Indians in the Twentieth Century*, ed. Peter Iverson. Norman: University of Oklahoma Press.

Kalt, Joseph, and Stephen Cornell. 1994. "The Redefinition of Property Rights on American Indian Reservations: A Comparative Analysis of Native American Economic Development." In *American Indian Policy*, eds. Lyman H. Legters and Fremont J. Lyden, 121–150. Westport, Conn.: Greenwood Press.

Lawson, Michael. 1982. *Dammed Indians: The Pick-Sloan Plan and Missouri River Sioux, 1944–1980*. Norman: University of Oklahoma Press.

Kinney, J. P. 1937. *A Continent Lost—A Civilization Won: Indian Land Tenure in America*. Baltimore: Johns Hopkins University Press.

Libecap, Gary, and Ronald Johnson. 1980. "Legislating the Commons: The Navajo Tribal Council and the Navajo Range." *Economic Inquiry* 18 (1) (January):69–84.

Mayhew, Stewart, and B. Delworth Gardner. 1994. "The Political Economy of Early Federal Reclamation in the West." In *The Political Economy of the American West*, eds. Terry L. Anderson and Peter J. Hill, 69–94. Lanham, Md.: Rowman and Littlefield.

McChesney, Fred S. 1992. "Government as Definer of Property Rights: Indian Lands, Ethnic Externalities, and Bureaucratic Budgets." In *Property Rights and Indian Economies*, ed. Terry L. Anderson, 109–146. Lanham, Md.: Rowman and Littlefield.

McCool, Daniel. 1987. *Command of the Waters*. Berkeley: University of California Press.

McDonnell, Janet A. 1991. *The Dispossession of the American Indians, 1887–1934*. Bloomington: Indiana University Press.

Meriam, Lewis, et al. 1928. *The Problem of Indian Administration*. Baltimore: Johns Hopkins University Press.

Pisani, Donald J. 1986. "Irrigation, Water Rights, and the Betrayal of Indian Allotment." *Environmental Review* 10, no. 3 (Fall):157–176.

Posner, Richard. 1974. "Economic Theories of Regulation." *The Bell Journal of Economics*, 6 (Autumn):335–353.

Preston, Porter J., and Charles A. Engle. 1930. "Report of the Advisors on Irrigation on Indian Reservations." In *Survey of Conditions of the Indians in the United States: Hearings Before a Subcommittee of the Committee of Indians Affairs*. U.S. Senate. 2nd sess., pt. 6:2210–2661.

Prucha, Francis Paul. 1984. *The Great Father: The United States Government and the American Indians*. Vol. 2. Lincoln: University of Nebraska Press.

———. 1990. *Atlas of American Indian Affairs*. Lincoln: University of Nebraska Press.

Rucker, Randal R., and Price V. Fishback. 1983. "The Federal Reclamation Program: An Analysis of Rent Seeking Behavior." In *Water Rights: Scarce Resource Allocation, Bureaucracy, and the Environment*, ed. Terry L. Anderson, 45–82. Cambridge, Mass.: Bellinger.

Smith, Rodney T. 1992. "Water Right Claims in Indian Country: From Legal Theory to Economic Reality." In *Property Rights and Indian Economies*, ed. Terry L. Anderson, 167–194. Lanham, Md.: Rowman and Littlefield.

Trosper, Ronald L. 1974. *The Economic Impact of the Allotment Policy on the Flathead Indian Reservation*. Ph.D. Diss., Harvard University, Cambridge, Mass.

U.S. Bureau of the Census. 1949. *Historical Statistics of the U.S., 1789–1945*. Washington, D.C.: GPO.

10

The Political Economy of the Hawaiian Home Lands Program

SUMNER J. LA CROIX
AND LOUIS A. ROSE

Captain James Cook's first contact with Hawaii in 1778 initiated a flood of fundamental changes for the Hawaiian people. The history of the nineteenth century is dominated by the tragic decrease in the Hawaiian population and sweeping changes in social, economic, and political institutions prompted by Hawaii's integration with the outside world. The rise of the sugar industry at midcentury led to increasing economic integration with the United States; in 1898 the United States annexed Hawaii. Political integration with the United States failed to halt the decline in the general welfare of the Hawaiian population, which faced increasing economic competition from Japanese and Chinese workers leaving the sugar plantations.

During World War I a movement arose among Hawaiians to rectify their declining situation. In 1921 Congress responded by passing the Hawaiian Homes Commission Act (HHCA). Its ostensible goal was to return Native Hawaiians to the land, thereby facilitating the "rehabilitation" of the Hawaiian race (Hawaiian Homes Commission Act 1921, 108).[1] The HHCA set aside 203,300 of Hawaii's 4,112,128 acres for establishment of small farms and ranches by Native Hawaiians. Yet by 1996 the Hawaiian Homes Commission (HHC) had awarded only 40,452 acres to 6,350 Native Hawaiians. Farms and ranches awarded to Native Hawaiians achieved only limited success, and in 1923 the HHCA was amended to allow Native Hawaiians to lease improved residential lots. Long waiting lists for residential lots appeared in the 1940s and have persisted into the 1990s. Hawaiian groups have accused the State of Hawaii of violating its trust obligations to Native

259

Hawaiians in its management and disposal of HHCA lands. By all accounts, the HHCA has had only limited success in achieving its original goal of reha-bilitation.

This chapter outlines the economic and political decline of Native Hawai-ians since Western contact; discusses the Hawaiian Home Lands (HHL) Program as the central response by the state and federal governments to rec-tify the diminished circumstances of Native Hawaiians; and most important, focuses on understanding how the program has performed, why it persists in its current form, and how it might be restructured to provide more benefits to Native Hawaiians. We begin with an outline of the complex factors lead-ing to the declining welfare of Hawaiians in the nineteenth century and the annexation of Hawaii by the United States. A discussion of the Hawaiian po-litical movement to return to the land, the enactment of the HHCA, and the HHCA's central provisions follows. An analysis of the transition of the HHCA from an agricultural homestead program to a quasi-public housing program is accompanied by a brief narrative outlining the program's opera-tion from the early 1920s to the early 1990s. The major political and eco-nomic factors affecting the program's performance are identified, and we compute a rough estimate of the economic losses induced by the program. We conclude by outlining several proposals for reform and identifying the institutional barriers to reform.

Hawaii in 1778

In 1778 Captain James Cook's ships encountered a group of eight small tropical islands populated by a people with social and political institutions re-markably similar to those in other more distant Polynesian societies. Al-though several distinct political entities actively competed with each other, the people of Hawaii were bound together by a common society. In each polity the populace was divided into three classes: chiefs (*ali'i*), commoners (*maka'ainana*), and priests (*kahuna*). Each polity was led by a ruling chief (*mo'i*) who held title to all lands and goods. In the manner of a feudal soci-ety, the ruling chief gave temporary land grants to lesser chiefs (*ali'i nui*) who then gave temporary land grants to their land managers (*konohiki*). The *konohiki* then subleased the land to commoners to grow taro and other trop-ical crops (Davenport 1969). Usually the land managers retained an active role in the management of their diverse lands (*ahupua'a*), which normally extended from the mountains to the coral reef fishing grounds. The com-mon people worked in a variety of occupations (canoe building, home build-ing, bird catching, fishing), with the bulk of the work being the cultivation of the land.

Work, like most other activities, was organized around an extended family unit, the *'ohana*. The term *'ohana* was used to cover relatives by blood, marriage, and adoption.[2] Many communal activities were conducted by the *'ohana,* such as planting and harvesting crops, clearing land, constructing irrigation works, and fishing beyond the shoreline's coral reefs. Land managers collected the chief's share of output from the family's headman (*haku*) rather than from individual farmers. In the absence of organized market institutions, the *'ohana* acted to reduce the cost of exchange among family members. It facilitated specialization in work activities and ensured the ability to consume a somewhat varied market basket of goods. In a similar fashion, the inclusion of diverse lands in the *ahupua'a* helped to make this production unit generally self-sufficient; without extensive market institutions linking these units, organization of production under the auspices of one large diversified firm further facilitated the expansion of opportunities for individual workers and consumers. Although occasional market fairs (where participants exchanged cloth, mats, baskets, pigs, dogs, dried fish, vegetables, poi, canoes, paddles, and spears) allowed for some regional specialization in production, the institutions of the *'ohana* and the *ahupua'a* were vital given the rough geography and shifting political boundaries in Hawaii.

Two missionary observers believed that the chiefs managed, via taxes, land rents, arbitrary confiscations, and voluntary offerings, to appropriate about two-thirds of the *'ohana*'s output.[3] There is some evidence that the net appropriation may have been lower, as the chiefs stored and ultimately redistributed a large fraction of their share of the produced goods. Marshall Sahlins (1972) has speculated that the storage and redistribution of goods was intended to redistribute income, to provide revenue for public works projects, and to ensure adequate stores during times of war and famine. In any case, even with these substantial appropriations, the common people lived well above subsistence levels. Tales of starvation are absent from the renderings of pre-1778 Hawaiian history. Theodore Morgan has observed that "in good times the food supply was adequate in quantity and variety" (1948, 51).[4] Ralph Kuykendall has emphasized that the common people "were probably less downtrodden than the lower classes of Europe in the eighteenth century," noting that they "regularly had time for cultural activities, sports, and games" (1938, 1:9).

Common people, unlike the serfs in Europe, were not bound to the soil, and their relative mobility contributed to their real incomes. The commoners' ability to vote with their feet placed constraints on the ability of chiefs to extract all income above subsistence levels; at the same time the high transportation costs associated with moving to another district allowed chiefs to extract a portion of the common people's income above the subsistence level. If the chiefs attempted to extract additional income, commoners had an additional option besides moving. The historical record contains numerous stories of rebellions against chiefs who oppressed the common people. David Malo, an early chronicler of the tales of prehistorical Hawaii, wrote that "for this reason . . . some of the ancient kings had a wholesome fear of the people" (1971, 195). As in other societies, competition between the ruling chiefs was not confined to the labor and product markets. Constantly waging war on each other, the ruling chiefs attained power by assembling loyal armies composed of large numbers of lesser chiefs. In precontact Hawaii chiefdoms expanded and contracted, formed and broke alliances, and apparently maintained this state of affairs for many centuries.

Despite the constant political flux, it is likely that after the initial Polynesian settlement, Hawaiian social, economic, and political institutions evolved substantially as a result of the large increase in population over the next 1,000 to 1,500 years. When Cook's ships arrived in Hawaii in 1778 they encountered eight small isolated islands where multiple political entities competed for power in a common yet constantly evolving cultural and economic environment. The Hawaiians cultivated numerous tropical root, tuber, and tree crops in "irrigated valley lands ranked among the most productive agricultural ecosystems anywhere in Polynesia" (Kirch 1985, 2). Although the commoners were poor, competition between the chiefs for their services prevented their incomes from being pushed to subsistence levels. Numerous institutions, such as the *'ohana* and the *ahupua'a*, were developed to exploit economies of scale in food production. To some observers, Hawaii's complex civilization—with its highly developed production technology; hierarchical, social, and political organization; art and culture; and religious beliefs and temple rituals—was an amazing achievement for an isolated people (Kirch 1985, 7).[5]

The Long Decline in Hawaiian Welfare: 1778–1920

Soon after Western contact King Kamehameha I conquered the other political entities and established a unified nation in 1795.[6] Yet between contact in 1778 and the passage of "rehabilitation legislation" in 1920, the economic and political condition of Hawaiians declined markedly.

Perhaps the signal event of postcontact Hawaiian history, commencing shortly after Cook's arrival in 1778, was the spread of new diseases (mumps, measles, influenza, smallpox, venereal diseases, cholera), to which the Hawaiian population had virtually no immunity. There is considerable controversy over estimates of the 1778 population. Robert C. Schmitt (1971) estimated 225,000; D. E. Stannard (1989) estimated 795,000; and T. Dye (1994) estimated 110,000. The first accurate census in 1849 revealed a much-diminished full-Hawaiian population of 78,854 and a part-Hawaiian population of 471. In the fifty-one years after the 1849 census, the resident Hawaiian population continued its precipitous decline, falling to 29,799

TABLE 10.1   Hawaii Population by Ethnicity

Ethnic Group	1778	1853	1900	1920
Full-Hawaiian		70,036	29,799	23,723
Stannard	795,000			
Schmitt	225,000			
Dye	110,000			
Part-Hawaiian	0	983	9,857	18,027
Caucasian	0	1,600	10,547	27,740
Japanese	0	0	61,111	109,274
Chinese	0	364	25,767	23,507
Portuguese	0	87	18,272	27,002
Filipino	0	0	0	21,031
Other	0	67	648	5,608
Total population	?	73,137	154,001	255,912

Sources: E. C. Nordyke, *The Peopling of Hawaii, 2nd ed.* (Honolulu: East-West Center, 1977); D. E. Stannard, *Before the Horror: The Population of Hawaii on the Eve of Western Contact* (Honolulu: SSRI, University of Hawaii, 1989); and T. Dye, "Population Trends in Hawaii Before 1778," *The Hawaiian Journal of History* 28 (1994):1–20.

full-Hawaiians and 9,857 part-Hawaiians. By 1920 the full-Hawaiian population had declined to 23,723 and the part-Hawaiian population had increased to 18,027, thereby registering the first increase in the broadly defined Hawaiian population since Western contact. Table 10.1 summarizes data on Hawaii's population and its ethnic composition.

The rapidly declining Hawaiian population affected all aspects of Hawaiian society in the nineteenth century. Sumner J. La Croix and J. Roumasset (1984, 1990) argue that a major effect of the population decline was to increase labor scarcity and thereby increase commoners' wage rates. The higher wage rates reduced the surplus realized by chiefs and land managers from their agricultural lands throughout the first half of the nineteenth century.[7] After 1820 the impact on the chiefs was magnified by growing urbanization, as commoners migrated to three villages (Honolulu on Oahu, Lahaina on Maui, and Hilo on Hawaii). The movement to urban areas disrupted the relationship between chiefs and commoners, inducing the development of new governmental institutions and stimulating competition between chiefs for tenants. Traditional systems of governance based on the hierarchy of common people and chiefs broke down with the rural exodus. As more common people pursued activities outside the traditional agricultural economy and divisions over the development of a code of law among chiefs grew, the enforcement of traditional practices by local chiefs began to break down in the late 1820s. In 1832 King Kamehameha III and his Council of Chiefs responded to the confusion over law enforcement by promulgating new laws designed to protect the public order and settle private disputes. In sum, the reduction in the chiefs' income and their loss of authority to new governmental institutions represented a severe shock to the traditional hierarchical structure of Hawaiian society.

The declining population and the shock of foreign influence were combined with a crisis in Hawaii's traditional religion. In 1819 King Kamehameha II and several high chiefs broke the religion's prohibition (*kapu*) on the sexes eating together. Defenders of the traditional religion rebelled against the king but were easily defeated. Wooden statues of the Hawaiian gods mounted on stone altars were burned by the common people.[8] The implosion of the traditional religion left a gaping religious void that was quickly filled by the arrival of Protestant missionaries from Massachusetts in March 1820. Conversion of the chiefs to the new religion was facilitated by the missionaries' instruction in the written Hawaiian language. By the late 1820s most high chiefs and many commoners had converted. The new religion suppressed traditional Hawaiian customs and games, such as the hula, and established U.S. missionaries as important advisors to the king. The precipitous destruction of the traditional religion and its replacement with a puritanical Protestant sect within a ten-year span are representative of the rapid social, political, and economic change of this era.

Government reform and religious change were followed in the 1840s by land reform measures establishing fee-simple property rights in land and redistributing the rights to land. The bulk of the lands were assigned to the king (984,000 acres), the Hawaiian government (1,495,000 acres), and 252 chiefs and land managers (1,619,000 acres). The commoners received only 28,600 of Hawaii's 4.1 million acres. The original land reform measure prohibited foreigners from owning land, but an 1850 law repealed this provision. Transferable property rights in land ultimately led to severely reduced land holdings by Hawaiians (La Croix and Roumasset 1990; Kame'eleihiwa 1992). Over the course of the next seventy-five years, major Hawaiian landowners voluntarily sold their lands, often to sugar plantations; lost land due to mortgage default; or assigned their lands to charitable trusts. Other lands were sold at auction after their owners died intestate. In addition, many commoners who were awarded small landholdings either abandoned or sold their lands to sugar plantations and migrated to the cities to work as clerks, stevedores, teamsters, construction workers, and day laborers. In 1920 over 50 percent of part-Hawaiians and 36 percent of full-Hawaiians lived in Honolulu, compared to 33 percent of the entire population (Fuchs 1961, 69). By 1919 part- and full-Hawaiians owned only 9.77 percent of the value of assessed real property in the territory.

One consequence of the land reform measures was that they enabled sugar planters to assemble large tracts of land (some of which were rented from individual Hawaiians, the king, or the Hawaiian government) for sugar production on plantations. The Civil War in the United States cut off the supply of Louisiana sugar to the Northern states, and Hawaii was one of several foreign suppliers that expanded production to fill the gap. A reciprocity treaty, implemented in 1876 and renewed in 1887, allowed Hawaiian sugar to enter the United States free of duty. Responding to the higher net price of sugar, planters increased the acreage devoted to sugar from 12,283 acres in 1874 to 125,000 acres in 1898. This spectacular growth established the economic power of sugar plantations, which were generally controlled and managed by Caucasian residents.[9]

The 1893 overthrow of the monarchy (by Caucasian residents assisted by U.S. marines) and the subsequent annexation of Hawaii by the United States in 1898 radically reduced Hawaiian political power. Sumner La Croix and Christopher Grandy (1997) attributed the 1893 overthrow to the large discrepancy between the economic and political power of foreign residents and the political dynamics unleashed by the 1876 treaty between Hawaii and the United States establishing free trade in Hawaiian sugar and U.S. manufactured goods. Annexation by the United States was, however, not inevitable and ensued primarily as a consequence of the increased strategic importance of the islands during the Spanish-American War. Although Hawaiians retained some political power in their role as the largest bloc of voters electing a two-house territorial legislature, most political power was transferred to a governor appointed by the president of the United States; to the U.S. military, which established several major military bases on government lands; and to the U.S. Congress, which could block amendments to the territorial constitution.

Immigration to Hawaii, both pre- and postannexation, also markedly affected the political and economic conditions of Hawaiians. Beginning in 1865 the Hawaiian government and the sugar industry cooperated to bring Chinese, Japanese, Portuguese, Filipino, Korean, and other workers to Hawaii to labor in the sugar fields (Nordyke 1989, 22–57). Combined with a falling Hawaiian population, the immigration rapidly reduced the proportion of full- and part-Hawaiians in the total population from 97.1 percent in 1853 to 24.5 percent in 1900 and to 16.3 percent in 1920. Beginning with annexation, U.S. immigration laws restricted the number of Chinese and Japanese workers who could enter Hawaii, prompting the sugar industry to substitute Filipino immigrants. Table 10.1 provides data on the changing ethnic composition of Hawaii's population.

The influx of foreign workers also quickly changed the ethnic composition of the sugar plantation workforce. In 1882 one of every four plantation employees was full-Hawaiian or part-Hawaiian; by 1900 Hawaiian representation had fallen to three out of every hundred workers (Fuchs 1961, 70). Many Hawaiians migrated to Honolulu, Hawaii's largest city, in search of alternatives to the back-breaking labor on the plantations. Table 10.2 presents

TABLE 10.2   Occupations of Hawaiians and Part-Hawaiians, 1900

Occupation	Employment	Percentage of Total Employment
Agricultural laborers	784	7.29
Farmers, planters, overseers	1,573	14.62
Other agricultural	340	3.16
Teachers	132	1.23
Government officials	78	.73
Lawyers	85	.79
Other professional service	141	1.31
Laborers	3,574	33.22
Servants	148	1.38
Watchmen, policemen and firemen	268	2.49
Other domestic and personal service	283	2.63
Boatmen, sailors	244	2.27
Clerks and copyists	290	2.70
Draymen, teamsters	398	3.70
Other trade and transportation	390	3.63
Fishermen	582	5.41
Carpenters and joiners	433	4.02
Painters	172	1.60
Machinists	21	.20
Other manufacturing	832	7.73
Total	10,758	100.00

Source: 1900 U.S. Census.

data from the U.S. census on the occupations of Hawaiians in 1900; over 33 percent were employed as "unspecified" laborers in a variety of fields, 14.6 percent had their own farms or were overseers on sugar plantations, 10.5 percent worked in agriculture, 5.4 percent worked as fishermen, 4 percent as carpenters, and another 9.6 percent in other manufacturing activities. The remaining 22.8 percent of the workforce was scattered across a wide variety of professional, government, and trade occupations.

Hawaiians were neither the first nor the last workers in the sugar fields to leave the plantation for the city. Chinese workers began to leave the plantations in the early 1880s and successfully established small businesses and rice farms. After 1900 many Japanese field workers also began to leave the plantations after their four-year contracts expired. In 1900 the Japanese comprised just 15.7 percent of Honolulu's population, but by 1910 Japanese made up 30 percent of the city's total (Fuchs 1961, 122). The increased competition with Japanese and Chinese immigrants for jobs and the contin-

TABLE 10.3   Occupations of Male Hawaiians and Part-Hawaiians, 1920

Occupation	Employment	Percentage of Total Employment
Agricultural laborers	1,843	15.23
Farmers, planters, overseers	360	2.97
Other agricultural	615	5.08
Teachers	431	3.56
Government officials	179	1.48
Lawyers	46	.38
Other professional service	682	5.64
Laborers	18	.15
Servants	204	1.69
Watchmen, policemen and firemen	299	2.47
Other domestic and personal service	344	2.84
Boatmen, sailors	236	1.95
Clerks and copyists	630	5.21
Draymen, teamsters, longshoremen	885	7.31
Laborers	1,178	9.73
Other trade and transportation	1,236	10.21
Fishermen	333	2.75
Carpenters and joiners	337	2.78
Painters	160	1.32
Machinists	183	1.51
Engineers, cranemen, hoistmen	203	1.68
Laborers	641	5.30
Other manufacturing	1,066	8.81
Mining	23	.02
Total	12,102	100.00

Source: 1900 U.S. Census.

ued exodus of Hawaiians to urban areas are both reflected in the 1920 census data on Hawaiian male workers' occupations (Table 10.3). Hawaiians with their own farms or working as overseers declined from 14.6 percent of the workforce in 1900 to 3 percent in 1920. Farm laborers expanded from 7.3 percent of the workforce in 1900 to 15.2 percent in 1920; this indicates that Hawaiian farmers sold their land, with many continuing to work as farm laborers and others moving to urban areas.

In 1890 approximately 7.7 percent of the male Hawaiian workforce were fisherman, and 79 percent of all fishermen were Hawaiian (Hawaii Bureau of Public Instruction 1891, 26).[10] Increasing competition from Japanese fishermen reduced the percentage of Hawaiians working as fishermen from 5.4

percent in 1900 to 2.8 percent in 1920. Only 26 percent of all fisherman were Hawaiian in 1920 (U.S. Bureau of the Census 1923b, 4:1277). In 1880 nearly all longshoremen were Hawaiian; during the 1880s they were gradually replaced by Chinese workers whose contracts on the sugar plantations had expired. By 1920 only 49.9 percent of the dock workforce were Hawaiian (U.S. Bureau of the Census 1923b, 4:1277). The number of Hawaiians working as clerks increased from 2.7 percent of the labor force in 1900 to 5.2 percent in 1920, indicating a movement from blue-collar jobs to low-status white-collar jobs. In spite of an increase in the percentage of the labor force working in professional services, the increasing competition from the children of Japanese and Chinese immigrants painted a bleak picture of the future for many Hawaiians.

The 1920 census also reveals that secondary school enrollment of Hawaiians lagged behind that of other ethnic groups. Among children aged sixteen to seventeen living in Honolulu in 1920, 56.5 percent of Japanese, 57.3 percent of Chinese, 63.8 percent of Caucasians, and 51 percent of Hawaiians were enrolled in school (U.S. Bureau of the Census 1923a, 3:1183, table 14). Adult male labor force participation rates also lagged behind those of other groups. In 1920, 78.8 percent of full-Hawaiian males, 60.5 percent of part-Hawaiian males, 85.6 percent of Japanese males, 82.5 percent of Chinese males, and 80.3 percent of Caucasian males participated in the labor force (U.S. Bureau of the Census 1923a, 3:1271, table 16). Adult female labor participation rates were also lower for full-Hawaiians (7.7 percent) and part-Hawaiians (13.7 percent) than the general population (20.1 percent).

After 140 years of Western contact, the economic, political, cultural, and demographic conditions of Hawaiians had, in many ways, severely deteriorated. The Hawaiian population was drastically diminished; the Kingdom of Hawaii's independence had been lost; Hawaiians had sold, lost, or abandoned most of their lands; increasing competition from Chinese and Japanese immigrants was reducing the relative economic position of Hawaiians; and Hawaiians were lagging behind other groups in educational attainment, thus providing a worrisome signal that their situation was unlikely to improve in the near future. Nonetheless, Hawaiians did retain some residual political influence, and the stage was set for an attempt to halt their deteriorating circumstances and to identify paths to political, cultural, and economic renewal.

The Hawaiian Homes Commission Act

Origins of the Act

The economic impact of World War I on Hawaiians appears to have been the trigger stimulating their expanded political activity. The general price inflation of World War I was coupled with relative price increases for such Hawaiian food staples as poi and fish. "In 1914 the selling price of a 100-pound bag of taro from the farmer to the poi mill was $1.25. . . . in the early part of 1918, it was $2.05" (McGregor 1990, 11). Disruptions in shipping during the war and meat rationing increased the price of fish "by almost 100 percent. For example, fish that normally had sold for 20 cents a pound sold for 35 to 40 cents a pound" (McGregor 1990, 10). Hawaiians complained about the higher prices and noted that poi, the traditional Hawaiian food manufactured from the taro plant, was now grown by Chinese farmers, processed in Chinese poi mills, and distributed by Chinese and Japanese trade networks. Local Hawaiian civic clubs bemoaned the concentration of Hawaiians in crowded urban tenements, blamed high death rates on the urban crowding, and began to contemplate plans for the "rehabilitation" of the Hawaiian race ("Back to Land Move" 1918). In fact, in 1919 the crude birthrate for full-Hawaiians (29.16 per 1,000) was somewhat lower than the rate for all groups (34.76 per 1,000), and the crude death rate for full Hawaiians (39.42 per 1,000) was substantially higher than the rate for all groups (15.36 per 1,000) (U.S. Department of the Interior 1919–1940, 65–67).

McGregor identified the November 1914 formation of the Hawaiian Protective Association as the signal event that prompted Hawaiians to undertake political activity to rehabilitate their people (1990, 1–4).[11] The association published a newspaper, engaged in social and educational work in the community, and was active in a 1918 campaign against run-down tenement housing. Public discussion among Hawaiians of their changed economic circumstances intensified.

During 1918 Princess Kawananakoa toured farm districts in the United States, gathering information about wartime measures to return urban workers to the farm. Upon her return to Hawaii, she urged Hawaiians to return to agricultural occupations and enterprises to avoid the ills of urban crowding ("Princess Will Urge Hawaiians to Go Back to the Land" 1918). The Hawaiian Protective Association drafted a resolution urging that Hawaiians be allowed to homestead government lands when leases to sugar companies expired. Leaders presented the resolution to John Wise, a Hawaiian Republican member of the Territorial Senate. In December 1918 Wise announced a plan for rehabilitation of Hawaiians that focused on reforming Hawaii's homesteading laws ("May Ask U.S. to Give Land to Hawaiians" 1919). They required that upon petition of twenty-five qualified individuals, state agricultural lands be opened to homesteading if unoccupied or leased subject to a notice of withdrawal.[12] Some leases of government-owned sugar cane lands had expired during World War I, but President Woodrow Wilson had issued an executive order preventing their release for homesteading during the War (A Proclamation 1919, 1804). Other leases were scheduled to expire over the next few years. Wise introduced a resolution in the Territorial Senate (HCR 2) asking the U.S. Congress (1) to open 80 percent of the government sugar cane lands for homesteading; and (2) to reserve a portion of these lands for Hawaiian homesteaders. The Territorial Legislature endorsed HCR 2 in April 1919. The Territorial Legislature also passed a second resolution (HCR 28) recommending changes to federal law desired by sugar interests, many of which were in direct contradiction to the goals of HCR 2.

After hearings in the U.S. Congress in February 1920, the two resolutions were merged into a single bill (HR 12683) and introduced to Congress by Jonah Kuhio Kalanianaole, Hawaii's nonvoting delegate to the U.S. House of Representatives. Significantly, the reformulated measure did not allow government-owned sugar cane lands to be opened for homesteading. Instead, it provided for a $1 million fund to finance development of second-class agricultural lands to be set aside for Hawaiian homesteading. Funding for this program would come from rents on government-owned sugar cane lands and receipts from water licenses. Leases to Hawaiians would be for 999 years, and individuals with any Hawaiian ancestry were eligible for the program. Congress retained the power to decide whether to release the sugar lands for homesteading or to continue leasing the lands at auction.

After the Territorial Legislative Commission returned to Hawaii in March 1920, its members became aware of opposition by Hawaiian groups, island newspapers, and the Hawaii Chamber of Commerce to the bill's provisions to return Hawaiians to the land. After discussions between the various parties and deliberations by the U.S. House Committee on Territories, a new bill (HR 13500) was introduced that made significant changes to HR 12683. Important changes included restricting access to individuals who were at least one-thirty-second Hawaiian, shortening the duration of leases from 999 to 99 years, specifying the particular tracts of lands to be placed under control of the rehabilitation program, and transferring from Congress to the territorial administration the right to decide whether to lease the territorial government's sugar lands or to open them to homesteading. HR 13500 passed the House in May 1920 but was not acted upon by the Senate during the 1920 or 1921 sessions of the Sixty-sixth Congress.

After the failure of HR 13500, Delegate Kuhio returned to Hawaii to fashion a more acceptable bill. After extensive discussions, the Territorial Legislature passed new resolutions endorsing amendments to HR 13500. The U.S. House and Senate passed S. 1881 in June 1921, and President Warren Harding signed the bill on July 9, 1921.

Provisions of the Hawaiian Homes Commission Act

The HHCA contained no preamble specifying its purpose, but it was generally recognized that its purpose was the "rehabilitation of the Hawaiian race." The HHCA did not open any of the government-owned lands leased to sugar plantations. Instead, it designated about 203,000 acres of very marginal public lands (approximately 5 percent of the islands' total land area) as "Hawaiian homelands" and transferred their control to the newly created HHC, consisting of the governor and four gubernatorial appointees. The HHCA enabled the HHC to lease the lands as homesteads to Native Hawaiians for a term of ninety-nine years; HHC lands that were not leased as homesteads were to be returned to the territorial land commissioner. Homesteaders could obtain 20 to 80 acres of agricultural land, 100 to 500 acres of first-class pastoral land, or 250 to 1,000 acres of second-class pastoral land. The annual rent on leases, regardless of the amount of land, was one dollar, and there was a moratorium on county property tax payments for five years. Lessees were required to occupy and to use or cultivate the site within one year after the lease was made and to continue to cultivate or use it; the HHC could terminate the lease if this provision was violated. Within any five-year period, the HHC could open no more than 20,000 acres for settlement.

Lessees had to be Native Hawaiian, that is, with 50 percent or more Hawaiian blood. Upon the death of a lessee, the lease passed to statutorily specified relatives only if these relatives satisfied the blood quantum requirement. A lessee was allowed to transfer or mortgage the lease only with the permission of the HHC and only to Native Hawaiians who satisfied the blood quantum requirement. Subletting was strictly prohibited.

The HHCA prohibited lessees from applying for loans under the 1919 Farm Loan Act of Hawaii. Combined with the prohibition on mortgaging the land to a non-Hawaiian, the HHCA's provisions effectively cut off the homesteader from most private and governmental sources of capital. The only source of capital for the homesteader, beyond personal savings and unsecured personal loans, was the Hawaiian Homes Loan Fund, which was authorized to loan up to $3,000 per homesteader. In effect, the HHCA set up the HHC as a monopoly supplier of capital to the homesteader.

The Hawaiian Homes Loan Fund was initially used to pay the commission's operating and capital costs as well as to make loans to homesteaders. All revenues from the leasing of public lands "made available" as Hawaiian homelands and 30 percent of the revenues from the leasing of territorial sugar lands and receipts from water licenses were to be accumulated in the fund until it reached $1,000,000. The legislature periodically increased the funding cap until it finally abolished the cap in 1959 (Spitz 1963).

Hawaiian leaders had originally proposed a government program that would rehabilitate Hawaiians by returning them to agricultural work on their own small sugar cane farms. The final legislation retained some of the original proposal's form but none of its substance. Hawaii's fertile government-owned sugar lands were closed to all homesteading. The territorial lands set aside for Hawaiians were marginal or submarginal agricultural lands, previously rejected by sugar, rice, and pineapple planters. Homesteaders' rights in the new homelands were limited by numerous restrictions on alienation and use. And financing for housing and business development could be obtained from only one source, the HHC. Although the HHCA set the stage for some Hawaiians to return to the land, its marginal lands and restricted opportunities were unlikely to be the catalysts for a rehabilitation of the Hawaiian race.

From Agricultural Homesteads to Public Housing

The HHC moved quickly to prepare the first settlement on Molokai. By February 1923 thirteen settlers had assumed leases at the Kalanianaole Settlement, and by August 1924 the settlement had 278 residents. Although the experiment with diversified farming was initially successful, the lack of irrigation water led many settlers to abandon their farmlands. A second settlement on the Ho'olehua Plain on Molokai was leased in October 1924, with the settlers continuing the experiment with diversified farming. In 1926 the HHC allowed homesteaders to enter into subleasing contracts with the pineapple grower, Libby, McNeil, and Libby, despite the HHCA's ban on such arrangements. The contracts with pineapple companies paid rents to the Native Hawaiian settlers but did not utilize their labor. The HHCA's goal of rehabilitating Native Hawaiians by encouraging their labor on homestead lands was apparently forgotten. The amount of land in pineapple cultivation expanded over the next few years, stabilized in the 1930s, and continues through 1995.

In 1923 Congress passed legislation amending the HHCA to enable Native Hawaiians to lease half-acre house lots. The limited success of diversified agriculture, the realization that other assigned lands were also likely to be marginal agricultural investments, and the demand by the highly urbanized Hawaiian population on Oahu for home lots induced the HHC to switch its primary goal from starting small-scale farms and ranches to developing residential areas. This goal was to provide improved residential lots of less than half an acre and loans to build homes on the lots at below-market rates. The first house lot development was on the island of Hawaii in South Hilo at Keaukaha in 1924. By 1927 it contained 158 improved lots. In 1928 Congress extended the HHCA from the islands of Molokai and Hawaii to the islands of Oahu, Maui, and Kauai. The popularity of the South Hilo development prompted the HHC to open a second residential settlement at Nanakuli, Oahu, in 1930. Settlements followed at Kawaihae, Hawaii (1936); Kewalo-Papakōlea, Oahu (1937); Waimānalo, Oahu (1938); Waimea, Hawaii (1952); Anahola, Kauai (1957); Kekaha, Kauai (1958); Paukukalo, Maui (1959); Kapaakea, Molokai (1950); Waianae, Oahu (1977); Lualualei, Oahu (1985); Kula, Maui (1986); and Waiehu Kou, Maui (1986). After the disastrous experience with diversified farming on Molokai, the HHC has issued relatively few pastoral and agricultural leases to applicants.[13]

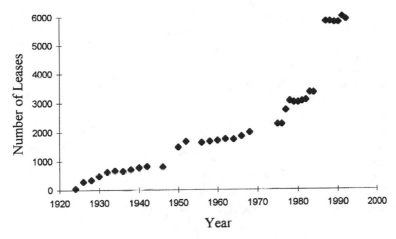

Figure 10.1   *Hawaiian Homes Leases*

A rough indication of the performance of the HHL Program between 1921 and 1989 is contained in measures of the assignment of HHL trust lands to Native Hawaiians. There are three closely related measures of such activity: (1) the number of homestead leases assigned; (2) the number of improved homestead house lots; and (3) the total land area leased for homesteads. Given the heterogeneity in the value of land leased, the total number of leases is the probably the best indicator of the diffusion of HHL Program benefits among the eligible Hawaiian population. The number of leases assigned increased throughout the period, with a significant increase in the growth of new leases being observed after 1977 (see Figure 10.1).[14] Nonetheless, the total number of leases allotted over the life of the program has been small.

Another indicator of the state's commitment to the HHL Program is estimated HHL Program expenditures.[15] This series includes all expenditures from all funds for administration, operation, and capital improvement projects (Figure 10.2). HHC expenditures began as a relatively high percentage of state revenues in the 1920s (10 to 19 percent) and declined rapidly in the 1930s (Schmitt 1977; State of Hawaii 1970–1992). Since 1950 HHC expenditures have been somewhat volatile, but have generally not exceeded 2 percent of state government expenditures. Although HHL Program expenditures increased in the 1970s, they declined again from the late-1970s to the mid-1980s. During the administration of Governor John Waihee (1987–1994), the state's first elected part-Hawaiian governor, HHL expenditures again assumed a slightly upward trend.

The 1959 Hawaii Statehood Act specified that the HHCA must be made a part of the Hawaii State Constitution and mandated the inclusion of a pro-

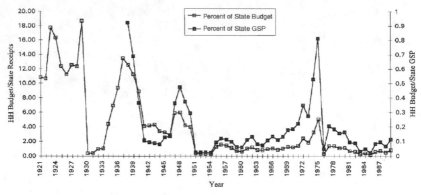

Figure 10.2   *Hawaiian Homes Expenditures, 1921–1989*

vision in the Hawaii State Constitution establishing a trust relationship between the federal and state governments over the program (Hawai'i Admission Act 1959, 4–13; Hawaii 1978, 17). Administrative control over the
program was granted to the state, but the act could be amended only with
the consent of Congress. The 1978 Hawaii Constitutional Convention
amended the act to make changes in the program's administrative and substantive requirements. The changes were approved by Congress in 1986.
The most important amendments included allowing homesteaders to leave
their homesteads to Hawaiians with at least a one-fourth Hawaiian blood
quantum and requiring the HHC to give preference to Native Hawaiians
when leasing unassigned lands (Parker 1989, 160–161).[16]

Beginning in the 1970s, Hawaiians lobbied and litigated to have the federal government enforce its trust over the state's administration of the program. Although federal courts agreed that the federal government had a
trust responsibility toward the HHL Program, they also concluded that neither individual Hawaiians nor Hawaiian groups have standing to sue to enforce the obligation.[17] In 1982 a joint federal-state task force was established
to investigate allegations of mismanagement and trust violations. The task
force's 1983 report substantiated many of the allegations, made recommen-
dations for reform, and suggested that the Department of Hawaiian Home
Lands (DHHL—the successor to HHC after statehood) end its policy of
distributing land only after it had been improved sufficiently to meet county
zoning and building codes (Parker 1989, 30). The DHHL responded by increasing the number of leases from 3,332 in 1984 to 6,068 in November
1994. Most of the new leases were, however, granted on unimproved land
that remains unimproved in 1995.

Since World War II, HHL residential programs have been characterized
by excess demand. Although the HHC compiled long waiting lists for vari-

ous projects, many applicants were never awarded a lease. Several times in the postwar period the HHC lost its waiting list. In 1994 the waiting list consisted of approximately 16,000 persons. Hawaiians have also frequently charged DHHL with irregularities concerning the allocation of lands. In 1991 the legislature established the Hawaiian Home Lands Claims Trust to review petitions from HHL Program applicants who may have been damaged by mismanagement of the program from 1959 to 1988.[18]

During the 1980s DHHL began to reclaim certain trust lands that had been illegally set aside by executive orders and proclamations for purposes not benefiting the trust. In October 1994 the state corrected many of these past wrongs by signing over to the HHL trust 16,518 acres of land. This brought the HHL trust up to 203,500 acres, the amount specified by the HHCA of 1921. In December 1994 the state administration proposed a major settlement for past breaches of the trust calling for payments of $30 million per year for twenty years to the trust. The 1995 state legislature appropriated funds for the first two years.

An Economic and Political Analysis of the HHL Program

Political Support for the HHL Program

Since annexation in 1898 Hawaii's politics have been heavily influenced by ethnic coalitions and ethnic bloc voting. Hawaiians were mostly aligned with Caucasians between 1900 and 1946, when a dominant Republican party controlled both the Territorial Senate and House. In the decade following World War II, the Democratic party gained strength by organizing the growing bloc of Japanese voters. The turning point in party control came in 1954, when the Democrats attained large majorities in both the Territorial House and Senate. During the fifteen years following World War II, Hawaiians switched their allegiance from the Republican party to the Democratic party. Since 1962 all state governors have been Democrats, and there have generally been overwhelming Democratic majorities in the state House and Senate.

The large potential Hawaiian voting bloc was an important factor inducing a Republican Congress to pass the HHCA in 1921. Hawaiian voters comprised 56 percent of the electorate in 1920. Yet between 1898 and 1920, neither the Territorial Legislature nor the U.S. Congress had passed major legislation to reward the Hawaiian bloc in the Republican coalition. The rise in organized Hawaiian political activity after 1914 and the continuing decline in the economic condition of Hawaiians increased the chance that Hawaiians would defect to the Democrats unless legislation specifically benefiting Hawaiians was enacted.

Although Hawaiians have managed to remain aligned with the winning coalition throughout the twentieth century, their political power declined markedly between 1920 and 1950. Hawaiian voters declined to 40 percent of the electorate in 1930, 25 percent in 1940, and 18 percent in 1950. After 1950 data on the race of registered voters were not collected. As a proxy for registered voters, we use the percentage of the overall population over the age of twenty composed of Hawaiians.[19] Our data show the Hawaiian percentage as 12 percent in 1960, 17 percent in 1970, 19 percent in 1980, and 21 percent in 1989. The decrease in Hawaiian numbers from 1920 to 1960 is reflected in declining program expenditures (see Figure 10.2), and the increase from 1960 to 1989 is mirrored in slightly increasing but volatile program expenditures.

The slightly higher expenditures (as a percentage of state government spending) on the HHL Program since the early 1970s may also reflect the large increases in the real value of land in Hawaii since the late 1950s, the period when tourism began to take off (La Croix, Mak, and Rose 1995). Higher real land values increase the subsidy accruing to each HHL applicant, who receives an improved housing lot for an annual rent of one dollar. The higher value of the housing lot award may have induced Native Hawaiians to organize and to lobby for more expenditures on the HHL Program. The increase in land prices has certainly been accompanied by increasing Hawaiian political activity, much of which has also been induced by other economic, political, and cultural forces.

Fine-Tuning a Program, or
Survival of the Fittest Bureaucrats?

The early history of the HHL Program is particularly important, as the program was originally structured to return Native Hawaiians to the land on owner-operated farms and ranches. The program's original goal of "rehabilitating" Hawaiians by returning them to work on their own small farms was, within just a few years, greatly deemphasized. Given the mixed results of the initial agricultural settlements on Molokai, HHC officials quickly petitioned Congress to allow the program to provide applicants with improved housing lots and mortgage loans in HHL residential subdivisions. Although the program still relocated Hawaiians from crowded urban tenements to single-family residences in all-Hawaiian neighborhoods, the rehabilitative work component of the program was essentially eliminated. The HHL Program had been deftly transformed from a program emphasizing the value of labor on small family farms into a housing subsidy program.

The HHCA's goal of locating Hawaiians on marginal and submarginal agricultural lands was ill-fated, and the swift move by the HHC to transform the HHL Program probably saved many Hawaiian families from a dismal future farming lands from which a living could not be obtained. The transformation of the HHL Program into a housing subsidy program had the potential to improve the general welfare of Hawaiian families if it was carried out properly. However, the new HHL Program was incapable of addressing more fundamental problems, such as low school enrollment rates.

It is possible that the transformation of the HHL Program was prompted not only by HHC bureaucrats' quick perception of the poor quality of HHL lands but also by the self-interested behavior of bureaucrats interested in perpetuating their newfound jobs. There is certainly precedent for such arguments in the context of federal programs for Native Americans. Fred McChesney (1990) has argued that other federal land programs have been modified to perpetuate the federal Indian bureaucracy. McChesney analyzed the Dawes Act, which allotted fee-simple rights in tribal lands to individual Native Americans and allowed non–Native Americans to purchase "surplus" tribal lands. He argued that the suspension of land allotments in the early 1920s was prompted by both bureaucratic and political incentives. Officials in the Bureau of Indian Affairs realized that as the stock of lands managed by the bureau dwindled, the agency would shrink and many staffers would lose their jobs. To perpetuate their jobs, officials in the Bureau of Indian Affairs lobbied Congress to stop allotment.[20]

Although bureaucratic self-interest may have played a role in transforming the HHL Program, coalition politics also influenced the course of the program. As we discussed above, political equilibrium requires that some government programs be directed to provide benefits to the large bloc of Hawaiians in the reigning Republican coalition. In the mid-1920s Hawaiians were still a powerful voting bloc; eliminating the HHL Program was probably not a viable option for most territorial politicians regardless of its performance or future prospects. Since some territorial revenues were earmarked for the program and it was endowed with a stock of land, it would not be surprising if enterprising bureaucrats developed a new program to perpetuate their jobs and to maintain political equilibrium. The critical question, which we address below, is whether the restructured HHL Program provided benefits to Native Hawaiians in an equitable and efficient manner.

An Equitable and Efficient Program?

Rose and La Croix (1995) have argued that the HHL Program has dispensed benefits to Native Hawaiians in a highly inequitable manner. By November 1994 the HHL Program had provided only 6,068 home lots to Native Hawaiian applicants. A 16,000-person waiting list remains. This is mainly because of the cost of developing an improved housing lot and providing a mortgage subsidy as well as the bureaucratic logjams and delays at DHHL. If housing lots are to be developed in the future at the same rate as they have been since statehood (1959), it will take eighty years until the median applicant on the 1994 waiting list receives an HHL Program award! Following this scenario, a few Native Hawaiians will receive a valuable housing package this year, whereas the median applicant will not receive an award during his or her lifetime.

The HHL Program has been also been structured so that it is likely to provide benefits in a highly inefficient manner. Housing programs that subsidize the production and control the distribution of housing generally deliver housing at a resource cost greater than the housing's market value to its recipients. A careful study of the production efficiency of the HHL public housing program has not been done, so one cannot say precisely how wasteful this program is. However it is noteworthy that in the case of the U.S. Public Housing Program, for every dollar expended, 43 cents of value are delivered to recipients (Mayo 1986).

Many of the inefficient features of programs providing subsidies to housing production are also found in the HHL Program. A few examples applicable to the HHL Program will illustrate. The difficulty of exchanging HHL Program lands for other lands results in project locations that are determined by historical accident rather than economic considerations. The use of tax-free bonds to finance infrastructure wastefully biases expenditures in favor of initial capital expenditures over recurrent maintenance expenses. Regulations requiring that union wages be paid on publicly supported housing projects also increase costs. Probably the greatest source of production inefficiency within the HHL Program is the lack of high-powered incentives within the public sector to control housing costs and to maintain quality. The private sector's construction industry is motivated by profit and undertakes a new project only when the production cost is less than the project's expected revenue. The DHHL is not required to satisfy such a test, and even if it were, bureaucratic incentives to enforce it effectively are weak.

DHHL provides three types of subsidy for each homestead. First, it leases the unimproved land to the homesteader for ninety-nine years at an annual rent of one dollar; typically the unimproved land would have a market value of about $35,000 (in 1995 dollars). Second, DHHL develops the lot at a cost of $58,000 (Loudat, Horn, and Lucas 1994). Third, it provides mortgage reinsurance on the homesteader's purchase of the structure, typically for $90,000. A half-point reduction in the interest rate attributable to this insurance on a $90,000 home loan over thirty years is worth about $4,000. Thus the total value of the DHHL subsidy to a successful applicant is $97,000. Applying the estimate of waste for federal programs subsidizing the production and distribution of housing ($.43 of value for every $1.00 expended) to HHL Program housing lots, the $97,000 package is only worth $42,000 to the successful applicant. However, the typical applicant is unlikely to receive $42,000 in subsidies now. Instead, due to the logjam of government planning, funding, and development, the delivery of the subsidy package to the median HHL Program applicant is likely to be pushed far into the future. We noted above that if homestead lots are developed at the same rate as they have been since statehood, it would be eighty years until the median applicant receives an HHL Program award. Suppose, instead, we assume that the State of Hawaii or a sovereign Hawaiian government lowers the median waiting period to just twenty years. After discounting at 15 percent (Mak and Fujii's [1979] conservative estimate of the discount rate of an average Hawaiian), the value of the HHL Program award falls from $42,000 to just $2,500.

Intangible Benefits from the HHL Program

There may be less tangible benefits to the HHL program that we have failed to include in our analysis. Possible intangible benefits to Hawaiians include (1) the knowledge that the program's lands are inalienable, (2) the creation of ethnically homogeneous Hawaiian neighborhoods, and (3) the possibility of using program lands as a land base for a sovereign Hawaiian government. Let us briefly discuss each in turn.

The knowledge that the program lands are inalienable may be of value to many Hawaiians given the small amount of land that Hawaiians currently own in Hawaii. Underlying some Hawaiians' desire to retain land ownership is a deeply held cultural belief that *āina*, or the land, is more than a mere commodity to be traded for other valued goods. Although some Hawaiians have traded their land away, many Hawaiians (and Polynesians generally) have respected and revered the land as a form of spiritual and emotional as well as material wealth. Those who still hold these beliefs will benefit from the knowledge that government's holding of the land in trust keeps it Hawaiian, forever out of the hands of foreigners.

Another intangible benefit of DHHL holding lands in trust for Hawaiians is based on the relative ease with which people living in close proximity to one another can preserve and enhance their culture. If Hawaiian residences were contiguous, there would be more opportunities for the occupants to interact as Hawaiians. Community centers, schools, churches, some businesses, and neighborhood associations would permit Hawaiian traditions to be passed along from one generation to another in an environment sheltered from the rest of society. This argument is not as strong today as it was in 1921. Due to technological advances, people can transport themselves and communicate across distances at greatly reduced costs. Moreover, in many cities and rural areas there are spontaneously evolved ethnic communities. Nonetheless, the government mandate of ethnically homogeneous Hawaiian communities may increase the probability that such communities will endure.

A third indirect benefit from holding HHL program lands in trust is to aid in reestablishing Hawaiian sovereignty.[21] The Native Hawaiian sovereignty movement has gathered increased support from Hawaiians and other ethnic groups over the last decade. DHHL trust lands may help to establish a new political entity in two ways. First, some Hawaiians argue that the existence of federal legislation, the HHCA, which recognizes a trust relationship between Hawaiians and the United States, is an implicit recognition of their inherent sovereignty. Second, Rose and La Croix (1995) have estimated that the DHHL controls assets (lands and dedicated revenues) worth $850 million. By promising to use and disperse these resources more efficiently, or perhaps to distribute them to their supporters, sovereignty leaders can consolidate support.

The intangible benefits that may stem from the HHL Program are difficult to value, and we do not attempt such an exercise. However, given the low value ($2,500) of the program's direct benefits to the median Native Hawaiian on the waiting list, the intangible benefits would have to be very large for the HHL Program to be considered successful.

Conclusion

Rose and La Croix (1995) have made three suggestions for reforming the HHL Program. One option is to eliminate all alienability restrictions or at least to allow a lessee, without DHHL approval, to sell the home/lease package to any Hawaiian with a positive blood quantum. This would provide Native Hawaiians with more mobility and with increased incentives to maintain and upgrade housing on program lands. A second option, providing a housing consumption subsidy rather than a housing production subsidy, would reduce the program's inefficiency. Production waste would be reduced, and Native Hawaiians who rent as well as purchase housing could be assisted. A third option is to liquidate many of the program's assets and to disperse the proceeds to Native Hawaiians on the waiting list. This option would enable a Native Hawaiian in the middle of the waiting list to receive HHL Program benefits now rather than many years in the future. In addition, it would allow the beneficiary to use the program's assets for other important activities, such as purchasing land, financing education, or reducing high debt burdens.

The structure of the HHL Program does not, however, lend itself to comprehensive reform. Fundamental revisions of the 1921 HHCA must clear multiple hurdles. They must be approved by both houses of the Hawaii State Legislature and the governor, they must be approved by both the U.S. Congress and the president, and although not required by law, they should be approved by a vote of Hawaiians, for whom the program's lands are held in trust. The multiple barriers to changing the program combined with the

controversial nature of government land trusts virtually ensures that fundamental change will not occur until there is a crisis in the program or until the
Hawaiian community becomes more informed not just of the low level of
benefits delivered to a typical Native Hawaiian applicant but also of the large
potential benefits that could accrue to Native Hawaiians from reforming the
program.

The multiple barriers to changing the HHL Program have been advantageous in one major respect: They have helped to ensure that the revenues
and lands dedicated by the HHCA to Native Hawaiians have been retained
by Native Hawaiians for three-quarters of a century. On the other hand, the
multiple barriers have also served to lock in a housing subsidy program that
is both highly inequitable and highly inefficient. Neither "improved" administration of the HHL Program nor its transfer to a sovereign Hawaiian government is likely to remedy its fundamental difficulties. The dilemma of how
to reform the HHL Program within the context of a trust relationship is
fundamental and applies not just to Native Hawaiian land trusts but also to
the numerous Native American land trusts in North America. Progress toward reform would help to ensure that land, an asset with cultural, economic, and political dimensions, is put to its best use.

Notes

Comments by participants at the May 1994 Barnard College–Columbia University
Conference, "Furthering Research into the Past: Current Research on the Economic
History of Native Americans" were very helpful in improving the chapter. We also
thank the Social Science Research Institute at the University of Hawaii for its financial support of our research and the University of California, Berkeley for its support
during Spring 1995.

1. We use the term "Native Hawaiian" to indicate a Hawaiian who would qualify
for the Hawaiian Home Lands (HHL) Program, that is, any person with 50 percent
or more Hawaiian blood. We use "Hawaiian" more inclusively to refer to any person
with any Hawaiian blood.

2. Some controversy exists as to whether the *'ohana* represents a single extended
family or a group of extended families; see Beechert 1985, 7.

3. See Letter of William Richards to Commander Charles Wilkes, U.S.N., commander of the U.S.A. Exploring Expedition (March 15, 1841) in Sahlins and Barrere
1973, 23; Dibble [1843] 1909, 74. Since Richards's letter was written in 1841, the
two-thirds figure may not be applicable to earlier periods. Also, Richards's figure is
not based on empirical investigations.

4. An evaluation of the nutritional merits of the ancient Hawaiian diet reveals that
it meets early-twentieth-century standards; see Miller 1927.

5. There was irregular communication with and possibly migration from the Society Islands and Tahiti.

6. Kaua'i was not integrated into a unified nation until 1810.

7. They also argue that the 1795 unification of Hawaii initially provided the victorious chiefs with some monopsony power over the common people.

8. La Croix and Roumasset (1984) have argued that the old religion represented an investment in legitimacy by the *ali'i*. In the absence of a clear-cut superiority in violence, the presence of the old religion allowed the *ali'i* to maintain their authority. With the acquisition of Western military technology, legitimacy became less important, relative to violence, in maintaining the prevailing order. As the religion became less valuable, it was eliminated at an opportune moment.

9. Many U.S. residents had given up their U.S. citizenship and pledged allegiance to the Hawaiian Kingdom.

10. The Census Report also observes that "[t]here is quite a common impression abroad in the community that the Chinese have superseded the Natives in this business to a much greater extent than these figures would indicate. It is quite possible that some of the Natives returned as fisherman may be working for Chinese bosses" (Hawaii Bureau of Public Instruction 1891, 26).

11. The following section draws extensively from McGregor's (1990) article and Vause's (1962) thesis detailing the history of the HHC Act.

12. The May 27, 1910, amendments to Section 73 of the Organic Act (a federal law establishing the territory's fundamental governmental institutions) provided that most land leases contain a provision that the territorial government could withdraw the land from the lease "for homestead or public purposes" (An Act to Provide a Government for the Territory of Hawaii 1900).

13. Information obtained from interviews with Kenneth Tokoguchi and Stanley Wong at the Department of Hawaiian Home Lands (DHHL) and annual reports of the HHC.

14. About 800 of the leases assigned in 1984 were unimproved, and most lots remain unimproved in 1995.

15. The authors constructed expenditure data using the following sources: the HHC's biennial reports to the Territorial Legislature, the DHHL's annual reports, the session laws and revised statutes of the territory and the state, and interviews during 1992–1993 with personnel at DHHL. The expenditures series (and all other series expressed in dollars) have been annualized and deflated to constant 1991 dollars.

16. The homestead can only be willed to one-quarter Hawaiians who are blood relatives of the lessee.

17. See Parker 1989 for a more extended discussion of the litigation; see also the report of the Federal-State Task Force on the Hawaiian Homes Commission Act (1983).

18. Native Hawaiian Trusts Judicial Relief Act 1993, chap. 674 provides details of the Review Panel's charge and procedures.

19. Data are from the annual *Report of the Governor of Hawai'i to the Secretary of the Interior* (U.S. Department of the Interior 1919–1940); U.S. Bureau of the Census 1950; Schmitt 1977; and State of Hawaii 1988–1992. After 1960, census data are not categorized by specific Asian and Polynesian races in Hawaii but by "White, Black, Other, and Hispanic." Regarding our proxy variable for Hawaiian voters, we recognize that various ethnic groups have different propensities to register to vote and that this proxy contains measurement errors. Since our estimate of the total population of voters after 1960 does not deduct a substantial number of unnaturalized

immigrants from the Philippines and Japan, the voting base is biased upwards, thereby biasing the percentage of Hawaiian voters downwards.

20. Leonard Carlson (1981) argued that the demand by non–Native Americans for tribal lands fell as real land rents declined in the 1920s. The declining land rents reduced the economic rents available from purchasing at congressionally specified prices, thereby dissipating political support from potential purchasers (whites) for the allotment program.

21. There is no consensus among Hawaiians regarding the meaning of sovereignty. It is sufficient for our purposes that sovereignty is some unspecified degree of independence from the existing state and federal governments.

References

An Act to Provide a Government for the Territory of Hawaii. 1900. *U. S. Statutes at Large* 36.

"Back to Land Move." 1918. *Honolulu Advertiser*, 16 July, sec. 2, p. 1.

Beechert, E. D. 1985. *Working in Hawaii: A Labor History.* Honolulu: University of Hawaii Press.

Carlson, L. A. 1981. *Indians, Bureaucrats, and Land: The Dawes Act and the Decline of Indian Farming.* Westport, Conn.: Greenwood Press.

Davenport W. 1969. "The 'Hawaiian Cultural Revolution': Some Political and Economic Considerations." *American Anthropologist* 71:1–20.

Dibble, S. [1843] 1909. *A History of the Sandwich Islands.* Honolulu, Hawaii: T. G. Thrum.

Dye, T. 1994. "Population Trends in Hawaii Before 1778." *The Hawaiian Journal of History* 28:1–20.

Federal-State Task Force on the Hawaiian Homes Commission Act. 1983. *Report to United States Secretary of the Interior and the Governor of the State of Hawaii.* Honolulu, Hawaii: N.P.

Fuchs, L. H. 1961. *Hawaii Pono: A Social History.* New York: Harcourt, Brace, and World.

Hawaii. 1978. *The Constitution of the State of Hawaii.* N.P.: N.P.

Hawai'i Admission Act. 1959. *U.S. Statutes at Large* 73:4–13.

Hawaiian Homes Commission Act. 1921. *U. S. Statutes at Large* 42:108.

Hawaii Bureau of Public Instruction. 1891. *Report of the General Superintendent of the Census, 1890.* Honolulu, Hawaii: R. Grieve, Steam Book and Job Printer.

Kame'eleihiwa, L. 1992. *Native Land and Foreign Desires.* Honolulu, Hawaii: Bishop Museum Press.

Kirch, P. V. 1985. *Feathered Gods and Fishhooks.* Honolulu: University of Hawaii Press.

Kuykendall, R. S. 1938, 1953, 1967. *The Hawaiian Kingdom.* 3 vols. Honolulu: University of Hawaii Press.

La Croix, S. J., and Grandy, C. 1997. "The Political Instability of Reciprocal Trade and the Overthrow of the Hawaiian Kingdom." *Journal of Economic History* 57:1–29.

La Croix, S. J., Mak, J., and Rose, L. A. 1995. "The Political Economy of Urban Land Reform in Hawaii." *Urban Studies* 32:999–1015.

La Croix, S. J., and Roumasset, J. 1984. "An Economic Theory of Political Change in Premissionary Hawaii." *Explorations in Economic History* 21:151–168.

_____. 1990. "The Evolution of Private Property in Nineteenth-Century Hawaii." *Journal of Economic History* 50:829–852.

Loudat, T. A., Horn, A. R., and Lucas, R. 1994. *An Historical Performance Review of the Hawaiian Home Lands Trust.* Honolulu, Hawaii: N.P.

Mak, J., and Fujii, E. T. 1979. "A Cost-Benefit Study Relating to the Native Hawaiian Education Act." Unpublished report. Department of Economics, University of Hawaii.

Malo, D. 1971. *Hawaiian Antiquities.* Honolulu: University of Hawaii Press.

"May Ask U.S. to Give Land to Hawaiians." 1919. *Honolulu Advertiser*, 15 February, p. 2.

Mayo, S. K. 1986. "Sources of Inefficiency in Subsidized Housing Programs: A Comparison of U.S. and German Experience." *Journal of Urban Economics* 20:229–249.

McChesney, F. S. 1990. "Government as Definer of Property Rights: Indian Lands, Ethnic Externalities, and Bureaucratic Budgets." *Journal of Legal Studies* 19:297–335.

McGregor, D. P. 1990. "ʻĀina Hoʻopulapula: Hawaiian Homesteading." *The Hawaiian Journal of History* 24:1–38.

Miller, C. D. 1927. *Food Values of Poi, Taro, and Limu.* Honolulu, Hawaii: Bishop Museum.

Morgan, T. 1948. *Hawaii: A Century of Economic Change.* Cambridge: Harvard University Press.

Native Hawaiian Trusts Judicial Relief Act. 1993. *Hawaiʻi Revised Statutes* 13:chaps. 673–674.

Nordyke, E. C. 1989. *The Peopling of Hawaii.* 2nd ed. Honolulu, Hawaii: East-West Center.

Parker, L. S. 1989. *Native American Estate: The Struggle over Indian and Hawaiian Lands.* Honolulu: University of Hawaii Press.

"Princess Will Urge Hawaiians to Go Back to the Land." 1918. *Honolulu Advertiser*, 2 October, p. 1.

A Proclamation. 1919. *U.S. Statutes at Large* 40:1804.

Rose, L. A., and La Croix, S. J. 1995. "Hawaiian Home Lands: Proposals for Reform." Unpublished manuscript. Department of Economics, University of Hawaii.

Sahlins, M. 1972. *Stone Age Economics.* Chicago: University of Chicago Press.

Sahlins, M., and Barrere, D. 1973. "William Richards on Hawaiian Culture and Political Conditions of the Islands in 1841." *Hawaiian Journal of History* 7:18–40.

Schmitt, R. C. 1971. "New Estimates of the Pre-Censal Population of Hawaiʻi." *Journal of the Polynesian Society* 870.

_____. 1977. *Historical Statistics of Hawaii.* Honolulu: University of Hawaii Press.

Spitz, A. A. 1963. *Organization and Administration of the Hawaiian Homes Program.* Honolulu, Hawaii: Legislative Reference Bureau.

Stannard, D. E. 1989. *Before the Horror: The Population of Hawaii on the Eve of Western Contact.* Honolulu: SSRI, University of Hawaii.

State of Hawaii. 1970–1992. *The State of Hawaii Data Book.* Honolulu, Hawaii: Department of Business, Economic Development, and Tourism.

U.S. Bureau of the Census. 1923a. *Composition and Characteristics.* Vol. 3 of *U.S. Census of Population: 1920.* Washington, D.C.: GPO.

_____. 1923b. *Population 1920: Occupations.* Vol. 4 of *Fourteenth Census of the United States Taken in the Year 1920.* Washington, D.C.: GPO.

_____. 1950. *Current Population Reports.* Series P–20. Washington, D.C.: GPO.

U.S. Department of the Interior. 1919–1940. *Report of the Governor of Hawai'i to the Secretary of the Interior.* Washington, D.C.: GPO.

Vause, M. M. 1962. *The Hawaiian Homes Commission Act, 1920: History and Analysis.* Graduate thesis, University of Hawaii, Honolulu.

About the Editor
and Contributors

Terry L. Anderson is Professor of Economics at Montana State University and Executive Director of the Political Economy Research Center (PERC), a research institute focused on market solutions to environmental problems. His recent books include *Sovereign Nations or Reservations? An Economic History of American Indians* and *Enviro-Capitalists* (with Donald Leal).

Linda Barrington is Assistant Professor of Economics at Barnard College of Columbia University. Her recent publications include "Estimating Earnings Poverty in 1939: A Comparison of Orshansky-Method and Price Indexed Definitions of Poverty" in *The Review of Economics and Statistics*.

Ann M. Carlos is Professor of Economics at the University of Colorado. Her recent publications include "Theory and History: Seventeenth Century Joint-Stock Chartered Trading Companies" (with Stephen Nicholas) in *Journal of Economic History*. She is also author of *The North American Fur Trade, 1804–1821: A Study in the Life-Cycle of a Duopoly*.

Leonard A. Carlson is Associate Professor of Economics and Adjunct Associate Professor of History at Emory University. He is the author of *Indians, Bureaucrats, and Land: The Dawes Act and the Decline of Indian Farming*. His recent publications include "Learning to Farm: Indian Land Tenure and Farming Before the Dawes Act" in *Property Rights, Constitutions, and Indian Economies* (edited by Terry Anderson).

Karen Clay is Assistant Professor of Economics at the University of Toronto. Her recent publications include "Trade Without Law: Private-Order Institutions in Mexican California" in *Journal of Law, Economics, and Organization* and "Trade, Institutions, and Law: The Experience of Mexican California" in *California and the Pacific Rim: Past, Present, and Future* (edited by Sally M. Miller and A. J. H. Latham).

Steven LaCombe was a Graduate Fellow at the Political Economy Research Center (PERC) in Bozeman, Montana. He is currently attending law school at the University of Washington.

Sumner J. La Croix is Professor of Economics at the University of Hawaii at Manoa. His recent publications include "The Political Instability of Reciprocal Trade and the Overthrow of the Hawaiian Kingdom" (with Chris Grandy) in *Journal of Economic History*.

Frank D. Lewis is Professor of Economics at Queen's University, Kingston, Ontario. His recent publications include "Growth and the Standard of Living in a Pioneer Economy: Upper Canada, 1826–1851" (with Mac Urquhart) in *The Economy of Early British America* (edited by John McCusker) and "Agricultural Property and the 1948 Palestinian Refugees: Assessing the Loss" in *Explorations in Economic History*.

Fred S. McChesney is Professor of Law at Cornell Law School. He is the author of *Money for Nothing: Politicians, Rent Extraction and Political Extortion*. His recent publications include "Raid or Trade? An Economic Model of Indian-White Relations" (with Terry Anderson) in *Journal of Law and Economics*.

Edward Murphy is Assistant Professor of Economics at Southwest Texas State University. His recent publications include "A Balanced Budget Game" in *Classroom Expernomics*.

James W. Oberly is Professor of History at the University of Wisconsin, Eau Claire. His recent publications include "Tribal Sovereignty and Natural Resources: The Lac Courtes Oreilles Experience" in *Buried Roots and Indestructible Seeds: The Survival of American Indian Life in Story, History, and Spirit* (edited by Mark Lindquist and Martin Zanger). He is also author of *Sixty Million Acres: American Veterans and the Public Lands Before the Civil War*.

Louis A. Rose is Professor of Economics at the University of Hawaii at Manoa. His recent publications include "Public Use, Just Compensation, and Land Reform in Hawaii" (with Sumner La Croix) in *Research in Law and Economics* and "The Political Economy of Urban Land Reform in Hawaii" (with Sumner La Croix and James Mak) in *Urban Studies*.

Vernon L. Smith is Regents' Professor of Economics and Research Director of the Economic Science Laboratory at the University of Arizona. He has published one volume of his *Papers in Experimental Economics* and is working on two more volumes.

David M. Wishart is Professor of Economics at Wittenberg University. His recent publications include "Building Institutions to Support National and International Markets for Water in the Jordan Valley" in *Water International* and "Evidence of Surplus Production in the Eastern Cherokee Nation Prior to Removal" in *Journal of Economic History*.

Index